Sowing the Seeds

of Democracy

in China

Sowing the Seeds of Democracy in China

Political Reform in the Deng Xiaoping Era

Merle Goldman

Harvard University Press
Cambridge, Massachusetts
London, England

Library of Congress Cataloging-in-Publication Data

Goldman, Merle.
  Sowing the seeds of democracy in China :
political reform in the Deng Xiaoping era /
Merle Goldman.
      p.   cm.
  Includes index.
  ISBN 0-674-83007-5 (cloth)
  ISBN 0-674-83008-3 (pbk.)
  1. China—Politics and government—1976–   2. Democracy—
China.   I. Title.
JQ1510.G65   1994
320.951—dc20

93-26965
  CIP

For my children,
Ethan, Avra, Karla, and Seth,
who may someday see democracy
flower in China

Contents

Preface

In an editorial cartoon from the mid-1980s, a portly Chinese man in a Mao suit first carefully plants a seed that bears the label "democracy." In the second panel he diligently waters it, and in the third he is delighted when a beautiful flower springs forth. But in the final panel, all has changed: the flower has turned into a gigantic Venus's flytrap, and the man runs away in terror, lest he be gobbled up.

In China in the 1980s, as some began to grapple with the theory and practice of democracy, the story this cartoon tells was repeated over and over again. I focus here on the group of intellectuals who attempted to move China's Leninist political system in a democratic direction in these years. Most of them formed an intellectual network around Hu Yaobang, until January 1987 the general secretary of the Chinese Communist Party. This book describes the evolving views and actions of this network and its associates from 1978 to June 4, 1989, in the aftermath of the Cultural Revolution and over the Deng Xiaoping decade of reform. The network's members differed in their concerns and emphases, but most of them were moving toward the same goal—to limit the party's power. This they sought to accomplish first by trying to implant democratic concepts into Marxism-Leninism and then by attempting to establish democratic institutions. When they found that their efforts to educate the public in these ideas were thwarted, they turned by the late 1980s to action of a more organized and more political nature.

The political role of those in the democratic elite was constantly changing throughout the decade, as was the degree to which the government tolerated their views. The evolution in the thinking and actions of the group's members was prompted in part by events in China, in part by the radical developments in the Communist and East Asian countries with which they identified, and in part by their exposure to Western ideas and institutions. The government crackdown of June 4, 1989, not only meant the failure to reach immediate goals but also marked an irrevocable change in the once close relationship between Chinese intellectuals and the Chinese state, which over the previous ten years had become one of increasing alienation. The relationship of the intellectual to the rest of society was also in flux, as the story of the emergence of the democratic elite both reflected and affected the experience of other important segments of the urban population. These elements came together at Tiananmen Square in 1989, and continue to evolve today.

This book is the first I have written for which the subjects could be interviewed. After China opened to the outside world in the post-Mao era, I became acquainted with a number of the protagonists—especially Liu Binyan, Ruan Ming, Su Shaozhi, Wang Ruoshui, and Xu Liangying—and have spoken with them periodically, both in China and in the United States. Their writings and those of their colleagues are voluminous; I have been inundated with materials by the participants in the events that I describe. Many of the main figures deserve a book of their own. David Kelly has already written extensively about Wang Ruoshui, David Bachman about Yan Jiaqi, James Williams about Fang Lizhi, and Orville Schell about Liu Binyan and Wang Ruowang as well as about Fang Lizhi. Some of the protagonists have written their own autobiographical accounts. I am grateful to all with whom I have spoken, and also to those who have written of their experiences, for their invaluable assistance.

I also thank the *China Quarterly* for permission to use material, now somewhat revised, from two articles of mine: "The Zigs and Zags in the Treatment of Intellectuals," no. 104 (December 1985), and "Hu Yaobang's Intellectual Network and the Theory Conference of 1979," no. 126 (June 1991).

I live in a nourishing scholarly environment. Boston University, where I teach, provides me with good students and with sufficient time and support for research; the Fairbank Center for East Asian Research at Harvard, where I have been an Associate since I was a graduate student, has been a source of inspiration and intellectual stimulation for almost thirty years. My late teacher John K. Fairbank and former teacher Benjamin Schwartz and my former classmates Paul Cohen, Roderick MacFarquhar, and Ezra Vogel have given me unstinting encouragement. In writing this book I have benefited immensely from the advice and help of Michael Schoenhals, visiting scholar at the Fairbank Center, and particularly Nancy Hearst, Center librarian, who rechecked all my notes diligently and accurately. I have also been aided by note checker Eric Marsman and typists Xiaoling Hong and Wei An. I am grateful as well to Elizabeth Gretz of Harvard University Press, who helped me shape the book in its final form. My colleagues Paul Cohen, Andrew Nathan, Tony Saich, and Jeff Wasserstrom have read the manuscript and provided constructive criticism. The Guggenheim Foundation made it possible for me to take time off from teaching to do research and writing.

Most important, my mother, my children, and especially my husband, Marshall, though at times impatient, have always been unqualified in their support and enthusiasm for my endeavors.

June 1993

Major Figures

Reformist Political Leaders

Hu Qili (1929–)
Member, Chinese Communist Party
Politburo, 1985–1989; Member,
Politburo Standing Committee,
1987–1989

Hu Yaobang (1915–1989)
General Secretary, Chinese Communist Party, 1980–1987

Wan Li (1916–)
Chairman, National People's
Congress, 1988–1993; Member,
Chinese Communist Party
Politburo, 1982–1992

Zhao Ziyang (1919–)
Premier, People's Republic of China,
1980–1987; General Secretary,
Chinese Communist Party,
1987–1989

Zhu Houze (1931–)
Director, Propaganda Department,
1985–1987

Democratic Elite

Newspaper Editors

Ge Yang (1916–)
Editor, *New Observer,*
1979–1989

Hu Jiwei (1916–)
Editor, *People's Daily,* 1977–1983

Qin Benli (1918–1991)
Founder and Editor, *World
Economic Herald,*
1980–1989

Sun Changjiang (1933–)
Deputy Editor, *Science and Technology News,* 1985–1989

Wang Ruoshui (1926–)
Deputy Editor, *People's Daily,*
1977–1983

Yang Xiguang (?–1989)
Editor, *Guangming Daily,*
1979–1983

Marxist Humanist Theorists

Guo Luoji (1932–)
  Philosopher, Peking University
Li Honglin (1926–)
  Historian, Fujian Academy of
  Social Sciences
Li Shu (1912–1988)
  Historian, Institute of History,
  Chinese Academy of Social
  Sciences
Liao Gailong (1918–)
  Deputy Director, Party History
  Research Center
Ruan Ming (1931–)
  Editor, *Theoretical Trends,* Central
  Party School, 1977–1982
Su Shaozhi (1923–)
  Director, Institute of Marxism-
  Leninism-Mao Zedong Thought,
  Chinese Academy of Social
  Sciences, 1982–1987

Yan Jiaqi (1942–)
  Director, Institute of Political
  Science, Chinese Academy of Social
  Sciences, 1985–1989
Yu Guangyuan (1915–)
  Director, Institute of Marxism-
  Leninism-Mao Zedong Thought,
  1978–1982; advisor to Hu Yaobang
Yu Haocheng (1928–)
  Legal jurist; Director, Masses
  Publishing House
Zhang Xianyang (1938–)
  Director, Marx-Engels Research
  Office, Institute of Marxism-
  Leninism-Mao Zedong Thought
Zhou Yang (1907–1989)
  Deputy Director, Propaganda
  Department, 1978–1983; Chair-
  man, All-China Federation of Liter-
  ary and Art Circles, 1978–1983

Disciples

Cao Siyuan (1948–)
  Theorist; Director, Stone Group
  think tank, 1988–1989
Ding Xueliang (1952–)
  Theorist, Institute of Marxism-
  Leninism-Mao Zedong Thought

Zhang Weiguo (1957–)
  Journalist, Beijing office of *World
  Economic Herald*
Zhou Duo (1947–)
  Sociologist, Stone Group

Literary Associates

Bai Hua (1930–)
  Writer, attached to military until
  1986
Liu Binyan (1925–)
  Journalist, *People's Daily,* until 1987
Liu Zaifu (1941–)
  Director, Institute of Literature,
  Chinese Academy of Social
  Sciences, 1985–1989

Wang Ruowang (1917–)
  Writer, Shanghai
Wu Zuguang (1917–)
  Playwright
Xia Yan (1900–)
  Playwright; Vice Chairman, All-
  China Federation of Literary and
  Art Circles

Scientific Associates

Fang Lizhi (1936–)
  Astrophysicist; Vice Chancellor,
  University of Science and
  Technology, Hefei, 1985–1987
Li Shuxian (1934–)
  Physicist, Peking University

Wen Yuankai (1946–)
  Chemist, University of Science and
  Technology, Hefei
Xu Liangying (1920–)
  Physicist, Institute of the History of
  Science, Chinese Academy of
  Sciences

Entrepreneurial Associate

Wan Runnan (1946–)
  Head, Stone Group, 1984–1989

Democratic Activists

Chen Ziming (1950–)
  Social and Economic Research
  Institute, Beijing

Wang Juntao (1958–)
  Social and Economic Research
  Institute, Beijing

Revolutionary Elders
(Participants in the Long March and members of the Central Advisory
Commission, 1982–1992)

Bo Yibo (1908–)
  Vice Chairman, Central Advisory
  Commission, 1982–1992
Chen Yun (1905–)
  First Secretary, Central Discipline
  Inspection Commission, 1978–
  1987; Chairman, Central Advisory
  Commission, 1987–1992
Deng Xiaoping (1904–)
  Chairman, Military Affairs
  Commission, 1981–1989;
  Chairman, Central Advisory
  Commission, 1982–1987

Li Xiannian (1909–1992)
  President, People's Republic of
  China, 1983–1988
Peng Zhen (1902–)
  Chairman, National People's
  Congress, 1978–1988
Wang Zhen (1908–1993)
  President, Central Party School,
  1982–1988; Vice President, People's
  Republic of China, 1988–1993
Yang Shangkun (1907–)
  President, People's Republic of
  China, 1988–1993

Disciples

Li Peng (1928–)
  Member, Politburo Standing
  Committee, 1987–; Premier,
  People's Republic of China, 1988–

Yang Baibing (1920–)
  Member, Central Military Affairs
  Commission, 1988–1993

Elders' Intellectual Network

Marxist-Leninist Theorists

Chen Xitong (1930–)
  Mayor of Beijing, 1983–1993
Deng Liqun (1915–)
  Director, Propaganda Department,
  1982–1985
Hu Qiaomu (1912–1992)
  President, Chinese Academy of
  Social Sciences, 1978–1982
Li Ximing (1926–)
  Secretary, Beijing Party Committee,
  1984–1993

Wang Renzhi (1933–)
  Director, Propaganda Department,
  1987–1992
Xu Weicheng (1930–)
  Director, *Beijing Daily,* 1985–1989;
  Deputy Director, Propaganda
  Department, 1989–

Yan'an Literary Associates

Chen Yong (1919–)
  Editor-in-chief, *Literature and Art
  Theory and Comment,* 1986–
He Jingzhi (1924–)
  Deputy Director, Propaganda
  Department, 1980–1987
Huang Gang (1919–1993)
  Editor, *Contemporary Reportage,*
  1979–1983

Lin Mohan (1913–)
  Vice Chairman, All-China Federa-
  tion of Literary and Art Circles,
  1979–1988
Liu Baiyu (1916–)
  Vice Chairman, Chinese Writers
  Association, 1978–1985

It is true that the errors we made in the past were partly attributed to the way of thinking and style of work of some leaders. But they were even more attributable to the problems in our organizational and working systems. If these systems are sound, they can place restraints on the actions of bad people; if they are unsound, they may hamper the efforts of good people or indeed, in certain cases, may push them in the wrong direction. Even so great a man as Comrade Mao Zedong was influenced to a serious degree by certain unsound systems and institutions, which resulted in grave misfortunes for the Party, the state and himself.

—Deng Xiaoping,
"On the Reform of the System
of Party and State Leadership,"
August 18, 1980

Abbreviations

ACFLAC	All-China Federation of Literary and Art Circles
CAS	Chinese Academy of Sciences
CASS	Chinese Academy of Social Sciences
CCP	Chinese Communist Party
CPPCC	Chinese People's Political Consultative Conference
CYL	China Youth League
Keda	University of Science and Technology, Hefei
NPC	National People's Congress
PRC	People's Republic of China
SERI	Social and Economic Research Institute

1

The Democratic Elite

China has been an agricultural society for most of its history, and
therefore it is not surprising that the Chinese use metaphors from nature and the weather to describe their political economy. In the early
decades of the twentieth century Chinese intellectuals used the word
"sprouts" *(mengya)*[1] to describe the beginnings of capitalism in their
country in the seventeenth and eighteenth centuries. Today many Chinese compare their budding capitalism to the bamboo shoots that
emerge after a spring rain. A similar metaphor is sometimes used in
talking about democracy in China. Although the shoots of democracy
have not been as plentiful, their roots more fragile and their buds
few, they emerged whenever the political atmosphere showed signs of
warming during the Deng Xiaoping decade of reform (1978–1989).
When buffeted by the cold winds of the political campaigns of 1981,
1983, and 1987 and the freeze of the military suppression on June 4,
1989, of the Tiananmen Square demonstrators, the shoots just as
quickly disappeared. Yet invariably they reemerged with the next
thaw in the political climate. Their resilience and intermittent budding
indicate that the ground had been prepared, the seeds sown, and the
roots nurtured to make possible their repeated appearance.

The sowers were members of China's democratic elite—individuals
and loose congeries of highly placed intellectuals, some associated directly, others indirectly, with Hu Yaobang, general secretary of the
Chinese Communist Party from 1980 to January 1987. At the center
of this elite was a group of Marxist theorists and editors, who, in
reaction to the Cultural Revolution, sought to humanize Marxist-
Leninist ideology. They were joined at times by writers such as the

journalist Liu Binyan, the Shanghai author Wang Ruowang, the screenwriter Bai Hua, the playwright Wu Zuguang, and the literary critic Liu Zaifu. In the mid-1980s, several prominent scientists—including the astrophysicist Fang Lizhi and the historian of science Xu Liangying—became part of the group. Various disciples and former students also followed the example of their mentors.

Over the course of the decade these individuals and informal groups gradually developed into an intellectual network, but not because of any concerted, organized action. Rather, their writings and speeches, though on a variety of topics, expressed the shared conviction that some kind of limit had to be placed on the power of the party in order to prevent another Cultural Revolution. Initially, members of the democratic elite sought to restrict party leaders by humanizing their ideology, but when these efforts were thwarted in the early 1980s, they increasingly emphasized the need to introduce democratic institutions as a means of curbing the party's power. Even though Hu Yaobang was in direct contact with only a few members of the democratic elite, he became their protector, both because he held similar ideological views and because he was supported by them in his power struggle within the party. When Hu was purged in January 1987, Zhao Ziyang, who became party general secretary (1987–1989), assumed Hu's patronage of the intellectual network. Both Hu's and Zhao's patronage of the democratic elite, however, was fraught with tension, because the elite sought to push political reforms much faster and further than did their patrons.

Members of the democratic elite did not have an overall political program or even a clear understanding of democracy. Like their literati predecessors, they believed that those who governed, even in a democracy, should belong to an educated elite, a view generally held by China's intellectuals. Until the late 1980s, most of them insisted that China's peasants did not care about politics and were not sufficiently educated to understand democratic principles or practices. The intellectuals' outlook, though rational, scientific, and technological, was not "democratic." In many ways the intellectual community's emphasis in the Deng era on professionalism and "scientific" methods of decision making was reminiscent of the literati's stress on meritocracy.

The democratic elite's simplistic idea of democracy derived from the concept of "rule by the people" (minzhu), used in China in the early decades of the twentieth century. The concepts of a legally protected voice for those in the minority, the existence of a plurality of views and interests, and the need for institutional limits on political power were not part of their initial understanding. They came to appreciate these additional ideas only after they themselves had been repeatedly repressed by both the Mao Zedong and the Deng Xiaoping regimes, to which they had given their full support. As they began to evaluate the damage inflicted on China as well as on themselves by the party and Mao in the anti-rightist campaign (1957–1959), the Great Leap Forward (1958–1960), the Cultural Revolution (1966–1976), and the continuing, though more limited, campaigns of the Deng era, and as they learned more about the workings of Western democracies, they called for a form of checks and balances: a stronger National People's Congress (NPC), a more independent judiciary, and freedom of the press. Some even called for civil and individual rights protected by laws and institutions. Through their writings, speeches, and debates on a myriad of issues—the causes of the Cultural Revolution, the relationship between the party-state and society, the existence of alienation under socialism, the role of individual conscience and neo-authoritarianism—this intellectual network disseminated a variety of democratic ideas that both influenced and reflected the views of important segments of China's urban society, including students, intellectuals, professionals, the new entrepreneurs, and reformist party cadres.

The ideas and actions of the democratic elite were not without precedent in China. Individuals and loose associations of literati and students returning from study in the West and Japan in the late Qing dynasty (1644–1911) were the first sowers of the seeds of democracy. For one hundred days in 1898, a group of younger literati attempted to reform the Confucian political structure by reinterpreting Confucianism, much as the democratic elite in Deng's era initially attempted to reform the party by reinterpreting the Marxist-Leninist ideology in which they had been indoctrinated. Although the literati's effort failed, the original founders of the Guomindang and other political activists, who carried out the 1911 revolution, established the first parliament in February 1913. It met for five months before it was disbanded by the military. During the chaos caused by the warlords who held sway between 1916 and 1927, the May Fourth movement of 1919 called for democracy as well as for "science," which was defined primarily as a critical view of Confucianism. The authoritarian rule of Chiang Kai-shek (1928–1949) that followed made a mockery of democracy, but the very incompetence and weakness of his regime permitted an ongoing discourse on democracy. When the Chinese Communist Party came to power in 1949, however, Mao Zedong and his colleagues created a party-state with more control over the population than that of any dynastic ruler, including China's most despotic emperor, Shi Huangdi of the Qin dynasty (221–202 B.C.). The party-state not only banned all discussions of democracy; it silenced, ostracized, sent to labor reform camps, or imprisoned virtually all advocates of political reform.

The Deng Xiaoping regime brought a thaw in the political atmosphere. Some of the controls of the Mao years (1949–1976) were lifted; others were loosened. The democratic elite was allowed to reseed the ground periodically and to cultivate the democratic seedlings that shot up with the slightest encouragement in the political climate. Despite recurring cool gusts, the shifting political winds were not as extreme as during the Mao period. And the radical economic changes that the Deng regime implemented not only moved China toward a market economy, opened it to the outside world, diffused economic decision making, caused rapid economic development of the coastal areas, and led to the emergence of an entrepreneurial middle class with a degree of economic autonomy but also helped to loosen control overall. These economic reforms have received much attention from Western as well as Chinese observers. The story of the emergence of the democratic elite and of demands for political reform, supported first by Hu Yaobang and later by Zhao Ziyang, is equally important and deserving of consideration.

Periodic student demonstrations and the establishment of politically oriented semiofficial and nonofficial newspapers, journals, publishing houses, and think tanks by former Red Guards and others also enriched the soil that bred these democratic shoots. Over time, a symbiotic relationship developed between the democratic elite and the former Red Guard and student activists. Sometimes, as in the late 1970s, they expressed parallel views; at other times, as in the late 1980s, they influenced each other. Briefly, toward the end of the decade, the democratic elite and the activists, particularly Chen Ziming and Wang Juntao, participated in joint actions. Together they came the closest in twentieth-century China to nurturing democratic seeds that had the potential for flowering.

The Traditional Soil

Despite the repeated crushing of democratic movements, first by military regimes in the early part of the century and then by the Communist totalitarian system in mid-century, something in the Chinese tradition has nourished intermittent democratic shoots over the past century. The mainstream of Confucian tradition, with its emphasis on ideological conformity and authoritarian rule, supports the contention of China's Long March veterans, the party's revolutionary elders, that democracy is inappropriate for China. Both the political reform tradition of Confucianism and aspects of Daoism, however, could lead China in a more democratic direction.[2]

Under Confucianism, the literati had a responsibility to speak out against abuses of power and to resist despotic rulers. They were to expose and criticize wrongdoings of officials even at the risk of their own lives. The Confucian system also had institutions, such as the Censorate and the practice of remonstrance, through which literati could criticize the misdeeds of higher officials and even of the emperor. Although the emperor had complete power over his subjects, stories of famous literati who remonstrated against abusive superiors reveal that in practice, if not in theory, Confucianism sought to restrain its rulers' power. Individuals, moreover, were to make independent moral judgments. Although not protected by laws or institutions, courageous individuals have criticized repressive rulers throughout Chinese history. These principled literati saw themselves as intermediaries between the government and the people. By interpreting the "murmurings" of the people to the leaders, they tried to draw the rulers and the ruled closer together so that the rulers might govern more effectively.[3]

The traditional system limited itself in other ways, as well. Even though the traditional political order theoretically presided over every aspect of Chinese society and economy, the historian Benjamin Schwartz points out that it did not directly interfere in everyday life. In practice, the government was self-limiting.[4] The political scientist Tang Tsou explains that the traditional system had "zones of indifference" upon which the political authorities, of their own volition, did not infringe.[5] The Confucian order, in addition, restrained political power by means of a vast array of rites, rituals, procedures, rules, and specific norms that the ruler and his officials were obliged to follow. If they did not, they risked provoking strong criticism from the literati. The exercise of power was internally rather than externally restricted, however. Restraint was exercised by custom and conscience, not by laws and institutions. This did not mean that the traditional order desired pluralism or freedom of thought; on the contrary, it prized conformity and hierarchy. But the consensus, as Schwartz observes, was very broad, including a variety of Confucian schools and even tolerating Daoism and Buddhism on the fringes.

The tradition of the principled literati continued into the Mao era, when a small number of intellectuals followed their predecessors in protesting against the abuse of political power. The writers Liu Binyan and Wang Meng, in accordance with Mao's Hundred Flowers policy in 1956 and the first half of 1957, published stories that exposed the conflict between educated, capable intellectuals and incompetent, oppressive party bureaucrats. For their actions, Liu and Wang were targeted in the anti-rightist campaign that followed. In the early 1960s the journalist Deng Tuo subtly criticized the irrational economic policies of the Great Leap Forward. This criticism along with other charges against him made Deng Tuo the first fatality in the Cultural Revolution's campaign against officials and intellectuals who Mao believed opposed his policies. Those like Liu Binyan and Wang Meng who survived the Cultural Revolution and were rehabilitated in the late 1970s initially resumed the role that they had tried to play in the Mao period. Like their literati predecessors, they saw themselves as a conduit through which the political leaders learned of the defects of their policies and heard about the wishes of the people. In the early years of the Deng regime, these intermediaries expected that the party's leaders would listen to their interpretations of the people's murmurings and respond accordingly.

The traditional view of government as humane also nurtured democratic efforts. The government was supposed to promote the people's happiness. If the ruler was unconcerned with the people's welfare, then the people had the right, through the Mandate of Heaven, to replace him. The ruler's ability to rule, determined by his behavior and effectiveness, was not a democratic concept; people could only accept or rebel against his rule. Nevertheless, it was ultimately based on the tacit consent of the ruled. In addition, the ruler was held accountable in a moral sense. But whereas in traditional times individuals were periodically punished for reminding the ruler and his officials of their ideals, in the Mao years the whole intellectual community, their families, and their acquaintances suffered for the courage of a small number of their colleagues.

Until well into the Deng period, most of the principled intellectuals, like their literati predecessors, never questioned the assumption that they could speak on behalf of the people or at least for the benefit of the people. Nor did they question the assumption that when properly informed of the people's wishes, the leaders would respond appropriately. Because of their continuing persecution under the Deng regime and the party's diminishing response to their pleas, however, some reluctantly acknowledged that the intellectuals' paternalistic presumption in "speaking for the people" had in part reinforced the repression. Even if the leaders supposedly listened to the people through intellectual intermediaries, the problems to which the intellectuals called attention and the abuses they pointed out were dealt with superficially or were not truly alleviated. In most cases the intellectuals' efforts to inform the leadership of its abuses had, in fact, provoked retribution. Their remonstrances, presented in the media and at meetings, proved to be counterproductive, leading to their own and others' persecution.

Even though the criticisms and campaigns against intellectuals in the Deng era were relatively limited when compared with the zealous, wide-ranging campaigns of the Mao era, by the second half of the 1980s, members of the democratic elite realized that even under the supposedly reformist Deng regime, they had no protection against retaliation. They concluded that methods more effective than ideological and moral persuasion were needed to close the gap between the rulers and the ruled: the government had to be held accountable in an institutional, legal, and social sense as well. A government not only of the people or for the people but *by* the people was needed. Instead of acting as the people's intermediaries, these intellectuals increasingly urged that the ruled express themselves directly to the rulers by means of elections, a free press, a legislature, and the formation of interest groups. Instead of the traditional view that emphasized "rule by sages," they emphasized the "rule of law." The Legalist school had introduced the basic concept of law during the Qin dynasty, but it was the law of punishment. The state used the law to control society; society did not and could not use law to restrain the state. Under Mao and Deng, similarly, law was a tool of power, not a tool for society.

The democratic elite in the 1980s increasingly emphasized that law should be used to protect civil and individual rights.

As in traditional times, in the twentieth century under the Guomindang and Communist systems the only restraints on political power were self-imposed limits. Even though the idea of rights had been included in all of China's constitutions since the late nineteenth century, in none of these constitutions were they referred to as "natural" rights.[6] Because rights were granted by the state, they could also be taken away by the state. Mao, especially toward the end of his life, increasingly regarded himself *as* the state; he exercised little self-restraint, and the party imposed few restraints upon him. And even under the reformist Deng regime, the intellectuals discovered they still had no rights vis-à-vis the state.

In the mid-1980s, consequently, some members of the democratic elite began to talk publicly about rights as inherent in the individual, impossible for the state to withdraw and in need of protection by independent judicial and political institutions. Among the strongest public advocates of this view were the astrophysicist Fang Lizhi and the legal scholar Yu Haocheng. They looked to Western ideas in trying to resolve their problems, but their efforts were prompted by internal events within China and by their own bitter experiences. Moreover, the demand for institutional protections was not altogether unknown in Chinese history. Wm. Theodore de Bary has written about the Confucian scholar Huang Zongxi (1610–1695), who called for the protection of morality with institutions and laws.[7] Huang was the most outspoken, but not the only, seventeenth-century scholar asking for such protections. This view was not a dominant one in Confucianism, but it was an important precedent for those seeking institutional restraints and protections in the twentieth century. The democratic elite's demand that certain rights be guaranteed by laws and institutions was thus not an alien concept in China. Even though some members of the network realized that if such institutions were established, they themselves would in time be replaced as intermediaries for the people and would lose their unique status, they became ardent advocates of the establishment of such institutions.

Though they had a symbiotic relationship with the student protesters of the Deng era, most of the democratic elite stayed away from the student demonstrations until the Tiananmen demonstration of the spring of 1989. In the late 1980s some members began to reach out to nonofficial think tanks and to the new middle class of urban and rural entrepreneurs spawned by economic reform, particularly those involved in private and collective enterprises. The new middle class, professionals such as lawyers and doctors, and students shared with the democratic elite a desire to limit the party-state's control over their activities and to protect themselves against its arbitrary interference. Yet despite the elite's acknowledgment of the need to build a broader social base for political reform, its activities still retained the traditional literati's bias toward the educated class.

Western Nourishment

Although the democratic elite's demands for institutions and laws to limit political power stemmed primarily from its Chinese experience, its members looked to Western democratic ideas and institutions for ways to impose restraints. The fall of the Qing dynasty in 1911 and the collapse of Confucianism as a political system, followed by a period of warlordism and weak governments, had opened China to all kinds of new ideas from abroad. In the years before and after the May Fourth movement of 1919, sparked by a student demonstration against warlord concessions to the Western powers and Japan, China's intellectual atmosphere was energized by a cultural pluralism and political discourse comparable only to the period of the Hundred Schools of Thought that existed early in its history (722–221 B.C.).

In the post-Mao period the indecisiveness of the political leadership, the irrelevance of Marxist-Leninist orthodoxy to China's problems, and China's openness similarly made possible the expression of ideas that had not been seen or heard since the establishment of the People's Republic in 1949. These ideas were some of the same ones that had excited the May Fourth participants, and ranged from individualism to Western Marxism, from Nietzsche to Freud, from existentialism to Christianity. As their predecessors had rebelled against the traditional culture and political system, so too did the democratic elite and students in the post-Mao period challenge the ideological and political system they had known since 1949. Their protest was impelled not only by their own experiences but also by their belief that the political system, instead of improving the lot of society, had made it worse. Equally important, they were well aware of the failure of the Soviet system that China had emulated and of the general movement toward democracy throughout the world.

Like the immediate successors of the May Fourth movement, they discovered that pluralism, both ideological and cultural, though it does not lead to democracy, is a precondition for democracy because it makes possible a politically conscious, relatively independent community. In the reform years under Deng, until the June 4, 1989, crackdown, wide-ranging, emotionally charged debates on topics such as the new authoritarianism versus democracy and Chinese culture versus Western culture were tolerated without the imposition of an orthodox view or a conclusive consensus. Open discussion of political as well as cultural issues took place in journals, newspapers, academic forums, and periodically on television.

The May Fourth period has been characterized as China's enlightenment,[8] and post-Mao China may also be characterized as a time in which intellectuals sought individual and intellectual autonomy. Like their May Fourth predecessors, however, they initially exerted little effort to organize politically to achieve these goals. Their original approach, as in traditional times, was to try to persuade the leaders of their views through ideological arguments and individual protest. The exception in the Deng period was the brief Democracy Wall movement, in late 1978 and early 1979, made up of ex–Red Guards and workers who formed their own organizations and published their own pamphlets. Some called for the establishment of democratic institutions among their demands. In the early days of the Deng era, few members of the democratic elite gave public support to this movement. Although they mentioned the need for institutions and laws, most of their discussions in those years focused on the need for more pluralistic, rational methods of decision making and a more humane form of Marxism and socialism.

Because most of the democratic elite had originally been Marxist theorists, the ideological approach was well suited to their training and interests and in accordance with Chinese tradition. In the late 1970s and early 1980s they were attracted to the revisions of Marxism-Leninism going on in Eastern Europe and in the West. With the exception of Fang Lizhi, most of them did not reject Marxism; they continued to believe in at least some of its original tenets, though they rejected the "distortions" of Lenin, Stalin, Mao, and the Gang of Four and the orthodox interpretations of Deng's elderly colleagues. The democratic elite sought to make ideology more relevant to the period of reform. In this effort they had the support of Hu Yaobang, who was also interested in East European and Western interpretations of Marxism. He encouraged China's theorists to revise and revitalize Marxism-Leninism in the hope that the ideology could regain the legitimacy it had lost during the Cultural Revolution. By the late 1980s, however, most intellectuals, a portion of the reformist political leadership, and the urban population in general had lost faith in orthodox Marxism-Leninism, not only because of its perversion in the Cultural Revolution but also because it was losing its hold elsewhere in the Communist world.

An ideology that had once appeared to be monolithic was now splintered into fragments. While older party and military leaders remained upholders of orthodox Marxism-Leninism of the 1950s, several reform political leaders, members of the democratic elite, and their younger disciples explored a variety of interpretations, particularly from Eastern Europe and the West. Like their foreign colleagues, they turned to the early Marx, where they found the concepts of alienation, humanism, and self-realization to be relevant to their present condition. In contrast to the ideology of the Cultural Revolution, these concepts treated people not as mere members of a class or political faction but as individuals, and they offered a form of Marxism that appealed to the ideologically disillusioned.

Only as their revisions of ideology and their remonstrances met with increasing rebuffs from the elders and Deng, and as they came into more direct contact with the West, did members of the democratic elite give more consideration to the need for establishing political institutions and laws that would guarantee and sustain the cultural and ideological pluralism they were promoting. By the mid-1980s, their ideological rhetoric became mixed with demands for specific institutions and laws to implement the civil rights stipulated in the Chinese constitution and specific measures to strengthen the power of the National People's Congress so it could truly act as a legislative check on the leadership. By the late 1980s, they began to organize politically and publicly for the first time by setting up their own journals and organizations outside the party's jurisdiction, just as former Red Guards had done in the late 1970s and as other less highly placed intellectuals had been doing since the mid-1980s.[9]

Democratic practices and organizations were not totally unknown in China. In the 1913 elections, a number of parties genuinely competed for political office. In the late 1920s and 1930s, Western-oriented intellectuals formed groups to criticize the Guomindang's abuse of human rights. In addition, they called for democratic elections, representative government, rule of law, freedom of speech, and an independent judiciary. Some advocates demanded that these practices be adopted not merely for their social and economic utility but for their own sake. Independent journals and organizations, such as the League for the Protection of Civil Rights, were established in the 1930s and early 1940s to fight for these rights. Because Guomindang repression was somewhat erratic, intellectuals were able to organize groups and establish journals to express such ideas.

The intellectuals' relative autonomy and freedom in the early decades of the twentieth century ended in the early 1950s with the Communist Party's imposition of economic, social, and ideological control over all sectors of society, especially the intellectual realm. The party needed the intellectuals in its drive for economic modernization, but it did not trust them and regarded them as rivals for authority. Controls on intellectuals were imposed to a much greater degree and much more systematically than in the traditional or Guomindang periods. And unlike under the Confucian order, there were no ideological or bureaucratic restraints on the leadership's exercise of power as Mao pushed Chinese society toward a utopian future. In 1956, when some of the writers of the post–May Fourth era and some of the same individuals, such as Luo Longji and Zhang Bojun, who had headed the League for the Protection of Civil Rights, tried to advocate views during the Hundred Flowers period similar to those they had expressed in the 1930s, they became prime targets of the anti-rightist campaign.

Yet Western concepts introduced into China in the early decades of the twentieth century did not disappear altogether. Ba Jin, the author of the popular 1930s novel *The Family,* wrote of his generation: "We were all the children of May 4 . . . One of the main reasons I did not give over to absolute despair during the tyrannical years of the gang of four was that I had my memories of the past."[10] The May Fourth legacy even influenced the generations who were educated under the Maoist regime, as seen in the semi-spontaneous demonstration in Tiananmen Square on April 5, 1976, against the dictatorship of Mao, the Gang of Four, and the Cultural Revolution. The influence of May Fourth was even more evident in the Democracy Wall movement of 1978–79, when the participants, who were young people brought up entirely under the Communist system with little contact with the West, called for democracy, human rights, a rule of law, and freedom of speech.

The Winds from Eastern Europe, the Soviet Union, and East Asia

The influence of the thaw in the Soviet Union after Stalin's death in 1953 and of the reform movements in Eastern Europe were as important as the May Fourth legacy in stimulating the movement for political reform in the post-Mao era. Some older members of the democratic elite had visited the Soviet Union and Eastern Europe when China was allied with them in the 1950s, knew the languages of these countries, and had read widely in their literature. After the Cultural Revolution they were initially inspired by the reform efforts of Yugoslavia, Poland, and Hungary, and they also learned of the early efforts by Bukharin to resist the Stalinist model. Liu Binyan, Wang Meng, and other writers were personally acquainted with Soviet participants in the freer intellectual atmosphere following Stalin's death, and theorists such as Su Shaozhi were in touch with Hungarian and Yugoslav reformers. Su supervised the translation of Bukharin's writings into Chinese. The democratic elite's positive view of the changes going on in the Soviet Union and Eastern Europe conflicted with that of China's leaders. In the 1980s, the leadership feared that Poland's Solidarity movement might inspire China's workers to organize an independent labor movement that would threaten the party; the democratic elite admired Solidarity as a spontaneous social movement challenging the regime from below in alliance with the intellectuals. In the late 1980s members of the democratic elite were particularly enthusiastic about Mikhail Gorbachev's policies of *glasnost* and political reform, and they urged China's leaders to follow the examples of Gorbachev and other reformist East European leaders.

The Deng regime was not totally devoid of political reforms. It introduced multiple candidates and a secret ballot in elections to the people's congresses from the local level up to the county level in the early 1980s, and even introduced multicandidate elections for the Central Committee at the Thirteenth Party Congress in 1987, when several associates of the elder leadership were voted out of office. Multiple candidates and secret ballot elections were also used at some academic institutions and professional organizations. Such elections had been unknown in the People's Republic since the early 1950s. But these political reforms were minor compared with the direct elections for the president of Russia and the emergence of opposition parties in Eastern Europe in the late 1980s. Moreover, China's local elections had little influence on policies made at the center, and candidates not approved by the party were not allowed to take their seats. Gorbachev's toleration of independent associations and journals and even public demonstrations goaded China's democratic elite to push harder for similar reforms at home. When in the late 1980s they began to establish their own journals and organize publicly, however, they were repeatedly thwarted by the authorities.

Like their East European and Soviet counterparts, those who made up the democratic elite expressed a variety of views. Some stressed a more democratic style of decision making within the party; others wanted a more humane socialism; some emphasized a freer party press and the establishment of a nonofficial press; others sought to make the National People's Congress into a legislative branch. Some stressed the rule of law; others stressed institutionalized procedures. All wanted to make Marxism more just and more relevant to the changing world. But by the mid-1980s, because of the continuing repression, most concluded that the revision of Marxism was not enough; institutional as well as ideological change was needed. At the same time, many former Red Guards and members of the younger generation were increasingly attracted to non-Marxist ideas and styles of life, including Western popular culture, music, and individualism in addition to Western political institutions.

Toward the end of the 1980s, as the four little dragons of East Asia, particularly Taiwan and South Korea, not only developed dynamic economic models but also moved toward democratic institutions, China's intellectuals began to look at their Confucian brethren more seriously. The party leadership was attracted to these nations because of their authoritarian leaderships and fast-paced economies. The democratic elite, however, was interested in their movement toward parliamentary governments, a freer press, and the emergence of opposition parties competing with the ruling party in free elections. The four little dragons demonstrated that the Confucian and traditional values that they and China shared were not obstacles to the introduction of democratic practices. This example encouraged the democratic elite to become still more critical of China's Leninist political system and Marxist-Leninist orthodoxy and less critical of the nation's traditional legacy as the major obstacle to change. Indeed, some well-known intellectuals also began to look to China's traditional culture to provide answers to the country's problems.

The Legacies of the Cultural Revolution

Even more important than traditional and external influences in generating demands for political change was the more immediate experience of the Cultural Revolution. Ba Jin describes these years as a "disaster without precedent in five thousand years of Chinese culture" and as a "specter" that "haunts post-Mao China." [11] The disaster left two fearsome legacies: on one side loomed anarchy, chaos, and the breakdown of order; on the other, despotism and ideological fanaticism. These two bequests provoked contradictory responses from the elders who were part of the post-Mao leadership and the democratic elite, though both groups had been equally persecuted during the Cultural Revolution. The elders and their associates, more concerned with preventing a recurrence of disorder, demanded the imposition of unity, stability, party authority, and orthodox ideology; the democratic elite, more worried about a recurrence of despotism, demanded restraints on political power and the regularization of political procedures.

The party, because it had been unable to prevent the Cultural Revolution and in fact had created the conditions that allowed a leader and a small group to dominate the political structure, immobilize the economy, and persecute millions of people, found its legitimacy as well as its ideology severely undermined. The party's failure to stop or to limit the Cultural Revolution raised questions about a political system that could not correct itself until the death of its leader. The elders blamed these events on the Gang of Four's distortion of ideology and repudiation of standard party practices; the democratic elite, some other intellectuals, and segments of society blamed the ideological orthodoxy, the political system, and the party itself.

Both the party leadership and the democratic elite also questioned various pre–Cultural Revolution policies and practices, particularly the nationwide campaign in 1955 against the writer Hu Feng and his disciples; the anti-rightist campaign of 1957–1959, during which over half a million intellectuals were persecuted; and the irrational economic policies of the Great Leap Forward, which had led to the death of thirty million people, primarily in the countryside. With a few exceptions, party leaders now admitted that they either had actively gone along with Mao's misconceived policies, as in the Great Leap Forward, or had passively stood by, as in the Cultural Revolution.

They thus admitted that they as well as Mao had contributed to the increasing alienation not only of the intellectuals but also of the peasants and workers, whose wages had remained relatively static since 1957, and, finally, of the party itself, which became Mao's chief target in the Cultural Revolution.

Although both the party leaders and the democratic elite sought to ensure that China would never again suffer such tragedies as the Great Leap Forward or the Cultural Revolution, consensus broke down over what safeguards were needed and how to institute them. The elders and their associates, who included the former head of the Beijing Party Committee Peng Zhen, the economic planner Chen Yun, the generals Wang Zhen and Yang Shangkun, and the theorists Hu Qiaomu and Deng Liqun, differed somewhat on economic issues, but they generally agreed that the only way to close the gap between the leaders and the led was to reimpose the party's authority and reindoctrinate the population with orthodox Marxism-Leninism. The reformist political leaders, led by Hu Yaobang and Zhao Ziyang, and the democratic elite, in contrast, encouraged the search for new approaches to ideology and governance, calling for "socialist democracy" and "socialist legalism." Although they defined these terms in different ways at different times, they generally sought a more predictable system, guided by laws and more rational decision making, guaranteed by institutions and feedback from society. They had concluded that the highly centralized Leninist-Stalinist political-economic system that China had copied from the Soviet Union in the 1950s was repressive as well as unsuitable for the approaching age of high technology. Even Deng Xiaoping himself admitted in a speech on August 18, 1980, that the party's excessive concentration of power at the top had led to the abuse of political power.[12]

The Decade of Reform

With such views emanating from reform-minded political leaders, Hu Yaobang encouraged a group of theorists to criticize Mao's ideology and policies and some aspects of orthodox Marxism-Leninism, as long as they did not threaten the party's dominant authority. But when some of these theorists disregarded this limit and began to discuss changing the political structure by instituting restraints on the party's power, their suggestions had an unintended result. Not only did they provoke the opposition of the elders, but they neutralized their own patrons, forcing them to desert and at times turn against the theorists at critical moments. Even Hu Yaobang, the reform leader most open to political change, wanted reform within the prevailing institutions and ideology rather than outside them. The reform-oriented political leaders as well as Deng and the elders continued to be influenced by the Leninist political structure they had long been part of and by the harsh experiences they had endured at the hands of the Red Guards. They acknowledged the need for greater scientific, professional, and technological input in decision making and tolerated some cultural pluralism and religious worship. But when their authority was challenged from below by demonstrations in the streets, they repressed the movements or individuals involved and incarcerated their leaders.

The political leaders who favored reform advocated the separation of the party from economic enterprises and even from government administration. They first permitted and then promoted the decollectivization of agriculture; the establishment of private, individual, cooperative, collective, joint, and foreign enterprises; and the move toward a market economy. They urged increased study abroad and invited foreign advisors to China. They acknowledged interest groups in different geographic areas, economic sectors, professions, and generations. They encouraged the reemergence of the eight "democratic" or small parties that had been established in the 1940s by intellectuals and professionals as a middle force between the Guomindang and the Chinese Communist Party but virtually eliminated during the anti-rightist campaign. They invited the members of these small parties to advise on policy, though all their activities had to be under the party's leadership. They opened channels for other nonparty elites to influence policy as well. Still, these groups could not participate in *making* policy; similarly, they could discuss ideology, but they could not change its fundamental tenets. The goal of the reform-minded political leaders, like that of the elders, was to revise and ultimately to strengthen the system, not to undermine it.

Although theoretically Deng rejected one-person rule, his regime evolved into an oligarchy over which he presided. Deng most often sided with the reform-oriented leaders, who themselves did not always agree. Hu Yaobang was more willing to consider changes in the political system and allow freer intellectual debates; Zhao Ziyang was more interested in far-reaching economic and administrative reforms than political reforms, but he too recognized the need to respond to the plurality of interests that were developing.

At important junctures, however, even before the June 4, 1989, crackdown, Deng periodically switched to the elders' side, for reasons of both ideology and personal history. He believed strongly in technocratic and economic reforms, but only within the prevailing political and ideological framework, very much in the tradition of the nineteenth-century self-strengtheners, a group of reformist Qing officials who were interested in Western science and technology, *yong,* but rejected Western political ideas and values, *ti.* Deng moved back and forth between the reformers and elders, using persuasion and compromise to achieve a balance between them. Although he was at times concerned about the abuses of power, his "cat theory" of development—that it does not matter whether a cat is black or white as long as it catches mice—sums up his pragmatic, technocratic bias.

Because of the fragmentation of the leadership, the Deng regime was beset by factional disputes and indecisiveness over policy. The regime consequently oscillated between periods of relative relaxation and periods of repression, as had occurred under Mao. But unlike during the Mao era, because the political leaders favoring reform were more often in the ascendancy, the periods of relaxation, particularly with regard to intellectuals, were much more far-reaching and longer in duration. In the periods of relative repression, in 1981 and especially in the campaigns against spiritual pollution in late 1983 and against bourgeois liberalization in the early months of 1987, some of the elders and their associates tried to extend the campaigns from the intellectual realm into the economic sphere. When that happened, Deng threw his support back to the reformers so as not to interrupt economic reforms.

The major targets of the campaigns of the Deng era were the democratic elite and their associates, but these campaigns were without the fanaticism, mass mobilization, and indiscriminate terror of the Mao period. Moreover, they were limited to a small number of individuals and the criticism of specific works. The attacks were not on a person's entire career or life's work, nor did they extend to one's family, colleagues, and profession. Perhaps most important, although the targets were silenced during the brief campaigns against them, they reappeared shortly after the campaigns ended and resumed arguing even more vigorously on behalf of the ideas for which they had just been criticized. In addition, when attacked in the Deng era, most of the democratic elite refused to criticize themselves or their colleagues as they had been forced to do under Mao. Nor did they suffer serious repercussions because of their refusal. Instead of being ostracized, as they had been under Mao, their selection for public criticism now enhanced their stature and made their views more appealing to the public at large. Moreover, as it became clearer that the targets of a campaign reappeared soon after its conclusion, resistance and noncooperation during the campaigns increased.

Members of the democratic elite may have lost their party membership and positions in the Deng campaigns, but they were not deprived of public forums for very long. There were still no laws or institutions to protect them, but there appears to have been a tacit recognition of a "loyal opposition" on both the reformist and the elders' sides. The reformist loyal opposition expressed itself not only in such semiofficial papers as the *World Economic Herald* (Shijie jingji daobao) and the nonofficial *Economic Weekly* (Jingjixue zhoubao) but also in the official journals and, most important, in the party's premier newspaper, the *People's Daily* (Renmin ribao), until June 4, 1989. The elders' loyal opposition also expressed itself in the party's official media, particularly its main ideological journal, *Red Flag* (Hongqi), and after 1987 its successor *Seek Truth from Facts* (Qiushi); the *Liberation Army Daily* (Jiefangjun bao); and sometimes even in the newspaper of the intellectuals, the *Guangming Daily* (Guangming ribao). The official patrons of the democratic elite, Hu Yaobang and then Zhao Ziyang, dominated the Secretariat and the Standing Committee of the Politburo. The elders dominated the Central Advisory Commission, established in 1982 to absorb retired high officials; the Central Discipline Commission, under Chen Yun; and the National People's Congress, under Peng Zhen until his retirement in 1988.

In another significant difference from the Mao era, both the elders and the reformers sought to make the NPC into a strong legislative institution. Peng Zhen's efforts to strengthen the NPC were not to restrain the party's overall power, as the democratic elite was trying to do, but rather to use it to counter the reformers' power in the Secretariat and the Standing Committee of the Politburo. By at times refusing to go along with the Secretariat and the Politburo, however, Peng Zhen inadvertently helped boost the democratic elite's efforts to make the NPC into a more meaningful, independent legislative forum where dissenting views could be voiced and which could periodically act as a check on party leaders.

As under Mao, the media and intellectual groups associated with the various political factions usually waited for a signal from their political patrons before publishing a controversial article or launching a provocative debate. Often the initiative from above led to an uncontrolled response from below; the words and actions of the intellectual clients of both the reform leaders and the elders were sometimes more daring than their political patrons desired. The reform leaders' call in 1986 for discussions of political reforms, for example, evoked demands by some members of the democratic elite, their associates, and others for a system of checks and balances, and even a multiparty system. A similar dynamic occurred with the elders and their associates. The 1983 campaign against spiritual pollution and the 1987 campaign against bourgeois liberalization in the intellectual realm were extended by associates of the elders into the economic realm. In such cases, however, Deng Xiaoping treated the elders' associates more leniently than he treated the democratic elite. The elders' associates might be charged with using "incorrect" methods; members of the democratic elite usually received the more serious accusation of "opposing the party and socialism." Nevertheless, as was true for associates of the democratic elite, the elders' associates were sometimes forced to resign from their official positions.

The Emergence of a Loyal Opposition

Until the Deng era, society and state in China were regarded as virtually the same. Even the principled literati of traditional times defined themselves with reference to the state or as serving the state at the same time that they served society and their own conscience.[13] When the party came to power in 1949 and became the state, service to the state became synonymous with service to the party. The party-state and society, therefore, were regarded as one whole, though the reality became quite different. Intellectuals, including ideological dissidents, gladly gave their full support to the regime in the belief that it was the only political entity that could unite the country and achieve the goal that China had been seeking since the late nineteenth century: to make China "rich and powerful." The fundamental harmony of interests of all groups and individuals within the party-state was assumed. Until the Cultural Revolution the government was regarded as basically good; to impose external constraints on the party leaders was believed to be unnecessary and even undesirable, because that would hinder them in their efforts to modernize China.

Intellectuals as well as the general population were therefore unconcerned with issues of human rights and the individual's relationship with the state. Even politically oriented intellectuals had little desire to limit the party's power. Moreover, whereas in the Confucian tradition, a literatus might be considered more loyal when he opposed an unjust ruler than when he gave him unquestioning loyalty, in the People's Republic it was virtually impossible to exercise independent moral judgment. One was "loyal" only when one gave unquestioning loyalty to the party-state and its leadership. The individual had to subordinate himself or herself completely to the economic, social, and ideological needs of the party-state and its leadership in order to aid in transforming society. At the same time, through the Hu Feng and anti-rightist campaigns, the Great Leap Forward, and the Cultural Revolution, the party-state repressed and purged anyone who refused to comply. Although the four constitutions of the People's Republic provided for the fundamental rights of freedom of speech, press, assembly, association, and demonstration, no laws or institutions were established to implement these rights. There was no independent judiciary, free press, or opposition party to carry out these provisions, prevent their violation, or call for their enforcement.

Despite the Deng regime's acknowledgment in the late 1970s of the impossibility of totally controlling society and of the willingness of the regime to permit certain freedoms, such as freedom of religious belief, academic research, and popular culture, as long as they did not conflict with the policies of the party-state, the leadership consistently crushed any organized activity outside the system that they believed challenged it. Thus they repressed the Democracy Wall activists and student demonstrators and obstructed the democratic elite's efforts to set up its own publications and organizations. Unlike Gorbachev in the Soviet Union in the late 1980s, Deng and his associates were unwilling to tolerate any politically oriented organization, group, or journal over which the party did not have some control, even if the control was only minimal or nominal.

Nevertheless, because the party leadership was indecisive and divided in its ideological stand and policies, a number of relatively independent think tanks and publications were able to function in the late 1980s, and some relatively open conflicts between the elders' associates and the democratic elite on political and ideological issues occurred in the party-controlled media and forums. In addition, the different groups and interests spawned by the regime's economic reforms and opening to the outside world further weakened the party's grip over society. Like Gorbachev, Deng and the reform leaders tried to stimulate the initiative of the population and mobilize the people's support for reforms by giving them some degree of freedom in their private, economic, and intellectual lives, and these actions further undermined party control. Similarly, the promotion of competitive elections and secret ballots at the local level, in some professional organizations, and in the Central Committee in 1987 was meant to rid the bureaucracy of older, less-educated officials, but it also had the effect of giving the population some choice in selecting leaders. Gail Lapidus has pointed out in the Soviet case[14] that as such political participation increases, it inevitably encourages autonomy for various groups and individuals.

Because the Cultural Revolution's legacy of challenging authority plus the Deng regime's fluid definition of what was permissible made possible public debate on fundamental issues such as culture, ideology, and at times even the political structure without the imposition of any one authoritative view, individuals and groups increasingly asked their own questions and provided their own answers. In addition, contact with peers in the outside world further weakened party control, as professional groups and intellectuals began to identify more with their international colleagues and their concerns than with their own country or even their own colleagues at home. The party still exerted control over the intellectual realm when it wished, but during periods of relaxation editors, journalists, writers, and intellectuals had more autonomy. The reform leadership was willing to permit the presentation of a variety of views in order to get more feedback so as to rule more responsively.

In fact if not in theory, there was a tacit acceptance of a more differentiated view of society, and at times the reform-minded political leaders acknowledged that the party-state's view of society as a unified harmonious whole did not necessarily correspond with reality. The revival of sociology after more than twenty-five years of suppression and the introduction of public opinion polling in the mid-1980s revealed that the views of the party-state and those of society were not the same. The polls indicated that segments of society held views and values that differed significantly from those of the party leadership as well as from one another, findings that challenged the party's right to speak in the name of society. Recognition of different interests and views did not mean that these interests could organize themselves, nor did it lead to a pluralistic political system. Only a minority of the democratic elite publicly called for a multiparty system, specific democratic institutions, or a system of checks and balances. Nevertheless, virtually all of the democratic elite and their associates called for some form of ideological pluralism, protected by institutions and laws, in order to strengthen society's role vis-à-vis the state. In the post-Mao era, they wanted to be citizens rather than the subjects they had been since 1949.

For the intellectuals as a whole and especially for the democratic elite, the experiences of the anti-rightist campaign, the Cultural Revolution, and the continuing campaigns during the Deng era, though less repressive than those under Mao, slowly but surely broke the bonds between the intellectuals and the party-state. As intellectuals began to define themselves more in terms of their profession, the members of the democratic elite began to define themselves more in terms of their responsibility to society than in terms of their responsibility to the party-state. Continuing persecution, increasing exposure to Western ideas, and the party's weakened control all influenced the evolution of the democratic elite over the Deng decade of reform from loyal courtiers into a loyal opposition. Although they did not and could not take the next step of setting up an opposition party, for the first time in the People's Republic, party intellectuals had by the late 1980s organized themselves into groups independent of the party and advocated an agenda different from that of the party.

Hu Yaobang's intellectual network and its associates formed the most influential of these groups. Although its members had diverse concerns, by the end of the reform decade most were moving toward a radical break with both their previous role in the People's Republic and the tradition of their literati predecessors. The nature of the Deng regime and the evolution of their own thinking had transformed them from remonstrators into opponents of the political leadership, party policies, and Marxist-Leninist ideology to which they had hitherto been loyal. Like their Western and Soviet counterparts, they had come to see themselves in conflict with the party-state and had joined with other social groups against it. They even associated with nonofficial groups, particularly one led by the well-known activists Wang Juntao and Chen Ziming, who in the late 1980s had established their own nonofficial think tank, journal, publishing house, and opinion-polling organization as alternatives to those of the party. Not only had this nonofficial group and others achieved a degree of respectability and efficacy, but the democratic elite had come to despair of achieving political reforms within the prevailing party system. Their increasing disillusionment with and detachment from the party-state both influenced and mirrored what was happening to China's urban population in general.

2

Hu Yaobang's Intellectual Network

Hu Yaobang was unique among the elders of the Long March. Unlike his fellow revolutionaries, he was willing to tolerate some public criticism of party policies and even to contemplate some reduction in the party's monopoly on political power. As he gained power early in the Deng era, he became the protector of intellectuals who expressed views that differed from those of the party leadership. His greater support for radical ideological revision and political change may have had its beginnings in his Hakka origins. The Hakkas, a branch of China's main ethnic Han group who have migrated from the central plains over the last 1,500 years to the west and south, are generally regarded as more questioning and less conformist than their fellow Han. Hu's personality—impetuous, activist, curious, and relatively independent—exemplified these qualities.[1]

Hu was born into a poor peasant family in Hunan in 1915. His father put great emphasis on his children's schooling, and provided Hu with educational opportunities that were rare for peasant children. Although at thirteen Hu left school to join the Communist revolution, he continued his education on his own. He studied mainly Marxism-Leninism and history, but also read Tang and Song poetry, modern fiction, and even some Shakespeare. Decades later, while the other elders continued to stress the importance of revolutionary values, Hu extolled intellectual achievement, technical skill, and professionalism as well.

In 1927 Hu participated in Mao's Autumn Harvest Uprising in Hunan, and in 1931 he went to Mao's Jiangxi base area, where he joined the Communist Youth League (CYL). In 1933 he joined the party.

During the civil war against the Guomindang he worked under Deng Xiaoping and with him established the party's authority in Sichuan and the Southwest. This was the beginning of a close professional and social relationship between the two men, who became bridge partners as well as fellow revolutionaries. In August 1952 Hu was transferred with Deng to Beijing, and in September of that year he became first secretary of the Youth League. In this post he appointed a vast network of able people, some of whom were to become part of his own intellectual network in the post-Mao period. He also became directly involved in the publications of the league, particularly *China Youth News* (Zhongguo qingnian bao). Even before the beginning of the Hundred Flowers period, he encouraged this publication to attack bureaucratism and to criticize the party's abuse of power. During these years he gained a reputation for openness to new ideas and a willingness to listen to others. He was not associated with party infighting.

Hu resisted the anti-rightist campaign of late 1957–1959 against those who had criticized the party during the Hundred Flowers. When the campaign was launched he was leading a delegation to Moscow, but on his return he reprimanded those in charge of the movement in the CYL who had labeled scores of his followers as "rightists." Some of Hu's associates believe that his experience of being falsely charged an "anti-Bolshevik" in the 1940s, when he came close to being executed, had had a profound effect on him and later impelled him to defend those who were falsely accused.[2]

He was successful in protecting some of his followers, but not all. One of these was Liu Binyan, who wrote for *China Youth News* and who had been specifically criticized by Mao.[3] When those in the Youth League accused of being rightists were about to be sent to the countryside and factories for labor reform, Hu convened a meeting and assured them that they would be welcomed back.[4] No other party leader at that time had dared to comfort those under attack. On the contrary, most had rushed to criticize their colleagues and subordinates to avoid being labeled rightists themselves and to better their own positions. Hu's ability and willingness to withstand the pressure to participate actively in such a campaign was highly unusual. Even he, however, was forced to criticize a few of his followers, including the editor of *China Youth News*. These acts he regretted for the rest of his life.[5] Although his speeches during the Mao and

Deng eras rarely deviated from the party's main policy line, his actions often did.

During the Cultural Revolution Hu was locked up in a "cow pen," a makeshift prison, for two and a half years. His captors denounced him at public meetings, paraded him through the streets with a dunce cap on his head, and forced him to do heavy manual labor. His children were branded as reactionaries and were also detained. Hu, accused of being a "capitalist roader," anti-party and anti-socialist, never acknowledged the charges against him, nor did he ever seek to help his cause by flattering Jiang Qing or Lin Biao. Although he was physically and mentally abused, he refused to confess his "crimes." In the early 1970s he became ill and was sent back to his home in Beijing, where he spent his time reading both ancient Chinese classics and Marxist works by East European and Western writers. He invited a number of intellectuals to discuss this literature with him.

Upon his mentor Deng's return to the party leadership in 1973, Hu was made a vice president of the Chinese Academy of Sciences (CAS) and was put in charge of reviving its academic activities. With Hu Qiaomu, Mao's former private secretary and the party's chief theorist, Hu Yaobang worked night and day to rid the academy of the Cultural Revolution's anti-intellectual policies. In 1975 the two men presented an important report calling for the revival not only of science and technology but of intellectuals and the pursuit of knowledge in general. After attacks were renewed against Deng Xiaoping in late 1975 for his revival of education, science, and technology, however, Hu was purged again, along with his mentor, in April 1976. Hu Qiaomu, always attuned to the way political winds were blowing, criticized himself at that time for following Deng and provided Jiang Qing with materials to be used against Deng. In the campaign against Deng that followed, the Gang of Four published the report of the two Hu's in order to repudiate Deng and Hu Yaobang and their emphasis on professionalism and education. The effect of the publication, however, was the opposite of what the Gang had intended. Instead of putting Hu and Deng in a bad light, the publication of their efforts to do away with Cultural Revolution policies increased their popularity.

In the spring of 1977, even before Deng's reappearance in July, Hu returned to power as a vice president of the Central Party School, the training center for high officials. At the Eleventh Party Congress that August he was elected to the Central Committee, and in December he became head of the Organization Department, the office of the party apparatus. Hu's arrival at the Organization Department was greeted enthusiastically. As his subordinates hoped, he immediately took out the long-ignored appeals for justice from those who had been purged and began the process of rehabilitation. One observer recalls that Hu convened a meeting at which he talked emotionally about the injustices committed during the Mao era, moving many to tears.[6]

Against very strong opposition, he rehabilitated virtually all those purged not only during the Cultural Revolution but also during the anti-rightist campaign. Mao's designated successor, Hua Guofeng, and the remaining Maoists in the top leadership had wanted just a few people rehabilitated; Deng himself thought that about 60 percent should be rehabilitated.[7] But Hu insisted that it was necessary to rehabilitate almost all victims of the campaigns, not only out of fairness, but also to heal the wounds of the past and to gain their cooperation in carrying out reforms.

Over three million officials, scientists, intellectuals, and skilled workers who had been imprisoned, detained, or suffered persecution returned to public life. Among those Hu personally rehabilitated were several elders from the Long March who were later to turn against him. In addition, at Hu's behest, the designation of landlords, rich peasants, and their children as reactionaries, in place since the beginning of the Mao era, was removed. The political atmosphere was suddenly infused with elation and expectation.

Although Hu was known as Deng's protégé, he differed with Deng not only on whom to rehabilitate but also on how to deal with contentious issues. Unlike Deng, who increasingly secluded himself in the manner of Mao in his later years, Hu remained directly and personally involved. He often made inspections of the provinces, where he met with local officials and was readily accessible to ordinary people. In May 1980 he even made an inspection tour of Tibet, with a team that included another reform official, Wan Li, who had been the first to allow the emergence of family farming and the beginning of decollectivization while first party secretary of Anhui from 1977 to 1980. Upset by the poverty he saw in Tibet, Hu proposed policies to improve the economy, revive Tibetan culture, and expand education. He was the first official to propose withdrawing certain Chinese personnel from Tibet and permitting freedom of religious worship there. He was later hailed by the Tibetans as "China's Buddha."

Of all the elders in the top leadership, Hu was the only one who believed that it was necessary to undertake not merely administrative reform, such as separating the party from the government, but also fundamental political reform. During his tenure as a vice president of the Central Party School (1977–1981), he often discussed with members of the Theory Research Office, which he established at the Central Party School in 1977, the obstacles socialist countries faced in establishing truly democratic governments and the ways they might overcome these difficulties.

These theorists, joined by some who had worked with Hu in the Youth League in the Mao era, others who had been labeled rightists in 1957–1959, and still others who had been activists in the Cultural Revolution, formed the core group of Hu's intellectual network. Within this group were the top editors and journalists of the *People's Daily* and the *Guangming Daily*. They were all committed Marxists, drawn together by a shared disillusionment with Maoist ideas and policies. They dealt more directly with ideological and political issues than had their literary counterparts who had been the main critics during the Mao era. Whereas the literary intellectuals in the late 1970s described the horrors of the Cultural Revolution and the abuses of power continuing into the Deng era, the theorists looked for the causes of the Cultural Revolution and for ways to prevent another such catastrophe. Their explorations led them to critique Mao and his policies dating back even before the Cultural Revolution, and these efforts in turn prompted them to look for ways to revise the ideology and to reform the political system.

The Intellectual Revival

With the blessings of Deng Xiaoping, Hu Yaobang and his associates first repudiated the anti-intellectual policies of the Mao era. Whereas Mao had disparaged expertise, most of the Chinese leadership, including the elders, believed that developing science and technology was crucial for China's modernization. On March 15, 1977, just a few months after the fall of the Gang, the *People's Daily* asserted that science must no longer be distorted by ideology: "Marxist philosophy cannot replace natural science."[8]

Soon after his return to power Deng took steps to redress the damage done during the Mao years not only to science, technology, and professionalism but to the entire intellectual community. In a speech at the National Conference on Science on March 18, 1978, Deng removed all intellectuals, not just scientists, from the category of the bourgeoisie, where they had been placed by Mao, and made them members of the still-honored proletariat. Deng went on to emphasize professionalism rather than ideology as the criterion for judging one's value to society. "We cannot demand that scientists and technicians or . . . the overwhelming majority of them, study stacks of books on political theory, join in numerous social activities and attend many meetings not related to their work . . . Comrades of different trades and professions are not divorced from politics when they do their best at their posts; on the contrary, this is a concrete manifestation of their services to proletarian politics and social consciousness." Equally important, he recommended that the party reduce its direct control over science. "It is impossible for Party committees to handle and solve all matters. We must admit that in scientific and technical work, there are many things we do not know . . . We should give directors and deputy directors of the research organizations a free hand." In addition, "we must listen closely to the opinions of the experts [and] leave them free to use all their skills and talents."[9] Deng's proposals echoed those suggested in the 1975 report of Hu Yaobang and Hu Qiaomu to the Academy of Sciences.

In November 1978 the Theoretical Physics Institute of CAS for the first time elected its director and its deputy director by democratic means.[10] The party did not present any official candidates, though the party committee of the institute made informal recommendations. The members then voted by a secret ballot. Although the incumbent director was reelected, the newly elected deputy director had never before held any leading position. This limited democratic procedure in effect rejected the party's past practice of imposing its own politically approved nominees. Its introduction at this time, however, was not so much to promote democratic procedures as to rid the scientific establishment of obstructive party bureaucrats and to stimulate scientific research. A "commentator article," which usually implies high-level official authorization, in the *Guangming Daily* complained that these bureaucrats "consider intellectuals as 'dissidents' . . . and hit intellectuals and deprive them of funds, bar them from party membership and . . . suppress their scientific achievements."[11] In the *People's Daily* another commentator article criticized "tyrants . . . [who] do

not understand that, without the fostering of a large number of qualified scientists and technicians and without the building of a scientific
and technical contingent joined by the masses in their millions, the
attempt to achieve the four modernizations will fail." [12]

As in the May Fourth movement, the modernization of science was
linked with developing a "democratic spirit." A *People's Daily* contributing commentator article declared: "The scientific spirit and the
democratic spirit are inseparable in the struggle to build a modern
and powerful socialist country . . . Raising the scientific and cultural
level of the whole Chinese nation must therefore be closely linked
with expanding the scope of the nation's democratic life." [13]

Although priority was given to liberating science and technology from ideological and bureaucratic controls, the social sciences
also felt the effects of this ideological relaxation. The social sciences
had literally been destroyed in the mid-1950s, by the imposition of
Marxist-Leninist ideology and party bureaucrats and by the outright
banning of disciplines such as sociology, political science, and anthropology. Science was regarded as of prime importance in modernization, but a *People's Daily* commentator article also acknowledged
that "development of social sciences is an important aspect[,] indispensable in building a modern and powerful socialist country." [14]

During the Mao era the social sciences had been incorporated into
the Academy of Sciences, but in 1978 they were separated into their
own Chinese Academy of Social Sciences (CASS) and thus given an
importance they did not have under Mao. Institutes within the CASS
were to become think tanks, and their members became advisors to
the political reform leaders. Fostering a variety of ideas in the social
sciences was also seen as necessary for enlivening China's cultural life.
A staff commentator of *Philosophy Research* (Zhexue yanjiu) wrote
that if there were "no difference of opinions and no clash of ideas in
our pursuit of knowledge, our minds would stop working. They might
even freeze and petrify. Science and culture can develop to their full
potentials and flourish only under conditions of free discussion." As
the natural sciences need free discussion, "so do philosophy and social sciences." [15]

Some even looked to the social sciences not only as aids to reform
but as important academic disciplines in themselves. The staff commentator of *Philosophy Research* continued, "Every branch of philosophy and social sciences, like natural sciences, deals with a specific

subject and follows a rigid logic of reasoning." Scholarly research and the collection of data were to be treated as intrinsically worthwhile. The commentator even suggested that Marxism-Leninism might be irrelevant: "Sometimes we cannot find guidelines of any kind in Marxist classics and must make creative exploration on our own." [16] Moreover, political interference hindered academic inquiry. "A major obstacle to . . . free discussion is the confusing of academic issues, especially those of philosophy and social sciences, with political issues . . . [W]e must foster a general awareness among the people that it is necessary to draw a well-defined line between political issues and academic issues." [17]

Yet while some academics, given their experiences under Mao, sought to separate academia from politics, others, reacting to the same harsh treatment, tried to encourage social scientists to comment on political issues. Mao's cultural czar Zhou Yang, who had been persecuted and imprisoned during the Cultural Revolution, criticized the Gang of Four's politicization of academia, though their action was in part an intensification of the politicization that he and his colleagues had begun in Yan'an in the early 1940s. Yet despite his criticism of the Gang, Zhou now again sought to use academia for political purposes, this time to help democratize political life. Hence he declared that to separate academia from politics completely was impossible. "Some comrades had some naive and mistaken idea in wanting to mark off a clear division between politics and academia." He, too, linked diversity in academia and culture with a democratic atmosphere. "Without a lively democratic atmosphere they will not develop soundly." [18] Like the *Philosophy Research* commentator, Zhou did not spell out what he meant by a democratic atmosphere, other than to define it as the expression of diverse and pluralistic views, but within the context of the People's Republic, which had hitherto regarded diversity and pluralism as negative phenomena, his view was a radical one.

As in prior periods of relative relaxation, the first signs of diversity appeared in literature. As early as 1977 a plethora of stories appeared that expressed pent-up grievances, particularly regarding the Cultural Revolution. These writings, which came to be known as "wounded literature," depicted the pain, violence, injustices, and destruction of the Cultural Revolution. Some even touched upon the earlier antirightist campaign. These outpourings of bitterness helped the reformers in their struggle against the remaining Maoists, because the accounts encouraged popular resentment against official holdovers from the Cultural Revolution. Similar writings were used by Khrushchev in the late 1950s against the remaining Stalinists and by Gorbachev in the mid-1980s against the holdovers from the Brezhnev era.

The wounded literature writers employed modernist literary techniques, introduced into China in the early decades of the twentieth century but suppressed by the party when the Soviet doctrine of socialist realism, as espoused by Mao's 1942 Yan'an "Talks on Literature and Art," became official party policy in 1949. The artists in the late 1970s now experimented with stream of consciousness, symbolism, flashbacks, internal monologues, and nonlinear plots, best exemplified in the stories of Wang Meng. These writers regarded modernist techniques as appropriate to describe the disruptive nature of the Mao years and to express personal and individual emotions that had been suppressed during the Cultural Revolution. Some of these works also exposed the evils that continued in the Deng era, such as rural poverty, the repressive treatment of intellectuals, and especially the arrogance, privileges, corruption, and abuse of power by party officials. The stories' protagonists were not the positive, heroic characters of the traditional or Mao eras, but usually somewhat negative, flawed individuals.

"Obscure poetry" *(menglong shi)* was another new genre that diverged from the traditional mode and from socialist realism. A group of young writers who had come of age during the Cultural Revolution wrote poetry that purposely did not carry a political or moral message. But while ostensibly apolitical, these poets were making a political statement by writing poems in which style and subject matter were determined by themselves and not by the party. The genre was not only incomprehensible to party officials but represented an alternate approach to the Soviet dogma, echoed by China's Communist leaders since the 1930s, that "writers are the engineers of human souls."

Initially not only the reform leaders but most officials welcomed the wounded literature, because it was consistent with their own desire to see the excesses of the Cultural Revolution exposed and Maoist policies rescinded. But as was true during the Mao period and in the Soviet Union and Eastern Europe, the party could not control creative literature, which ultimately undermines a totalitarian regime precisely because it is creative. Furthermore, these works exposed both the hor-

rors of the Cultural Revolution and those of the anti-rightist campaign, which had been led by the elders, particularly Deng and Peng
Zhen. The wounded literature therefore raised questions about a political system and a leadership that had allowed such abuses to take
place and proved unable to stop them once they occurred.[19]

A revival of Confucianism in the late 1970s similarly stressed not
only traditional values favored by the leadership, such as education,
harmonious social relationships, and conciliation between the leaders
and the led, but also other values not necessarily desired by those at
the top, particularly the principle that intellectuals have a responsibility to criticize the abuse of political power. Plays were performed
about upright, honest officials, such as the impartial Judge Bao, the
typical virtuous official of the Song dynasty, who defied tyranny and
oppression. People had in the past looked to such upright figures to
champion their desire for justice and fair play. In traditional society,
with no institutional restraints on power, the populace had to rely
on exemplary officials to protect them from the arbitrary power of
other officials.

Several Chinese intellectuals, however, argued that in a modern society the establishment of democratic institutions, not upright officials, was the only way to protect oneself against arbitrary power.
They referred to their constitution, as Soviet and East European intellectuals were doing in this same period, as the basis for the introduction of democratic institutions and procedures. As a number of
researchers at CASS pointed out, China's constitution stipulated
"freedom of speech, correspondence, the press, assembly, association,
procession, demonstration and the freedom to strike."[20] An article of
November 24, 1978, in the *People's Daily,* however, asserted that
these rights were infringed upon precisely because they were "only
principles." It was necessary to draw up a "civil code before they can
be effectively implemented."[21] A New China News Agency release
stated: "It is urgent that a civil code be instituted as quickly as possible
if the four modernizations are to be achieved."[22]

Although the reform leaders were merely recommending a more
democratic style of party rule, some of the intellectuals associated
with them, and even some of their own official media, believed that
China would not be able to modernize economically without substantial institutional and judicial reforms. At a conference at the Institute
of Law, 160 participants were told by Yu Guangyuan, a vice president

of the Academy of Social Sciences, a deputy director of the State Science and Technology Commission, and an advisor to Hu Yaobang, that "without democracy there can be no modernizations."[23] This view was repeated in an editorial in the *People's Daily* on January 3, 1979, which stated: "The four modernizations must be accompanied by political democratization."[24] In direct opposition to the position of the elders, the editorial asserted that democracy was not a destabilizing but a stabilizing force, because it allowed the government to hear a range of differing opinions.[25] The intellectual revival thus reclaimed not only the May Fourth movement's emphasis on science and expertise but its call for democracy.

Opposing Mao's Thought and Maoist Leaders

Renewed interest in democracy was accompanied by a critique of Mao, his thought, and his Cultural Revolution associates. In the spring of 1978 the theorists in the Central Party School launched a campaign-like discussion of the slogan "Practice is the sole criterion of truth." Although they were using a Maoist technique, their purpose was to use pragmatic criteria to criticize publicly Mao's ideas and practices, specifically Mao's cult of the personality, emphasis on the power of the will, and use of class struggle in party conflicts. The Swedish sinologist Michael Schoenhals has pointed out that this discussion marked the first time since 1949 that Mao, his ideology, and policies had been directly contested from within the political system.[26] The same theorists also used this slogan to undermine the authority of Hua Guofeng and other high-level Maoists, whose claim to leadership was based on continuing Mao's policies. These remaining Maoists had been labeled the "two whatevers" faction by their opponents after they published a joint editorial in the *People's Daily*, *Red Flag*, and *Liberation Army Daily* on February 7, 1977, entitled "Study Documents Well and Keep Hold of the Key Link." It declared: "Whatever policy decisions were made by Chairman Mao must be resolutely upheld by us. Whatever instructions were given by Chairman Mao must be firmly and unwaveringly followed by us at all times."[27]

In July 1977 the journal *Theoretical Trends* (Lilun dongtai), established by Hu Yaobang and theorist followers in the Central Party School, launched the first public attack on the "two whatevers" faction. Its editor, Ruan Ming, was an associate of Hu's from his Youth

League days. The journal sought to correct the ideological distortions of the Gang of Four and to reverse the policies of the Mao era. Soon after the first issue appeared on July 15, a number of its articles were reprinted in the major national newspapers, the *People's Daily, Guangming Daily,* and *Liberation Army Daily,* and in other papers under the byline "special commentator." By being published in the Central Party School's publication first, the articles avoided the censorship of the party vice chairman, Wang Dongxing, who had been Mao's bodyguard and was still in charge of propaganda.

Of the many influential articles reprinted from *Theoretical Trends,* the most important was "Actual Practice Is the Only Criterion for Examination of Truth," originally written by Hu Fuming, a teacher at Nanjing University. He had submitted the article to the *Guangming Daily,* whose editor, Yang Xiguang, and head of the newspaper's party group, Ma Peiwen, were also associates of Hu Yaobang. Feeling that the article was too moderate in its criticism of Mao's ideology, in April 1978 Yang Xiguang introduced Hu Fuming to Sun Changjiang, a former activist during the Cultural Revolution who was now on the staff of the Theory Research Office and a lecturer at People's University. Sun was writing an article on the same subject. With the assistance of Wu Jiang, a veteran theorist and director of the Theory Research Office, Sun fashioned one article out of the two, which was published in *Theoretical Trends* on May 10.

Hu Yaobang then made the important decision to reprint this article in the chief newspapers of the party and the army. Sun and Wu Jiang had persuaded Hu that ideology should continue to play a role, but its validity had to be proven in actual practice. Their purpose was to make ideology more relevant to new conditions and to restore the legitimacy Marxism had lost in the Cultural Revolution. The practice criterion article was reprinted the next day as a special commentator article in the *Guangming Daily* and on the following day in the *People's Daily, Liberation Army Daily,* and through the New China News Agency. Except for Hu's associates at the Central Party School and the *Guangming Daily,* the only other people who knew of its origins were Hu Jiwei, editor-in-chief of the *People's Daily,* and some of his associates in the Theory Department of the paper, headed by the philosopher and deputy editor Wang Ruoshui. Both Hu Jiwei and Wang Ruoshui had been allied with Hu Yaobang in the past.

Although it was Hu Yaobang who made the decision to publish the article in the national media, Deng Xiaoping's ideas were very much in accordance with the article's content at this time. When Deng made his first formal reappearance after the Cultural Revolution in July 1977, he used a slogan that was both Maoist and traditional: "Seek truth from fact." His pragmatic statement was the first salvo against Mao's policies. Even before that, on May 24, Deng mentioned in a conversation with colleagues that he had told the remaining Maoists' leaders: "If you stick to the 'two whatevers,' then to overturn the verdict on me [*wei wo fan an*] makes no sense . . . It just won't do to take words spoken by the chairman at one point, under one set of conditions, and apply them to a different issue, a different event, or a different situation."[28]

Nevertheless, in contrast with Khrushchev's harsh treatment of Stalin at the Twentieth Congress of the Soviet Communist Party in February 1956, Deng's treatment of Mao was much gentler. To repudiate Mao and his policies, Deng often said, would also implicate most of China's current leaders, including himself, who had either actively carried out Mao's policies, in the anti-rightist campaign and the Great Leap Forward, or passively followed his orders, during the Cultural Revolution. Deng would later say: "We should not create a false impression that . . . only one person made mistakes. I am eligible to say so, because I myself have committed mistakes. In the anti-rightist movement in 1957 . . . we were all activists, and I was responsible for the mistake of making the scope of this struggle far too broad, for I was the party's general secretary. During the Great Leap Forward in 1958 . . . we were also hot-headed . . . The mistakes involved in all these cases should not be imputed to a certain person. We should admit that there is no infallible man."[29] Yet while Deng criticized the anti-rightist campaign for being too broad, he did not reject the need for the campaign itself. For this reason Hu Yaobang was unable to remove the rightist labels on the last handful of those purged in that period, among them Lin Xiling, the charismatic woman student leader at People's University during the Hundred Flowers, and Luo Longji and Zhang Bojun, the former leaders of the League for the Protection of Civil Rights, who had headed the largest small party, the China Democratic League. Deng could not continue to justify the campaign if there were no rightists. To exonerate these individuals would imply a total repudiation of the anti-rightist campaign and Deng's leadership role.

The remaining Maoist faction considered the practice criterion article a threat to its authority. Because the article was reprinted in the *People's Daily* without his approval, Wang Dongxing called on May 17 for an investigation to find out who was behind it. The head of the Propaganda Department, Zhang Pinghua, another remaining Maoist, told his associates in the department to feel free to criticize the article.

Some associates of the elders also considered the article a threat. The day that the article was reprinted in the *People's Daily*, Wu Lengxi, who had been the paper's editor-in-chief from 1958 until the Cultural Revolution, called up Hu Jiwei, his former deputy, and chastized him for publishing the article.[30] Wu angrily charged that the article "supports the notion of doubting everything" and even "argues that some of Mao's instructions are incorrect and that we must not deal with Mao's instructions as if they were dead dogma or worship them as if they were the Bible." If Mao's ideology were to be questioned and revised as the article suggested, Wu asked, would China "still be able to remain united as one? Will there still be stability and unity in our country?" Wu's arguments were similar to those that would be used by the elders Chen Yun, Li Xiannian, Wang Zhen, Peng Zhen, and others, as well as their spokesmen Hu Qiaomu and Deng Liqun, in their later conflict with the reform-minded political leaders and their intellectual associates. Wu articulated the fear that was later to obsess them—that any political change would destabilize the country.

Although Deng appears to have been unaware of the specific details of how the article had been written, by late May or early June the controversy it had provoked had aroused his curiosity. On June 2, at a conference on the political work of the army, he publicly took sides in the debate by criticizing those comrades "who think that it is enough to just copy or borrow what was originally said by Marx, Lenin, and Mao Zedong in its entirety."[31] Deng's clear stand swung wavering party leaders to Hu Yaobang's side against the remaining Maoist faction. Hu Jiwei gave Deng's June 2 speech front-page coverage in the *People's Daily*, seemingly according it the party's imprimatur. Nevertheless, as Wu Lengxi's phone call revealed, Hu Yaobang and his associates encountered opposition very early in the Deng era from the other revolutionary elders, who agreed with Hu in removing the Maoist faction but not in rejecting Mao's thought and pre–Cultural Revolution policies and in revising ideology. Hu Qiaomu visited Hu Yaobang on June 20 to urge him to stop the debate on the practice criterion immediately and to stop *Theoretical Trends* from publishing any more articles on the subject. Not wanting to antagonize the elders further, Hu Yaobang asked Wu Jiang and Ruan Ming to suspend the discussion for the time being.

But even Hu could not control his intellectual associates. Wu Jiang, with the assistance of Sun Changjiang, wrote a new article to rebut Wu Lengxi's criticism and brought it to the attention of Luo Ruiqing, then the secretary general of the Central Military Commission. Like his fellow elders, Luo had suffered greatly during the Cultural Revolution, but unlike them, he was not as fearful of repudiating Maoist practices. He agreed to publish the rebuttal in the *Liberation Army Daily* and assumed responsibility for the article after he made some revisions. This article, "A Most Fundamental Principle of Marxism," was published on June 24, again under the "special commentator" byline. It reemphasized the need to revise ideology in light of the changing times. Luo died six weeks after the article appeared. Hu Yaobang then called for a third article, expressing similar ideas. "All the Subjective World Must Be Examined by Practice" was first published in *Theoretical Trends* on September 10, and reprinted in the *People's Daily* as a special commentator article. Although these articles infuriated the elders, they attracted widespread attention and helped prepare the ideological ground for Deng's reform program approved at the Third Plenum of the Eleventh Central Committee in December 1978.

Despite the trauma that China's intellectuals and others had endured during the Mao years, for many it was not until this discussion on the practice criterion in the spring of 1978 that they began to criticize Mao's ideas and policies openly. Even Ba Jin had continued to refer to Mao and his writings as "brilliant" and "great" in the aftermath of the Cultural Revolution. Only after the practice criterion discussion did he begin to think about writing *Random Thoughts,* a collection of essays in which he chastised both his colleagues and himself for carrying out Mao's orders without question.[32]

In September 1978 another conflict erupted between Hu Yaobang and the remaining Maoist faction, this time over the *China Youth* (Zhongguo qingnian) journal, which was to reappear on September 11 after a twelve-year suspension. But Wang Dongxing opposed its publication in order to counterattack against Hu, who as former head of the Youth League played an important role in reviving the journal.

Its inaugural issue, moreover, contained several articles expressing approval of the April 5, 1976, Tiananmen protest against Mao and the Gang of Four, which hitherto had been labeled "counterrevolutionary," and it denounced the security police who had suppressed the demonstrators. In addition, a contributing commentator article, "Eliminate Blind Faith, Get a Good Grasp of Science," compared the cult of Mao to blind religious faith or superstition.

Despite Wang Dongxing's opposition, the issue appeared about September 20. Wu De, a remaining Maoist who had been mayor of Beijing in 1976 and who had led the crackdown on April 5, was dismissed from his position on October 11, 1978, and hundreds of participants in the April 5, 1976, demonstration were released from prison. The poems recited during the demonstration, a number of which compared Mao to the despotic Shi Huangdi of the Qin dynasty, were published with a title page inscribed with Hua Guofeng's personal calligraphy, which Hu Yaobang had requested, giving the stamp of approval. On November 14, 1978, it was announced that the verdict on the April 5, 1976, Tiananmen protest had been officially withdrawn.

Although the writings and actions of Hu Yaobang and his intellectual associates were explicitly directed against the remaining Maoists, they implicitly attacked the Leninist system of democratic centralism that gave unlimited power to a few leaders. Concomitantly, Hu and his associates were searching for new political approaches to constrain that power. *China Youth* became a major forum for the discussion of new approaches. Two young authors of a November 1978 article, "It Is Necessary to Bring Democracy into Full Play," asked: "How could the 'gang of four' have run amuck in such a way over the past several years? Why were the Chinese people tolerant of them? . . . Why couldn't the hundreds of millions of our people have exposed and overthrown them in time to prevent such a disaster?"[33] The authors answered that such a disaster could not be attributed solely to one individual or small group; it was the product of China's political structure and history. But instead of employing the two standard explanations for the Cultural Revolution, China's "feudal" past and the machinations of the Gang of Four, they pointed to the "absence of reliable organizations and systems to safeguard socialist democracy."[34] Their absence had given the Gang and Lin Biao the opportunity to oppress the people.

The authors recommended the establishment of a "disciplined judiciary" and genuine democratic elections as institutions that could prevent another Cultural Revolution. "Among the various people's democratic rights stipulated in the constitution and law, the most important are the people's right to vote, dismiss, and supervise the personnel of the state's executive and administrative organs." They insisted: "It is now imperative to implement firmly the measures that call for electing the people's representatives through secret ballot." In addition, the tenure of leading officials should be limited so that "there will be no such thing as 'the position assured forever' whether or not one's work performance is satisfactory."[35] Moreover, they demanded freedom of the press in order to expose officials' abuses and mistakes. These political reforms were necessary because, they explained, "the Chinese people have lived too long under an autocratic system."[36]

Thus by the fall of 1978 articles in the official media were calling for democratic elections, limited terms of office, freedom of press guaranteed by law, and a "disciplined judiciary" in order to restrain abusive officials. The editors' note to the "Democracy into Full Play" article commented that the "four modernizations" in agriculture, industry, science and technology, and the military could not be achieved "without an adequate people's democracy and a healthy legal system." It advised members of the Youth League to "be concerned about the affairs of the party and state, constantly consider and actively participate in the study and discussion of bringing democracy into play" in order to prevent another Cultural Revolution.[37] Even before Wei Jingsheng of the Democracy Wall movement coined his famous slogan on the need for the "fifth modernization"—democracy as necessary for the four modernizations—the concept was already being discussed in the official press under Hu Yaobang's jurisdiction.

It is within this context that a seething underground protest, expressing similar views, was allowed to explode overground in late 1978 and early 1979. In part the protest echoed views that Hu Yaobang's intellectual associates were already discussing in the official press.

Democratic Activists and the Democratic Elite

Like the democratic elite, the activists in the Democracy Wall movement of late 1978 to early 1979 sought reform of the political system. But with no access to the official media, they made their demands known through a mass movement of wallposters, mimeographed pamphlets, and demonstrations in front of a long wall in the center of Beijing. Huge crowds gathered there daily to read the posters, air their views, and buy the pamphlets printed by the activists. Soon other walls in Beijing and in other major cities were being used as well. Although the active participants were small in number, several hundred to several thousand at any one time, they expressed the widespread, deep revulsion felt by both officials and ordinary citizens at Mao's use of terror and chaos for his own political purposes and utopian visions.

Following Mao's example, Deng first used these spontaneous demonstrations in the streets as leverage against his Maoist opponents in the leadership and as a means of consolidating his position at the upcoming Third Plenum of the Eleventh Central Committee in December 1978. And just as Mao had used genuine grievances against the party to conduct an intraparty struggle during the Cultural Revolution, so did Deng in its aftermath. Like Hu Yaobang's associates, the Democracy Wall activists attacked Mao's policies and his followers in positions of leadership, but they went further than Hu's associates by referring to Hua Guofeng, Wang Dongxing, and other Maoists specifically by name.[38] The activists' words and actions, with those of the democratic elite, helped Deng oust Hua as party chairman, Wang as a vice chairman, other Maoists from their posts, and formally abrogate the April 1976 decision to dismiss Deng from office that had been passed under their auspices. At the same time, many of the activists' wallposters effusively hailed Deng and Hu Yaobang as supporters of modernization, democracy, and science and as "honest servants of the people."

Initially Deng praised the activists' wallposters as normal phenomena permitted under China's constitution. The *People's Daily* and *Guangming Daily* asserted that it was legal for people to put up wallposters. On November 16, 1978, Deng and Hu went to view the posters at Peking University and Qinghua University and urged party leaders at all levels to encourage their posting. Hu even invited several of the Democracy Wall activists to his home. Among them was Wang Juntao, who had participated in the April 5 protest and who was an editor of the relatively moderate nonofficial journal *Beijing Spring* (Beijing zhichun).[39] Hu talked with the group for four spirited hours about the political issues raised by their movement. Although this official tolerance was more a political ploy than an indication of a genuine desire for a spontaneous mass movement, in late 1978 and early 1979 Deng, Hu, and their supporters were willing to open wide the avenues of expression, the *yanlu,* as the emperors had done in traditional times of reform, and Hu at least was willing to debate with the participants. Because Deng and Hu did not initially demarcate where the avenues should go, ordinary citizens enjoyed more freedom than at any other time since the Hundred Flowers period.

Although these ex–Red Guard Democracy Wall activists used the same techniques of wallposters, pamphlets, and open debate that they had used when Mao summoned them to rebel against authority in the Cultural Revolution, their goals were now very different. A substantial minority, like Hu's intellectual associates, were not looking for new leaders as much as for a revised ideology and new political institutions. Most of the articles in their nonofficial journals, like those of the democratic elite in the official media, still used the traditional and Marxist terminology in which they had been indoctrinated. Outside of Marxism-Leninism they had read little in Western political thought. Nevertheless, because they too had suffered during the Cultural Revolution, some called for institutional and legal procedures to guarantee freedom of speech and protect civil liberties in order to prevent such oppression and arbitrary treatment in the future. In language similar to that of the democratic elite, most of them called for a system of "socialist democracy" and "socialist legality," democratic elections, rule of law, and the expression of diverse views.

But the Democracy Wall activists were a more fragmented and diffuse coalition than Hu Yaobang's associates. Although most wanted to establish procedures and laws within a Marxist and socialist framework, a small number advocated a much more radical approach. Their youthful idealism had been dashed during the Cultural Revolution, making them feel much more alienated and betrayed than their elders. These activists urged their followers to go out and fight for their rights, which, as in the West, they regarded as inalienable. Wei Jingsheng was the most daring of this radical fringe. An electrician at the Beijing Zoo and a former Red Guard, he echoed the democratic elite's statement that there could be no modernization without democracy. His call for a fifth modernization—"without democracy, the four modernizations would not be achievable"—captured their ideas in an ingenious slogan.

Wei Jingsheng and his associates differed from the democratic elite and most of the other democratic activists in their total rejection of the Marxist-Leninist system. They believed that despotism was inherent in Marxism-Leninism and in rule by the Communist Party. They expressed these views in their nonofficial journal *Exploration* (Tansuo), which observed that Confucianism had more relevance for China than did Marxism-Leninism. "The Confucian saying that 'an oppressive government is worse than a tiger' which has been widely repudiated nowadays seems more easily appreciated than the fashionable 'Marxism-Leninism.'"[40] Moreover, as to "the Marxist socialist experiment of using dictatorship to achieve the equal rights of man . . . Actual facts have demonstrated once and again that it simply won't work . . . A concentration of powers is bound to fall into the hands of a few."[41] Another *Exploration* article asserted that the Leninist party-state derived from Marxist ideology "explains why all social systems based on Marxist socialism are without exception undemocratic and even anti-democratic autocracies."[42]

Wei and his followers believed that genuine reform was impossible within the existing system and under the leadership of Deng Xiaoping. One of Wei's followers wrote that the party "does recognize the people's freedom and rights, provided these rights are channeled to unite the minds of hundreds of millions of people by a single ideology, a single political party, a single life style . . . Isn't it a religious cult when people are compelled or willing to follow a well-prescribed pattern to think, to work, to live, to struggle, and to die . . . [and] to induce people to toil like beasts by promising them happiness in the next world?"[43] The article asked, "What justifications are there to say that the country would be thrown into chaos unless all opposing views are eliminated, and unless all explorations for systems different than the socialist system are suppressed?"[44] Concluded the author: "If the existence and triumph of Marxism-Leninism must rely on bloody suppression of all opposing views, we as clear-headed youths of the twentieth century are not prepared to tolerate it."[45]

In the early months of 1979 some of the more radical Democracy Wall activists helped organize protests of peasants who came to Beijing to express their grievances. When one of the organizers of the protests, Fu Yuehua, was arrested, *Exploration* immediately called for the punishment of her captors. The journal also exposed the conditions in China's prisons by describing in graphic detail the brutality of their isolation cells and their use of mental and physical torture. A Chinese Human Rights League was established in Beijing in January by Ren Wanding, another former Red Guard. The league urged President Jimmy Carter of the United States to support the struggle for human rights in China just as he had in the Soviet Union.

Even for Hu Yaobang and his intellectual associates, these more radical democratic activists went beyond the limits of acceptable criticism and action. Not only had they organized peasant protests, exposed prison conditions, and called for foreign intervention, but they had directly attacked Marxism-Leninism and the party. For Deng Xiaoping, the Democracy Wall activists' critiques of Mao were not the kind of criticisms he had expected. Whereas Deng had wanted Mao denounced for undermining party organization, the activists had denounced him for suppressing and persecuting his critics. Moreover, they had challenged the Leninist one-party state, a basic tenet of Deng's thinking. Despite Deng's enthusiasm for economic reform and his willingness to allow some local political reform, he never deviated from his belief in the dominance of the Communist Party.

A crackdown was virtually inevitable by early 1979. The Democracy Wall activists were no longer needed in Deng's struggle to oust the remaining Maoists, whose power was already in decline by December 1978. He had expected that once he had won the power struggle and consolidated his position, which occurred at the Third Plenum, that the Democracy Wall activists would retire quietly. But instead they continued to speak out and to organize. Even more disturbing, Wei denounced China's February invasion of Vietnam, a protest that Deng regarded as traitorous.

Annoyed by the democratic activists' unwillingness to retreat or to be controlled, Deng launched his offensive. Official newspapers in February 1979 labeled the activists "anarchists" who, masquerading under the banner of democracy, were causing worsening economic conditions and social instability. *Exploration* responded to these charges with an editorial comparing Deng's suppression of the Democracy Wall movement to the "habitual practice of all new and old dictatorial fascists." The editorial warned people to "heighten their vigilance and no longer lightly believe in any ruler who is not subject to the people's supervision and control . . . The people must maintain vigilance against Deng Xiaoping's metamorphosis into a dictator."[46] Although Deng had given priority to the people's interests when he came to power, he was "no longer worthy of the people's trust and support, because his actions have shown that he does not want to pursue democracy." The journal again charged that Fu Yuehua's arrest was illegal. "We would like to know if it is legal or not for a vice premier and a vice chairman [Deng Xiaoping] to announce the arrest of people rather than for the courts and the people's representative organs to do so?"[47]

On March 29, almost immediately after this issue appeared, Wei was arrested. Six months later at a show trial from which his family and friends were excluded, he was sentenced to fifteen years in prison and was placed in solitary confinement as an example to deter others. A transcript of Wei's trial came into the hands of the editors of *April Forum* (Siwu luntan), another nonofficial journal. It printed Wei's final statement, which rejected the charges against him and claimed his innocence on the basis of the Chinese constitution. One of the editors, Liu Qing, wrote that although he did not completely agree with Wei, he defended him because he believed that the way in which Wei's case was handled would tell "how far China had proceeded on the road of democracy and rule of law"—not very far, he was to discover. Shortly after Wei's statement was published in *April Forum* in November, Liu Qing was also arrested.

After the arrests of the more radical activists, some of the more moderate leaders of the Democracy Wall movement tried to organize a united front of democratic activists and continue with the publication of nonofficial journals, but they were subjected to constant harassment and in April 1981 were arrested in a nationwide crackdown. They were not even given show trials; their homes were searched and their books, papers, and letters confiscated. A few were released in the mid-1980s and some in the early 1990s, but most of them remained in prison. By the spring of 1981, the party had crushed the Democracy Wall movement by breaking its network and intimidating its sympathizers into silence. The rights to publish, speak, and assemble freely, guaranteed in the constitution, were treated by the party as criminal acts. The spontaneous protest of 1978–1979, however, despite its suppression, was a precursor of later student protests to come.

Equally important, the arguments of the Democracy Wall activists, though not those of the more radical Wei Jingsheng group, continued to be echoed in the official media by the democratic elite. Some members of the democratic elite had gone to observe the Democracy Wall protests and a few even expressed public support, but most stayed clear of the demonstrators. Possibly they feared that they might lose the public forum they had only recently been given. And by temperament and rank, they still had the Confucian literati's disdain for mass protest movements. They saw no need to engage in organized public actions. Like the literati of old, they viewed themselves as advisors and spokesmen of the reform leadership, a leadership that had given them privileges they had long been deprived. They welcomed their alliance with Deng Xiaoping and Hu Yaobang, and they did not want to do anything to jeopardize it.

In the late 1970s, moreover, most of the democratic elite still believed in Marxism and socialism and had faith that the Deng leadership and reforms would ultimately bring China into the modern world. They did not agree with the views of the more radical activists, such as Wei Jingsheng's rejection of Marxism, socialism, and Deng's leadership. They regarded Deng and Hu as the only leaders who could repair the damage of the Mao era, and they feared that the activists could undermine the reform leaders and their reforms by provoking the elders and their associates into returning to Mao's more repressive practices.

There were a few important exceptions. An unusual revolutionary elder, Ge Yang, a woman who was a former rightist and the editor-in-chief of the journal the *New Observer* (Xin guancha), offered positions as editors to a number of the talented poets writing in the "obscure poetry" genre, such as Bei Dao and Gu Cheng, the editors of the nonofficial literary journal *Today* (Jintian). Wang Ruoshui and Yan Jiaqi, a younger social scientist, had often gone to observe the activists at the Democracy Wall, and Yan even published an essay in one of their journals. Guo Luoji, a younger theoretician connected with Hu in the late 1970s, criticized the arbitrary arrest of the activists and the suppression of their nonofficial journals. But generally the democratic elite did not protest Deng's crackdown, although they continued to echo the more moderate activists' call for a revision of Marxism and the institutional reform of the socialist system.

The Theory Conference, January–April 1979

The Third Plenum in December 1978 marked Hu Yaobang's as well as Deng's ascendancy to power. Having orchestrated the ideological attacks on the remaining Maoist faction, Hu was rewarded with a promotion to the positions of secretary general of the Central Committee and director of the Propaganda Department. He also retained the services of the theorists from the Central Party School who had taken part in the practice criterion discussion and assisted in the assault on the "two whatevers" faction; they were to be his ghostwriters in the early 1980s. Several of them helped draft the communiqué of the Third Plenum that officially marked the beginning of what became a ten-year era of reform. Although a group associated with Hua Guofeng and Wang Dongxing was originally scheduled to draft the documents for the plenum, pressure from the official media, the democratic elite, and the Democracy Wall activists for the ouster of the Maoists, plus a November 10, 1978, work conference in preparation for the plenum also criticizing the remaining Maoist leaders, gave Deng the power to hand over the task to Hu and his intellectual network.

Deng's views appeared to be in accord with those of Hu and his associates. In a speech on December 13, 1978, which in essence became the keynote address for the Third Plenum, Deng declared: "Democracy has to be institutionalized and written into law, so as to make sure that institutions and laws do not change whenever the leadership changes, or whenever the leaders change their views or shift the focus of their attention." Moreover, "these laws should be discussed and adopted through democratic procedures."[48] The words and actions of the reform leadership, with the assistance of the democratic elite from above and the protests of the Democracy Wall activists from below, made possible the beginnings of an era of reform.

Nevertheless, as revealed in the objections of Wu Lengxi and Hu Qiaomu to the practice criterion discussion and to certain criticisms of Mao, party leaders, especially those who were elders, opposed too sweeping a repudiation of the Maoist past. The party's theoretical journal, Red Flag, the sociologist Ding Xueliang has pointed out, even resisted using the term "practice criterion."[49] Following the plenum, one of the Long Marchers, Ye Jianying, suggested that a theory conference, presided over by Hu Yaobang, be convened in order to bring about ideological consensus and to lay the ideological foundation for the forthcoming economic reforms. This emphasis on ideology, even at a time when ideology was being downplayed, reflects the continuing strength of the Confucian belief that rectification of ideas is a prerequisite for the rectification of officials and policies.

Although the theory conference was meant to achieve a consensus, it produced just the opposite. Ostensibly it was sponsored by the party's Propaganda Department and the Academy of Social Sciences, but since these organizations were then under Hu Yaobang's direction, the conference was really his product. Yu Guangyuan, who during the Hundred Flowers period had been in charge of science and technology in the Propaganda Department and had presided over a debate on genetics challenging the prevailing Lysenko dogma, became Hu's chief advisor on preparations. With Yu's advice, Hu chose five chairmen, who were to head five discussion groups. Four of them—Hu Jiwei, Zhou Yang, Wu Jiang, and Yu Guangyuan—had been actively involved in the practice criterion discussion. Hu also asked Deng Liqun, Liu Shaoqi's former political secretary, to be a chairman, but Deng declined. Although Deng Liqun had helped to purge the remaining Maoist faction, he may not have agreed with Hu's willingness to contemplate far-reaching political reforms and ideological revisions. In his place Hu appointed Tong Dalin, a close colleague of Yu Guangyuan and a member of the Science and Technology Commission. In traditional Chinese fashion, the five chairmen each chose ten participants, who in turn each chose fifteen more participants, bringing the total number of participants to over two hundred.

The first half of the conference, from mid-January to mid-February 1979, was dominated by Hu's intellectual network. In addition to the five chairmen, Hu's associates from the Central Party School—Sun Changjiang and Ruan Ming—also participated. Also taking part were several newspaper editors—Yang Xiguang and Ma Peiwen of the *Guangming Daily* and Wang Ruoshui, deputy editor of the *People's Daily*. They all had played important roles in publicizing the practice criterion discussion. Theorists who were later to become associated with the Institute of Marxism-Leninism and Mao Zedong Thought—Su Shaozhi, Zhang Xianyang, and Feng Lanrui—also attended. They advocated a radical revision of ideology. Other prominent participants included several members of the Academy of Social Sciences, such as the director of the Institute of History, Li Shu, and several younger political thinkers. One of these, Yan Jiaqi, was to become the first director of the Institute of Political Science of CASS in 1985. Older theorists such as Liao Gailong, Li Honglin, and Yu Haocheng were also active participants, as was Bao Tong, a member of the Science and Technology Commission with Yu Guangyuan and Tong

Dalin. Bao had helped write Deng's speech for the 1977 National Conference on Science and would later become Zhao Ziyang's political secretary and director of the Research Center for the Reform of the Political Structure under the Central Committee.

Ideological theorists associated with the elders likewise attended. Hu Qiaomu, his close associate Hu Sheng, and Wu Lengxi were supposed to be leaders of the conference along with Hu Yaobang and his five chairmen. Followers of the elders participating in the discussion groups included the Maoist poet and propaganda official He Jingzhi, the *Red Flag* editor Xiong Fu, and literary officials in the General Political Department of the army, Lin Mohan and Liu Baiyu. Although Hu Qiaomu and Deng Liqun did not attend much of the first part of the conference, their associates who attended reported back to them on the proceedings.

The conference included few plenary sessions. Hu Yaobang's opening address and short closing remarks and Deng Xiaoping's speech of March 30 announcing the four cardinal principles—to uphold the socialist road, the dictatorship of the proletariat, the leadership of the Communist Party, and Marxism-Leninism and Mao Zedong Thought—were heard by the whole conference, but otherwise most participants attended only their own discussion groups. In addition to the regular sessions, there were informal sessions such as the one given by Yu Guangyuan, praising Yugoslavia's effort to move away from the Stalinist emphasis on planning and heavy industry toward a market economy as an example for China to follow.

Although the atmosphere at the conference has been characterized as relatively open and relaxed, at the end of each day all documents and printed materials had to be returned to the authorities. With the exception of Deng Xiaoping's speech and Hu Yaobang's opening address calling for explorations into new ideological areas, few of the speeches from the meeting have been published. What was discussed can only be gleaned from the articles published by participants around that time or from what the participants have said since.[50]

One of the most controversial speeches was given by Zhang Xianyang, later to become a member of the Marxist-Leninist Institute. He prepared a three-thousand-character critique of Mao's Cultural Revolution policies and Mao's concepts of total dictatorship, continuing revolution, and taking class struggle as the key link. Born in 1936 to a longshoreman father and a peasant mother, Zhang had graduated from the philosophy department of People's University, where he subsequently taught. Like other young faculty members in philosophy departments during the Cultural Revolution, he became a "revolutionary rebel," a slightly older version of the Red Guards. His subsequent experience of being suppressed by Mao for having done as his leader had asked was profoundly disillusioning, and shortly after the Cultural Revolution Zhang and several associates began to challenge Mao's policies. As early as June 11, 1977, in an article in the *People's Daily,* he traced the Gang's "fascist dictatorship" back to the repressive practices of the anti-rightist campaign and also implicated the elders, including Deng Xiaoping.

During the conference Zhang and Wang Guixiu, who also taught at People's University, published another article in the *People's Daily.* In it they traced the "fascist dictatorship" back even further, to the supposedly "golden age" of the early 1950s. They described the Cultural Revolution not as an aberration of the Gang of Four but as a result of earlier policies. "We constantly waged struggle between the two lines after the founding of the PRC and . . . we invariably opposed right deviation . . ." As a result, "a taboo thus developed in which opposition to right deviations was only allowed, not opposition to 'left' deviations. Whoever opposed left deviations was considered as one who committed a heinous crime . . . The outcome was that the party and country were pushed almost to the verge of destruction." [51] This taboo, which should have been eliminated with the fall of the Gang, Zhang asserted, continued to shackle people's minds. Part of this critique was later incorporated into the official evaluation of the Cultural Revolution, the "Resolution on Certain Historical Issues of Our Party since the Founding of the People's Republic of China," adopted at the Sixth Plenum of the Eleventh Central Committee in June 1981.

Wang Ruoshui's speech at the conference, also a critique of Mao's policies, was to appear in an appendix to the resolution, but by June 1981 it was deemed too radical. Wang characterized the Cultural Revolution as a "gigantic catastrophe for our party and our people." He asked, as did others, how it was possible for just a few people, led by Mao, to "throw a great nation of 800 million people . . . into such utter chaos?" [52] He too found its source in the anti-rightist campaign: "From that point on many intellectuals no longer dared to speak and to criticize shortcomings in the party's work" and "speaking out was

treated as a crime." He warned that the fear of speaking out continued into the present. "That the masses dare not criticize the party is
very harmful to the party and is very dangerous." [53]

There were calls for a government accountable to the people rather
than to the party leadership. Yan Jiaqi, a student of Yu Guangyuan
who had moved from the study of physics to philosophy and then to
the social sciences in an effort to find answers to China's political
problems, gave a talk to his group on February 4. There he recommended limited terms of office for political leaders. He did not, however, mention elections or any other specific procedures for limiting
terms, until sometime after the conference. A former deputy of the
Theory Section of the Propaganda Department, Li Honglin, also
urged an end to life tenure for party officials, including the top leadership. The "rights of the leaders and cadres," he said, were "given by
the people" and not "dropped from the sky." [54] The leaders should
therefore be loyal to the people, rather than the reverse. Li called for
a government chosen by and accountable to the people.

Guo Luoji was one of the few participants to defend the Democracy
Wall activists publicly at the conference. At the age of sixteen he had
joined the underground Communist party, and after 1949 he had
taught at Peking University. He had made a name for himself in the
post-Mao era when, as a deputy from the Peking University area to
the Beijing People's Congress, he voted against the election of Cao
Yi'ou, the wife of Mao's head of public security, Kang Sheng, as delegate to the National People's Congress. Guo's was the first negative
vote at any provincial or municipal people's congress. As a result of
this unprecedented act the Beijing People's Congress continued for five
extra days, in order to criticize Guo for his "rightist" act. He was also
one of the first to call for the "full emancipation of the mind," which
later became a slogan of the Hu Yaobang network. By "emancipation" he meant dispensing with the Maoist distortions of Marxism,
particularly its emphasis on the "all-importance of will." [55]

Guo's most important contribution to the emancipation of the
mind was to come in an article "Political Questions Can Be Discussed," later published in the reformist People's Daily on November 14, 1979. He criticized the post-Mao party policy of allowing
free discussion on academic issues, but not on political issues. Even
though this distinction was made to counter the politicization of academia that had occurred under Mao, Guo insisted that it was some-

times impossible to separate the academic sphere from the political sphere, particularly in the fields of political science, jurisprudence, history, and philosophy. Moreover, merely allowing people to speak out was not democracy. In traditional times, "autocrats who let others air their views were enlightened autocrats, but such actions on their part did not change the nature of autocracy." By contrast, the concept that "all men are endowed by their creator with certain inalienable rights, advanced by the bourgeoisie, signified another step forward for man in history." Therefore, Guo insisted, "socialist democracy" did not mean giving certain people the privilege of speaking their minds on certain issues; "the people must have the right to express their opinions extensively on all kinds of political issues and to unfold discussions."[56]

All views, including counterrevolutionary ones, said Guo, could be aired. The line of demarcation should be drawn between thought and action: "So long as people do not take any action that contravenes the Constitution or the laws, they must be allowed to express all kinds of opinions on either political or academic subjects."[57] The way to oppose anyone who expresses counterrevolutionary views is not to arrest him, but to "start up a debate with him and criticize him."[58] Ding Xueliang has observed that Guo's arguments, especially his call for "all the people" to discuss political issues, were most upsetting to the elders, including Deng Xiaoping, because Guo implied that not just the democratic elite but the Democracy Wall activists also had the right to comment publicly.[59]

Su Shaozhi, with his collaborator Feng Lanrui, whose husband Li Chang was a close associate of Hu Yaobang's from his Youth League days, advanced the concept that China was moving into, but was not yet at, "the primary stage of socialism." They used the term "undeveloped socialism" *(bu fada de shehui zhuyi)*. The view that China was already at the primary stage of socialism would become party doctrine at the Thirteenth Party Congress in the fall of 1987. Su and Feng explained that a lack of understanding of the stages of socialism and, in particular, the failure to realize that China did not have the necessary conditions for even the primary stage had led to mistakes in policy, such as the imposition of complete state ownership of the economy, that had resulted in serious setbacks.[60] In their view any form of economic organization—private, cooperative, collective, state, or even foreign—was permissible at China's current stage of development. Their powerful critique of Mao's economic views helped to build support for the move toward a market economy.

The theorists associated with the elders used the Spring Festival break, from mid-February until the third week of March, to attack the ideas presented by the democratic elite during the first part of the conference. They found Deng Xiaoping responsive to their criticisms. During the break, China encountered difficulties in its war with Vietnam, and Deng began the crackdown on the Democracy Wall activists. Moreover, in addition to the reports of the five chairmen that Deng received on the conference's group discussions, Hu Qiaomu personally reported to Deng that some of the conference participants had made anti-Maoist, anti-party statements, which he characterized as more dangerous than those heard during the Hundred Flowers period. Deng asked Hu Qiaomu to organize a group of twenty to thirty to draft a speech he planned to give at the start of the second half of the conference.

When the draft was circulated ahead of time among the conference's original participants, it evoked much consternation. Hu Yaobang's associates offered many suggestions for revision that Hu relayed back to Hu Qiaomu and Deng. Yet although a few statements were deleted, such as "rightism is currently the major danger," the changes were minor and much of the draft remained as it was. Apparently Hu Yaobang was unable or unwilling to take a stand against the mentor who had made it possible for him to convene the conference in the first place.

When Deng delivered the speech, its ideas were warmly received by his listeners. But those participating in the second half of the conference were quite different from those of the first half, and the whole tone had changed. Now over four hundred people were in attendance, and they were mainly provincial party secretaries and provincial and army propaganda officials allied with the elders. The conference speakers in the second half were no longer theorists associated with Hu Yaobang but party propaganda cadres associated with Hu Qiaomu. They warned of dangers from the "right" and the need to struggle against them. Some of the participants during the first half did not even attend the second half, and those who did were relatively quiet. Nevertheless, Hu Jiwei continued to oppose leftist ideas publicly and Zhang Xianyang, on the day after Deng's speech, expressed views at a small group meeting similar to those he had expressed earlier.[61]

The shift in Deng's views in these months can be seen in the talks he gave over the course of the conference. On January 20, during the first half of the meeting, he called for the discussion of democratic and legal institutions, and in a speech on January 27, he spelled out what this meant. Although the latter speech, at the suggestion of Hu Qiaomu, was not included in Deng's *Selected Works,* transcripts exist. Not only did he admit that democracy had not been realized in socialist societies since the October Revolution, but he also praised the Western bourgeoisie for practicing democracy and recommended that China "should develop the good points of the bourgeoisie in this respect. So far we have not done this well. Stalin made mistakes, so have we." Moreover, he lauded the bourgeoisie for having made itself the "masters of the country" by establishing an elective and legislative system to control the government. "We should find a way to let people feel that they are the masters of the country." [62]

By contrast, "Uphold the Four Cardinal Principles," the speech written under Hu Qiaomu's direction that Deng delivered on March 30, expressed an unswerving belief in the supremacy of Lenin's one-party state and party domination, thereby contradicting his January calls for institutional controls. Much of his March 30 speech condemned the Democracy Wall activists, whom Deng charged had "raised such sensational slogans as 'Oppose hunger' and 'Give us human rights,' inciting people to hold demonstrations and deliberately trying to get foreigners to give worldwide publicity to their words and deeds." He was particularly incensed with the plea of the China Human Rights League to President Carter "to 'show concern' for human rights in China." [63] Although he had praised bourgeois democracy in his January 27 speech, Deng now blamed the disruptions during the Democracy Wall movement on ideas from abroad, specifically the United States. He expressed his desire to learn from the capitalist countries in science and technology, but not from the ideas and values that accompanied the science and technology.

Deng made it clear that he would not countenance any protest movements that the party or he did not control. Much of this speech reiterated his basic belief in Leninist party control—a belief that he had held ever since joining the party in 1924. Of the four cardinal principles, he emphasized obedience to the party. "In the China of today we can never dispense with leadership by the Party and extol the spontaneity of the masses." He admitted that the party had made "many errors, but each time the errors were corrected by relying on the Party organization, not by discarding it." [64] His interpretation of democracy was decidedly Leninist, resting on the concept of democratic centralism. "We must link democracy . . . with centralism, legality, discipline and the leadership by the Communist Party." [65] If China departed from the Leninist party-state, this would "inevitably lead to the unchecked spread of ultra democracy and anarchism, to the complete disruption of political stability and unity, and to the total failure of our modernization program." [66]

One part of Deng's March 30 speech appeared to be directed at the participants in the first half of the theory conference. He specifically criticized "certain people (even if only a handful)" who, instead of recognizing the danger of ideas that undermined the four cardinal principles, supported them. Like his elderly colleagues, he was clearly displeased with sweeping criticisms of Mao. "Comrade Mao, like any other man, had his defects and made errors. But how can these errors in his illustrious life be put on a par with his immortal contributions to the people?" His defense of Mao was also a defense of himself and his colleagues. Mao's errors were "likewise those of his comrade-in-arms, the Party and the people." [67]

Hu Yaobang assumed a defensive position during the conference break. In a talk at a journalists' conference convened by the Propaganda Department on February 28, he commented that the theory conference had "gone well." Many participants "expressed very good opinions and offered very good views; this is an important achievement." Nevertheless, Hu admitted, "since so many people spoke at the meetings it was hard to avoid some ideas and views which were not so satisfactory, but at the least we can continue to discuss!" Still, he advised: "We should not assume that the speeches given at the conference are the views of the Central Committee and are definitive." [68] He added, "I am not saying that we should hide Mao's mistakes and errors," but he cautioned, "we should vigorously check the facts . . . [and] when we write and speak, we should do so with reservations." [69] The criticism of the Cultural Revolution could continue, but Hu urged journalists to report more on present-day modernization than on past injustices. He proposed less use of the terms "left" and "right" and advised that during the war with Vietnam, journalists should build up a spirit of patriotism.

Despite some compromises with the elders and especially with Deng, Hu still expressed greater tolerance of spontaneous movements than they had. His approach was to respond positively, urging that party organizations, for example, be more responsive to the needs of society so that "spontaneous demonstrations would not be so popular."[70] This positive approach was to remain an article of faith with Hu, leading eventually to his break with Deng during the student demonstrations of December 1986.

The Aftermath of the Theory Conference

By the spring of 1979, the sense of exhilaration that had filled the intellectual community before and after the Third Plenum began to wane. A few of the participants in the first half of the theory conference were punished, particularly Guo Luoji, who became the chief scapegoat. His articles and actions, even before the conference, had angered several leaders, including Deng. Meetings were held to criticize him, and in 1982 he was transferred to Nanjing University, where he was deprived of his status as a party cadre and denied the right to hold an official position. For some time thereafter, he wrote articles under a pen name.

Guo's fellow participants in the theory conference, however, continued to speak out with relative impunity in the party press against the policies and ideology of the Mao era. Although Hu had urged them to stop, they still characterized Maoist practices as "leftist." At the same time they indirectly criticized the domination of the Leninist party-state that Deng had just reinforced with his enunciation of the four cardinal principles. Li Honglin, for example, in an April 1979 article in the *People's Daily,* was one of the first in the country to draw a distinction publicly between the nation and society on the one hand and the party and the political system on the other. "A great majority of people love the motherland and hope that China will become prosperous. What they are skeptical about is this 'ultra-leftist' socialism." This kind of socialism, he asserted, alienated Chinese society from the political system.[71] In another *People's Daily* article two months later he pointed out that Lin Biao and the Gang of Four were able to seize political power and suppress the Chinese people "because of the lack of democracy."[72] "At that time the power to elect party and state leaders was not in the hands of party members and the people," he explained.[73] He implied that the present-day government had not yet resolved this problem. China's proletarian dictatorship cannot "ensure that the Chinese people have effectively grasped national political power and cannot guarantee that this political power will not be usurped by bad people."[74] For Li, democracy was not just a question of officials acting less bureaucratically; rather, a political system quite different from that of Lenin's democratic centralism needed to be established. Like the Democracy Wall activists, Li insisted that democracy was not to be bestowed as a favor, but to be won by the people.

Because academic journals spoke only to small circles of intellectuals, they were allowed more leeway in the Deng period. A number of the democratic elite or their associates were the editors of the major journals, and thus scholarly essays and forums went even further than the articles in the national media in urging that political commentary as well as intellectual debate be institutionally and legally protected. Li Shu, a historian who participated in the first half of the theory conference, published several articles after the conference on this topic. He admitted that until recently he had believed that the only way to achieve intellectual vitality was to draw a clear demarcation between academic discussion and political discussion, but he had now concluded that there could not be freedom of speech on academic issues without freedom of speech on political issues.

In *Historical Research* (Lishi yanjiu), of which he was editor-in-chief, Li Shu declared that intellectual debate "tolerates neither prejudgment nor interference from the high level authorities or the majority of the people . . . questions of right and wrong in the arts and sciences [should be settled] through free discussion in artistic and scientific circles."[75] He criticized Mao's hitherto revered Hundred Flowers policy that had supposedly promoted debate, however, because in his view, it did not work. "It remained an idea carrying neither legal protection of citizens' inviolable democratic rights under the socialist system nor legal functions of punishing those who violated them. Many people who mistook this personal idea for constitutional rights were soon humiliated . . . Facts showed that in the absence of a sound socialist democratic system, the people would be in constant danger of losing not only their freedom of speech, but their academic freedom as well."[76] It was "our failure to foster an extensive legal sense in our country's political life [that] gave Lin Biao and the 'gang of four' a big opportunity to usurp and abuse power."[77] Intellectual endeavors need a democratic system, with guaranteed rights, because the prerequisite for the development of science and culture is an "atmosphere in which a hundred schools of thought will be able to contend."[78] Moreover, academic work should not merely explain policies; intellectuals should propose and advise on social and economic policies as well.

At a symposium of the Beijing Political Science and Sociology Group called to revive these disciplines, several participants demanded a genuine "democratic system on a sound footing," where people had "the right to elect and the right to dismiss" and where "freedom of speech means that citizens should enjoy the freedom of expressing agreement or disagreement with political issues and state affairs." Even though practice had proved that "public opinion cannot be unified," people still suffered and were arrested for expressing differing and critical views.[79] The participants also criticized the party's assumption of the functions of the judiciary; they insisted that the power of law should be "higher than that of policy, higher than that of instructions of any leader and higher than that of the decision reached by any party organizations."[80]

Despite Deng's criticism and the imprisonment of Democracy Wall activists, some scholarly journals, while dissociating themselves from the activists, continued to argue for human rights. The journal *Studies in Law* (Faxue yanjiu) published a number of articles in the fall of 1979 observing that even though concern for human rights arose with the emergence of the bourgeois class, the desire for these rights had become universal. The interest of the Chinese people in human rights derived from their own experiences in the Cultural Revolution and their worries about the future.

Even several national newspapers discussed human rights in relatively positive terms. The *Workers Daily* (Gongren ribao), for example, though criticizing the China Human Rights League for using the issue to serve their "ulterior purposes,"[81] nevertheless insisted that "such criticism does not in any way mean simplistically negating the issue of human rights. Neither does it mean that we should treat anyone who mentioned human rights as a reactionary and a member of the bourgeoisie."[82] It was not surprising, the article noted, that people doubted whether human rights could exist in a socialist society, because "some bureaucrats do not respect and even severely violate the democratic rights of the people . . . the people's freedom of person and trample upon the people's basic right to life."[83] The article praised the Chinese League for the Protection for Civil Rights, which it described as an independent organization set up in the 1930s, and praised its founders, the former president of Peking University Cai Yuanpei, Sun Yatsen's widow Song Qingling, and the writer Lu Xun. Two of the league's other founders, Luo Longji and Zhang Bojun, were not mentioned because they had been imprisoned by Deng and his colleagues in the 1957 anti-rightist campaign. These two were among the few "rightists" whom Hu Yaobang had been unable to rehabilitate. The article noted that whereas the founders of the league in the 1930s had been motivated by their opposition to Chiang Kai-shek's policies, those who demanded human rights in the late 1970s did so because of their experiences during the Cultural Revolution. Therefore, "we must overcome all interference and steadfastly fight for the effective protection of the democratic rights of the people."[84]

Despite Deng's promulgation of the four cardinal principles, some of the ideas presented by the Democracy Wall activists and the democratic elite in the first half of the theory conference and in subsequent discussions in 1979 appear to have had an impact on policy. At the Second Session of the Fifth National People's Congress in June–July 1979, it was decided that elections for the local people's congresses should be carried out in a more democratic way. Even though the party still had final approval, the eight small parties and any other citizens were entitled to nominate candidates whom the party would consider. In addition, direct elections were extended from the local-level people's congresses to the county-level people's congresses, and elections would be conducted by secret ballot. The introduction of contested local elections, however, was motivated more by a desire to oust remaining Maoist officials and to stimulate the initiative of the masses than to make China more democratic at the local level.

Nevertheless, a *People's Daily* editorial, seemingly taking its cues from the arguments of the democratic elite, rejected the idea that democracy was merely a question of work style or strategy. The editorial declared, as did the democratic elite, that the democratic system that restrained and punished officials according to laws would prevent encroachments on people's rights and interests and at the same time produce a more stable polity and a vibrant economy. The editorial stressed that political reform was as important for China's moderniza-tion as economic reform. "We are painfully aware that democracy and the legal system, like food and clothing, are things that people of a socialist country cannot do without even for a moment. Without democracy and without the legal system, there is no socialism and there is no powerful country and happy people."[85] The editorial acknowledged that laws were not enough; they should be enforced by the courts, which must "administer justice independently, subject only to the law."[86] Like the democratic elite, the editorial called for rule by law, not by man. The Fifth Plenum of the Eleventh Central Committee, held February 23–29, 1980, not only added Hu Yaobang and Zhao Ziyang to the Standing Committee of the Politburo and reestablished the Secretariat, headed by Hu, but also discussed the need to end lifelong political tenure.

The democratic elite's calls for contested elections, limited terms of office, human rights, freedom of the press, and rule of law expressed in 1978–1979 went far beyond the adoption of Western science and technology, or *yong,* advocated by the elders. The democratic elite urged the adoption of some of the Western "essence," or *ti,* as well. Their calls were tacitly and at times publicly supported by a sizable number of intellectuals who shared the belief that ideological and political changes were necessary in order to assimilate Western science and technology.

The democratic elite's interest in assimilating the Western essence, however, was primarily motivated by a desire to restrain unchecked political power so as to prevent another Cultural Revolution. The practice criterion discussion and the theory conference marked the beginning of an effort to revise ideology and to introduce institutions that would make this possible. These events also marked the beginning of the conflict between Hu Yaobang and his intellectual network and the revolutionary elders and their spokesmen, with Deng Xiaoping moving back and forth between the two sides. The conflict was over power, but it was also a debate over which way China should proceed—back to a pre–Cultural Revolution, modified form of a Leninist political system or on to a new future that envisaged fundamental institutional and ideological change. Despite increasing attacks and even campaigns against specific individuals in Hu Yaobang's intellectual network, for the next ten years its members and their associates intermittently but steadfastly continued to call for political reform and ideological revision.

3

Political Openness, Literary Repression

Despite Deng Xiaoping's reinforcement of the Leninist party-state with his enunciation of the four cardinal principles in March 1979, the avenues of expression, the *yanlu,* expanded and extended further in 1980. In addition to fostering the decollectivization of agriculture and overall economic development, Deng continued to call for the promotion of expertise, openness, and an end to political campaigns and control over cultural life. But though this stance represented a radical departure from the Mao era, it was still purely a self-limitation of power, as in traditional times. The reform leadership, including Hu Yaobang, did not contemplate the establishment of organizations or institutions to check the party's power from without. Restraint of the party-state depended exclusively on the decision of the party leaders themselves to curb their own power. Memories of the repression of the Cultural Revolution, still vivid, encouraged self-restraint.

Deng Xiaoping's Critique of the Political System

Nearly all of Deng's speeches at this time touched directly or indirectly on Mao's "mistakes" in his later years. Transcripts of Deng's talks, not included in his selected works, reveal that the negative lessons of the Cultural Revolution remained very much on his mind. In one of these talks, given on May 31, 1980, to propaganda officials, among them Hu Qiaomu and Deng Liqun, Deng criticized a current slogan that had emerged after the repression of the Democracy Wall movement—"Foster political ideology and eliminate bourgeois ideology"—as "flawed and incomplete." He described a visit with Li Weihan, a vice chairman of the Chinese People's Political Consultative Conference (CPPCC) and an old friend. Li had urged Deng to shift the present emphasis from criticizing bourgeois ideas to criticizing "feudal" practices. In agreement with Li, Deng warned his listeners against underestimating "feudal" influence, which he said had "caused serious damage to the normal political life of the party" and had made the words of the top leaders become "law."[1] Despite his four cardinal principles, Deng's definition of "feudal" influence could also be applied to the rule of a few leaders implicit in the Leninist party-state.

Although Deng had denounced a "handful" of the democratic elite as well as the Democracy Wall activists in his March 30, 1979, speech, he still recommended some of the same reforms they had proposed to diminish "feudal" influences. The life-long tenure of cadres and leaders, for example, "must be abolished."[2] He also recommended the establishment of proper rules and regulations for governance. The Propaganda Department organized a meeting on June 11, 1980, to convey Deng's views. They were treated as another breakthrough in Maoist dogma—similar to the initial presentation of ideas in the practice criterion discussion.

In a speech given a few weeks later, Hu Yaobang, while also blaming "feudal" practices, attributed China's problems specifically to its existing political system. In referring to the rise of Lin Biao and the Gang of Four, for example, Hu said: "First, we have to associate it with the problems of our system; second, we ought to trace its social and ideological origins." He explained: "In most socialist countries, the communist parties have failed to establish a successful system after the victory of the revolution." Like Deng, he traced the sources of the problem to the "life-long tenure of our party cadres and the concentration of power." These phenomena have "prevented the emergence of a vivid and vigorous political atmosphere . . . Anyone who dares to put forward different opinions can be punished if the top leaders disagree with these views." Therefore, "we must make up our minds to change the system this time." Hu lamented that China "had not gone through the baptism of bourgeois democracy" and that the rule of "one person alone has a say" remains law.[3]

Deng was circumspect in his criticism of Mao; Hu was unequivocal. Although he praised Mao's leadership style from 1935 to the early 1950s as one of "willingness" to listen to a variety of views, Hu declared that Mao "brought much misfortune to our party in his later years . . . He brought us disasters." Only "by admitting this fact," he asserted, "can we make progress and be respected by our descendants." Hu Yaobang was particularly upset by Mao's use of the personality cult to suppress anyone who differed with him. Unless the system were changed to lessen the power of the top leader, Hu warned, they would "face the danger of ruining the party, the country, and [them]selves."[4]

The calls for criticism of "feudal" practices by Deng and Hu evoked a negative response from the elders' spokesmen. As early as mid-1980 they warned of the dangers of "bourgeois liberalization," an epithet used for Western political ideas and values. On June 25, Hu Qiaomu wrote Hu Yaobang, cautioning him: "We must clearly define what should be opposed and corrected and how to carry out the reform . . . Otherwise, people will rush ahead into mass action, which might cause turmoil ideologically, politically, and organizationally."[5] Hu Qiaomu felt that criticisms and reforms would undermine stability and unity. In opposition to Li Weihan, he stressed that bourgeois liberalization should be criticized along with feudalism. Further, he sought to shift the focus of the attack from "feudalism" to Western political and economic practices.

In this period Deng continued to side with Hu Yaobang, as he had in the discussion of the practice criterion. Deng himself initiated the discussion on the need for fundamental political reforms in the party in his extraordinary speech of August 18, "On the Reform of the System of Party and State Leadership." In it he sharply criticized not only the feudal legacy but also the party's prevailing overconcentration of power. He called for an end to the common practice of high party officials also holding government posts, saying that it was "not good to have too many people holding two or more posts concurrently."[6]

Deng sought to reduce the party's domination over virtually all aspects of life. Despite his commitment to the Leninist party-state, he made a penetrating critique of its fundamental features:

> In addition to sharing some common characteristics with past types of bureaucracy, Chinese bureaucracy in its present form has characteristics of its own. That is, it differs from both the bureaucracy of old China and that prevailing in the capitalist countries. It is closely connected with our highly centralized management in the economic,

political, cultural and social fields, which we have long regarded as essential for the socialist system and for planning. Our leading organs at various levels have taken charge of many matters which they should not and cannot handle, or cannot handle efficiently. These matters could have been easily handled by the enterprises, institutions and communities at the grass-roots level, provided we had proper rules and regulations.[7]

Deng charged that the "overconcentration of power in the hands of an individual or of a few people" inevitably impaired democratic and socialist life.[8] "The long-standing failure to understand this adequately," he insisted, "was one important cause of the 'Cultural Revolution,' and we paid a heavy price for it. There should be no further delay in finding a solution to this problem."[9] He attributed the overconcentration of power to practices introduced in 1949. "We did not consciously draw up systematic rules and regulations to safeguard the people's democratic rights. Our legal system is far from perfect and has not received anywhere near the attention it deserves."[10]

Although in the past Deng had blamed Mao and others for this overconcentration of power, he now placed the major blame on the system itself.

It is true that the errors we made in the past were partly attributable to the way of thinking and style of work of some leaders. But they were even more attributable to the problems in our organization and working systems. If these systems are sound, they can place restraints on actions of bad people; if they are unsound, they may hamper the efforts of good people or indeed, in certain cases may push them in the wrong direction. Even so great a man as Comrade Mao Zedong was influenced to a serious degree by certain unsound systems and institutions, which resulted in grave misfortunes for the party, the state, and himself. If even now we still don't improve the way our socialist system functions, people will ask why it cannot solve some problems which the capitalist system can . . . Stalin gravely damaged socialist legality, doing things which Comrade Mao Zedong once said would have been impossible in Western countries like Britain, France, and the United States. Yet, although Comrade Mao was aware of this, he did not in practice solve the problems in our system of leadership . . . Some serious problems which appeared in the past may rise again if defects in our present systems are not limited.[11]

Deng's remedies for the defects, however, harked back to traditional cures—administrative reforms and the promotion of younger, more professional officials.

Nor did Deng's remedies include significant change for the party. In good Leninist fashion he did not want the party subject to any external constraints, though he sought to limit its power by internal constraints, recommending that three internal committees act as checks on one another. The tragedy is that Deng, like Mao, accurately perceived that China's problems lay in its political system, but despite some half-hearted efforts, he too was unwilling to carry out fundamental political reforms, much to the misfortune of the party, state, and himself. When he and the party felt threatened, Deng, like Mao, took advantage of the same overconcentration of power to assert his will.

Deng promised never again to launch political campaigns. "There should be no political criticism of the kind that has been directed at some individuals in the past, and still less should there be struggles directed against either the cadres or the masses. Historical experience has shown that no problem of mass ideological education was ever solved by launching a mass movement instead of organizing exhaustive persuasion and calm discussion, and that no currently functioning systems were ever reformed or new ones established by substituting a mass movement for solid, systematic measures." He proposed that specific units convene conferences at which they would have "the right" to make decisions on questions of importance to the units, such as instituting procedures to recall incompetent administrators and, "within appropriate limits," electing their own leaders.[12] In these elections the party secretaries would be entitled to only one vote and could not make unilateral decisions as they had in the past. These radical proposals, however, were meant primarily for experts and professionals. Moreover, Deng concluded his speech by reiterating that the core of the four cardinal principles was to "uphold leadership by the Party."[13] With this statement he undermined the very reforms he was proposing.

The Democratic Elite's Elaboration on Deng's Critique

While intellectual and theoretical circles were enthusiastic about Deng's August 18 speech, some within the elder leadership found it upsetting and even threatening. Their spokesmen Hu Qiaomu and Deng Liqun wrote to Hu Yaobang, advising that Deng's speech not be publicized. Nevertheless, though parts of it were not to be published until 1983, word of it leaked out and set the tone for subsequent discussions of political reform, especially among members of the democratic elite. Shortly thereafter, several of them elaborated on Deng's speech in public forums.

The most controversial elaboration was by Liao Gailong, who had been at the theory conference and was a member of the Policy Research Office of the Central Committee, the office that set forth policy options for the leadership. At a seminar on party history on October 25, 1980, Liao went further than Deng in calling for the party's separation from not only the government and the economy but also cultural activities, mass organizations, and the media. He favored an independent press: "We should permit, require and encourage the media, the journalists and commentators to independently assume the responsibility of reporting or publishing news, letters from the masses and comments."[14] Liao too called for improvements in the legal system, but not so much to reinforce prevailing regulations as to help safeguard "the personal freedom and other civil rights of all citizens."[15] Furthermore, when the judiciary conducted a trial, no one should "be allowed to interfere in the independent activities of the judicial officials in their work. In short, the judiciary must be independent. Even party committees will not be able to interfere in this independence."[16] His proposals for reform resonated with practices in Western democracies. He had had little experience with their institutions or procedures, but he found them appropriate for limiting political power in order to prevent another Cultural Revolution.

Liao also proposed various concrete political reforms that were being experimented with in Eastern Europe and would eight years later be tried in the Soviet Union under Gorbachev, such as giving more power to the legislative branch of the government. In China's case, the legislative branch was the National People's Congress, which hitherto had done little more than rubber-stamp party leaders' decisions. He recommended reducing the size of the congress from 3,000 to 2,000 delegates and turning it into a two-chamber legislature, one representing regional interests and the other representing various professional groups. The two chambers would make laws jointly and supervise each other. Its Standing Committee would be reduced from

300 to 60–70 members, who would serve full-time as professional legislators. Liao hoped that this legislature would in time become powerful enough to limit the power of party leaders.

Ironically, the elders, rather than the reformers, were the first to use the National People's Congress as a check on the leadership. Peng Zhen, serving as its chairman, used the body to water down the reforms and curb the power of the reform officials in the Standing Committee of the Politburo and the Secretariat under the control of Hu Yaobang and Zhao Ziyang. Some of the more orthodox Marxists also called for freedom of the press when they found it difficult to publish their own works at times when the national media was controlled by Hu's network. Although the orthodox Marxists' advocacy of these institutions derived from political battles rather than from a genuine commitment to democracy, their periodic repression under both Deng and Mao likewise gave some a greater appreciation of the need to limit political power.

Liao Gailong added specificity to Deng's recommendation that internal committees check the overconcentration of power in the top party leadership. He suggested that a Discipline Inspection Committee, an Advisory Committee, and a Central Executive Committee mutually restrain one another. The Central Discipline Inspection Commission, established in 1978, and especially the Central Advisory Commission, established in 1982, became filled with retired officials, however, as again the elders used reform for their own purposes. In time these commissions became their power bases through which they limited reforms proposed by the Politburo Standing Committee and restrained Hu Yaobang, Zhao Ziyang, and their intellectual networks. Instead of curbing the elders and their spokesmen, the internal committees became a check on the reform leaders and their reformist policies.

Liao's most radical recommendation was the establishment of independent labor unions. He criticized the current situation: "The workers are not permitted to elect the officials of the so-called trade unions. The party arbitrarily appoints the officials. Thus the unions do not represent the workers' interests." Whereas the elders and Deng were fearful of independent trade unions because of their potential for creating a Chinese "Solidarity" movement, Liao urged their establishment precisely to prevent a similar move in China. "We all know what has happened in Poland. If we do not change our course, the same things will happen to us."[17] He also urged that professional organizations become independent of the party and be allowed to work for their own interests. Liao's recommendations for reform, especially regarding independent unions and autonomous interest groups, went well beyond Deng's more limited proposals.

Similarly, the discussions of democratic institutions in the media that had preceded Deng's August 18 speech and that continued after it also went much further than Deng had. An article in the journal *Ideological Liberation* (Sixiang jiefang), for example, explained that "democratization" meant "to legalize and regularize, according to definite systems, the democratic rights and demands of the people into a common norm of conduct."[18] In this way, democratization "is the political foundation of stability and unity."[19] At present, however, "the basic recognition of the people's democratic rights is inadequate, and we need concrete systems and concrete laws to protect such rights, threading the democratic principles through all the systems and laws for otherwise the constitution will turn into a mere empty paper."[20]

Demands for a good system countered the age-old and now increasingly loud demands for good leaders. In June the *Beijing Evening News* (Beijing wanbao) began a series focusing on the symbol of the "emperor." One column criticized those who called for a modern leader who would be similar to the upright Emperor Taizong of the Tang dynasty, or for good officials resembling his senior official Wei Zheng, who admonished the emperor many times. This column explained that principled intellectuals worked well under a "good" emperor, when they were not necessary, and they were completely ineffective under a "bad" emperor, who might chop off their heads. Even when a "good" emperor, such as Taizong, listened to Wei Zheng's admonitions, "his majesty often flew into a rage."[21] The desire for "a good emperor to emerge," the column acknowledged, "is not surprising at a time when people aspire to return order to society in the wake of a catastrophe that lasted ten years." China's problem, however, had been not lack of "good rulers" but "our failure to . . . protect people's democracy and inner-party democracy from being undermined by feudal fascist elements . . . Ours is a choice between . . . democracy and autocracy, and between rule by law and rule by man, rather than a choice between good and bad emperors."[22]

Liao Mosha, who along with his associates Wu Han and Deng Tuo,

under the pseudonym "three-family village," had subtly tried to per
suade Mao to become a "good emperor," wrote: "During the 1960s,
an article by Comrade Wu Han entitled 'Hai Rui Admonishes the
Emperor' caused him not only his job but also his life. This memory
remains fresh to us today."[23] Deng Tuo was also cited as a principled
intellectual who lost his life for daring to criticize the ruler. This traditional approach had proved not only ineffective but counterproductive.

Another formative debate in 1980 focused on whether democracy
was a means or an end. Deng Xiaoping saw political reform as a
means to a more efficiently run economy; Hu Yaobang, in a speech
on October 15, described democracy as "not only a means but an end;
it is our basic system."[24] An article in *Philosophy Research* asked, "If
socialist democracy were regarded merely as a means for realizing
modernization and not as an end itself," what value would there be
in achieving economic modernization? The article warned that such
an approach had already resulted in "great damage."[25] It specifically
criticized the Leninist concept of democratic centralism, which regarded democracy as "merely strengthening centralization."[26] Moreover, "centralism divorced from democracy can only be a kind of autocracy. Perceiving democracy as a means of centralism most
conspicuously illustrates . . . taking democracy merely as a means.
Those comrades who adhere to this point often mainly understand
democracy to be a work style and method."[27] Such a view meant that
"when [democracy] may be used and when it may be discarded, when
it is too much and when it is too little, when it should be in a 'mass'
proportion and when it should be 'limited' must all depend on certain
subjective political needs. Thus, the people's power and rights are all
forgotten, and the so-called democracy becomes purely an instrument
of utilitarianism . . . or even a political trick."[28] The people had already paid a very heavy price for this view of "democracy as a means
and not an end."[29]

Yu Haocheng, the legal expert and a participant at the theory conference, was a vociferous opponent of the view of democracy as
merely a means. Born in 1927 in Manchuria, the son of a professor
of Chinese literature at Yenching University, Yu joined the party in
1942 but was criticized in the rectification campaign of that year.
After 1949, because of his fluency in English and Russian, he worked
first for the Tianjin Foreign Affairs Office and then, in October 1956,

for the Ministry of Public Security, which asked him to establish a publishing house to be called the Masses (Qunzhong). During the Cultural Revolution he was imprisoned in the infamous Qincheng prison, supposedly for collecting inflammatory materials on Jiang Qing. From 1968 to 1971 he was kept in solitary confinement in a very small cell, where he survived by reciting poetry, songs, and operas he had memorized as a youth. Because his self-criticism was regarded as insufficiently abject, Yu was also tortured. In 1971 he was sent to labor in Hubei. When he was rehabilitated in 1978, he returned to the Masses Publishing House as its chief editor.

As opposed to most members of the democratic elite, who worshiped the party and Mao unquestioningly in the 1950s, Yu had begun to have doubts at the time of the 1955 campaign against the writer Hu Feng, who had written a long report to the Central Committee calling for more freedom for writers. Yu wondered how Hu Feng's report on various interpretations of art could be considered counterrevolutionary.[30] He was also influenced by Khrushchev's 1956 denunciation of Stalin. Yu did not write about his doubts until the Gang of Four had been toppled, but then he challenged the Leninist system directly. He opposed the traditional desire for enlightened leaders by explaining that a leader's "acceptance of dissident opinions by his subjects" is not democracy; it is merely the tradition of placing one's faith in "sagacious rulers, virtuous prime ministers, honest officials." Such a view only reinforces the age-old belief that granting permission to speak is the right of the leaders, who therefore can also withhold the right to speak when they disagree with what the subject has to say. "Such a work style, of course, cannot be designated as democratic, as it falls very short of really letting the people act as masters and exercise their own freedoms and rights."[31]

The traditional methods were no longer appropriate, Yu explained, because they did not protect those who had the courage to protest the abuse of power. "How many masterful article writers like Deng Tuo and Wu Han . . . have died miserably under the sword of the executioner?"[32] The constitution's guarantees of freedom of speech and press had not helped them, because "realistic life indicates that these prescriptions [are] merely things on paper and not actualities." He therefore called for institutions and laws to protect the freedom of the press and enact the constitution. Equally important, he called for the establishment of independent newspapers: "Why must newspaper offices and publishing houses be run only by party committees and government organs . . . and [why can they] not be managed independently under the conditions of compliance with pertinent laws and edicts?" He explained that "everything [is] subjected to state monopoly."[33] Until that monopoly was eliminated, he implied, there could not be real freedom.

Despite Yu's stated belief in Marxism, his view of the rule of law was much closer to the Anglo-Saxon than the Marxist perspective. When the Gang of Four and the military leaders connected with Lin Biao were put on trial in November 1980, in part to embarrass Hua Guofeng and the remaining Maoist leaders connected with them, Yu took the unpopular position that "to organize a public trial when the party committee has already ruled on the guilt or innocence of the accused" was "useless."[34] Without referring to any specific case, he stressed that the judiciary should act strictly in accordance with the law and render justice independently.

Seemingly in response to the elders' concern that political change meant chaos, a number of articles emphasized that it was democracy and the rule of law, not an imposed unity, that brought stability. The democracies of capitalist countries were relatively secure because "their state apparatus always operates along the course determined by law," no matter which party gains power or who becomes president or prime minister.[35] The law under an autocracy "often constitutes a demonstration of individual whim and tyranny"; the law under democracy is "the will of the people expressed through their own representative organ in legal form . . . no one can substitute his words for the law."[36] Therefore "from now on, we must establish a principle: the effect of a law . . . is greater than that of any written or unwritten individual opinion, order, or talk."[37] Furthermore, "people should have the power to supervise the execution of the law, so that the law becomes a powerful weapon for the protection of the people's democratic rights."[38]

A collection of articles published in fall 1980 introduced Western Enlightenment thinkers to the Chinese reading public. Among the authors was Montesquieu, who was described as having "put into effect the separation of three powers, distinguishing between the legislative, executive, and judicial powers as the necessary condition for securing people's political freedom." Montesquieu was also quoted as having said that when these powers are arrogated to an individual or one

organization, then "the masses live without security and in poverty
... Therefore, it is necessary to divide power in order to limit the
power of the ruler, protect people's political freedom and safety." This
collection also quoted Rousseau to the effect that officials must be
responsible to the people and that no one could place himself beyond
the law, no matter who he might be.[39]

Accompanying the praise of Western Enlightenment thinkers was
increasing criticism of orthodox ideology. Before Guo Luoji was sent
to Nanjing, he published an article in the Shanghai paper *Wenhui
News* (Wenhui bao) in which he attributed the loss of ideological belief and commitment to the Cultural Revolution: "The revolutionary
leaders were made into 'gods' and the science of revolutionary theories was made into a theology. They further promoted a set of rites,
such as the so-called 'morning instructions,' 'evening reports,' 'loyalty
dances,' and quotations, calisthenics and a religious atmosphere prevailed everywhere ... [P]eople's faith in the theories reached a state
of superstition."[40] But when the people found out after the Cultural
Revolution that they had been betrayed, "their enthusiasm ... turned
into despair and their suspicions into doubt, ... particularly [among]
the younger generation."[41] Like others in the Hu Yaobang network,
Guo did not reject Marxism, only its distortion. He too hoped to relegitimize the ideology by making it more relevant to the present. Guo
explained: "If Marxism is not allowed to be doubted and criticized,
then there is no way to recognize a false Marxism when it appears."
In refuting those opposed to any change in the ideology, he asked:
"Is it not true that the criticism of Marxism is protected under the
constitution?" Individuals "should not be charged and punished because they have expressed doubt about Marxism or made statements
criticizing Marxism."[42]

In July 1980 Wang Ruoshui continued Guo Luoji's arguments at a
forum of over forty political theorists. He urged: "We must seek to
emancipate our minds from all forms of superstitions, dogmatism,
stereotyped writing, forbidden zones, outdated modes of thought, ...
and false conclusions born of limited experience." Reiterating the
practice criterion, he insisted that "according to Marx, all theories
must be subjected to the test of practice." When discussing ideology,
members of the democratic elite often reverted to the idiom of their
literati predecessors, whose prime commitment was not to any political authority but to "the truth." Typical was Wang's assertion that

"the truly emancipated person is not one who spews forth patent lies to please the authorities. He is one who speaks the truth at the risk of being labeled a 'rightist' and 'conservative.'"[43]

In the late 1970s and early 1980s, Wang and his colleague Ru Xin, then deputy director of the Institute of Philosophy of CASS, argued that Marxism included humanism. Their view stemmed from their Cultural Revolution experiences and the reinterpretations of Marxism being debated in Eastern and Western Europe at the time. Wrote Ru Xin: "It is wrong to set Marxism and humanism in fundamental opposition to each other." He revealed that his interest in humanism had been sparked by an elderly poet who, after experiencing the brutality of the Cultural Revolution and the campaigns against humanism during the Mao period, swore "never to participate in any so-called criticism of humanism" again. Although humanism, Ru explained, referred to an "ideological and cultural movement launched by the rising bourgeoisie during the European Renaissance . . . [in] the broad sense, it refers to . . . attaching importance to the value of man . . . Man himself is the highest aim of mankind and man's value is in himself." This fulfills the Marxist desire to enable "man to fully and freely develop himself."[44]

Wang Ruoshui, a slight, soft-spoken, and intensely serious philosopher as well as journalist, went further and raised the controversial issue of the existence of alienation in a Marxist-Leninist state. He referred to Marx's early work *The Economic and Philosophical Manuscripts of 1844* as the source of the view that alienation can exist under socialism as well as under capitalism. It had been translated into Chinese in June 1956, at the beginning of the Hundred Flowers period, along with the Marxist humanist interpretation of Georg Lukacs. When Mao began his attacks on Soviet revisionism in 1963–64, Wang and Ru Xin as well as Ruan Ming became members of a small group of scholars who, under Zhou Yang's leadership, studied European interpretations of Marxism in order to repudiate them and to reinforce Mao's attacks on revisionism.

When Wang became a victim of the Cultural Revolution, however, he found the concept of alienation relevant to his own experience; he had become alienated from the very system he had helped to establish.[45] That Wang's experience paralleled that of other intellectuals can be seen in the great interest in 1979 in the retranslation and republication of Marx's *Manuscripts* and many East European works on the topic as well as in the writings of Western Marxists, including Herbert Marcuse, members of the Frankfurt School, and the Freudian-Marxist Erich Fromm. Translations of Sartre, Camus, and Kafka, whose writings depicted individuals trying to make sense out of an absurd world, captured the imagination of younger Chinese intellectuals.

Yet despite the availability of these foreign writings, it was the intellectuals' own experience in the Cultural Revolution, rather than outside influences, that made the concepts of alienation and humanism seem so powerful and compelling. Ruan Ming explained: "The realities of China and nothing else . . . caused the Chinese people to be drawn to these all but forgotten works of Marx. Their interest in the young Marx came from the real needs of the people, who rejected the calcified Marxism, which had disregarded man and caused the abuse of human rights, freedom, dignity, and talent and brought on China 'the ten years of holocaust.'"[46]

In a 1980 article Wang Ruoshui asked, "Why does the question of estrangement once again attract so much attention today? This is, in my opinion, because the practice of socialism has given rise to the question of estrangement and it has taken on new significance." Even though "socialism should have eliminated estrangement," nevertheless, he emphasized, "we must admit that realities prove that there is still estrangement."[47]

Wang identified three types of alienation—ideological, political, and economic. Ideological alienation was caused by the cult of the individual. "The playing up of the cult of the individual results in the alienation of the leader from the people . . . Is that not turning the leader into a god?" Complete obedience to Mao meant "one person laying down the law."[48] Wang blamed this phenomenon not only on Mao but on those who obeyed him. He was one of a small number, with Ba Jin, the literary critic Liu Zaifu, and a few other writers, to accept some public responsibility for the excesses of the Mao era. "We should not blame Lin Biao and the Gang of Four alone for all this. Many people, including myself, took part in propagating the cult and did so out of warm feelings," resulting in the loss of control over one's actions. The experience of the Cultural Revolution fit Wang's general definition of alienation all too well: "A thing originally of our creation has developed and become an estranged force, which has gone out of our control and has turned round to dominate and oppress us."[49]

Political alienation, in Wang's view, occurs when the leaders of a society, who are supposed to be its servants, become its masters. "Once power is in their hands there is the danger that some of these leaders do not use this power to serve the people, but serve themselves. As a result servants of the people become lords of the people who ride roughshod over the people . . . When a government becomes a lord out of control of the people, it becomes an estranged force." [50] In addition to calling for the more traditional remedy of humanism to reduce the alienation, Wang also proposed meaningful competitive elections and freedom of speech, so that self-serving officials could be removed from office.

The political alienation that had begun under Mao, Wang believed, was continuing into the present. "Now that the 'Gang of Four' has been overthrown, we must not think that everything is just fine." Although present-day cadres were not as bad as the Gang, "they act the high and mighty officials and are indifferent to the interests of the people." Furthermore, they might not even represent the people's interests. "Promoting democracy, perfecting the legal system, laying down the rules guiding life in the party and abolishing the system of life-long appointment of cadres" are necessary in order to overcome political alienation. [51]

Alienation in a socialist economy, Wang insisted, was different from that in a capitalist economy. It was caused less by exploitation than by a lack of understanding of objective economic rules, the imposition of bureaucratic controls, and the priority given to heavy industry. Although the purpose of socialist society is supposedly to meet the needs of the people, "high speed growth and the development of heavy industry are sought after one-sidedly." These policies "bring sufferings to the people, and the harder they work the greater their sufferings." [52] Voluntarism and ignorance of economics, a description of Mao's utopian policies since the Great Leap Forward, had produced economic alienation. Wang insisted that this condition could be overcome only by understanding economic realities and responding to the people's demands. The proposition that alienation could exist in socialism provoked vigorous debate, pro and con, in the intellectual community.

While Wang and other members of the democratic elite critically reinterpreted Marxism-Leninism, some reevaluated China's traditional dominant belief, Confucianism. Through most of the Mao period Confucianism had been regarded as a repressive ideology. In the

Deng era a more positive view was presented, but perspectives varied. The mainstream position stressed the Confucian emphasis on education, responsibility, and harmony; a minority view emphasized the values Confucianism shared with Western humanism, including the Western stress on independent moral judgment. In fact, a *Wenhui News* article pointed out that a similar "world view was already expressed in the humanist doctrines of Confucius almost 2,000 years before the Renaissance, and it became later the fine tradition of Confucianism."[53] This long tradition, the article declared, should be reaffirmed in the present.

Grass-roots Democratic Practices

As extraordinary as the discourse on Western values and democratic practices in the national media and at public forums in Beijing and other urban centers were the elections occurring on the local level. Most areas continued the practice of the last thirty years of only nominating candidates approved by the party, but in a few districts candidates who had not been nominated by the party were allowed to run in competitive elections for seats in county and district people's congresses. Although the local congresses had little real power, former Red Guards and Democracy Wall activists who had been silenced by Deng's crackdown on the Democracy Wall movement seized the opportunity to work for democratic reform by running in these elections. They used the skills of debate, speech making, and campaign mobilization that they had learned as political activists in the Cultural Revolution.

The most competitive elections were held in university districts. An especially contested election occurred in Haidian District, the location of Beijing's universities. In addition to the official candidate, Zhang Wei, several nonofficial candidates also ran for the seat. Among them were a well-known graduate student in philosophy, Hu Ping; another graduate student, Yang Baikui, who later became a political scientist; and Wang Juntao, who had participated in the April 5, 1976, Tiananmen demonstration and had been a co-editor with Chen Ziming of the nonofficial journal *Beijing Spring* in the Democracy Wall movement. Their political platforms were critiques of the thirty years of party rule. In fact, the Beijing Spring group promoted candidates in 9 out of Peking's 12 universities.

In debates during the campaign, Wang Juntao distinguished himself by displaying extraordinary debating skills that inspired and even evoked cheers from his listeners. To be a charismatic speaker[54] was a rare quality in Chinese political figures, who did not need to campaign for office among the ordinary people. In a campaign speech given on November 3, 1980, Wang's distaste for the Leninist system and his desire for democracy were vigorously expressed. In his view China's difficulties, its poverty and backwardness, continued because "China's politics are dictatorial."[55] He urged that "political reforms be carried out at the same time as economic reforms and mutually influence each other."[56]

Wang Juntao recommended comparative study of the Soviet and U.S. political systems as points of reference for China's reforms, but the political reforms he proposed strongly resembled the American system of checks and balances. Although he had no personal experience with and little knowledge of such a division of power, he called for an independent judiciary, a strengthened National People's Congress, and an independent press.[57] He criticized the state-owned press: "It cannot objectively and in a timely fashion criticize the government and publish news that the government believes inappropriate for ordinary people to know." He suggested that the small parties and mass organizations be allowed to run their own newspapers. As Liao Gailong had proposed a month earlier, Wang declared that mass organizations (unions of workers, peasants, students, scientists, and writers and artists) should be "completely independent of the state," and he insisted that "the government should not encroach on all kinds of basic civil rights and freedoms."[58] He acknowledged that these reforms amounted to a "qualitative revolution," but he urged that they be carried out "harmoniously" and with "moderation."[59] Equally bold was his criticism of Mao. Wang insisted that Mao had not fully understood Marxism, which was "why he made serious mistakes."[60]

Though the content of Wang's critique of Mao did not differ much from that of the democratic elite, it was his direct criticism of the leader that supposedly led to his loss of the election by a small margin to Hu Ping, who had been an activist at the start of the Cultural Revolution, serving as editor of the first nonofficial journal in Chengdu. His journal had published an article by Yu Luoke, one of the first individuals to be executed in the Cultural Revolution for repudiating leftist ideas. In 1970 Hu Ping himself wrote a critique of "ultra leftism," which he defined as "making Mao into a god," and as a result was sent away to the countryside for five years. Having achieved the highest grades in the entrance examination to Peking University in 1978, Hu Ping was immediately allowed to study for a research degree in philosophy. During the Democracy Wall movement, he edited another nonofficial journal, *Fertile Soil*. In it he published one of his own articles, "Freedom of Speech," which formed the basis of his platform in the election campaign.

"Freedom of Speech" became well known in intellectual circles. In it Hu Ping charged that the party leaders' definition of democracy meant "nothing but an enlightened autocracy. Freedom of speech, as they understand it, is not different from the submitting and accepting of remonstrances and widening access for public opinion to reach the ruler as practiced in feudal society . . . This system of remonstrating . . . was not truly freedom of speech because the sphere of what might be stated by ministers or the people was actually decided by the will of the emperor . . . At times [it] was somewhat wider and at times extremely narrow, . . . [depending on] the character of the rulers."[61] This kind of freedom of speech "does not depend on whether the rulers are willing to lend an ear and will tolerate critical opinions, but on whether the rulers have the power to punish those who hold opposing views." Hu Ping therefore called for institutions and laws to protect people's rights: "True freedom of speech exists . . . only when the right to free speech exists independent of whether it enjoys the protection of an enlightened ruler, and only when the people have learned to resist power in its attempt to interfere with free speech."[62]

Other Democracy Wall activists who won seats in local congresses were Chen Ziming, Wang's co-editor at *Beijing Spring;* Fu Shengqi, a worker who had been an editor of the nonofficial journal *Voice of Democracy* (Minzhu zhisheng) in Shanghai; and Liang Heng of Hunan Teachers College, who ran as a non-Marxist candidate. Their victories were short-lived, however, for the party did not allow Hu Ping or any of the others to take their seats. Thus the efforts to introduce democratic practices at the local level in 1980 were thwarted. The experience was a disillusioning one, not only for the nonofficial candidates, but for all who had voted for them.

Equally disillusioning for a segment of intellectuals and former Red Guards was the regime's withdrawal of "the four great freedoms" Mao had inserted in the 1975 constitution: putting up wallposters, conducting debates, launching demonstrations, and carrying out strikes. These practices, which Mao used against party officials in the Cultural Revolution, were regarded by the elders as disruptive and dangerous. In contrast to the Second Session of the Fifth National People's Congress in June 1979, at which there had been a spirited debate on whether or not to retain "the four greats," the Third Session, in September 1980, decreed that because "the four greats" had never played a "positive" role, they should be discontinued. They were ultimately removed from the 1982 constitution. Some members of the democratic elite who had been attacked by "the four greats" nonetheless resisted their withdrawal. Hu Jiwei supported putting up posters, "if and when people wish to write [wallposters *(dazibao)*] that are well reasoned, based on facts and are signed with real names . . . Posting a *dazibao* is not a violation of the Constitution."[63] Despite his dissent, the plenum welcomed the end of "the four greats" with virtual unanimity, declaring that they would now no longer be used to undermine stability and economic development.

The retreats that began in the fall of 1980 were also influenced by events in other Communist countries, particularly Poland. That summer the shipyard workers in Gdansk and other Polish cities had gone on strike to protest the rise in food prices and had formed the independent workers' union Solidarity. The development evoked opposing responses in China. The democratic elite was encouraged to believe change was possible in a Leninist party-state; the elders were frightened into retreating on political reforms and repressing dissent in order to prevent the development of a Chinese Solidarity that would threaten the party-state.

Deng Xiaoping continued to advocate radical economic reforms in late 1980, but politically he shifted closer to the elders' views on the need for tighter controls. Despite his call for some degree of fundamental political change in his August 18 speech, Deng, like his elderly colleagues, never questioned the supremacy of the party, its ideology, or its leadership. Yet even though the elders Li Xiannian and Chen Yun had complained about a crisis of confidence, and Peng Zhen had stressed absolute party leadership and use of law to enforce party policies since the late 1970s, Deng had appeared relatively unaffected by their views until late 1980, when at a work conference on December 25, 1980, he too expressed concern about dissident views, especially in the party. "What is particularly serious," he said, "is that in the party press and also in party life, very few people have boldly stepped out to wage serious ideological struggle against these incorrect viewpoints."[64] He warned that people could not be "allowed to go to excesses in talking about [Mao's] mistakes, that can only damage the image of our party and state and the prestige of the party and the socialist system, and can only sap the unity of the whole party."[65]

Deng also supported his elderly colleagues' criticism of bourgeois liberalization. "We must criticize and fight the tendency toward worshipping capitalism and advocating bourgeois liberalization. We must criticize and fight the decadent bourgeois idea of being selfish and greedy for money[,] . . . anarchism and extreme individualism."[66] He continued to urge contact with Western countries, but "in the ideological and political fields, we must carry out the above-mentioned struggle to the end . . . [and] carry forward the spirit of patriotism."[67] Class struggle was no longer the main contradiction in Chinese society, but it "really does exist and cannot be underestimated."[68]

By the end of 1980, therefore, the coalition between the reform leaders and the elders formed in the aftermath of the Cultural Revolution against the remaining Maoists in the leadership, which had begun to split in the course of the practice criterion discussion and the theory conference, widened even further. In early 1981, with Deng's acquiescence, the elders' spokesmen intensified their efforts to impose ideological control. Document no. 7, issued in February 1981, called on the press to comply more strictly with Central Committee policies. All writing about the anti-rightist campaign and the Cultural Revolution was to cease. A *People's Daily* commentator article complained, "Some comrades have 'raised self-expression' to the plane of 'the highest artistic principle' without taking into consideration that there are certain unhealthy tendencies and moods."[69] Provincial newspapers echoed this stress on party discipline. The symbol of obedience in the Mao era, Lei Feng, the young soldier who described himself as a "screw in the party machine," was resurrected, and the slogan "Learn from Lei Feng" again became a familiar refrain as the Deng regime moved into a period of retrenchment.

The need to develop the economy, science, and technology before contemplating political reforms was another recurring theme in the retrenchment. Political reforms without a sustained period of economic development, the elders and their spokesmen repeatedly stressed, would cause chaos *(luan)*—a perennial Chinese fear. A

Guangming Daily article pointed out: "It is obviously unrealistic to seek to act in too great a hurry, pay no heed to objective conditions and attempt to attain a high degree of democracy all at once . . . chaos is bound to result." The bourgeois system of democracy was not "the panacea for solving all our problems . . . it is bound to cause confusion and clashes within our society."[70]

Literary Repression

Even as theorists and others were calling for political reforms and ideological revisions and nonparty candidates were running in local elections, the elders and their associates were already tightening controls in the literary realm. Both in dynastic times and in the Mao era dissent had usually been expressed in literature, and these leaders almost instinctively focused their attacks on writers. The elders had Deng's cooperation in this effort. Although in his 1979 speech at the Fourth Congress of Writers and Artists Deng had declared that literature was no longer to be subordinated to politics, by early 1980 he had reverted to a more Maoist view: although literature was not to serve politics, it was also not to be separated from politics. Hu Yaobang was forced by his mentor's switch in emphasis to take a position contrary to the tolerance of dissent he had hitherto displayed. In his keynote address at the Playwrights Conference of February 12–13, 1980, Hu criticized several plays, focusing particularly on "If I Were Real," written in 1979 by Sha Yexin and two other writers of the Cultural Revolution generation. Sha had been born in 1939 in Shanghai and worked at the Shanghai People's Art Theater. "If I Were Real," modeled on Gogol's "Inspector General," depicted a young man who deceived officials in Shanghai by pretending to be the son of a high military official in Beijing. Because of his supposedly good connections *(guanxi),* he was given privileges ranging from theater tickets to having a friend released from prison. When he was finally found out, he protested that he had done nothing wrong, explaining, "If I were really the son of [some high party official], then everything I've done would have been completely legal."[71]

Not only was the play's morally flawed protagonist a departure from the heroic protagonists of China's traditional and socialist realist literature, but the work satirized party officials. Although the party had called on writers to expose bureaucratic abuses and official corruption, it was not willing to tolerate such ridicule. The play was performed at the Central Drama Academy in November 1979, but only forty-six times and to a restricted audience of party officials. Nevertheless, ten thousand copies of the script were printed. Hu Yaobang's criticism of the play was intended to warn writers against portraying such official behavior and privileges as systemic to socialism rather than as "evils" of the "feudal" past. In making such a warning Hu seemed to reverse his previous attribution of bureaucratism primarily to the existing system rather than to Chinese tradition.

Even though Hu's speech was not published until a year later, word of this warning from China's most reformist leader spread and had a chilling effect on playwrights. Although Hu admitted that his opinions might not necessarily be correct and that he had made mistakes in the past, he declared that "If I Were Real" had "quite a few shortcomings."[72] He called Sha a talented playwright with a bright future, but cautioned: "If the play is not successfully revised, I think it should not be presented. It can be temporarily suspended."[73]

Hu may have issued this warning to writers reluctantly. In his original speech, for example, he had also included a caution against labeling a particular writer or a particular work "counterrevolutionary." But when his speech was published nearly a year later, that advice was deleted. In an interview Hu gave to a Hong Kong magazine in 1980, he acknowledged that the party had made mistakes during the past thirty years in its treatment of literary works. "Some of our policies . . . were incorrect before Lin Biao and the Gang of Four . . . Our system is not perfect."[74] Significantly, he also declared that the use of satire was still appropriate.

In contrast to Hu Yaobang's relatively moderate criticism of a small number of plays, associates of the elders took the offensive against literary dissent. They directed their attacks against two different kinds of writers: one group, represented by Wang Meng and younger writers of the Cultural Revolution generation, wanted to separate literature from politics for artistic reasons; another group, represented by Liu Binyan and the Shanghai writer Wang Ruowang, used literature to make political statements.

The milder attack was against writers whose work was less directly political. Party criticisms of relatively apolitical writers were more nuanced than criticisms of politically oriented writers. Artistic experimentation was not rejected, but it was criticized because it could not be easily appreciated by the masses. In reality, the authorities felt threatened by a genre of literature that could not be totally understood or controlled by the party. The official critique by the literary critic Feng Mu exemplified this nuanced approach. At a forum of the editorial department of *Poetry* (Shikan), China's most prestigious poetry journal, he praised experimentation in artistic forms. Works that combined realistic description with a symbolic approach—for example, the works of Kafka—were acceptable as long as they were well written. Nevertheless, writers were still expected to use the "era's most advanced ideology as their guide."[75] Although he also praised a number of Wang Meng's works for their depiction of the "complicated changes in people's ideas, emotions, and psychological state in a diversified and complicated society," he criticized Wang's stream-of-consciousness style and hoped that he would adopt more "solid techniques."[76]

Feng Mu also specifically criticized the younger poets, primarily the "obscure poets," who "create high-brow literature and cannot care less about what the 800 million peasants might wish to read . . ."[77] Instead of criticizing the obscure poets directly, the party used an older generation of poets against them. The older poet Gu Gong criticized his son Gu Cheng, a prominent "obscure" poet. Other famous elderly poets such as Ai Qing, Zhang Kejia, and Tian Jian similarly criticized the obscure poets for the incomprehensibility of their works. These older poets had used their poetry to help mobilize the masses for the revolution in the 1930s and 1940s, and their criticisms may have been sincere. The more sophisticated Feng Mu also insisted that "innovation" could not "depart from the traditional base or from the time in which our country finds itself."[78] Nevertheless, he admitted that he appreciated some poems of Gu Cheng and of another obscure poet, Shu Ting, even though he did not understand other poets. But while Feng Mu declared "we can only let them exist and let the people themselves decide whether or not to accept them,"[79] articles in *Red Flag* were less tolerant. One charged that these poets would rather "create the spring snow for 1,000 people than create the song of the rustic poor for the 800 million people."[80] Such poets would "definitely have no future in their career if the 'self' in their works . . . is only satisfied in expressing their selfish and trivial desires."[81] Most important, the article warned that artistic experimentation might lead to ideological and political experimentation.

While avant-garde literature was rejected and accessibility praised, the party's science policy still stressed China's need to catch up with advanced scientific research. The Shanghai newspaper *Liberation Daily* (Jiefang ribao) urged eliminating the "erroneous 'leftist' influence on the science and technology front,"[82] because it hindered theoretical research. Increasingly the Deng regime differentiated between scientists, who were to absorb the latest developments from the West and do highly specialized work, and nonscientific intellectuals, particularly writers and artists, who were to remain rooted in their native traditions and engaged in work easily appreciated by ordinary people. But the regime remained much more willing to tolerate experimentation in artistic style than in ideas. Though criticized, Wang Meng and others continued to explore stream of consciousness, fantasy, symbolism, and psychological nuance. China's premier literary journal, *Literary Gazette* (Wenyi bao), became a forum for debates on literary modernism. Participants pointed out that some modernist methods were not as new or as foreign as the term implied; these techniques could be found in traditional Chinese poetry and ancient Chinese writing.

The regime was more concerned with writers who used literature for specific political purposes. At the Fourth Congress of Writers and Artists, Liu Binyan had forcefully upheld the May Fourth view that literature must expose the ills of society. He described his surprise when he was sent to the countryside during the anti-rightist campaign and encountered the harshness of the peasants' life and the indifference of the local officials. He found that rural life was just the opposite of its idealized portrayal in literature and the media. In the manner of his Confucian predecessors, he exhorted his fellow writers to assume their responsibility by telling the truth. And he denounced officials who would rather "blame the mirror" that the writers held up than use it to correct the ugly picture it reflected.[83]

Liu's mirror in the post-Mao era, as in the Hundred Flowers period, reflected the ugliness of the new class of officials spawned by the Leninist system. But instead of enthusiastic, idealistic youth in conflict with opportunistic officials whom Liu had depicted during the Hundred Flowers, his focus shifted wholly to the corrupt, abusive officials. In his first major work in the Deng era, *People or Monsters,* written in the form of an investigative report *(baogao wenxue),* he described a female official in his home area, the Northeast (Manchuria), who used her connections to establish a widespread system of corruption.

She embezzled huge sums of public money to build a financial empire that became a powerful political-economic organization unrestrained by law, institutions, or moral code. The party members under her jurisdiction were obedient to her rather than to the party. Liu's description of her empire recalls Lu Xun's condemnation of traditional society as "man-eating." "Party and government cadres slowly degenerated into parasitical insects that fed off the people's productivity and the socialist system."[84] Unlike the authors of the wounded literature, Liu did not treat this phenomenon as merely an aberration due to the Cultural Revolution that could be resolved with a return to party norms; he saw it as inherent in the system itself. "The Communist Party regulated everything, but would not regulate the Communist Party."[85] And in this work no young hero came forth to rectify the system.

Liu Binyan and others who advocated using literature to expose the party's abuse of power received the harshest criticisms. Attacks came not only from literary officials allied with the elders but from a number of former rightists who had been allied with Liu in the Hundred Flowers period. The persecutions that writers and others had endured in the anti-rightist campaign and the Cultural Revolution had led some to a more liberal stance, others to more conservative positions. One of these former rightists was the writer Liu Shaotang, who had been the first in the Hundred Flowers to criticize Mao's Yan'an Talks as obsolete. Yet he was also one of the first to attack his former colleague Liu Binyan in the post-Mao era. Liu Shaotang said he understood why writers were "bitter" and critical to the point that "their affection for the party and socialism" was "almost nil."[86] Nevertheless, because memories of his 1957 persecution were still fresh in his mind, Liu Shaotang expressed gratitude to the present leadership, which, instead of "wielding the big stick," had invited writers to debate their views and to publish them relatively easily. He envied the younger writers who could now enjoy the "full democratic freedom of expression" that he had been deprived of as a youth. But he feared that "this right to practice democracy in the political and artistic fields" would be abused and provide "an opportunity to promote anarchism and extreme individualism."[87] In another article, directed specifically at Liu Binyan, Liu Shaotang urged him to return to literary work and to stay away from politics.

Some of the older writers from the 1930s and the 1940s, such as

Ding Ling, who had been persecuted in 1942 and even more severely persecuted during the anti-rightist campaign, also expressed their gratitude. Like Liu Shaotang, Ding Ling was so appreciative to the regime for having rehabilitated her and given her some freedom in her old age that she was willing to support views that contradicted her earlier ones. Perhaps continuing to be loyal to the party, which had virtually ruined twenty-two years of her life, was the only way she could accept what had happened to her.

At the same time, some of the persecutors of the Mao years came to the opposite conclusion. The most prominent, Zhou Yang, Mao's cultural czar, and his ally the playwright Xia Yan joined with the Hu Yaobang network in resisting any return to pre–Cultural Revolution literary repression. Zhou and Xia had endured nearly ten years of imprisonment in terrible circumstances during the Cultural Revolution. Reverting to a more Western view of literature that he had held in the late 1920s, Zhou Yang in the late 1970s urged his colleagues to respect a writer's independence and individuality. Under some pressure at the Fourth Congress of Writers and Artists, he apologized to all those whom he had hounded in the past. Appointed president of the All-China Federation of Literary and Art Circles (ACFLAC) after his rehabilitation, Zhou's reformist stance came into conflict with that of the elders' literary spokesmen, many of whom had been his close colleagues during the Mao era.

In late 1980, the cultural atmosphere was darkened by increasing criticism of politically bold literary works. Using the pen name Che Dan, Sha Yexin lamented in a *Literary Gazette* article entitled "Talking 'Nonsense'" that after "If I Were Real" was criticized, "Playwrights were afraid to write." Referring to Hu's speech at the Playwrights Conference, he warned that "a bit of wind from above produces the beginning of a thunderstorm from below."[88] Less than two years after Deng had launched his reform program, writers again feared the kind of campaign they had suffered under Mao. But Hu Yaobang's blocking tactics and resistance from writers diverted the "thunderstorm" of which Sha had warned for a time. When the storm finally hit, it had weakened to a "gust of cold air."

4

The Campaign
against Bai Hua
and Other Writers

Although delayed and weakened, the storm of criticism that had been threatening in the first half of 1981 finally hit its target, the playwright Bai Hua and several other writers, in the summer of that year. The campaign revealed the limits of the Deng regime's reform program. The regime would tolerate a degree of artistic and academic pluralism, but would suppress any potentially popular work that it believed challenged it politically.

There were factional as well as ideological reasons for the choice of Bai as main target. He was a writer attached to the army, which like the elders was not very enthusiastic about Deng's reforms. Although Bai had joined the Red Army in the 1940s to fight against the Guomindang and to help bring the Communists to power, he was designated a rightist in 1957 for having urged less party interference in the writing of younger authors.[1] He was rehabilitated in 1961 but still had trouble publishing his works, and in May 1966 he once again came under attack. For the next seven years, he was unable to visit or correspond with his wife and child. Released again in 1974, he was not allowed to publish until the fall of the Gang of Four.

In the early days of the Deng Xiaoping decade, Bai was not associated with the theorists around Hu Yaobang or with other writers, but acted as a lone conscience of the regime. He found a model in Qu Yuan, one of the first principled literati in Chinese history, who killed himself in 195 B.C. when his remonstrances with his ruler over prevailing policies were ignored. Qu became a symbol of politically engaged literati willing to protest against unjust policies and even to sacrifice their lives for the good of society. This tradition of individual protest was continued by Bai Hua, described by a friend as "a rooster crowing at midnight instead of in the morning," upsetting people because they did not like to be so awakened.[2] Despite his continuous persecution from the 1950s on, he remained a strong and dashing figure, an actor and artist as well as a playwright.

With a colleague, Bai published a letter in the *People's Daily* protesting the ban on "If I Were Real," and in the early years of the Deng regime he wrote several historical plays criticizing official abuses. A film scenario, "Tonight the Starlight Glitters," an account of the Red Army's Huai Hai campaign against the Guomindang during the civil war, depicted the fears of the soldiers going into battle. This scenario so infuriated some high-ranking military officers that they demanded that Bai be relabeled a rightist for denigrating brave soldiers. At the time, however, the party did not concur, though Bai was not allowed to leave Wuhan, where he was stationed, to spend the Spring Festival of 1981 in Shanghai with his wife, a former actress, and his son. His son complained: "For other people the Cultural Revolution has ended, but not for our family."[3]

The Controversy over "Unrequited Love"

It was not until the army media attacked Bai's scenario "Unrequited Love" (Kulian) in the spring of 1981 that the army finally won party support for an open attack on Bai. The script had been published in September 1979 in a popular literary magazine, *October* (Shiyue), but it did not generate concern from Deng and the elders until it became a movie in 1981, though even then it was seen only by a small select group of military and party officials.[4] "Unrequited Love" is the story of an intellectual who dedicates himself to his country out of a strong sense of patriotism, but is repaid only with repression and cruelty. The protagonist, an artist, is forced to flee China in the 1940s at the time of the Japanese occupation and goes to the West, where he becomes famous and wealthy. Yet when the 1949 revolution occurs, he returns to China because of his love of his country and his desire to help it modernize. But very quickly his love of his country is distorted into the worship of an individual, Mao. This distortion is described symbolically in a scene in which the artist is taken as a child to visit a Chan Buddhist temple. He asks, "Why is this Buddhist statue so black?" "The incense smoke of many good men and pious women has blackened it," is the reply.[5] These lines imply that not only have the leader and the party created this blackened idol, but the people themselves have willingly participated. Their sense of patriotism has degenerated into the "deification of one man." Like Ba Jin and Wang Ruoshui, Bai Hua implicated himself and his countrymen in the blind obedience to Mao.

Despite repeated persecution, the artist never ceases to love his country. When his daughter tells him of her plan to marry an overseas Chinese and live abroad, he objects. His daughter replies: "Papa! You love this nation of ours . . . But does this nation love you?" Michael Duke has noted that throughout "Unrequited Love," Bai describes the artist as returning to China because of his love of *zuguo*.[6] *Zuguo* refers to the Chinese people, the homeland, and the motherland, but not necessarily to the state, government, or political party. The only significant departure from this usage is in this conversation with his daughter, who uses the term *guojia*, which refers to the government or state as well as to a geographic unit. Bai Hua later confirmed that in using these two terms he intended to distinguish the intellectual's love of his country and society from the government and its policies that had persecuted the intellectuals,[7] and to protest the distortion of love of one's country into blind obedience to a particular leader, party, or government. The daughter, unlike her father, is unwilling to give unquestioning loyalty to the party or to equate love of her country with loyalty to her government.

Not long after the conversation with his daughter, the artist, fleeing a band of Red Guards, suddenly collapses, and in the film's last scene he lies dying in the snow. His body forms a large question mark, as if to ask whether his life of unrequited love for his country had been worthwhile. Few intellectuals in China had ever asked this question publicly before.

Bai's view of patriotism as loyalty to country that does not necessarily include loyalty to party, government, or leaders angered the military and the elders. Traditionally, the Chinese view individual interests as inseparable from those of society, and society, at least theoretically, is indistinguishable from the state, which is identified with the ruler.[8] Because the ruler's intentions are regarded as good and in harmony with the people, the relationship between state and society is not seen as one of confrontation or opposition, as it is in the West, but as one of unity. When principled literati remonstrated with an abusive ruler or officials, they hoped to persuade them to rectify their actions so as to be more in accord with society and to rule more effectively. Thus to criticize the ruler or officials expressed true loyalty to the state, because the criticism was meant to improve governance and, therefore, society. But with China's emulation of the Stalinist model after 1949, for an intellectual to exercise his or her individual conscience and protest against unjust policies became virtually impossible.

Bai had also antagonized the party leadership in other ways. His speech at the Fourth Congress of Writers and Artists boldly asked, "What sort of socialist country is it where communists do not dare speak the truth at party conferences, fathers, sons, brothers, sisters and friends do not have heart-to-heart talks among themselves, writers do not dare take notes and citizens are afraid to keep diaries?"[9] He went on: "Shall we keep silent before a bureaucracy which ties hand and foot?" Warning that writers and artists were still not safe, Bai quoted Liu Binyan's statement about officials in *People or Monsters:* "They are afraid of offending this man or that man. However, they are not afraid of offending the 'masters' of the people's republic—the people."[10]

Even more significant, Bai was among the few to defend the participants in the Democracy Wall movement publicly, particularly the literary participants. He complained that talented young writers had "no vehicles for the dissemination of most of their works, so they must resort to publication in mimeographed periodicals . . . They are seldom approached by people in literary circles, who find their thought 'frightening' . . . rather, it is the product of a frightening era."[11] Also an artist, Bai had supported the "Star, Star" (Xingxing) exhibition of unofficial painters and sculptors, experimenting with new techniques and materials, held briefly in November 1979 in Beijing before it was closed down by the authorities.

By early 1981 Bai's speeches and actions as well as his scenario alarmed both party and military leaders. On March 27, in a speech to the General Political Department of the army, Deng Xiaoping gave permission for public criticism of Bai and "Unrequited Love," because, he explained, "the issue involved is the upholding of the four cardinal principles."[12] He expressed agreement with the military that a "right deviation" had emerged in the process of rectifying the "Left" that must "also be corrected."[13] In addition, he seconded Chen Yun's suggestion that more attention be given to ideological works, particularly those by Mao.

Just as the last leaders of the Democracy Wall movement were being arrested in April, the military fired the first volley in its campaign against Bai. The *Liberation Army Daily* unleashed a series of editorials and articles by unnamed "special commentators" denouncing Bai and "Unrequited Love." Liu Baiyu, a former ally of Zhou Yang in the persecution of writers in Yan'an and of rightists in the Mao era and now the head of the Cultural Department in the General Political Department, masterminded the army media's criticism. On April 23, these critics were joined by another Maoist writer, Huang Gang, editor-in-chief of *Contemporary Reportage* (Shidai de baogao). Huang was known as "Yao the second" after Yao Wenyuan, the zealous literary figure of the Gang of Four. Born in Hubei in 1917, the son of a senior party official, Huang Gang had gone to Yan'an with other intellectuals in the late 1930s, where he entered the literary department of the Lu Xun Arts Institute. After graduation, he worked in Yan'an for the *Liberation Army Daily* and later for the New China News Agency. While there he became a close friend of Liu Baiyu, developing a relationship that gave him a direct connection with the army in the post-Mao era. Several army writers also worked with him at *Contemporary Reportage*.

The army media attacked Bai for being "unpatriotic." One article in the *Liberation Army Daily* charged that Bai's use of the "term 'this country' *(guojia)* and not the 'motherland' *(zuguo)*" in "Unrequited Love" revealed his belief that "'this country' is no longer the people's country and is dominated by the 'gang of four.'"[14] Bai himself had said that the scenario stood in opposition to not only the Gang but "powerholders through all ages" and "'those people professing to be the symbol to the motherland,' of course including people past and contemporary."[15] His words, therefore, implicated Deng as well as Mao. He was also charged with confusing Mao's and the present regime's treatment of intellectuals with that of the Gang of Four.

Mindful that the Cultural Revolution had begun with criticism of Wu Han and his play "Hai Rui Dismissed from Office," Hu Yaobang attempted to protect Bai from these vollies. The fear that an attack on a writer and one piece of writing might escalate into a political movement was still very real for the reform leaders and intellectuals, who sought to prevent such a recurrence. Hu was committed to the promise made at the Third Plenum as well as in Deng's August 1980 speech that there would be no more political campaigns, and he gave several talks in which he urged that criticisms not be allowed to escalate. He sent word to Bai Hua through his son Hu Deping, who was an authority on the famous eighteenth-century novel *The Dream of the Red Chamber,* assuring Bai that he was trying to stop the criticisms against him.[16]

While the General Political Department and Huang Gang took the offensive, those associated with Hu attempted to deflect the charges. Hu personally urged Zhou Yang, Xia Yan, and others in the literary establishment to limit the attacks. From April to June, numerous articles in the party media under their control called for *literary* analysis rather than *political* criticism in discussing creative works. Xia Yan, speaking at a meeting of the Chinese Film Artists Association, which he headed, asked: "Were not the poems of Li Bai and Du Fu and the 'Li Sao' of Qu Yuan all voicing discontent? Are the Chinese people who suffered 10 years of misery not to be allowed to voice their discontent? Of course there have been excesses . . . [but] prohibition and suffocation are both bad."[17] Zhou Yang, at a meeting of the All-China Federation of Literary and Art Circles, urged writers not to fear speaking out on issues. Hu Yaobang himself at a symposium in May denounced the strident quality of the criticisms of "Unrequited Love": "Some criticism was certainly permissible, but if more appropriate methods of criticizing had been adopted then the effect would have been somewhat better."[18] He encouraged countercriticism and urged that criticisms be made by individuals, not by party organizations or editorial departments, which would give them the party's imprimatur. He insisted as well that criticism of a work be separated from criticism of the author. Above all he sought limits: the debate on the scenario "must be brought to an end soon."[19]

Hu's efforts circumscribed the attacks to some extent. Even though the General Political Department, under the leadership of Wei Guoqing, pressured the *People's Daily* to reprint the *Liberation Army Daily*'s criticisms of Bai, the paper, edited by Hu's associates Hu Jiwei, Wang Ruoshui, and others, ignored them. Instead writers in the *People's Daily* echoed Hu's call for restraint. An article on June 8 urged opposition to practices such as "finding faults, vilification, framing charges, exaggerating mistakes and driving one to the wall . . . The one subjected to criticism also has the right to state his own views and vindicate himself." It called for the end to "the use of a political movement or one in a disguised form to handle literary and art problems." [20]

In addition to the resistance by Hu and his network, Bai's literary peers also opposed the army's attack. The *Literary Gazette* reported that ten of twelve articles submitted to the journal on Bai Hua expressed disagreement with the *Liberation Army Daily*'s critique. [21] In contrast to the Mao era, most writers now refused to join in the criticism of one of their colleagues. Because the party no longer demanded their public allegiance, writers could express their opposition through passive resistance, though no individual or group openly challenged the attacks on Bai. Apart from Huang Gang few writers joined the General Political Department's criticism of Bai Hua, and Huang was ostracized by the literary community. Students at the universities in Beijing put up wallposters defending Bai Hua and posted issues of the *Liberation Army Daily* and *Contemporary Reportage* in which they crossed out the criticisms of Bai. Bai himself said that he had received over a thousand letters of support.

Even nonliterary journals opposed the attacks on him. The *Beijing Science and Technology Newspaper* (Beijing keji bao), in May and June, criticized *Contemporary Reportage*'s treatment of Bai, particularly its editorial in a special edition in late April, which had stated: "We are resolved to stand on the side of the masses of workers, peasants, and soldiers, cadres and patriotic intellectuals." The science newspaper devoted thirteen issues and twenty-six articles to criticizing the prefix "patriotic," used before "intellectuals" but not before the other groups. Of the hundred letters it received on the subject, only four agreed with the use of the term "patriotic intellectuals." [22]

Hu Yaobang and his associates seemed to be defusing a campaign that was about to be launched. Contrary to past practice when a campaign was imminent, the Central Committee did not issue a directive to newspapers and writers coordinating the criticisms. Nor did the condemnation of a particular work now automatically preclude praise of the author's other writings. Hu set a precedent in praising Bai's past works and urging that he not be "bludgeoned" for one particular scenario. Bai was given an award for a poem written in 1979 that had eulogized the new course set at the Third Plenum, though he was not allowed to receive the award in person.

A few institutions under Hu's purview did break with him on the issue of "Unrequited Love." The Central Party School held a meeting to criticize the scenario and reported its proceedings to the Central Committee. Hu chastised the school, reminding its members not to attack others lightly.[23] The head of the Propaganda Department in Shanghai, Chen Yi, a former rightist who had attacked his old literary colleague Wang Ruowang and opposed Hu's reform policies, coordinated attacks on Bai in Shanghai literary journals with the *Liberation Army Daily* and *Contemporary Reportage*—though some papers in Shanghai, such as the *Wenhui News* and *Shanghai Literature and Art* (Shanghai wenyi), refused to reprint the *Liberation Army Daily* articles. Elsewhere the *Liberation Army Daily* attacks on Bai were reprinted in twenty provincial newspapers. Yet by late spring the criticisms of Bai seemed to be waning and the offensive appeared to have been repulsed.

A Different Political Campaign

With Hua Guofeng's formal resignation as chairman of the party at the Sixth Plenum of the Eleventh Central Committee in June 1981, however, the elders shifted their attention from attacking the "left," specifically the remaining Maoists, to attacking the "right," focusing on what they called the lack of attention to ideological indoctrination. In this they had Deng Xiaoping's acquiescence. In a July 17, 1981, speech to high officials of the Propaganda Department, Deng criticized the laxity on ideological issues that he claimed had encouraged the emergence of bourgeois liberalization. He cited the film "Unrequited Love" as an example of such liberalization, charging that it "gives the impression that the Communist Party and the socialist system are bad. It vilifies the latter to such an extent that one wonders what has happened to the author's Party spirit."[24]

Deng was particularly upset by Bai's view of patriotism as love of country exclusive of party and socialism. He asked: "If you don't love socialist New China led by the Communist Party, what motherland do you love?" He insisted that "above all, we demand [that] writers, artists and ideological and theoretical workers in the Communist Party observe Party discipline."[25] Deng's inclusion of theorists among those in need of discipline presumably referred to those associated with Hu Yaobang, though his primary concern at this time was "Unrequited Love." Yet Deng, like Hu, also sought to limit the attack, by publishing criticism only in *Literary Gazette* with reprints in a few party newspapers. He chastised the *Liberation Army Daily* for publishing articles that were "not always entirely reasonable" and for tactics that were "not carefully thought out."[26]

Deng's comments from March to June 1981 on the draft of the "Resolution on Certain Historical Issues of Our Party since the Founding of the People's Republic of China" that was to be adopted at the Sixth Plenum in June 1981 reveal his reasons for siding with the elders against his disciple Hu Yaobang. Even though the draft was written by a group headed by Hu Qiaomu, Deng was disturbed by its inadequate reaffirmation of Mao's historical role. Deng acknowledged that Mao was overly enthusiastic about the Great Leap Forward, but he cautioned that no other leader—including Liu Shaoqi, Zhou Enlai, and he himself—had objected at the time. Even Chen Yun did not speak out. Deng therefore concluded that "on no account can we discard the banner of Mao Zedong Thought. Otherwise, we would be negating the glorious history of our party." He admitted that the party had committed some "big mistakes in the past, including the three decades after the founding."[27] He also agreed with the draft's assertion that "in comparison with the mistakes in the seventeen years preceding it, the 'Cultural Revolution' was a grave error affecting the overall situation."[28] Nevertheless, he insisted that the present discussion of "Mao Zedong's mistakes" had been "too excessive . . . Responsibility for some past mistakes should be born collectively, though chief responsibility, of course, lies with Comrade Mao Zedong."[29]

Thus Deng, like the military and the elders, concluded that criticism of Mao like that expressed by Bai Hua, especially in his image of the blackened Buddha, would undermine the party and its current leaders as well. In July Deng called for public criticism of "Unrequited Love" and bourgeois liberalization, and the storm that Hu, his network, and the literary intellectuals had been trying to stave off finally hit. Nevertheless, in comparison with campaigns of the Mao era, this one was limited. It was restrained not only because of the more moderate approach of both Deng and Hu Yaobang but because the elders themselves, having experienced persecution during the Cultural Revolution, wanted to prevent any new campaign from veering out of control. A *Guangming Daily* article explained: "After 1957, . . . an article of criticism indicated the coming of a political campaign."[30] This fear "remains fresh in people's memories."[31]

Although Mao's use of class struggle and mass mobilization was now rejected, some of his views were endorsed, especially those in his Yan'an Talks that stressed that literature should emphasize the positive rather than the negative view of the present as well as of the future. A China News Agency (Zhongguo Xinwenshe) commentary declared that in some works, "not only is there a mood of dejection, but the ideas of pessimism, nihilism, and ultra-individualism are propagated. A few of the works have even thrown patriotism away." [32] The *China Youth News* criticized advocates of bourgeois liberalization because they "vilify the party's leadership, defame the socialist system, calumniate Mao Zedong Thought and bring shame on our motherland through literary and art works, articles, speeches . . ." [33] Moreover, "some comrades only pay attention to the harmful effects of 'leftist' ideas and unhealthy trends, but fail to realize the perniciousness of the bourgeois liberalization." [34]

As usual, Hu Qiaomu presented the elders' definitive statement. In a speech on "Unrequited Love" on August 8 at a meeting on ideological indoctrination convened by the Propaganda Department, not only did he implicate the reformist policies associated with Hu Yaobang and his network, but he reminded the participants that the Sixth Plenum resolution had been directed against both the leftist ideology of the Cultural Revolution *and* the ideological trends of bourgeois liberalization. Furthermore, "quite a few" of the trends had "cropped up in the name of carrying out the policies of the Third Plenary Session of the Eleventh CCP Central Committee and emancipating the mind . . . [and] seeking truth from facts." [35] He specifically criticized "a very small number of cadres who . . . have personally expressed their sympathy and support for the liberalization trend. This laxity in organization, weakness in work and slackness in discipline is certainly detrimental to the struggle against [the] ideological trend of bourgeois liberalization . . . We must admit that the central Secretariat has not adopted enough practicable and effective measures to solve the existing problems on ideological work, though it has discussed them many times." [36] This "very small number" seemed to refer to Zhou Yang and Xia Yan, in charge of ideological matters in the literary realm, and the condemnation of the ineffectiveness of the "central Secretariat" in carrying out ideological indoctrination was an attack on Hu Yaobang.

The campaign was concluded with the *Literary Gazette* article that

Deng had demanded, written by associate editors Tang Yin and Tang Dacheng and published in October 1981. In opposition to Bai's distinction between love of country and love of party, they reaffirmed Deng's definition: "The patriotism of today is inalienable from love for the party and love for socialism." [37] They also criticized Bai's use of the blackened image of Buddha as a symbol of Mao. "The trust and respect accorded by the masses to Chairman Mao definitely cannot be simply summed up as a personality cult." [38] They absolved both Mao and the people from the excesses of Mao's policies. Neither Mao nor the Chinese people but the "Lin Biao and Jiang Qing counterrevolutionary cliques were able to instigate and create a personality cult until it reached a fanatical degree." [39] Despite these criticisms, Bai regarded the *Literary Gazette* article as more "comradely" than the attacks of the *Liberation Army Daily* and *Red Flag*. As had Hu Yaobang, the *Literary Gazette* article also praised Bai for having written good works in the past.

Although this article was widely reprinted in an effort to end the whole affair, the *Liberation Army Daily* and *Red Flag* continued to condemn Bai for vilifying the party. A *Red Flag* article charged that Bai did not give the party enough credit for setting things right. The intellectual in Bai's scenario, for example, died in the snow, his body forming a question mark, at the very time that the Gang of Four had been smashed. This symbolism, the article asserted, showed "a lack of confidence in the party and socialism" [40] and implicated the party in the tragedies it depicted.

Bai made a self-criticism at a party meeting of the Political and Cultural Department of the Wuhan Military Command to which he was attached. He then made a further self-criticism in a formal letter to the editors of the *Literary Gazette* and *Liberation Army Daily*, admitting that he had failed to describe the intellectuals' love of the party appropriately. He also acknowledged that he had wallowed in the tragic stories of the intellectuals in the Cultural Revolution, creating "a sense of gloom and despondency." [41] In addition, he declared: "I should definitely not have attributed the personality cult to the ignorance of the masses." [42] He explained, however, that he had been "perplexed by Comrade Mao Zedong's mistakes in his later years and the blind faith in him by the people, including myself." [43] He did not, therefore, exonerate Mao or the party from building up the personality cult. Under obvious pressure from the military, he concluded that now "[I] must . . . eulogize the magnificent contributions of the People's Liberation Army."[44] At several points in his self-criticism, he implied that great pressure had been put upon him. He described what he called "the heart-to-heart style, earnest and repeated"[45] admonishments of officials. But unlike under Mao, when he would have been sent away for labor reform or to prison, he retreated to his home.

Although Bai was forced to make a self-criticism, others who were not publicly criticized refused. One article described their negative reaction: "They invariably 'fly into a rage' and try to 'reject it.'" Some intervene to prevent others from having to make self-criticisms. Even worse, if one is criticized, "he becomes a 'hero,' . . . comrades who dare to make criticism and self-criticism are isolated."[46] Others protested publicly against the revival of a campaign against intellectuals. Sun Changjiang, a participant in the practice criterion discussion and the theory conference, pleaded in a September article in the *People's Daily*: "We must learn from historical experience."[47] He later recalled that he had had tears in his eyes while writing the article, feeling that "our historical experiences are too painful and what is more painful is that we have not absorbed their lessons."[48]

Still, the bold resistance to the campaign revealed that some had absorbed the lessons of history. Even at the meeting of the Propaganda Department at which Hu Qiaomu had presented the definitive critique of "Unrequited Love," several participants objected that the campaign against Bai Hua and bourgeois liberalization was incompatible with the guidelines of the Third Plenum. Hu Qiaomu attributed the resistance to "feelings of skepticism and despair toward the party and socialism"[49] engendered by the Cultural Revolution. He cited a question intellectuals had asked when confronted with efforts to reindoctrinate them: "Why should we make such a fuss as soon as a mistake is committed in ideological work, while we can forgive a failure in a scientific experiment and even a serious mistake in economic work?"[50] Hu responded that the "losses" from a failed experiment involved only a small number of people. As for economic mistakes, he claimed that the "relatively unimportant mistakes in economic work" had only an indirect impact. About the mistakes of the Great Leap Forward, which caused the deaths of over 30 million people, he said nothing.

Hu Qiaomu articulated the elders' chief concern that "a wrong ideological trend with a widespread social influence . . . will spread like an epidemic and will harm the spiritual health, stability and unity of the whole society." Therefore, "our criticism of 'Unrequited Love' and the ideological trend of bourgeois liberalization is precisely a criticism of an important political tendency that has truly existed for a long time. It is not making a fuss about some trifling thing."[51] He warned: "We must not hold endless debates on fundamental questions of actual politics and turn our party and the People's Republic into a club for holding daily political debates as though only this situation can be considered springtime." Because he and the elders did not welcome such a "springtime," Hu insisted: "We must thoroughly change the situation of having so many policies that it is difficult to decide which one is right."[52] Since the party had resolved the problems arising from the Cultural Revolution, writers need no longer write about the past. Rather, he exhorted them to "shift the focus of their creative work to the current struggle to build a new life," warning that one "who looks back too often can hardly make progress."[53] Hu expressed the elders' reluctance to come to grips with the tragedies of the Maoist past and their desire to suppress those, like Bai Hua, who believed such an examination to be crucial to the reform of the political system.

Although Bai Hua was the major target of the campaign, the veteran literary officials Zhou Yang and Xia Yan were criticized indirectly. Huang Gang called them Bai's "behind-the-scenes backers."[54] Zhou Yang was hospitalized at this time. Physically and mentally broken by the experience of the Cultural Revolution and by feelings of guilt for his previous actions, he also sought to avoid assuming a role in the campaign and being castigated once again as a "hatchetman." Even his patron Hu Yaobang had complained at the Propaganda Department's August 1981 meeting about "slack" leadership in the cultural realm. In contrast to Zhou's relative inaction, most of his former colleagues from the Yan'an period, such as Lin Mohan, He Jingzhi, and Liu Baiyu, were vociferous in denouncing Bai Hua and bourgeois liberalization. That they also kept their distance from Zhou made him all the more depressed. Feng Mu, the editor-in-chief of the *Literary Gazette,* likewise engaged in passive resistance by taking ill. Despite its definitive article on "Unrequited Love," the *Literary Gazette* was attacked in *Red Flag* for having published Sha Yexin's pseudonymous article "Talking Nonsense," rebutting Hu Yaobang's criticisms at the Playwrights Conference. *Red Flag* called the publication of "Talking

Nonsense" another indication of weak leadership in the literary realm.[55] In addition, *October* magazine was reprimanded for having published the scenario of "Unrequited Love."

The divisions between reformers and supporters of the elders, however, were still not clear-cut in this campaign. Although Hu Qiaomu played a leading role, his associate Deng Liqun did not. Similarly, the elder Chen Yun sent a letter to the Politburo in which he criticized the campaign. "I am convinced that our party launched too many political movements during the more than thirty years following liberation . . . The people are tired of political movements . . . and the party members and masses still have a lingering fear about political movements."[56] Moreover, he warned that criticisms of controversial literary works was the old road of the anti-rightist campaign and the Cultural Revolution, in which intellectuals were the first targets. Chen reminded his colleagues: "The Great Cultural Revolution should not be completely described as the mistake of Mao alone, but should be called the biggest mistake our party has ever made. Since we are determined to rectify such a mistake, we should not be afraid of our misdeeds being exposed by the people. If the mistakes are covered up, they cannot be thoroughly rectified." He asserted that "Unrequited Love" was "more or less based on real life." Because intellectuals had been oppressed, it was "excusable for them to use the pen to struggle against the mistakes that have occurred in the party." Chen counseled that "we will be aiming at the wrong target if in opposing 'bourgeois liberalization' we criticize questionable works like 'Unrequited Love.'"[57] He urged a return to attacks on the "ultra-left," gradually stopping the "wind of criticism against those controversial works."[58]

Although the elders had not yet mobilized as a group against Hu Yaobang, his position was undermined by the campaign. Indications of his weakened political authority surfaced in the summer and fall. The *People's Daily,* supposedly under Hu's jurisdiction, came out strongly against Bai Hua and bourgeois liberalization after Deng's July speech criticizing "Unrequited Love." Similarly Huang Gang, though he had been relatively quiet after his initial attacks, joined in the campaign with his journal *Contemporary Reportage* in the fall of 1981 and defended the earlier use of the term "patriotic intellectuals" as correct. A *Beijing Daily* article emphasized the need to oppose a "small number of people" from "freely belittling and even totally negating Mao Zedong's philosophical thought."[59]

Given Deng's lead, Hu Yaobang had little choice but to go along with the campaign to a certain extent. In his speech at the centennial of Lu Xun's birth in October 1981 he warned against those who spread discontent in their writings. Yet he also spoke against "certain leading comrades in leading party organizations" who "stick to old rules, show no interest in necessary reforms; they are highly irresponsible bureaucrats, not carrying out the tasks given them by the party." [60] He charged them with being more concerned with their own individual and department interests than with the interests of the party and the nation.

After Bai Hua's letter in the *Literary Gazette* and his self-criticism were published, Hu's position gradually appeared to improve. By the end of 1981, at a conference of film producers, Hu declared: "The issue of 'Unrequited Love' is thus satisfactorily settled. Comrade Bai Hua is still a party member. He is still a writer and will continue writing." [61] With this statement, released by the New China News Agency and published nationwide, reformist intellectuals once more came to the fore. Hu Feng, the first writer against whom Mao had launched a campaign after 1949, was rehabilitated and restored to membership in the Chinese Writers Association. At a Writers Association meeting in December, Ba Jin was elected chairman to replace Mao Dun, who had died. Whereas Mao Dun had been relatively silent about the persecutions of the Mao era, Ba Jin had become eloquent in his denunciations. Yet despite the reemergence of the democratic elite, their opponents were still strong enough to retaliate. Although the People's Publishing House had announced at the beginning of 1982 that two volumes of Ba Jin's controversial *Random Thoughts* would be published, they did not appear.

By early 1982, the attacks on bourgeois liberalization began to wane and a more positive view of Bai Hua developed. Bai was even described in glowing terms. His twin brother, Ye Nan, also a well-known writer, publicly praised Bai for the very qualities the campaign had repudiated. "I cannot equal Bai Hua in ideological openness," he said. [62] He also lauded his brother for "exploring literary creation," which is "also worth emulating." Since Bai was a child, Ye said, he had "always dared to think and dared to act," [63] as demonstrated by his protests against the Guomindang and his poems against Chiang Kai-shek that led to his expulsion from school. An interviewer described Bai in April 1982 as "full of life and spirit, his eyes shining." [64]

Yet despite the efforts to picture Bai in a cheerful mood, his own work following the campaign reveals anything but that. In a narrative poem published in February 1982, "Clouds of Yunnan," he contrasted his somber mood with that of the energetic workers he met in Yunnan, where he had been sent during the anti-rightist campaign and was sent again after his 1981 self-criticism. "I was once proud of myself, being a man optimistic and strong / But now, in contrast to you, how dispirited I am." [65] Bai's suffering had more than one source. He had been the major target of a campaign, with all the stress and humiliation that entailed. But he was also chastised by his colleagues for having made a self-criticism. Their reproaches may also account for the depressed feelings expressed in his poem. Furthermore, despite the official conclusion to the campaign, Hu Qiaomu continued to attack "Unrequited Love" in *Red Flag* well into 1982. Again and again, Hu charged that the scenario had negated socialist China and its party leadership and had instilled despondency. "Unrequited Love," Hu insisted, gave the impression that "there is not the slightest brightness and freedom in China and that intellectuals deserve no better fate than persecution and humiliation." [66]

Other Targets of the 1981 Campaign

The authorities maintained that the criticisms of "Unrequited Love" and Bai Hua were not a campaign, but their impact was similar. In this case only one person was the ostensible public target—unlike the Mao era, when hundreds and sometimes thousands of people were singled out for public attack. Nevertheless, behind closed doors high officials and other writers and a few lesser-known local writers were also criticized.

One of these was Sun Jingxuan, a Sichuan writer, who had written "A Phantom Is Wandering Over the Land of China," a poem published in 1981 in the *Changlan Literary Monthly*. The lines of the poem that disturbed the authorities were those that rejected the Lei Feng view of absolute obedience to the party: "Originally, we thought that we were masters of our lives / And we could live happily in our own land, ... / But, we are actually nothing but screws which are firmly screwed to the steel machine." [67] As had Bai Hua, Sun in his self-criticism admitted that he had confused the Gang of Four's actions with those of Mao and even with those of the post-Mao regime.

In addition, when he attempted "to investigate and analyze the historical, social and ideological roots of the mistake of the [Cultural Revolution] . . . I did not take the Marxist-Leninist view as my guiding ideology."[68] Like a principled literati, he declared, "I considered myself . . . 'someone who is concerned about his country and his people.'" But because "I was full of grievances . . . influenced by my traumatic experiences . . . I could only see the negative aspects and the dark side of life." The poem was "written when I was in such a mood."[69]

Sun's self-criticism revealed that he too had been put under great pressure to confess. When he heard after the Sixth Plenum that the Sichuan authorities planned to criticize him, he became "agitated," though he had assumed an attitude of "I couldn't care less." The officials of the Sichuan Federation of Literary and Art Circles educated him "meticulously several times," and then sent him to a construction site at Gezhou Dam to learn about life. Sun described that experience as transformative. When he began his journey to Gezhou, "my hair was long and I was full of melancholy," but when he boarded the first boat to pass through the world's "largest lock" "amid the sounds of gongs, drums, and applause," Sun declared, "my confidence in socialism was strengthened."[70]

Another and more major target of the 1981 campaign was the less compliant poet Ye Wenfu. He, like Bai, was attached to the military. In his July 17 talk to Propaganda Department officials, Deng had also criticized Ye by name. Deng was not so much disturbed by Ye's poetry as by a speech that Ye had given at Beijing Normal University on April 10. In that speech, Ye referred to several emperors in Chinese history who had become corrupt and incompetent after achieving power, causing a change in dynasty. Ye had also compared the present-day China to the "age of Wen Yiduo," an outspoken poet of the Guomindang period who had criticized the "darkness" of his times and was reportedly assassinated by the Guomindang in 1946. The implication of Ye's speech was that today's poets and students should emulate Wen Yiduo's spirit of criticism.

Even more infuriating to Deng than Ye's speech per se was the thunderous applause it evoked from the audience of six hundred students. "The university party committee was aware of this matter but took no measures," Deng observed.[71] This example of laxness in ideological leadership had been brought to Deng's attention by a woman student who had tried in vain to get the party committee to criticize it. Although Deng specified Ye by name in his original talk, when the speech was published in his *Selected Works* three years later, Ye was referred to as the "young poet." In August 1981, when the Central Committee issued Document no. 30 calling for criticism against bourgeois liberalization, it mentioned Ye's name along with that of Bai Hua as the targets.

Whereas Deng had been upset by Ye's speech, it was Ye's poems of the late 1970s criticizing the special privileges of military officials, that had infuriated the military authorities. The first and most well known was "General, You Cannot Do This," published in August 1979 in *Poetry.* It concerned a Long March general, who had torn down a nursery school in order to build a private multistory residence for himself. Ye received many letters praising his poem, which encouraged him to ridicule the military further. A 1981 poem, "General, Give Yourself a Good Bath," portrayed an army general who wanted to install a modern bathtub in his basement. One line of the poem read: "Yes, generals, you should have a good wash . . . but not in this kind of bathtub." [72] Even though the poem's sentiments were in accord with the party's call since the Third Plenum to expose special privileges, its sarcasm, especially when directed at the military, was not. Another line of the poem was even more taunting, implying that the party was despotic: "Turn around and look at the unfortunate history of yesterday / The appendages of Qin Shi Huang had wormed their way into our party meetings." [73]

Like the principled literati, Ye wrote poetry in the hope that the military and party officials would be persuaded to reform and live up to their stated high ideals. In "General, You Cannot Do This," Ye asked: "Do you simply not want the oath you took when you joined the party?" [74] The army reacted angrily to Ye's mockery. Twenty-five generals signed a petition recommending that Ye be given a dishonorable discharge. Still Ye refused to be intimidated. When an investigative official of the Central Discipline Inspection Commission demanded that Ye name the commander who had installed the bathtub, Ye sarcastically suggested that Lu Xun should have been asked who his character Ah Q was. The military media used the context of the Bai Hua campaign, therefore, to intensify their attacks on Ye. In November–December 1981 the attacks on Ye were harsher than those on Bai. Unlike Bai and Sun Jingxuan, Ye refused to make a self-criticism.

Ye himself had predicted his own fate. He commented in 1980 that "in a country led by communists, to speak one's mind is to invite trouble. This is a tragedy."[75] Not only was Ye banned from publishing, but unlike Bai, who had some political patronage and was thus allowed to remain in his own home, he was confined to a room in which the temperature was five degrees below zero in winter. One of his friends reports that he often contemplated suicide.[76] Yet Ye, despite his harsher treatment, was not totally ostracized as he would have been during the Mao era. When the party organization of Ye's unit sent an investigative group to find out the circumstances of Ye's speech at Beijing Normal University, representatives of students and teachers challenged the investigators and defended Ye. When Ye attended a film at a showing organized by the Chinese Writers Association at the time he was being attacked, initially no one dared speak to him. But when the veteran poet Ai Qing and his wife, Gao Ying, entered the room, Gao called to him in a loud voice: "Ye, come over here." They then both greeted him warmly. Although Ai Qing had criticized the "obscure" poets for being unintelligible to the masses, he was demonstrating by his actions the kind of independence he had shown in Yan'an before the 1942 rectification and during the early 1950s, before he was labeled a rightist.

Wang Ruowang was another writer criticized publicly, but primarily in Shanghai. An old revolutionary writer, Wang had the relatively unique experience of having been jailed by both the Guomindang and the Communist Party.[77] As a youth he had written satires against the Guomindang and was jailed by them at the age of sixteen for underground party activity in a Shanghai factory. Like other writers from Shanghai, he made his way to Yan'an in 1937 and joined the party, but he was attacked in the 1942 rectification for a wallposter criticizing the bureaucratic airs of party leaders. In 1957, he was branded a rightist. Although the label was removed in 1961, because of his subsequent criticism of the Great Leap Forward he spent most of the Cultural Revolution in prison as a "counterrevolutionary." Perhaps because of his ability to survive so many terrible ordeals, he reemerged in the late 1970s, in feisty, irrepressible spirits. He exuded tremendous energy, which he poured into a continuous flow of articles criticizing the leadership and political system that had allowed the Cultural Revolution to happen. When the party tried to limit writing about the Cultural Revolution in 1979, he responded with a piece entitled, "A

Gust of Cold Wind in Spring," in which he asserted that no boundaries should be put on detailing the crimes committed in the Cultural Revolution.[78]

"Governing by Doing Nothing" (Wuwei er zhi), an article of Wang's published in *Red Flag* in 1979 when it had not yet been completely taken over by the elders' associates, became a famous critique of the party's control over writers and artists. Wang protested the party's treatment of writers as "kindergartners or elementary school students who have to be led by nannies."[79] "Inaction" *(wuwei)* is a Daoist term, but Wang attributed it to former vice premier Chen Yi, who commented at a conference in Guangzhou in 1962, "If we exercise leadership over everything, we may produce bad results. It is better to leave some things alone."[80] Although Wang was referring to the creative realm, the party attacked his call for inaction as applying to the political realm as well. In another controversial piece, "Trilogy," Wang described the starvation he endured in the Great Leap Forward and as a prisoner during the Cultural Revolution, both party-created disasters, saying he had less to eat in those years than he had had while imprisoned by the Guomindang. He asked: "Does such a political regime deserve to be called a proletarian political power?"[81]

Although Wang was criticized in the *Liberation Army Daily* and *Contemporary Reportage,* most of the attacks on him originated in Shanghai, from its propaganda head Chen Yi, who was also active in attacking Bai Hua. Although Chen Yi was a writer and a former rightist like Wang Ruowang, in the late 1970s he became involved in a factional struggle with Wang over the leadership of the Shanghai literary community. Wang served as the head of the Shanghai Writers Association and the editor of the influential *Shanghai Literary Monthly.* Under Chen Yi's direction, the Shanghai *Liberation Daily* attacked Wang's literary views and, on orders from higher-level officials, refused to print Wang's rebuttals. In January 1982, even *October,* which had published controversial works by Bai Hua and Ye Wenfu in the past, criticized Wang and refused to publish his articles. But in March the journal *Anhui Literature* (Anhui wenxue), which had also published Ye Wenfu's works and a broad spectrum of views, published Wang's counterattack, "Answers and Explanations," in which he refuted the criticisms Chen Yi had inspired and defended his proposal for "inaction"[82] in the cultural realm.

Liu Binyan was another writer primarily criticized behind closed doors at this time. A few public criticisms appeared in Huang Gang's *Contemporary Reportage,* where Liu was accused of making factual errors in his reportage, especially in *People or Monsters.*[83] *Contemporary Reportage* charged Liu with giving the impression that he had brought the case of corruption in the Northeast to public attention, whereas in truth the party organization had done so. This criticism sought to discredit both Liu and his genre of investigative reporting. Most of the articles did not mention his name, however, even though they denounced his type of reporting for presenting a totally distorted view of society.

Lingering Effects

Although the campaign against Bai Hua was supposedly concluded in December 1981, there were still serious aftershocks. Some members of Hu Yaobang's network were criticized for previously stated views. Hu Jiwei, for example, who had urged newspapers to criticize party policies when they were unresponsive to the demands of the people and whose paper had initially refused to reprint *Liberation Army Daily* articles against Bai, was "promoted" from editor-in-chief of the *People's Daily* to director in May 1982. In reality, however, this move was a demotion to a more ceremonial position. His deputy editor Wang Ruoshui lost some power as well. Ruan Ming, editor of *Theoretical Trends,* and other followers of Hu at the Central Party School who had been active in the practice criterion campaign were dismissed when Wang Zhen became president of the school in 1982. Wang Zhen also moved to have Ruan Ming expelled from the party, charging that his essays on political reform were opposed to communism. The purge of this group implicitly challenged Hu Yaobang and ultimately Deng, who had mobilized this group against the "two whatevers" faction. While the elders were also opposed to the faction, once it was ousted they regarded Hu's intellectual network as an increasing threat to themselves.

As some members of Hu's network lost their positions, those associated with the elders gained positions. Most important was the appointment of Deng Liqun, as director of the Propaganda Department. Deng Liqun, formerly Liu Shaoqi's political secretary, was closely associated with Chen Yun. He was also a close colleague of Hu Qiaomu, the party elders' principal theorist. As the efforts to revive Marxist orthodoxy and some aspects of Mao's thought continued into 1982, Deng Liqun, at a meeting with philosophers and social scientists, stressed that the social sciences must use Marxist ideology in analyzing philosophical and social science questions. During the summer of 1982 students at Qinghua University were required to attend classes in Marxism-Leninism. The *People's Daily* explained that these students were not being forced to study ideology, but when they discovered that Western existentialism and pragmatism were "unable to extricate them from perplexity and emptiness," they had turned "to Marxism-Leninism." [84] As early in the Deng era as 1982, therefore, concern existed that Western modernist thinkers were corrupting China's youth.

Revival of Mao's ideological thought was most conspicuous in the army. On the eve of the Twelfth Party Congress held in September 1982, the *Liberation Army Daily* published a controversial article by Zhao Yiya, who had been its deputy chief editor in the early stages of the Cultural Revolution, when he echoed the ultra-leftist line of Jiang Qing and her associates. With the support of Wei Guoqing, director of the General Political Department, Zhao's article attacked the capitalist system, which in the context of 1982 represented an attack on Deng's economic reforms. "No matter what kind of 'automatic production lines' there are, they are always weapons for the bourgeoisie to squeeze out the sweat and blood of the proletariat . . . As to the rotten bourgeois ideas, the decadent and debauched spiritual life in capitalist society . . . these we must all the more resolutely refuse to accept." [85] He then specifically criticized those in theoretical work, literature, and journalism who publicized bourgeois liberalization. He charged that if opposing liberalization was considered "ultra-left," then "upholding the party's leadership and the four basic principles" was also "ultra-left." [86]

This article, which was reprinted in Shanghai's *Liberation Daily*, provoked the reform officials, seemingly with Deng's support, to pressure the *Liberation Army Daily* into publishing an editorial refuting the article. The editorial described the article as a "grave political and organizational mistake," which in the name of opposing bourgeois liberalization had spread leftist views. As for the capitalist "automatic production lines," the editorial charged that instead of exploiting workers, these lines were actually an "important result of mankind's scientific and technological development, [and] have no class character."[87] Zhao Yiya's effort to explain every phenomenon in society in class terms was denounced, and the editorial charged that Zhao's views reflected the "pernicious influence of the 'left' ideas which have not been eliminated yet."[88] It continued: "That Comrade Zhao Yiya's article was published in this paper shows that among a very small number of comrades in the party and the army, there indeed remains the pernicious influence of 'left' ideas."[89] And it called on the army and media to "obey the party's absolute leadership."

Yet while the *Liberation Army Daily* went along with the rebuttal to the "left," one of its commentator articles criticized those who in their talks and writings attempted to "introduce" the bourgeois parliamentary system, the two-party system, election campaigns, freedom of speech, individualism, and the worship of money. It charged that "from the economic sphere to the political sphere and from the ideological and cultural sphere to other social spheres, hostile elements carry out sabotage acts of all forms."[90]

Contemporary Reportage was also criticized in 1982 for leftism. As the fortieth anniversary of Mao's Yan'an Talks approached in May 1982, the journal had initiated a column entitled "Renew Studies of the Talks," praising Mao's literary ideas and denouncing as "unhealthy" any deviation. An editorial note was added to an article published in February 1982 asserting that in "the sixteen years since the Great Cultural Revolution . . . Mao Zedong's thinking on literature and art was distorted and altered . . . in the first ten years ultraleftist ideas were the main trend while in the latter six years right deviationist ideas [were] . . . subsequently landing ourselves in the quagmire of bourgeois liberalization."[91] By combining the Cultural Revolution with the early Deng era, the note equated Deng's reform policies with those of the Gang of Four.

The editorial note provoked a major debate in the national media. *Literary Gazette* responded by publishing an article about a meeting of the editors of *Anhui Literature* and several theorists in April 1982 at which the participants described the Cultural Revolution as entirely different from the period since the Third Plenum. *Anhui Literature*'s June issue raised additional critical questions about the note: "Then why are not the forty years, but only the sixteen years, mentioned? Can it be said that interference did not exist before the Cultural Revolution? The Cultural Revolution did not just drop from heaven!"[92] The implication was that Mao's Yan'an Talks were responsible for the distortions that *Contemporary Reportage* had described. The participants in *Anhui Literature*'s April meeting had also criticized another article in *Contemporary Reportage* that had exhorted writers to "shift their standpoint to the side of workers, peasants and soldiers."[93] Some interpreted such advice as a call for a return to the ideological remolding of the Mao era. A *People's Daily* editorial on October 21, 1982, cautioned: "We should not and need not distinguish intellectuals from the workers and peasants . . . [and] still treat intellectuals as the petty-bourgeoisie or the bourgeoisie."[94]

Despite these criticisms, *Contemporary Reportage* responded in its July issue by reprinting its editorial note and publishing letters in support of its views. It accused the *Literary Gazette* of carrying out the orders of officials behind the scenes in mobilizing public opinion against it. And its next issue accused the *Literary Gazette* of trying to prevent the celebration of the fortieth anniversary of the Yan'an Talks. Some individuals were indeed in need of ideological remolding, it asserted: "There are some among our literary and art workers, including members of the Communist Party, whose world outlook is outmoded, semi-outmoded or bourgeois."[95]

Contemporary Reportage's effort to uphold the pre–Cultural Revolution Mao proved futile. With the reassertion of Hu Yaobang's authority, once again backed by Deng Xiaoping after the Twelfth Party Congress in September 1982, China began to move into another phase of ideological relaxation as an accompaniment to accelerating economic reforms. Those journals and officials who had attempted to revive Maoist views and practices were punished. *Contemporary Reportage* published a self-criticism in its first issue of 1983, in which it admitted that it had published erroneous views on "the sixteen years" and other important questions. Deng Liqun, newly appointed director of the Propaganda Department, was put in charge of dealing with *Contemporary Reportage* and Huang Gang. Deng's ideological stance in this period was more orthodox than Maoist. Huang Gang and his editorial board were dismissed, and the military members attached to the journal were sent back to their units. The publication was dissociated from the General Political Department and a new party group was put in charge. Wei Guoqing was removed from his position as director of the General Political Department. The *Liberation Daily* admitted in late 1982 that its reprinting of the Zhao Yiya article had been a "grave" organizational as well as ideological mis-

take: "Without permission, without asking for instructions beforehand ... [We] seriously violated the party's organizational principle." [96] Finally, on January 8, 1983, the *Liberation Army Daily* carried
an article declaring that it was "essential to eliminate the 'leftist' prejudice and build up a good atmosphere in which intellectuals are respected and importance is attached to learning, culture, and science." [97] China was about to enjoy another thaw.

The Bai Hua campaign demonstrated that while Deng Xiaoping
was willing to open up the economic realm, he was not willing to
permit the same openness in the cultural realm. At the same time,
however, it also revealed that he was reluctant to allow any crackdown in the cultural realm that might completely silence it, extend to
the economic sphere, or escalate out of control. Any moves in such
directions would undermine Deng's economic reforms and China's
concomitant openness to the outside world.

5

The Revival and Suppression of Political Discourse

By mid-1982 the Bai Hua campaign appeared to have been merely a brief aberration in the Deng regime's overall program of reform and openness. Hu Yaobang, in his report to the Twelfth Party Congress on September 1, sparked a revival of the political and ideological discourse begun in the late 1970s. China's socialist society was "still in its initial stage," Hu declared.[1] This concept was close to the one that Su Shaozhi and Feng Lanrui had presented at the theory conference, though they had said that China had not even reached the initial stage. Hu's definition of the initial stage, moreover, was limited to "productive forces" and did not touch on the different forms of production relations that Su and Feng had discussed. But like them, Hu also pressed for the continuation of reform in both political institutions and the leadership system. He repeated Deng's argument of August 18, 1980, that the party should not take responsibility for everything, including government administration and business enterprises. And as had others in his network, Hu complained about the party's undemocratic practices, misuse of privilege, arrogance, and abuse of power. He called for the rectification of the party over a three-year period, beginning in the latter half of 1983.

Like Liao Gailong, Hu urged: "Socialist democracy should be extended to all fields of life; political, economic, cultural and social; and it is necessary to extend democratic management to all enterprises and institutions and encourage self-management of community affairs by the masses at the grass-roots level."[2] Others followed his lead in putting renewed emphasis on developing democracy at the grass roots. Radio Beijing insisted that deputies elected to the local people's congresses "must maintain close contacts with the voters, accept their supervision and reflect their aspirations."[3] The legal expert Zhang Youyu talked of the need to build democracy at the local level, where neighborhood committees and village committees would act as "autonomous organizations."[4] He also called for the institutionalization and legalization of socialist democracy, which he said would "fully protect democratic rights."[5]

Yu Haocheng elaborated on Hu's proposal that people be allowed to assume more control over their own activities. He pointed out that the new 1982 constitution stipulated that citizens could "exercise their rights directly in managing various economic and cultural undertakings and all social affairs."[6] He also praised the new constitution for increasing the power of the National People's Congress by stipulating that its deputies not be subjected to reprisals for speeches or votes and by abrogating life-long tenure and limiting the terms of leading cadres to five years and no more than two terms. Yu and other members of the democratic elite continued their efforts to make the congress into an institution strong enough to limit the power of the party leadership.

Another member of the democratic elite, Li Honglin, even suggested the establishment of political parties as a means of limiting autocratic rule. Some months before Hu Yaobang's September speech, an article of Li's appeared in the *People's Daily,* calling political parties "component parts of the various classes . . . [I]t is truly inconceivable not to have political parties participate in present-day political life."[7] Li's vision of how parties might function contradicted the Leninist view that parties undermine political authority. Li reiterated that democracy had not taken root in China "because of the deficiency in our system and laws." Even if the system and laws for promoting democracy existed, it would be "difficult to implement them in practice because people are not accustomed to or know very little about them." Worse, "those who defended the principle of democracy and opposed the pernicious influence of autocracy" had often been "branded as traitors and heretics and isolated as well as persecuted."[8]

Encouraged by Liao Gailong's elaborations[9] on Deng's August 18, 1980, speech and Hu's speech at the Twelfth Party Congress, several members of the democratic elite recommended that intellectuals form their own organizations and professional associations with their own norms and leadership, relatively independent of party control. Zhou

Yang, for example, called for giving the All-China Federation of Literary and Art Circles more autonomy so that it could protect the rights and interests of its members. He saw the establishment of autonomous organizations as one way to prevent the alienation of the intellectuals from the party, a growing concern since the Cultural Revolution. He granted that the writers must obey the Central Committee politically, "but on the question of science and art, full freedom should be granted." [10] The federation attempted to move in this direction. Zhao Xun, its secretary, announced that ACFLAC would adopt democratic methods for the election of its leadership in order to overcome the bureaucracy and become more independent. The organizations that made up the federation were "to function less as government departments and more as mass organizations for writers and artists." [11] Zhao Xun further explained: "Mass literary and art organizations should be established and run by all people in literary and art circles, but not by people outside them." [12] A Hu Yaobang disciple from the Youth League, Li Ruihuan, a former carpenter who became the mayor of Tianjin in 1982, also called for more independence for intellectual organizations. [13]

Some younger well-known professional writers expressed their independence by choosing not to join the federation or the Chinese Writers Association. They became freelance writers, earning their own incomes rather than being paid by the federation or the association, another unprecedented phenomenon. In addition, for financial rather than ideological reasons, the government proposed that theater and opera troupes use their box-office receipts to pay their members' wages rather than being dependent on state subsidies. As a result of these moves to the market in the cultural arena, the party exerted less ideological or economic leverage over literary and artistic activities. To allow intellectuals and artistic groups as well as the decollectivized peasants a degree of autonomy marked a shift away from the tight state control that had existed since 1949.

In late 1982 there were also renewed efforts to enhance intellectuals' political status. Even though the Bai Hua campaign revealed the party's continuing suspicion of intellectuals, in its aftermath, Lu Jiaxi, president of the Academy of Sciences, extolled the intellectuals' devotion to the party: "Despite their heavy burdens, low salary, poor housing conditions and tremendous difficulties, they are always loyal to the party . . . They do not demand too much—mainly political trust—

and they just hope their opinions and suggestions can gain attention and their roles in [their] work can reasonably and fully be brought into play."[14] Lu repeated Hu Yaobang's earlier proposal that the Academy of Sciences be run primarily by scientists rather than by political cadres.

Anger at those responsible for the Bai Hua campaign and its criticism of intellectuals for bourgeois liberalization was vigorously expressed. The writer Zhang Guangnian rejected the view that "this trend seems to prevail everywhere in literary, art, academic and press circles and many people are dissenting from and even opposing the leadership of the party and the socialist path." He warned: "If we act out this erroneous estimate, the result will be dreadful to contemplate."[15] The possibility of another Cultural Revolution continued to haunt China's intellectuals, and a *People's Daily* article acknowledged that they had good reason for their fears. Those influenced by the left "adopt a suspicious and negative attitude toward them." Some of them "want to retain the erroneous things which existed before the third plenary session or even during the 'Cultural Revolution' . . . In fact, there is a small minority . . . who still hold leadership positions, waiting for the opportunity to stir up trouble."[16] Despite its circumscribed nature, the Bai Hua campaign had intensified the sense of alienation that the intellectuals and others had felt in the Cultural Revolution and earlier.

The Debate on Alienation and Humanism

In the more relaxed atmosphere of late 1982 and early 1983, the intellectual community returned to the question of whether alienation could exist in a socialist state. Although the Bai Hua campaign had interrupted the discussion of this issue that had begun soon after the theory conference in 1979, over six hundred articles on the subject had been published in major newspapers and journals. Alienation had also been a theme of the wounded literature. The Deng regime had tolerated the discussion of alienation and humanism in its early years because these concepts fit with its own critique of the dehumanizing nature of the Cultural Revolution and its factional struggle with the remaining Maoists.

Whereas in the late 1970s and early 1980s Wang Ruoshui had used the concepts of alienation and humanism to stress the need for both ideological and political change, by 1983 he and other associates had shifted their emphasis to ideological change, perhaps because, with the purge of the remaining Maoists and in the aftermath of the Bai Hua campaign, revisions of ideology seemed more likely to be tolerated than calls for political reform. Pursuing the reinterpretation of ideology rather than institutional reform was also more in accord with Chinese tradition. Again Wang Ruoshui played a leading role in the discourse on alienation, but in 1983 he and his associates focused more on the concomitant, but less controversial, concept of humanism as a way of overcoming alienation. Although their own traditional ideology of Confucianism was humanistic, they identified humanism with the Western Renaissance and Enlightenment and with the Western emphasis on the inherent value of the individual. They also found in Marx's early works the humanist elements they now believed were needed to liberate mankind, spiritually and physically, from dehumanizing conditions. Wang begins his article "In Defense of Humanism," written in January 1983, with a dramatic variation on the first words of the *Communist Manifesto,* in which "humanism" replaced "Communism": "A specter, the specter of humanism, has loomed large in China's intellectual circles." Humanism was not only a phenomenon of bourgeois societies: "We require socialist humanism . . . it means resolutely discarding the 'all-round dictatorship' and cruel struggle in the ten-year period of internal disorder, doing away with the cult of the personality which deifies an individual and belittles the people, and upholding the principle that all men are equal before the truth and the law and that a citizen's personal freedom and dignity are inviolable." [17]

Some of the views held by Wang and others were published in major newspapers such as the *People's Daily* and *Wenhui News,* but the discussion was primarily limited to academic circles until the centennial commemoration of Marx's death in March 1983. In an atmosphere of increasing openness on ideological issues, the speeches of the democratic elite and reform party officials called attention to the inadequacies of the orthodox ideology and Mao's thought. Su Shaozhi pointed out that in regard to today's problems, "Marx, Engels and Lenin . . . did not formulate for us—and could not possibly have done so—any systematic and specific theories in this respect due to lack of practice or time." Mao, furthermore, "made gross miscalculations." [18] Su observed that changes under way in China, such as the responsibility system in agriculture, were not dealt with in Marxism-Leninism. Revision of ideology was therefore crucial, because otherwise it "provides a sanctuary and hotbed for the 'left' ideology and offers an ideological ground on the basis of which exponents of such ideology can censure the current reforms."[19]

Even more important than the democratic elite's views in providing impetus for radical ideological reform were the statements of the reform officials at the centennial. Hu Yaobang, although he did not discuss alienation and humanism directly, admitted that since the end of World War II, Marxism had "experienced severe setbacks and failures, undergoing a bewildering process of turbulence and division" to the point that some people had "lost their confidence, describing Marxism as being in a state of 'crisis.'"[20] In an indirect admission of alienation, Hu implied that the "crisis" had been caused by the system itself, as Deng himself had implied in his August 18, 1980, speech. Paraphrasing Deng, Hu charged: "Even such a great Marxist as Comrade Mao Zedong could not avoid going astray and making distressing mistakes."[21]

Like the theorists associated with him, Hu Yaobang also expressed the desire to make ideology more relevant to the present. He praised current efforts to do away with the personality cult, increase consumer goods, and develop the market. He was particularly pleased by the reforms in the countryside, which he described as giving China's "800,000,000 peasants a free hand to tap fully their tremendous labor potential, develop a diversified economy and expand production." Nevertheless, he lamented, "there still exist many erroneous ideas and models that do not suit China's actual conditions and that had long fettered people's minds and seriously hampered the development of the productive forces."[22] One of these was the cadres' continuing contempt for intellectuals, whom they stigmatized as "bourgeois." Hu countered that a large number of intellectuals "loved their socialist motherland and had made important contributions to socialist construction."[23] The speech was another effort to refute the Bai Hua campaign's attacks on intellectuals for lack of patriotism. Expressing his fear of another Cultural Revolution, Hu warned: "The grave consequences of the prolonged 'Left' mistakes are far from being liquidated either in our ideology and public opinion or in various political, economic and organizational measures adopted."[24]

Zhou Yang, however, gave the centennial speech that received the most attention. Although at the end of 1981 he had offered his resignation as a deputy director of the Propaganda Department, supposedly because he had been held responsible for the Bai Hua affair and the laxity in ideology, his resignation was rejected. Thereafter he became increasingly more daring. In May 1982, at a meeting of the All-China Federation of Literary and Art Circles, he emphasized the relevance of the concepts of alienation and humanism in early Marx to present-day China. This view caused official consternation at the time, but it did not receive much broader attention until Zhou's centennial speech on March 8, in which he repudiated the Maoist assertion that "humanitarianism was absolutely incompatible with Marxism"[25] and the orthodox view that alienation existed only in capitalist societies: "The emancipation of mankind projected by Marx and Engels calls for emancipation from not only the system of exploitation . . . but also the bond of all forms of alienation."[26] Repeating arguments that Wang Ruoshui and other members of the democratic elite had made earlier, Zhou pointed out that because of the lack of democracy and a legal system, "the people's servants would sometimes abuse the power vested in them by the people to become, instead, the masters of the people. This means alienation in the political field, or power alienation. As to alienation in the ideological field, the most typical case is the personality cult . . . Therefore, 'alienation' is a phenomenon existing objectively . . . Only by admitting alienation can we overcome alienation."[27] His ringing words were enthusiastically received by his listeners at the Central Party School.[28]

There were less enthusiastic reactions as well, however. Wang Zhen, who presided over the meeting, told Zhou Yang during an intermission that he had benefited from his "very good" speech and asked Zhou to write down for him the characters for alienation, *yihua,* an indication that Wang did not understand the concept. Whether or not they fully understood the concept, most of the elders found it objectionable. Though Deng Liqun had earlier said it was permissible to discuss alienation and humanism as academic subjects, Zhou's speech abruptly ended the tolerance of even scholarly consideration of these topics. The day after Zhou spoke, the Marx centennial was hastily concluded. On March 10, two days later, Hu Qiaomu went to Zhou's home to talk with him and his close friends Xia Yan and Wang Ruoshui. As was his style in personal confrontation,[29] Hu Qiaomu was ostensibly very polite. He did not mention Zhou's speech, but he said that he too was interested in humanism. He said nothing about alienation, perhaps because, as Wang Ruoshui believes, he too did not truly comprehend the concept at the time. While Hu praised Wang Ruoshui's writing style, he criticized him for having substituted humanism for communism in his articles. In a telephone call the day before, Hu Qiaomu had told Deng Liqun that Zhou's speech had very serious "political mistakes" that could not be resolved simply by editing. In his view the speech gave the impression that socialism was opposed to humanism, and he directed Deng Liqun not to publish it in the party media and to arrange for criticisms to be written against it. Hu suggested that Zhou's speech be published only in *Philosophy Research,* a scholarly journal with a small circulation of several thousand.

But before these instructions could be relayed, Wang Ruoshui published Zhou Yang's speech in the *People's Daily,* on March 16. With a circulation of several million, the paper gave Zhou's words wide circulation and seemingly official endorsement. Shortly thereafter Wang, Zhou Yang, and Qin Chuan, the editor-in-chief of the *People's Daily,* were ordered to a meeting at the Propaganda Department, where Hu Qiaomu and Deng Liqun read them a department report accusing Zhou and Wang of creating "chaos" in literature, art, and theory, and suggesting that Wang be reprimanded. Wang was removed from his position as deputy editor of the *People's Daily.* Wang's mentor, the paper's director Hu Jiwei, had not been in Beijing when Zhou's speech was published, and consequently Qin Chuan was held responsible.

Nevertheless, discussion on the need to revise Marxism continued into the summer of 1983. Wang's colleague Ru Xin also called for radical revisions of ideology: "There [have] been earth-shattering changes throughout the world and China over the last three decades. But the Marxism of which we speak today is the system used in the 1930s, taught in pedagogical institutes in the Soviet Union." He lamented that Marxism had no ready-made answers for new challenges and urged that advances in the sciences, such as cybernetics, systems theory, biotechnology, and computers, be incorporated into ideology. Ru was one of the few intellectuals who also urged incorporating elements of "China's traditional culture and ideology," which he insisted had "many positive factors which should be given more expression."[30]

By early June, however, the opponents of the concepts of alienation and humanism dominated the media. Deng Liqun and his allies at the Central Party School began to categorize the democratic elite's efforts to revise ideology as "spiritual pollution." Four months before the Second Plenum of the Twelfth Central Committee in October, when Deng Xiaoping would echo the epithet, Deng Liqun denounced "a handful[,] including party members," who used the pretext of emancipating the mind to oppose Marxism-Leninism, Mao's thought, socialism, and the party. He charged that their articles on humanism and alienation were a bad influence, particularly on students. A campaign against spiritual pollution was launched at the Central Party School, where the windows thrown open by Hu Yaobang in the late 1970s were being closed by Wang Zhen.

Throughout the summer of 1983 Deng Liqun's repeated and increasingly louder fulminations against spiritual pollution made him, like his colleague Hu Qiaomu, a political as well as an ideological force to be reckoned with. Deng also became the member of the Secretariat in charge of intellectual matters. The prominent roles of Deng Liqun and Hu Qiaomu in articulating the elders' views may have been motivated as much by factional struggle as by ideology. Considering himself a great theoretician, Deng Liqun was annoyed that Hu Yaobang, in his position as general secretary, had replaced him as the major party theoretician. Unable to attack Hu directly at this time, he attacked Hu's ideological associates Zhou Yang, Wang Ruoshui, and Hu Jiwei. But he and Hu Qiaomu may have opposed them less for their ideological views than because they had refused to follow their lead.

The Second Plenum, October 1983

By the fall of 1983 Deng Liqun had won Deng Xiaoping's support for an attack on members of Hu Yaobang's intellectual network. Deng Xiaoping had encouraged the family responsibility system for peasants and had allowed some autonomy for artists and academics, but he was unwilling to tolerate a discussion of philosophical concepts that implied the party's political system had alienated the population. The Second Plenum of the Twelfth Central Committee, with Deng Xiaoping's speech as its cornerstone, was supposed to have launched the rectification of party cadres that Hu Yaobang had called for the previous year. Instead, provoked by the reports of Deng Liqun and Hu Qiaomu on the discussions of Hu Yaobang's network, Deng launched a campaign against spiritual pollution and Hu's theoretical network of associates. With the remaining Maoists no longer a threat to his regime and with the regime's supposed correction of the "mistakes" of the Mao years, Deng believed that continued discussion of alienation was undermining confidence in the political system and its capacity to reform. The question also remains whether Deng fully understood the concept. When Deng asked Hu Qiaomu and Deng Liqun what alienation meant, they are said to have told him simply that it was against socialism.[31]

Consequently, Deng Xiaoping's speech at the plenum charged that spiritual pollution was spreading "distrust of socialism, communism and leadership by the Communist Party."[32] Its propagators were "a number of theorists" who "have engaged in discussions of the value of the human being, humanism and alienation and were only interested in criticizing socialism, not capitalism . . ."[33] Beyond this, "some people preach abstract democracy, even advocating free expression of counterrevolutionary views. They set democracy in opposition to the Party leadership . . . Even today there are still comrades who have doubts about the need to uphold the Four Cardinal Principles."[34] He also lambasted writers and artists who depicted alienation in their literary and artistic works. They "are not interested in portraying and extolling the revolutionary history of the Party and the people and their heroic deeds in the struggle for socialist modernization . . . Instead, they make a point of writing about the dark side of life, they spread pessimism . . ."[35] He admitted that only a small number spread this spiritual pollution, but he complained that they had not been sufficiently criticized or stopped from publicizing their ideas. Like his predecessor Mao, Deng warned: "Spiritual pollution can be so damaging as to bring disaster upon the country and the people."[36]

That meetings to criticize spiritual pollution convened immediately after the plenum and that articles on the subject in the media trumpeted the same themes all over the country indicated that the campaign had been planned well before the Second Plenum. The speeches and actions of Deng Liqun and Hu Qiaomu over the summer had prepared the ground. Like the campaigns of the Mao era, this one sought to force compliance with the party's political line. Thus the elders tried to use the campaign to return China to the ideological unity and greater isolation of the pre–Cultural Revolution period. Several elders urged that the method of criticism and self-criticism used in the 1942 Yan'an rectification be used against the propagators of spiritual pollution, as a way to achieve unified thinking. And as in Yan'an, the campaign charged specific intellectuals—this time Wang Ruoshui and Zhou Yang—with disrupting ideological unity.

The speed with which the campaign spread suggests that it may have also expressed the dissatisfaction of a substantial segment of party cadres with the economic reforms and openness to the West. Some local cadres took this opportunity to oppose everything from the family responsibility system to Western-style dress and rock music, much of it coming into China via Hong Kong. Again as with Mao's campaigns, various groups used the campaign to attack their rivals. There were reports of local cadres freezing the bank accounts of rich peasants and budding entrepreneurs as the campaign quickly spread to the economic realm. National editorials reinforced such actions. A *People's Daily* editorial declared: "Some peasants have been influenced by decadent capitalist ideas and remnant feudal ideas . . . the idea of 'putting money first' and disregarding the interests of the state and collectives . . ."[37] An *Economic Daily* (Jingji ribao) editorial warned: "Some leading comrades on the economic front . . . do not realize the seriousness of spiritual pollution and regard it as something pertaining to the theoretical and the literary and art circles which has nothing to do with the economic front."[38]

But an attack on the economic reforms was not Deng Xiaoping's intent. He therefore stopped the counterattack against economic reforms just six weeks after it began, because it threatened productivity in the countryside. It also slowed industrial production as workers were forced to participate in ideological study sessions. Moreover, to reassure scientists and engineers that their efforts to modernize the economy would not be interrupted, the campaign was further restricted to literature, the arts, and ideology. And even in these areas, distinctions were made. To read Western classics such as Shakespeare was permitted, but not Western writers such as Sartre, Freud, Kafka, and the European neo-Marxists whose works directly challenged an authoritarian system. Even in economics there were distinctions. The acquisition of Western methodologies, such as statistics, econometrics, and quantitative forecasting, was encouraged, but any interest in Western economic theory was decried. A *Guangming Daily* article cautioned: "A small number of comrades are blindly blowing the trumpet of bourgeois economic theories and other non-Marxist economic theories of the West."[39] Even the respected economist Liu Guoguang complained in the *Economic Daily* that "because of the influence of the economic theory of the Western bourgeoisie, some comrades have lost their faith in the basic theory of the political economy of Marxism."[40]

Although the attack on pornography and Western styles received the most publicity, it was relatively brief. The campaign in the ideological realm was more hard-hitting, by contrast, and it continued into the spring of 1984. Lin Mohan, at a conference in November 1983, pointed out that while the spiritual pollution of pornography and commercialization "is easily recognizable by everyone . . . and it is easily rectified . . . a theoretical and academic form which often attacks Marxism, is not so easily identifiable . . . it permeates and exerts a subtle influence on people's thoughts."[41] Various concepts were denounced—humanism, existentionalism, modernism—but the main emphasis was on denying that alienation was produced by the Leninist party-state or party leadership. The cadre journal *Semi-Weekly Chats* (Banyue tan) explained: "We never deny that there are problems, shortcomings, malpractices and mistakes in the socialist society, but they did not emerge out of socialism." Rather they came from "decadent ideological influence left from the old society or seeping in from abroad."[42]

A Different Kind of Campaign

The campaign against spiritual pollution was the most widespread, intense campaign of the Deng era so far, but it was much more limited and constrained than the movements launched by Mao. When young people in various parts of the country were reported to be donning red armbands, breaking into people's homes, and chopping off high-heeled shoes in behavior reminiscent of the Red Guards, both the elders and the reform leaders pulled back from mass mobilization. A more significant restraint on the movement was the effort of reform officials, Hu Yaobang and Zhao Ziyang in particular, to circumscribe the campaign almost as soon as it started. Believing the potential still existed for another Cultural Revolution, they warned Deng and others that the campaign had gone too far. At an emergency Politburo meeting on November 19, 1983, Hu Yaobang and Zhao Ziyang expressed their fear that some would take advantage of the campaign to negate the Third Plenum and that foreign businesspeople might withdraw from China.[43]

As early as mid-November a commentator article in *China Youth News* called for an end to attacks on Western styles, and the Secretariat then ordered the Propaganda Department to have this article reprinted in other newspapers. The article asserted that "young people who want their lives to be fuller and more interesting cannot be accused of pursuing a 'bourgeois way of life.' Proper aspirations for a better life are not ideological contamination . . . After all, what is the goal of socialism? Is it not gradually raising the material and cultural life of the people?" A Cultural Revolution–style campaign, the article warned, could produce "socialist poverty" and a population of "a monotonous sea of blue and gray."[44]

When after November the campaign was restricted primarily to the field of ideology, the media associated with Hu Yaobang began attacking the "left" as well as the "right." In early December a *Workers Daily* commentator article declared: "We should not regard the problems which have emerged in the institutional reform of the economy as well as the contention among differing opinions as spiritual pollution . . . [W]e should not only oppose spiritual pollution on the ideological front but also continue to limit 'leftist influence' in economic work."[45] In addition, even before the retreat in the spiritual pollution campaign, there were attempts to moderate the attacks on those accused of spreading spiritual pollution. A front-page commentator article in *People's Daily* reminded its readers that those who write on alienation were their "own comrades." Their problems "should never be solved by resorting to exaggeration of shortcomings, based on the 'leftist stand.' At the same time, persons who have committed mistakes in terms of spiritual pollution should not be treated the same as those persons who have committed crimes in the economic field or in the nature of a criminal offense."[46] Another *People's Daily* commentator article urged: "we should calmly present the facts, reason things out, and allow those receiving criticism to describe the situation and make arguments . . . Still less is it allowed to launch movements as we did in the past . . ."[47]

Shortly thereafter Deng Liqun was criticized at a meeting of the Secretariat. Under pressure, he seemed to pull back from the campaign in late November in his address to the National Conference of Cultural Departments, saying, "We must continue to carry out economic reform and implement the open-door policy. In the course of this process some different views and suggestions will arise; they should be allowed even though they may not be so correct."[48] Another associate of the elders, Yu Qiuli, director of the General Political Department of the army, gave a talk circulated to the public in which he warned that if the campaign "expanded as to hit out in all directions, problems will arise . . . We must not confuse spiritual pollution with the improvement of material and cultural life." Though he approved of the confiscation of obscene videos and books, he advised that "some books and periodicals, whose main themes are good . . . should not be confiscated, sealed up for safekeeping or destroyed as spiritual pollution." He warned that using "oversimplified, one-sided, crude and excessive practices such as those used in past movements . . . will cause artificial nervousness, affect the unity of the army, [and] cut us off from the masses."[49]

Despite these warnings, some stubbornly held out against winding down the campaign. One was the Shanghai *Liberation Daily,* which had been so active in the attacks on Bai Hua. Another was the *Beijing Daily,* the newspaper of the Beijing Party Committee that was run by former followers of the Gang of Four and sustained its Maoist reputation throughout most of the Deng era. Well into January 1984 the *Beijing Daily* continued to call for extending the anti–spiritual pollution campaign indefinitely. Zhou Yang's erstwhile disciples from the Mao era also persisted in Maoist-like attacks on writers for their depictions of the Cultural Revolution. In *Red Flag,* which continued to provide a platform for their attacks, they used Maoist slogans not only in literary matters but also on political issues. Lin Mohan even repeated slogans of the Cultural Revolution, such as "Without destruction, there cannot be establishment."[50] Liu Baiyu attacked those who called alienation a result of the "'strengthening' of the state apparatus by the party."[51] These Maoist critics were able to continue their attacks because of the tacit support of some elders and because Deng did not personally and publicly announce an end to the campaign.

Nevertheless, Hu Yaobang and Zhao Ziyang could never have reined in the campaign so quickly without Deng's support, which had shifted back to them in mid-November when the campaign proved to be disruptive to daily life. The campaign's duration was brief not because Deng disagreed with his elderly colleagues on the need for tighter ideological controls but because remaining Maoists and others had used it as an opportunity to obstruct the economic reforms. But deviating somewhat from his mentor, Hu Yaobang appeared to have wanted to stop the campaign for ideological as well as for economic reasons. One of his supporters, the economist Ma Hong, who became the president of the Academy of Social Sciences in late November 1983, had urged not only guarding against "rightist" trends, "but also guard against and resist interference from the 'left'" in the social sciences.[52] On a personal level, Hu seemed to agree with Wang Ruoshui about the existence of alienation under socialism. Hu's son Hu Deping borrowed a tape of a Wang speech on alienation that the Hu family was reported to have listened to sympathetically.[53]

Hu Qiaomu's speech at the Central Party School on January 3, 1984, brought the campaign to a formal conclusion.[54] The speech was published as a 40,000-word article in *Red Flag* on January 26 and in the *People's Daily* on January 27, and then reprinted as a booklet in 20 million copies, an indication of its authoritative nature. A group effort by scholars at Peking University, *Red Flag*, CASS, People's University, the Central Party School, and the *Liberation Army Daily*, the speech had taken three months to write. It went through four drafts and was discussed at a series of seminars. The final version reads as if it were written by a committee and is a relatively mild denunciation of alienation, despite the ferocity of the early stages of the campaign. Although Hu Qiaomu rejected the use of the concept of alienation in analyzing the problems of socialist society, he compromised on the concept of humanism. He accepted humanitarianism as an ethical value that was appropriate in times of emergencies such as floods and famines, though not as an overriding principle. He rejected humanism, which he identified with the bourgeois phase of history and individual rights.

Although the speech did not mention Wang Ruoshui by name, it was a direct attack on his views. His ideas were called ahistorical and classless because they supposedly applied bourgeois concepts to the present "proletarian" stage of history. To claim, as Wang and others did, that "man is the starting point of Marxism" was wrong, Hu asserted, because Marx did not use abstract concepts such as "man" and "human nature." Hu granted that there were hints of such an approach in the younger Marx, whom he said was influenced by idealism, but certainly not in the more mature Marx. Because Marx later discussed these concepts only in their social, historic, and class context, they could only exist in a capitalist system. Alienation, therefore, could not exist in a socialist system, where state ownership had replaced private ownership. Hu insisted that China's continuing lack of democracy, its personality cult, and its repressive bureaucracy were legacies of the old society, not the present one.

Wang Ruoshui was in the audience when Hu gave his speech and heard Hu urge those who disagreed with him to present their views. On January 12 Hu's secretary sent Wang a copy of Hu's speech, asking for comments. Initially Wang did not wish to reply. He knew that Document no. 3 of 1984 had called for study and discussion of Hu's speech and had urged those with "mistaken" ideas to make self-criticisms. But in late February the editor of *Philosophy Research* also asked Wang for a reply. He decided, after many sleepless nights and against the advice of his friends, to respond to Hu's criticisms, even though Hu had already organized a task force to counter his response. Wang's act was another unprecedented step. To refute publicly an authoritative statement of the party's chief theoretician had been unthinkable during the Mao era.

In his rebuttal, Wang charged that Hu Qiaomu's claim that Marxism and humanism were incompatible was a view of the Mao era which, after the Cultural Revolution, was no longer acceptable. Even though Hu had claimed that the party had already corrected its "leftist mistakes of disregarding the rights and interests of the people," Wang insisted that "we should also admit that this problem has not yet been completely solved . . . More efforts should be exerted to oppose those who do not admit the value of man." [55] Unlike Hu, Wang characterized these unresolved problems not as phenomena of the old society but rather as carryovers from the Mao period into the Deng era. He cited as an example the cadres' continuing persecution of intellectuals. Wang's antidote for this abuse of power was a restatement of his Marxist humanist view: "We should attach importance to the study of the Marxist theory of man which has been neglected for a long time." [56]

This article, originally written for *Philosophy Research,* was inadvertently published in the Hong Kong journal *Mirror* (Jing bao) in June 1984. Wang had sent out sixty copies of the manuscript for comments and suggestions and unknown to him, one of the copies was sent to the *Mirror*. Hu Qiaomu ordered an investigation, and on June 20, 1984, the editorial board of the *People's Daily*, Wang's unit, held a meeting at which he was severely criticized. Although Wang defended himself by explaining the circumstances of his article's publication, he was reprimanded. Wang's former wife, an actress, turned over evidence to Deng Liqun to be used against him. The criticisms of Wang at the June 20 meeting were then published in an internal bulletin of the *People's Daily*, which concluded that Wang had stirred up a controversy that undermined stability and unity and challenged the party and Deng Xiaoping.

Nevertheless, Wang was not totally ostracized as would have occurred under Mao. Shortly after his reprimand he married a twenty-five-year-old journalism student, Feng Yuan, who agreed wholeheartedly with his views. Although no one openly defended him or publicly protested the unjustness done to him, many sympathized with him. His supporters passively resisted by refusing to denounce him and by keeping in contact with him. Such acts had been rare in the Mao period. Wang no longer worked at the *People's Daily*, but he continued to receive his salary and had the use of a *People's Daily* car. After a short interval he was able to find other outlets for his articles. In January 1984 he published an article, "Pain of Wisdom," in *Youth Forum* (Qingnian luntan). Although its context was the Mao rather than the Deng period, it described in a very personal way his waning enthusiasm for the revolution: "I gradually discovered that reality was not as perfect and flawless as I imagined and that the new society had its maladies . . . I often had a feeling of oppressiveness." [57] Although his mentor Hu Jiwei, like Wang, lost his position at the *People's Daily* in late 1983, he continued as president of the Federation of Journalism Societies, and Hu Yaobang put him in charge of formulating the first law on journalism in the People's Republic.

Unlike the Bai Hua campaign, however, this campaign was not limited to a group of relatively unknown writers. In addition to Zhou Yang, Wang Ruoshui, and Hu Jiwei, other famous writers—Ba Jin, Xia Yan, and Wang Ruowang—were publicly criticized. Their works also were not published for a time. Ba Jin was criticized for his continuing objections to the party's interference in literary activities, his refusal to denounce modernist literary techniques, and his demands for a museum on the Cultural Revolution. Xia Yan was made a target not only because of his close association with Zhou Yang but because of his article, "Reply to a Letter of a Friend," carried in *Shanghai Literature* in early 1983. Xia expressed a dislike for modernism, but he cautioned that "by no means must we repeat the past practice of 'immediately responding to a call and rallying together to attack somebody or something.'"[58] Wang Ruowang's suggestion of "governing by inaction" was again denounced, this time as a retreat to Daoism.

But in contrast to what occurred in the Mao years, these targets of attack were able to withstand the party's pressure to recant, by turning in a superficial self-criticism, remaining silent, or counterattacking. They were supported by letters to the editorial departments of various newspapers and party organizations complaining about intimidation and expressing fears of another Cultural Revolution. Perhaps they were also emboldened by Wang Ruoshui's refusal to write a self-criticism and by the perfunctoriness of Zhou Yang's self-criticism. Possibly as a way to protect himself, Hu Yaobang had personally asked Zhou to recant, and Zhou's "comrades" at a meeting of the Central Advisory Commission sternly criticized him. Zhou's self-criticism, however, did not even refer to the issue of alienation that he had stressed in his Marx centennial speech. Instead he criticized the manner and timing of his remarks rather than their content. He granted that his speech at the centennial was inappropriate for such a "solemn" occasion. In addition, he said, his "paper was open to distortion and misuse by people with ulterior motives or anti-socialist sentiments."[59] But Zhou then explained that because of his own personal experience and that of party members during the Cultural Revolution, he felt strongly that "leftist" tendencies had caused alienation that could gravely endanger the revolutionary cause. "Being preoccupied with opposing 'Leftist' errors," he nevertheless acknowledged that he had underestimated "the serious effects caused by spiritual pollution."[60]

Those criticized in 1981 were criticized again. Bai Hua was reprimanded, this time for a new historical play, "The Story of King Goujian," which premiered to a full house in Beijing in March 1983. This work, depicting a once benevolent king who forgot the lessons of the past and indulged in imperious, despotic behavior, was seemingly a symbol for Mao or perhaps even for Deng. Even though Bai had ostensibly collected materials in order to write another self-criticism, he kept revising it and finally did not write one at all this time. Although Liu Binyan was not publicly singled out, he was again criticized behind closed doors. An indirect attack on Liu as well as Hu Jiwei was expressed in articles denouncing those who presumed to act as the spokesmen of the people. A *People's Daily* commentator article observed: "There are people who talk a lot about opposing 'saviors,' while actually regarding themselves as 'saviors' wiser than the people and the party."[61] Su Shaozhi's Marxist-Leninist Institute was threatened with closure. When his collaborator Feng Lanrui, who still had good contacts with the elder Bo Yibo, complained about this to Bo's wife, Bo responded that no institutes were to be closed during the party rectification. The institute remained open. Even between the reformers and the elders, connections *(guanxi)* still mattered.

The intellectuals who were denounced in this period not only retained the respect of their colleagues but were able, to a certain extent, to continue their work. Being singled out for attack in fact became a mark of honor, an even more significant difference from the Mao era. The regime's criticisms of the intellectuals, published in the party media, spread their ideas far beyond the academic or literary worlds to a broader and receptive public. A target of criticism was no longer shunned. Commented a *Guangming Daily* article, "People who are criticized often win sympathy and support."[62]

Nevertheless, as under Mao, some intellectuals still sought to "clarify" their positions in the hope that they could avoid attack. One of them was Wang Ruoshui's colleague Ru Xin, who wrote a very long self-criticism, published in the *People's Daily,* in which he repudiated his previous views on humanism in favor of those of Hu Qiaomu. Another colleague, Xing Bensi, director of the Institute of Philosophy and a vice president of CASS, who had also been in the original Zhou Yang group studying alienation in 1963, repudiated the concept of alienation early in the campaign[63] and became a member of the group who helped write Hu Qiaomu's definitive statement against humanism and alienation.

Even the avant-garde writer and former rightist Wang Meng denounced his literary colleagues who wrote about individualism, irrationalism, and decadence. Of himself, he said: "There was indeed a certain amount of smugness and complacency to be seen in my character . . . and I did not quickly or fully understand and recognize all the various erroneous ideological trends and manifestations of spiritual pollution that were present at the time."[64] The poet Zhang Kejia and the much-persecuted writer Ding Ling composed abject self-criticisms. They attacked their colleagues for their reluctance to face up to the spiritual pollution within themselves. Despite past persecution, their readiness to comply with every twist in the party line made these two writers objects of ridicule by their colleagues.

Yet most intellectuals refused to attack their colleagues publicly. *Red Flag* complained that it was "not easy to find support for practicing criticism." On the contrary, those who criticized were shunned. Such treatment was characterized as "in violation of party discipline."[65] The New China News Agency singled out the leading organs of CASS for failing to criticize the small number of people in their ranks who spread spiritual pollution.[66] The campaign against spiritual pollution thus had little elite, let alone mass, support. It was suspended after a short time not only because it was incompatible with the economic reforms but also because it could not be sustained without at least the cooperation of the colleagues or the officials in charge of those under attack.

By the spring of 1984, passive resistance turned into active resistance. Eight members of the literary and art section of the National Committee of the CPPCC, among them the popular playwright Wu Zuguang, submitted a motion at the May meeting criticizing the campaign and reminding the party of its promise never again to launch a political campaign against intellectuals. In June the last resisters to ending the campaign finally fell silent. Hu Yaobang and the reform leaders, with the help of their intellectual associates, appeared to have won the second drawn-out round in their struggle with the elders and their associates. They had blunted another countermove against opening up the cultural sphere, though doing so took longer and the forces arrayed against them seemed to have grown stronger since the effort to blunt the Bai Hua campaign. As the spiritual pollution campaign gradually faded away, a slow thaw began in the second half of 1984, creating a genial climate for future reforms.

6

Radical Revisions
of Ideology and
Political Procedures

The warming political atmosphere precipitated a variety of different
currents in the winter of 1984–85. Some currents were generated by
the reform leadership; others by members of the democratic elite,
pushing for more change than the reform leaders intended and provoking crosscurrent responses from the elders.

A new, more responsive relationship between intellectuals and the
party-state seemed possible. As their base of power became more secure, the reform leaders began to consult with the scientific and economic community on policy matters to a much greater degree. They
regarded the expertise of this community as crucial to economic modernization. Hu Qili, a member of the Secretariat, a protégé of Hu Yaobang, and, with a degree in mechanical engineering from Peking University, one of the few higher officials with a university education,
organized scholars and experts to advise on the urban reform program launched on October 20, 1984. These same experts were also
asked to explain the reform program to the public through the media.
Zhao Ziyang established a number of think tanks and sought advice
from the relatively young experts staffing them. The most influential
of these, established in 1984, was the Institute for Economic Structural Reform (Tigai Suo), headed by Zhao's agricultural policy advisor, Chen Yizi. In addition, intellectuals were for the first time encouraged to establish private consulting services, research institutes, and
schools. The state also announced its gradual withdrawal of financial
support from the Academy of Sciences and the Academy of Social
Sciences in the expectation that their institutes would become increasingly self-sufficient by establishing their own enterprises.

The party renewed its rectification in 1984. The reregistration of the party's 40 million members was one way of purging cadres who obstructed Deng's reforms. Hu Yaobang led an effort to replace older, less educated officials with younger, more professional cadres in the expectation that they would be less obstructive and more helpful to the reforms.[1] The party's Organization Department acknowledged that only 4 percent of party members had a college education.[2] The attempt to appoint younger, better-educated officials was not a new one: similar efforts had been carried out in periods of reform in Confucian China as well as in modern times. Nor did a generational change necessarily mean a fundamental change in making policy. Nevertheless, the call to put intellectuals in positions of leadership had the potential to produce structural change in the People's Republic. A *Guangming Daily* commentator article noted that in contrast to Confucian and Maoist China, when intellectuals were advisors but did not make decisions, at present "the four modernizations drive has pushed into leading posts intellectuals who . . . not only make suggestions and carry out decisions, but also have to make policy decisions and supervise and examine implementation."[3]

Su Shaozhi, since 1982 the head of the Marxist-Leninist Institute, and his disciple Ding Xueliang were forthright in their assertion that intellectuals had more to contribute to China's modernization than did party officials. Marx himself, they said, had emphasized the important role to be played by scientific intellectuals. And now that the world was moving into what the American sociologist Daniel Bell called the "post-industrial society" of advanced technology,[4] they insisted that "professionals and technicians . . . have replaced manual laborers and [play] a leading part in the labor force."[5] Because the party supposedly represented the proletariat, their analysis implied that it too would lose its leading role. They further charged that China's interpretation of Marxism-Leninism hindered the training of those who had the high levels of knowledge necessary for competing in the modern world. "Our present theoretical circle is found to be unsuitable to a certain extent for the development of the era of new technological revolution."[6]

Attacks on the "left" without balancing them with attacks on the "right" became more and more the norm. Even *Red Flag* charged that there had been insufficient acknowledgment of the harm wrought by the Cultural Revolution: "Certain comrades . . . are still bound . . .

by the 'leftist' trappings of the 'Great Cultural Revolution.'"[7] Instead of the usual criticism of "weakness and laxity" toward the "right," the *People's Daily,* again expressing the views of the reformers, declared in an April 1, 1984, commentary that "failure to face squarely 'left' influence . . . is an extremely serious weakness and laxity."[8] Based on a summary of a talk by Hu Yaobang, this commentary urged the eradication of leftism and shifted the attack, as in the late 1970s, from the right to leftist views. On May 17, 1984, Hu Yaobang met with army officers in the Shenyang Military Region and directed them to overcome leftism.[9] Shortly thereafter the army began to teach its troops more about the negative consequences of the Cultural Revolution.

With renewed discussion of the Cultural Revolution came renewed debate over the role of ideology, once more led by members of Hu Yaobang's network. Li Honglin explained that it was impossible to import Western technology and filter out the ideas that produced that technology. His statement implied that some of the Western spirit, the *ti,* as well as the Western function, the *yong,* was necessary for modernization. He pointed out that even if China again closed itself off from the outside world, the action would not "ensure the purity of our internal spiritual world. This is because there are not only the dirty things originally existing in our house but also those which enter through the cracks from the outside." China should open its doors even wider, not only to enhance its intellectual and cultural life, but also to reinvigorate Marxism.[10] Marxism needed to develop in an open atmosphere so that it could absorb a variety of views from many different sources.

As usual, discussion in academic journals went further than in the mainstream media in proposing radical reforms. Much attention, for example, was given to Western legal procedures, and several new journals dealing with the law appeared. An article in one of them, *Judiciary Quarterly* (Faxue jikan), emphasized the need to rely on laws rather than on policies. The policies of the party are changeable, but "once a law is formed it has a more extensive and stable application than that of the policies of the party both in scope and in time . . . It explicitly and concretely stipulates what the people should, can or cannot do."[11] Moreover, "the party must operate within the limits of the laws." When a contradiction exists between the party's policy and the law, "we must act in accordance with the law."[12]

In opposition to the Leninist view that the party was the state, the article stressed that the party was only one part of the state. "We must not totally equate the policies of the party with those of the state."[13] Furthermore, the party's policies could only become the will of the state and be enacted into law by going through democratic procedures. Not only did this article renew the discussion begun in 1980 concerning the separation of the party from both the government and the economy, but it also suggested a limited role for the party overall. The party "is not an organ of power for issuing orders to the masses, nor is it an executive or judicial organ."[14]

Renewed emphasis was put on strengthening the local people's congresses and the National People's Congress so that they would become more than merely rubber-stamp organizations. One method was to make them more truly representative at the local level. In a few areas—for example, in Shanxi—the candidates for the provincial party committee were nominated by the party committees at the county level, instead, as was usual, being imposed by the higher level. The only conditions set by the party were that the candidates be under sixty years old and have some higher education. Even though the final list of nominees had to be approved by the party, supposedly the central or provincial authorities intervened only at this point, and not earlier. The reform leaders may have allowed this new procedure not because of any commitment to grass-roots democracy but because of their desire for younger, better-educated party cadres in positions of leadership. Nevertheless, a People's Daily commentator article praised these reforms because they "fundamentally change the outmoded method of relying on the ideas of a small number of people in deciding the appointment of cadres."[15] Although those voting remained only leading party officials at the county level and above, the new procedures still gave them some practice in democratic methods of choosing from multiple candidates in a secret ballot.

Such political reforms as well as the move toward a market economy continued to impel efforts to revise orthodox ideology. A front-page commentator article in the People's Daily on December 7, 1984, entitled "Theory and Practice," reportedly based on a talk that Hu Yaobang had given to propaganda officials,[16] stated that Marx's "works were written more than 100 years ago. Some were his tentative ideas at that time, and things have changed greatly since then. Some of his tentative ideas were not necessarily very appropriate . . . We cannot expect the writings of Marx and Lenin of that time to provide solutions to our current problems."[17] The next day, in a partial retreat, "current problems" was corrected to read that Marx and Lenin could not solve "all of our current problems." Although the revision of the December 7 article indicated opposition to it, two weeks later another front-page commentator article in the *People's Daily,* "More on Theory and Practice," announced that Marxism could be not only irrelevant, but even harmful. Marx, for example, "predicted that commodities and money would be unnecessary under socialist conditions. However, the practice of China's socialist construction has proved that commodities and money are necessary for socialist society and that we must develop commodity production." The article called for wiping out "outdated ideas, customs and conventions" that "hinder[ed]" China's development.[18]

Both *People's Daily* commentator articles still referred to Marxism-Leninism as the "guiding force," indicating that the question was not over whether to retain Marxism-Leninism but over how to reinterpret it for a changing world. Yet the official ambiguity on the ideology's relevance and even its potential for harm made possible public debates on fundamental ideological questions and even experimentations with political procedures. The Fourth Congress of the Chinese Writers Association held in late 1984 and early 1985 became an arena for debate and experimentation.

Springtime in the Literary Realm

Literature, with ideology, remained a sensitive barometer of changes in the party's configuration of power and policy. As 1984 turned into 1985, the literary atmosphere shifted from a freeze to springtime even more abruptly than it did in ideology. The change in climate from early fall 1984 was a dramatic one. In September, without the knowledge of the Politburo or the Secretariat and under the pretext of preparing for the forthcoming congress of the Chinese Writers Association, associates of the elders convened a forum of fifty participants who were carefully selected for their orthodoxy. He Jingzhi, a deputy director of the Propaganda Department, delivered the opening address, in which he stressed the need to resume the anti-rightist and anti–spiritual pollution struggle in literary and art circles. Although he did not mention the playwright Wu Zuguang by name, in the second part of his address he criticized Wu for criticisms he had made of the spiritual pollution campaign while he was abroad. The elders were also angry with Wu and his literary associates for their condemnation of political campaigns at the May 1984 CPPCC meeting. Wu was charged with violating discipline in his behavior abroad, and legal sanctions were threatened against him.[19]

The Hong Kong journals reported that when Deng Xiaoping and Hu Yaobang heard about the forum and read He's opening address, they were enraged that the organizers had failed to report their real intentions to them.[20] Hu Yaobang then sent the Secretariat member Hu Qili to take charge. Hu Qili directed the drafting of the closing address, which was also read by He Jingzhi, but was quite different from his opening message. It stressed the need to struggle against the "left" instead of the right in literary circles.

Soon after the forum's conclusion, the literary climate began to warm. At an October meeting on writing about the urban reforms, the writer Yuan Ying praised the attack on leftism in the economic realm, but he pointed out that "to oppose 'leftism' in economics and oppose 'rightism' in literature and art" was "both illogical and unrealistic."[21] He described the literary atmosphere as one in which there were sudden changes from "fair to cloudy" and then from "cloudy to overcast."[22] Moreover, some comrades, he declared, exaggerated the functions of literature and art, claiming that they would negatively influence young people's view of life and morality. Whatever influences literature and art might have, Yuan Ying protested they could "certainly not reach the stage of 'ruining the party and the state' which we often played up in the past. No precedent can be found in the world of a nation coming to grief due to literature and art."[23] The publication of Yuan Ying's talk two months later in the *People's Daily* indicated that his views conformed to those of the reform leaders, particularly Hu Yaobang.

The Fourth Congress of the Chinese Writers Association, convened in the brightening atmosphere of late December, not only opened up a new era for the literary community but also made possible an ideological and political counterattack on the elders, their associates, and like-minded literary bureaucrats. On the same day the congress began, December 29, the New China News Agency called for the retirement of forty senior army officers to make way for younger, more technologically trained officers. Both these events signaled an intensified offensive against those resisting reforms. The eight-day congress of over

800 delegates was dominated by calls for creative freedom, expressed much more openly than at the Fourth Congress of ACFLAC, held in the fall of 1979. With Hu Yaobang sitting conspicuously behind him, Hu Qili opened the congress with a call for "freedom of literary and art creation," receiving thunderous applause. In criticism clearly directed against the elders' literary spokesmen, he urged an end to the persecution of controversial writers and the "leftist" practices of political interference, discrimination, and character assassination in the literary realm.

As in the past, however, even this direct offer of freedom to writers was qualified. Hu Qili explained that writers' work "must be compatible with the environment of freedom the party and the state [has] provided them." Writers can write freely so long as they "understand the interests of the state and the people, the laws of social development and changes and their own social responsibilities, and reject the pernicious influence of decadent capitalist thinking and feudalism."[24] Ideological constraints, therefore, could still be invoked against any writer venturing beyond the unclear parameters set by the party. As had virtually all Soviet and Chinese party leaders since Stalin, Hu Qili called writers the "engineers of the soul," which in the context of late 1984 meant that they were to help the reformers by depicting characters who championed reforms and by denouncing characters who obstructed reforms. Although Hu encouraged writers to write about anything they pleased, his speech stipulated that they provide a positive characterization of the reforms.

Just as they had in previous years when leaders offered a limited degree of freedom, writers attempted to push the limits as far as they could. A vice chairman of the Chinese Writers Association, the poet and literary critic from the 1930s Zhang Guangnian, pointed out that because of "leftist" influence, "many writers had been afraid of even mentioning the 'freedom' of creation."[25] He urged literary officials, critics, and editors to ensure writers' freedom. Several writers noted that even though similar calls for freedom and independence had been expressed by officials as well as by writers in 1979, an atmosphere of repression had virtually enveloped the entire literary community for the past five years. Some described the state of fear and psychological constraint they felt due to the attacks on Bai Hua and spiritual pollution, and recalled how they had tried to retrieve their manuscripts shortly after they sent them out for publication.

The writer Wang Meng delivered the concluding speech at the congress, an indication of his increasing official role. Even he, soon to become a member of the Central Committee, did not hesitate to depict a literary community seething with factionalism, intimidation, and retribution. He blamed this frightening atmosphere on "leftists" who used their official positions to repress others. "They are used to treating the problems in literary works . . . [as] equivalent to . . . 'enemy movements' and reporting them to upper level authorities in a secret . . . manner." He decried such meddling in the creative process: "When I think of . . . our competent and outstanding writers who are loved by their readers and are not in a position fully to use the splendid freedom of writing to do their writing with one heart and one mind, but have to use their precious time and energy to cope with interference and disruption, I really want to cry." [26]

The most electrifying speech of the congress was given by the playwright Wu Zuguang, who attacked the party's thirty years of persecution of writers. His thirty-minute speech, interrupted by applause twenty times, was not only a personal statement of his own persecution since the 1957 anti-rightist campaign but an expression of the bitterness felt by most writers. Wu had been deprived of an opportunity to publish for nearly three decades and had been sent to Heilongjiang for several years of harsh labor reform. His wife, the actress Xin Fengxia, had been repeatedly harassed because of her refusal to denounce him and had suffered permanent physical harm. Because of her lingering fears, she at first tried to prevent him from speaking at the congress; she relented only after Wu promised not to criticize anyone by name.

In an intensely emotional speech, Wu declared: "Although the freedom of creative work should be a normal phenomenon and a democratic right enjoyed by everyone, this is the first time it has been guaranteed in no uncertain terms by the party Central Committee in more than thirty years since liberation. This is the result for which we have gone through all kinds of hardships and difficulties, made enormous sacrifices and paid in blood and tears. Therefore, I want to especially express the deep grief I feel for the comrades and friends who have died with unrighted wrongs and uncleared of the false charges against them." [27] Despite the Central Committee guarantees, he pointed out, "the persecution we are subjected to has not stopped to this day." He described his own continuing persecution for having ridiculed the spiritual pollution campaign while in the United States, where he had said that "to eliminate atmospheric or river pollution, let alone ideological contamination," was "impossible."[28] It was this remark that had supposedly so infuriated Hu Qiaomu and Deng Liqun and caused them to have Wu investigated. Wu was greatly moved by Hu Qili's guarantee of freedom of creation, but his own experience made him fear it would not become a reality.

Wu was not alone. Although most of the speakers at the congress hailed the free atmosphere and the reform officials' offer of freedom, the older screenwriter Ke Ling, one of the friends to whom Ba Jin apologized for having denounced him during the Mao era, added that official promises were not enough; laws were needed to protect writers. He declared: "Fundamentally it is a matter of whether it is rule by law or rule by individuals. With regard to the rights and obligations of writers and artists there should be explicit and rational regulations to allow for individual achievements and shortcomings, rewards and penalties, . . . There should be laws to follow and regulations to base their work on. The aim is . . . to free them of bureaucratic restrictions." Ke Ling also implicitly criticized the use of censorship in his demands for copyright laws to protect writers from having their work cut or excerpted at will. He understood, however, that laws alone could not protect writers if officials did not enforce them: "Of course, even if there are laws to follow, problems of deviations in exercising the law may still emerge."[29]

The 1979 ACFLAC congress had also called for freedom to choose one's own theme and style, but at the 1984 congress these freedoms were stipulated in a new constitution for the Chinese Writers Association. Equally unusual, the new stipulations were debated and revised on the congress floor before they were adopted. In addition, the association, rather than the party, was designated as the institution that was to protect writers' freedom of creative writing, international exchanges, members' rights, and economic interests. The group's constitution, like the national constitution, was still subordinate to the party's policies and Marxism-Leninism, and therefore the party could simply ignore the constitution if it wished. Nevertheless, even if the association's guarantees did not in reality limit the actions of the party leadership, the writers now had their own constitution that they could cite to give legitimacy to their demands for freedom of expression.

Democratic Procedures

More unprecedented than the speeches and the revised constitution were the methods used at the Fourth Congress of the Chinese Writers Association to shift the balance of power in the leadership of the association. The use of a cultural forum for political purposes has been a time-honored practice in Confucian and Communist China as well as in other Communist countries; this congress was different in its use of democratic methods to carry out changes. Such novel procedures were due in part to the encouragement of Hu Yaobang, whose power was increasing in late 1984. At a meeting of the Secretariat just before the congress, with prompting from Xia Yan, Hu recommended that instead of the usual procedure, in which a small number of party officials determined the makeup of the association's leadership beforehand, the congress should elect their own leaders in democratic elections.[30] Wan Li, also at the Secretariat meeting, supported Hu's recommendation, arguing that since the association was supposedly a nongovernmental organization, the party should not interfere in its deliberations. Although Hu's recommendation for democratic procedures may have been primarily motivated by his efforts, as elsewhere, to replace older, politicized bureaucrats who obstructed reforms with younger professionals and artists who favored reforms, the effect was to initiate an embryonic democratic process in intellectual and professional organizations.

Writers used the opportunity to attack their persecutors as well as to remove literary bureaucrats. The democratic procedures began first with the elections to the association's council, consisting of about 220 members, who receive more privileges than ordinary members. Although an official list of nominees for the council was presented, the names of over 70 others were added by various delegations or by recommendations from the floor. In the end there were 292 candidates for 220 positions, giving association members a choice for the first time. Bai Hua was one of those not on the official slate who was added from the floor and then elected to the council. Bai had not even been on the original list of delegates designated by his army unit to attend the congress. But in another effort to break the dominance of the elders' literary bureaucrats, Hu Yaobang shortly before the congress ordered another, more open election of members of the various delegations to the congress. In the second round of elections, Bai Hua received the highest number of votes in his unit. By contrast, a Shanghai literary bureaucrat, Xia Zhengnong, who had persecuted Ba Jin and had been on the original list of delegates to the congress, failed to be elected and did not attend.[31]

Ba Jin, who had been criticized by Hu Qiaomu, Deng Liqun, and the Shanghai Propaganda Department under Chen Yi, was elected chairman of the Writers Association at the December congress by an overwhelming majority of its members. Just four months earlier, at the instigation of Deng Liqun and Hu Qiaomu, the Shanghai Federation of Literature and Art Circles had ousted Ba Jin as its chairman and replaced him with the bureaucrat Xia Zhengnong. A few outspoken writers such as Wang Ruowang and Sha Yexin protested, but Ba Jin was not reinstated. Soon after, however, the Shanghai cultural authorities were chastised for falling behind the rest of the country in cleaning out leftist influences. The *Literary Gazette* called such influences "deep-rooted," having been planted at the beginning of the Cultural Revolution.[32] Anything associated with the Cultural Revolution was now repudiated.

The most dramatic vote of the congress, however, was the unexpected election of Liu Binyan as a vice chairman of the association. Liu had been criticized behind closed doors during the Bai Hua and spiritual pollution campaigns and had been castigated in several newspapers for his investigative reporting. He had continued to work and had uncovered several cases of extensive bureaucratic corruption, but had been unable to publish them in the *People's Daily*, the unit to which he was attached. Although his name had not been included on the official list of candidates for vice chairman, he was nominated from the floor. In the election he came in second only to the revered Ba Jin in the number of votes received. The spontaneous support indicated the high regard in which Liu was held by his colleagues. Those on the party's official list who had participated in the spiritual pollution campaign, however, did not fare so well in the voting. Ouyang Shan, a well-known writer from Guangdong, was voted to the council but lost his position as a vice chairman, while another Guangdong writer whom Ouyang had criticized, Qin Mu, was voted in as a vice chairman. Similarly Liu Baiyu, who had participated actively in the campaign against Bai Hua, lost his position as a vice chairman, as did He Jingzhi.

In addition to winning a vice chairmanship, Liu Binyan used the relatively open forum of the congress to redress some of the injustices of the past few years. He attacked Huang Gang, one of the first writers to criticize Bai Hua's "Unrequited Love," as a "leftist." Liu argued that if Huang Gang could be a candidate for the council, then the reformist editor Mei Duo, who had not been on the original slate, should also be a candidate. Mei Duo was subsequently elected to the council; Huang Gang, who did not attend the congress, was not elected.

Bai Hua greeted the support he received from his colleagues and the defeat of his attackers with jubilation. In an article in the *People's Daily* at the time, he praised Hu Yaobang's understanding of the needs of writers. "How familiar he is with the current situation in the literary circles and with the writers' aspirations." He described conversations with colleagues on the telephone about the happenings at the congress: "Our voices quivered on the phone and we could not help holding back our joy and excitement."[33] In another article he described himself as "a man walking against the wind on a snow-covered plateau who suddenly comes upon a valley grown all over with flaming azalea flowers, and before whom the world suddenly turns gloriously bright."[34]

Bai Hua also quoted from a letter that he had earlier received from his son. It poignantly revealed, as had Wu Zuguang's description of his wife's opposition to his giving his speech, how devastating the party's campaigns had been to the families of the victims. His son had asked: "Papa, can't you change to some other way of life? Why do you think your mission in literature is so important?" Bai Hua replied: "Literature is my life . . . I cannot, my son, even though since the time of your birth you have suffered because of me, living in isolation, helplessness and fear, and I am very sorry." He admitted that "for the sake of spending my remaining years in peace, naturally I should give up my work, and we would then have a tranquil and comfortable home like others. But I cannot. Forgive me, my son." Just before the congress he had received another letter from his son, pleading: "Papa, don't speak, don't take a stand, don't show your feelings and don't write articles. Don't discuss anything, not even in private. Don't do it even if everybody else does, papa, for your sake and also for us. I know there are hundreds of thousands of people who understand your utter sincerity, but they cannot help you."

In his reply, Bai Hua acknowledged that his son's fears were the result of persecutions in the Deng era as well as under Mao. "Even today it is difficult for me to assure you and your mother that from now on the sky over our roof will always be bright and cloudless. That is an illusion I have naively cherished time and again in the past, and each time it has come to nothing." Yet, like his Confucian predecessors, he declared: "To change a formula of an absurd political concept, we may have to pay with many people's lives plus decades of precious time."[35] He believed that an enlightened political leadership would help in this endeavor; the congress, he noted, demonstrated that "the party Central Committee and Comrade Hu Yaobang have held our hands and crossed the bridge together with us."[36]

Whereas Bai Hua and Liu Binyan were conspicuous in their presence at the congress, Hu Qiaomu and Deng Liqun were conspicuous in their absence. When their telegrams of greetings to the congress were read aloud, there was dead silence. By contrast, when the telegram from the rehospitalized Zhou Yang, one of the targets of the spiritual pollution campaign, was read, there was an enthusiastic five minutes of applause.[37] Liu Binyan, Bai Hua, Wu Zuguang, and over 400 other writers at the congress signed a public letter to Zhou, expressing their appreciation and wishing him well. But Ding Ling, whom Zhou Yang had ruthlessly persecuted during the Mao era and who had initially evoked great sympathy when she was rehabilitated after twenty-two years in labor reform, was shunned at the congress because of her active participation in the spiritual pollution campaign. A number of prominent writers petitioned the Central Committee to rehabilitate Zhou Yang. The contrast between the positive attention paid to the targets of the spiritual pollution campaign and the negative reaction shown the attackers was blatant, and another way of expressing the preferences of the participants. The writers' behavior was exactly the opposite of what it had been during the Mao era. In the words of a China News Agency correspondent: "At the congress, the writers also exercised their democratic rights on many occasions, something which seldom happened in the past." They voted "in light of their own judgment and desires."[38] Both directly and indirectly they expressed their own preferences rather than those of the party.

Another unprecedented event was a press conference held at the conclusion of the congress, at which some of the participants spoke as freely as they had at the congress itself. Wang Meng used the occasion to emphasize the limited nature of their "freedom." He pointed out that one could not praise, for example, leftists such as Jiang Qing. Other writers, such as the deputy editor of the *Literary Gazette* and party secretary of the Writers Association, Tang Dacheng, pleaded for legal and constitutional guarantees in order to protect "writers from being jailed unjustly, as during the 1966–1976 'Cultural Revolution,'" unless they broke the law by inciting opposition to the government. He asserted that "differing views and artistic differences" did not "constitute a crime."[39]

Although these actions may have coincided with the wishes of the reform leadership at the time, other unprecedented actions of the congress participants must have been embarrassing, especially for Deng Xiaoping. One concerned the poet Ye Wenfu, who was not at the congress and whose work had not been published since Deng had specifically singled him out for criticism in 1981. In the past, no one had dared to inquire about a "nonperson" at a public meeting, especially one condemned by China's paramount leader. Yet during the proceedings delegates from two provinces publicly asked what had happened to Ye.

The events of the congress led some to believe that persecution had finally ended. The last surviving member of the "three-family village," the first target of the Cultural Revolution, Liao Mosha, wrote: "Nothing like that has ever happened at previous conferences, whether inside or outside the party, or in newspapers. What we are witnessing has no historical precedent."[40] Others, however, expressed anxiety amid their jubilation. The Manchurian writer Deng Youmei, who was elected a vice chairman, described the congress as bringing "spring in winter," and he acknowledged that the Deng years had provided a much better climate for creativity than the Mao era. But he also cautioned that one could not rely on the party's promises. "Whether it is possible to truly realize 'freedom of creation' depends mainly on the writers' own efforts."[41] He became another voice urging his colleagues to fight for their own freedom. The writer Chen Dengke expressed a similar unease. "Despite the repeated declaration of the party central leadership that no political movement will be carried out,"[42] campaigns had been staged every three or five years from the early 1950s to the present. "My God! Our writers and artists have been tortured by 'leftist' ideas for so many years and have been criticized by both violent and nonviolent means . . . [T]he residual influence of the ultra leftist ideas in the field of literature and art has not been thoroughly criticized and eliminated."[43]

In early 1985 other signs of spring appeared to allay these apprehensions. Two poems by Ye Wenfu were published in the February issue of *Poetry,* and a number of the obscure poets, including Shu Ting, Bei Dao, and Gu Cheng, were again published in literary journals. Even more auspicious were the plans made by other professional organizations to use election procedures similar to those used at the Writers Association congress. Liu Binyan predicted: "The democratic election of the leading organs of the Writers Association will have a far-reaching impact on the elections of the provincial, regional and municipal branches of the Federation of Literary and Art Circles." Yet he warned that "the extent of the real power of these democratically elected leadership corps is still a problem awaiting clarification."[44]

The impact of the writers' congress was felt far beyond the literary world. As news of the congress spread, demands for more autonomy and freedom in academic research, publication, and comment were heard from virtually all professional organizations. The journalists' and dramatists' associations wanted to use the new procedures of the Writers Association to elect their officials and protect their members. Hu Jiwei, president of the Federation of Journalism Societies, called for legislation to protect freedom of the press. A group of Hong Kong journalists with whom he visited in Shenzhen encouraged him to demand additional rights, an indication of the liberalizing impulses coming from Hong Kong. Subsequently, in the magazine *Journalist* (Xinwen jizhe), Hu called on the regime to define exactly what it meant when it charged that journalists "start[ed] rumors and divulge[d] secrets." Such vagueness about journalists' rights and actions, he asserted, hindered their ability to gather news freely.[45]

The climax of this period of liberalization came in March 1985 with the publication of Liu Binyan's "A Second Kind of Loyalty," whose title became a slogan describing the intellectuals' critical yet loyal stance vis-à-vis the party-state. In this investigative report Liu contrasted the loyalty of the party's icon Lei Feng, who unquestioningly carried out the party's and Mao's orders—"the first kind of loyalty"—with two protagonists who dissented from the party's and Mao's orders when their individual consciences led them to believe that the leadership's policies betrayed Communist ideals.[46] As Liu had done in his 1979 speech "The Call of the Times," the protagonists distinguished between loyalty to one's country, society, and ideals and loyalty to the party's leadership and shifting political line.

Because of the lack of an independent judiciary, people from all over the country told Liu of their grievances in the hope that his report on their case in the press would help them redress the injustices they had suffered. "A Second Kind of Loyalty" is an account of Chen Shizong, a mechanical engineer, and Ni Yuxian, a former soldier, who had sought Liu's help. Despite great personal risk, each in his own way had challenged policies he believed were harmful to the Chinese people. In the manner of their literati predecessors they had written "remonstrances" to party leaders, taking them to task for actions that diverged from their purported ideals. But whereas China's dynastic leaders occasionally responded positively to such entreaties, China's Communist leaders invariably punished the messenger.

Chen Shizong returned to China in 1963 after studying mechanical engineering in the Soviet Union and became upset at the leftist policies he found being carried out. He wrote letters to Mao and Khrushchev, urging both leaders to join together to reform their countries. Two months later he was jailed for breaking into the Soviet Embassy in order to deliver his letter to Khrushchev. In jail he wrote another letter, admonishing the party for fostering blind faith in Mao. When he was released after spending eight years in prison, he continued to remonstrate, this time against a case of injustice he observed in prison. A prisoner had been shot and left to die of his wounds for inadvertently walking across a security boundary. Chen worked tirelessly to win compensation for the prisoner's widow and child.

Like Chen, Ni Yuxian remonstrated with the leadership when he found that its policies conflicted with his ideological principles.[47] At the age of eighteen, he wrote to Mao, telling him that contrary to party propaganda, the destructiveness of the Great Leap Forward policy had been caused by man rather than by natural disasters. He suggested various agricultural reforms to alleviate the distress the leap had caused. Because of his impudence, he was discharged from the army and entered the Shanghai Maritime Academy, where during the Cultural Revolution he put up posters attacking associates of the Gang of Four. Using his own funds, he also published ten thousand copies of selected quotations from Lenin in order to demonstrate that Mao's ideas differed from orthodox Marxism-Leninism. Although he was expelled from the academy, he continued to protest against the Gang with posters urging that Deng Xiaoping be returned to power. He was imprisoned and sentenced to death a month after Deng returned to power. A letter of appeal he wrote to Ye Jianying from death row postponed his execution, and he was finally released with other political prisoners in 1979. When he returned to the Maritime Academy, he criticized its party branch secretary, who had been a Cultural Revolution activist and had persecuted many individuals and their families. Nevertheless, the branch secretary continued in his post. When Liu Binyan's report was published, the academy threatened to bring suit against Liu. Shortly thereafter, Ni went into exile in the United States.

Both of Liu's protagonists expressed themselves in the language and style of their literati predecessors. They professed loyalty to the government at the same time that they criticized the government's policies for leading the country to disaster. Even their idiom resonated with the moral indignation of their ancestors. Chen advised: "For the last time I give you most sincere advice . . . I think the Central Committee . . . has committed a series of serious mistakes, and among them are some mistakes in principle . . . The main one is the worship of the individual, or the cult of the individual." Then, specifically addressing Mao, he admonished: "You . . . do not permit others to criticize your shortcomings and mistakes. If there is some criticism on principle that is a little sharp, you immediately turn hostile and carry out ruthless struggles and attacks." Prophetically, he warned: "In the course of time, those around you who will be left will be a group of villains holding sway . . . I am extremely worried about the destiny of the party and the state. With feelings of utmost sincerity . . . I hope you will distance yourself from petty men and bring men of noble character close to yourself." To have a nation of "Lei Fengs," Chen pointed out, was dangerous: because Lei Feng is blindly obedient, he never says "no" to his superior's wrong decision.[48] Like their biographer Liu Binyan as well as their ancestors, Chen and Ni tried at great personal risk to persuade the leadership to reform its ways and to replace bad officials with officials of integrity, in the belief that such changes would resolve China's problems.

"A Second Kind of Loyalty" portrayed its two protagonists as independent characters whose courage in criticizing the leadership made them more genuine patriots than the Lei Fengs, whose acquiescence in their leaders' judgments reinforced the repressiveness of the system. Even when the political leadership did not correct injustices and continued their abuses, Liu believed that politically engaged individuals, as represented by Chen, Ni, and, for that matter, himself, must continue to speak for the abused and persecuted despite the personal risk involved.

Liu was criticized both at home and abroad for being too idealistic in expecting the party leadership to respond positively to such admonitions.[49] Men of independent conscience may have had an ameliorating influence in the Confucian era, but under Deng it was unlikely that individuals of courage and nobility would have any more success than Chen and Ni had had with Mao in persuading the leadership to mend its ways. Few of the protagonists in any of Liu's reports had been able to right wrongs; their efforts were more often punished than rewarded.

Liu's critics also charged that he focused only on local officials, not on the top leadership, and that he criticized only abuses, not the system itself. As was true of his protagonists, Liu's sense of responsibility to the government and his prophetic lone voice were very much in the traditional mode. In the mid-1980s he still hoped that political reform would come from more enlightened party leaders. Nevertheless his exposés, despite their limitations, were implied critiques of a leadership and a system that had allowed such abuses to occur and had failed to correct them. Moreover, in order to be published and read by the Chinese public, Liu found it necessary to temper his criticisms, especially after the launching of the 1981 and 1983 campaigns.

Even with self-imposed restraints, Liu had great difficulty in getting "A Second Kind of Loyalty" published. Only when He Jiadong, an editor at the Workers Publishing House—who in 1957 had been labeled a rightist for publishing a collection of Liu's reportage—established a new magazine, *Pioneer* (Kaituo), was Liu's piece published in March 1985. Shortly thereafter the magazine was banned, and He and his associates were removed from all their posts. He Jiadong was sent back to his native province; Liu himself encountered so much criticism that he threatened to stop writing altogether.

In April 1985 a cold political gust again withered the democratic sprouts that had budded at the Writers Association congress. The elders and their associates mobilized their forces to smother the fragile blossoms of winter.

An Uncertain Spring

Signs of an imminent storm had appeared even earlier in a tough speech against freedom of the press given by Hu Yaobang at a meeting of the Secretariat in February 1985. Under pressure from the elders, who were particularly disturbed by journalists' subsequent demands for the same freedom of expression granted to writers, Hu stated un-equivocally that there could be no freedom of the press—the press must be the "mouthpiece of the party."[50] It should present the "main-stream of socialist society," which he said was "bright." Although Hu acknowledged that China had a "seamy side," he described it as "non-essential."[51] The press should devote 80 percent of its space to positive stories and achievements and only 20 percent to negative stories and shortcomings.[52] Even the 20 percent was qualified, because it should not evoke "gloomy feelings."[53] Moreover, before reporting important news, journalists must seek permission from higher authorities. Hu strongly implied that only the party's view of the shortcomings in Chinese society was to be presented in the media.

Commenting on the widely heralded creative freedom granted at the writers' congress, Hu explained that writers and artists were dif-ferent from journalists. They were indirect, rather than direct, mouth-pieces of the party and less specifically involved in political issues. Writers could consequently write whatever they wanted in any style they wished, but, he warned, that did not mean their works would be published: "The editorial boards of our publications, papers, and publishing houses can also make a choice and have the right to decide whether or not to publish a work . . . [W]riters can never use their own freedom to deprive the editorial boards of freedom."[54]

Perhaps even more threatening to intellectuals was Hu's revival of the specter of another attack on spiritual pollution. Hu admitted that references to "eliminating" spiritual pollution had frightened people at home and abroad. Criticism should be handled more judiciously and with milder language than in the spiritual pollution campaign, Hu advised, so as not to frighten away China's foreign friends. But he insisted that "this certainly does not mean that there is anything wrong with the principle of opposing spiritual pollution, and still less does it mean that we need not resist . . . erosion caused by decadent and moribund exploiting-class ideas."[55] His words revealed not only his inadequate understanding of the concept of freedom of the press but also his inability to withstand pressure from the elders without the support of Deng.

Delivered in February, the speech remained an internal document until April, when Hu Qiaomu took advantage of Hu Yaobang's ab-sence abroad to have it published in the *People's Daily* without Hu's permission or revisions and despite the opposition of the director Qin Chuan. Its publication sparked a retightening of controls not only in journalism, but in the whole intellectual realm. Hu Qili's promise of creative freedom did not prevent persecution of writers and intellectuals any more effectively than statements in the past. Chen Yun was reported to have denounced Hu Qili's call for "creative freedom" as counter to party tradition.[56] The demands by other professional groups for the kind of democratic procedures used at the writers' conference, moreover, troubled Deng Xiaoping. In March 1985, at a science and technology conference, he again spoke of the need for compliance with party decisions, emphasizing: "We must have discipline as strong as iron and steel."[57] When the elders and their associates launched a counterattack, therefore, they had Deng's support. There were no political institutions or laws to guarantee the freedoms promised at the writers' congress.

The relatively open expression of views in late 1984 and early 1985 became noticeably reduced by April 1985. The democratic procedures used at the writers' congress were not allowed in other professional organizations and were not to be repeated at later congresses of the Writers Association. Other artistic professions were denied creative freedom. Even though the Secretariat member Xi Zhongxun had urged the delegates at the opening session of the Fourth Congress of Chinese Dramatists to "speak their minds freely,"[58] that did not occur. The dramatists' congress and a subsequent Chinese Film Artists Association meeting were marked not by elections but by confrontations between the elders' associates and the younger members, who proposed that those over sixty years of age not be allowed to hold leadership positions. The Fifth Congress of ACFLAC, originally scheduled for June 1985, did not take place, perhaps because the authorities feared that its participants too would demand the same democratic procedures and creative freedom offered at the writers' congress.

Hu Yaobang himself withdrew much of the freedom that he and his colleague Hu Qili had promised. In a speech given in April, he emphasized writers' responsibility to society. Although claiming he was reluctant to speak out because "anything said by our central comrades now is likely to stir up quite a big wind,"[59] he reaffirmed the past criticisms of "If I Were Real" and Bai Hua. Once again he defined writers, artists, journalists, and theorists as "engineers of the soul." While cautioning against closing China off from the outside world and treating those with dissident views harshly, he called for constant vigilance against foreign influences.

The elders' spokesmen, again becoming active, renewed their defense of orthodox Marxism-Leninism and reattacked their old targets. For once Hu Qiaomu and Deng Liqun enthusiastically praised and promoted a speech by Hu Yaobang—his February talk on journalism.[60] Deng Liqun resurrected the obedient model of Lei Feng, and Hu Qiaomu defined patriotism as the love of socialism and the party, the same symbols used during the Bai Hua campaign. In an article in *China Youth News,* Hu Qiaomu declared: "In today's China, communism not only conforms with patriotism, but is also the highest development of patriotism." He quoted Deng Xiaoping as asking: "How can we say that the motherland is an abstract concept? If we do not love the new socialist China under the leadership of the Communist Party, what should we love?"[61]

The elders themselves became increasingly active in mid-1985. They joined in renewed denunciations of spiritual pollution and bourgeois liberalization. Although at this time these terms were used primarily against party officials engaged in money-making schemes and selling pornography, particularly in South China, these "sins" were attributed to the Western values and ideas that had accompanied the import of Western technology and management. Bo Yibo warned party members to "guard against the growth of the psychology of worshiping foreign things and the ideology that everything foreign is good."[62] At a conference on party work style, Chen Yun declared: "Communist Party members should constantly bear in mind that we are working for socialist modernizations, not modernizations of another brand."[63]

With the return to orthodoxy, the elders' associates attacked several theorists associated with Hu Yaobang. Deng Liqun criticized Li Honglin, with whom he had worked during the Mao period. Li voluntarily transferred from the Academy of Social Sciences in Beijing to the Fujian branch in order to forestall his removal altogether. Yu Haocheng became another target. Yu still objected to the party practice of deciding on important cases before they were tried, and in a recent article, "Democracy, Rule of Law, and Socialism," he had argued that China could have no independent judiciary as long as its legal approach was based on class struggle, similar to the judicial system of the Soviet Union. Even more upsetting to the elders was his depiction in the Hong Kong paper *Mirror* of the party practice of incumbent leaders appointing their successors as "undemocratic." Yu was retired at age sixty from his position as chief editor of the Masses Publishing House. Nevertheless he soon became a vice president of the Society of Political Science and secretary general of the Chinese Law Society. Professional societies like these were nominally under the control of the party, but they were able to engage in relatively freer discussion and activities than the professional "federations" and "unions," which the party more tightly controlled.

In the seemingly golden aftermath of the writers' congress Liu Binyan had written that the time when writers "were subjected to persecution and exile [was] gone for good,"[64] but behind closed doors he too was again subjected to attack. The publication of excerpts from his diary during the congress in the *Wenhui Monthly* (Wenhui yuekan) was suspended, with the explanation that Liu was about to go abroad. Yet though he had been invited to visit West Germany, he was not given permission to leave. The Central Discipline Inspection Commission, headed by Chen Yun, sent a work team to the *People's Daily* to investigate charges that Liu's reports contained slander.

In September 1985 Liu was forced to write a self-criticism. Despite tremendous pressure, he used the opportunity to justify rather than condemn his works and actions. He admitted to some mistakes on unimportant matters, but he reaffirmed the validity of his investigative reporting. He cited the report of a previous work team, headed by Tang Dacheng, an editor of the *Literary Gazette*, sent by the Propaganda Department to see whether his depiction of corruption in Heilongjiang in *People or Monsters* was accurate. The report had concluded that the problem with Liu's piece was not that it was untruthful, but that it had been insufficiently thorough in exposing the corruption that persisted after the fall of the Gang of Four. Liu reiterated one of the conclusions of his exposés—that too many people still in power were holdovers from the Cultural Revolution who opposed the reform policies of the Deng regime. By contrast, he said of himself, "As I look back on my writing over the last six years, I feel that politically I have been in active support of the party line, principles, and policies implemented since the Third Plenum."[65] He revealed that comrades had advised him to stop writing in order to protect his family and himself from further attacks, but he declared that he could not. Over the past six years he had received over 40,000 letters and a constant stream of visitors seeking help in redressing injustices that the party had refused to handle. He asked, "As a citizen and a member of the Communist Party, not to mention a reporter and writer, can I sit back and do nothing?"[66]

Liu also rebutted the view of the press presented by Hu Yaobang in February. On the contrary, he said, the experience of the Mao years showed that if journalists had spoken with different voices rather than in the one official voice of the party, the Cultural Revolution might have been prevented. He rejected the criticism of his investigative reporting, asserting that the phenomena he exposed "have not only not abated or disappeared; rather, in the majority of cases, they are becoming more and more intense and rampant."[67] He suggested that the party could resolve its problems more effectively if, instead of sending in work teams, it allowed an independent judiciary and independent press. Furthermore, their relative independence would produce not only a more humane society but a more efficient economy. "While the legs of the economic reforms are very long, those of [reform in] politics and the legal system are very short, and the imbalance will eventually pose as an obstacle to the implementation of the economic reforms."[68]

Such a rebuttal, virtually impossible in the Mao era, was courageous even in 1985, but it seems to have had Hu Yaobang's indirect backing. In an interview with Lu Keng, the editor of the Hong Kong journal *The Masses* (Baixing), who had been imprisoned as a rightist for many years, Hu Yaobang again complained about the continuing ill-treatment of intellectuals and criticized some of his colleagues for not sufficiently updating their ideological views in light of changing times. He specifically criticized Hu Qiaomu for working "too long by the side of Chairman Mao and [having] failed to go down among the lower levels for a sufficiently long time—and he . . . knows too little about economics."[69] Hu Yaobang admitted that he too suffered from the same shortcomings. More important, he modified somewhat his earlier statement on the press. In reply to Lu Keng's criticism of his stated view that the press must be the party's mouthpiece, Hu quoted Liu Shaoqi's criticism of the press during the Great Leap Forward: "If the comrades of *People's Daily* had not exaggerated the situation at that time, our mistakes in the Great Leap Forward would not have been so serious."[70] Lu Keng then asked: "Why can't you allow other voices to speak?" To which Hu replied: "Yes, yes. Why not?"[71]

A Congenial Summer and Fall

By late summer, some members of Hu's network had recovered their voices. Hu Jiwei went so far as to refute Hu's February view of the press in the first issue of a new journal, *Journalist Bulletin* (Xinwen xuekan). The old rules of journalism used during the revolutionary period, Hu Jiwei asserted, were inappropriate in the present period of modernization, especially "the long-standing evil practice of . . . throwing one's weight on people who have different opinions."[72] Although he did not call directly for freedom of the press, Hu Jiwei ingeniously insisted that since journalism was a "branch of learning," it should be allowed the freedom of exploration accorded to academic subjects.[73] Hence, when attending journalists' seminars and writing in journals, "comrades holding different opinions should be able to air their views freely and to carry out comradely discussions on an equal basis." In these seminars there should be a free atmosphere in which participants could express a variety of viewpoints and, through free discussion and debate, "judge what is right and what is wrong."[74]

Another sign of a thaw was the retirement of some of the elders' spokesmen, principally Deng Liqun as director of the party's Propaganda Department in August 1985, though he remained active in the Secretariat, in charge of intellectual matters. Deng Liqun was replaced by Zhu Houze, a disciple of Hu Yaobang's from his Youth League days, who had become known for the reforms he carried out in the poor province of Guizhou when he became party secretary there in 1983. Zhu had spent fourteen years in political exile during the Mao years because he opposed class struggle. Like his mentor, he had used his exile to read extensively on a wide range of topics. As the new director of the Propaganda Department, he gradually helped create a congenial climate for the reemergence of Hu's intellectual network.

In the fall of 1985 younger, more professional directors took over some of the institutes at CASS. Among them were Yan Jiaqi, who at forty-three became the director of the Institute of Political Science, and Liu Zaifu, a Fujian-born literary critic who at forty-four became director of the Institute of Literature and the youngest of its 131 members.[75] Su Shaozhi had already replaced Yu Guangyuan in 1982 as head of the Marxist-Leninist Institute. Even more significant than their rise to such important positions was that they were elected by their peers instead of being appointed in the usual way by the party leadership.

Hu Yaobang and Wan Li also took a personal interest in fostering educational reform. Research institutes and universities were given more independence in their curriculum as well as their finances. As a consequence some universities discontinued classes in Marxism-Leninism because of student disinterest. Party organizations at a number of universities were limited to ideological and political activities, and several university administrators were appointed on the basis of academic merit and given more autonomy. One of the new administrators was the astrophysicist Fang Lizhi, appointed vice chancellor at the prestigious University of Science and Technology in Hefei, Anhui.

Interest in emulating the rigorous academic programs of China's Confucian cousins in East Asia was expressed at the National Education Conference in May 1985. Wan Li noted that Japan and Singapore, despite their lack of abundant natural resources, had developed their economies very quickly and successfully because of their emphasis on education. Confucian China too had understood the importance of learning, and yet "some comrades" were still totally unaware of the extreme importance of education.[76] The reform leaders also allowed a limited degree of religious practice. Zhao Fusan, a Christian and a vice president of CASS, categorically dismissed the Marxist view of religion as the opiate of the people. He praised China's cultural heritage, such as the Dunhuang grottoes, the Potala Palace in Lhasa, and the stone carvings of Datong, as being inspired by religion.[77]

In the latter half of 1985 several controversial figures returned to public life. Although Hu Yaobang had earlier criticized Sha Yexin's play "If I Were Real," at Hu's prompting Sha was admitted into the party in June 1985 and was made director of the Shanghai Art Theater. Sha's party membership in no way limited his outspokenness. In an interview with a Hong Kong magazine, he expressed his admiration for Liu Binyan's "A Second Kind of Loyalty," which was still being attacked at that time. In opposition to the party's criticism, he declared that he had much more respect for Liu's kind of loyalty than the slavish loyalty epitomized by Lei Feng. Sha insisted that Liu "loves the party and the people."[78]

Even more controversial was Sha's production of the play "Us" (Women). The play, written by Wang Peigong, a writer attached to the political department of the air force, is the story of seven young people, exiled to a rural village during the Cultural Revolution. "Us" portrays the increasing disillusionment and alienation of the Cultural Revolution generation. The seven are first shown being captivated by Mao's utopian vision, then being terrorized by its violence, and finally in the Deng period suffering from a sense of aimlessness and numbed feelings. The play went through a number of dress rehearsals, but was canceled in June 1985 by the political department of the air force, under whose auspices it was initially staged. The play's director was dismissed, and the work was criticized because it failed to show the revival of hope after the Cultural Revolution. The play's main characters, rather than overcoming their difficulties, all suffered lasting effects from their trauma, becoming alcoholic, suicidal, ill, or divorced. Such morally flawed protagonists were unusual in both traditional and socialist realist literature and stood in sharp contrast to the unreservedly positive Lei Feng image.

Nevertheless, shortly after its cancellation, Sha restaged the play at his Shanghai Art Theater, where it made a dramatic comeback in October 1985. The China Opera and Drama Society then raised special funds to produce it in Beijing, an indication that as theaters became more financially independent, they were able to stage controversial works. "Us" played to packed houses in Shanghai and Beijing, competing with the revival of several of the revolutionary operas of Jiang Qing, whose idealized heroes were the mirror images of the flawed protagonists of "Us." Yet despite the *People's Daily*'s characterization of the play as an important experiment in theater, it was canceled for a second time in Beijing in November, after pressure from the Beijing Party Committee, and was soon closed in Shanghai as well.

Another controversial work published in 1985, *Half of Man Is Woman*, was also enthusiastically received. This autobiographical novel by Zhang Xianliang relates the experiences of a political prisoner in a labor camp who loses control over his life, including his sex life, suggesting that political oppression emasculates its victims physically as well as mentally.[79] Even though in the end the hero regains his manhood, the novel provoked heated debates. Zhang Xianliang, born into a well-to-do family in Nanjing in 1936, had been labeled a rightist at the age of twenty-one for writing nonconformist poetry. He spent the next twenty years either in prison or in a labor camp in Ningxia, China's gulag. In an interview with a Hong Kong newspaper, he acknowledged that at first he had not questioned the party and believed that he was guilty of all the evils attributed to him during the anti-rightist campaign. But like Liu Binyan, when he discovered during the Great Leap Forward that the "heroic" peasants suffered from hunger as much as he did as a political prisoner, he began to wonder if the party might be "capable of error." [80]

Half of Man Is Woman is Zhang's most politically controversial work, but it was attacked not so much for its powerful indictment of the system's repression as for its open discussion of sex, a subject still avoided even in post-Mao literature. Several women writers criticized the treatment of women in the novel as sex objects. Another woman writer, however, Zhang Xinxin, called it a "serious piece of literature" that was "psychologically and physiologically accurate." [81] She was one of the few to touch on its political theme, describing it as an analysis of "the essence of surviving in an environment which distorts and changes the most basic, the most important human instincts." [82] This controversial work and others, though criticized, could thus be seriously discussed in the media. Such debate would have been impossible in the Mao era.

Also unprecedented was the return of the principal victims of previous campaigns to public life. Although Wang Ruoshui was no longer allowed to publish in the *People's Daily*, he began publishing again in other media outlets. His first article after the spiritual pollution campaign appeared in the *Workers Daily* on June 21, 1985. Many magazines and newspapers then asked him to write articles, and he was invited to participate in several symposia. He also taught a graduate course for editors and journalists at the Institute of Journalism at CASS. Most important, while the elders' spokesmen were reasserting an orthodox interpretation of Marxism-Leninism, in the summer of 1985 members of Hu Yaobang's network resumed arguing for the revision of Marxism-Leninism based on present-day realities. Again Wang as well as others articulated a humanist interpretation of Marxism.

Though he did not mention Hu Qiaomu by name, Wang's June 21 *Workers Daily* article countered Hu's treatise on humanism by explaining that the party's negative view of humanism had led to the Cultural Revolution, when "brutal acts in violation of humanism were commonplace." Despite Hu Qiaomu's seeming acceptance of "socialist humanitarianism," Wang protested that "we have not . . . criticized the viewpoints that call for the total negation of humanism." [83] Su Shaozhi and members of the Marxist-Leninist Institute again called for ideological pluralism. Su's associates Zhang Xianyang and Wang Guixiu, in an article in the *People's Daily,* claimed Marxism had become stagnant because it was not challenged by different opinions and because it was not allowed to be debated.[84]

Concomitantly, demands for academic freedom resumed. A Central Committee directive of March 19, 1985, setting up a Chinese Science Foundation, modeled on the National Science Foundation in the United States, stated: "Truly respecting scientists and engineers means guaranteeing them freedom of academic inquiry and discussion so that they can pursue truth fearlessly."[85] Although only the sciences, and not other disciplines, were specified as the beneficiary of this academic freedom, *Red Flag* now recommended that laws on freedom of publication be passed to guarantee the right of academic freedom stipulated in the constitution.[86] In May Ma Hong, CASS president, called for freedom of the social as well as of the natural sciences. Members of the democratic elite and others spoke out strongly for academic freedom in all areas of intellectual inquiry. Su Shaozhi declared in the *Wenhui News:* "So long as they do not defy the Constitution and law, all academic questions can be freely discussed, and the right to do this should be treated with respect and protected."[87]

Two Politically Charged Controversies

That two apparently academic controversies in 1985–86 were subsequently turned into political conflicts, however, seemed to reveal how little China had changed. Nevertheless, because the conflicts were not allowed to turn into full-scale political campaigns and were conducted as debates, they also indicated the extent to which China had changed.

An Economic Controversy: Ma Ding   The most controversial work on the subject of contemporary capitalism and Western economics was that of the scholar Ma Ding, who suggested that Western economic methods were more helpful to China's development than Marxist political-economic theory. Ma Ding, originally named Song Longxiang, was born into a peasant family in 1957. He graduated from the Philosophy Department at Nanjing University, but studied economics as an avocation and audited classes on the subject. With the help of a friend who was an editor, he published a four-page article, "Ten Major Changes in China's Study of Economics," on November 2, 1985, in the *Workers Daily*. He proposed that because Marx provided "no ready answers" for present-day problems and "never indulged in Utopian fantasies on future societies," China's economists "must free themselves from Marxist books, and should start not from dogmas but from vivid facts, and found a new branch of economics in building socialism." Moreover, since economics was not an ideology, "it should not simply and directly become an appendix or a mouthpiece and means of demonstration for the current economic policies." Until now, Ma Ding complained, China's economists' only task had been to justify prevailing economic policies, such as the rash decisions of the Great Leap Forward and the Cultural Revolution. They criticized capitalism, but did not objectively present ideas from the West that might be helpful to China, such as Keynes's theory of using fiscal and monetary policy to stimulate economic activity and the neoclassical economists' view of the regulatory role of the market. Nor did they use input-output analysis, linear programming, or other forms of measurement. They stressed qualitative analysis to the neglect of quantitative methods. Consequently, Ma Ding lamented, they were incapable of understanding the magnitude of China's problems and providing any solutions.[88] In addition, they made "'a fetish of gross national output,' while neglecting the quality of life."[89] Their knowledge of Marxist economics was of no help in devising "new methods of analysis" for new situations.

Initially Ma's article was warmly received. On December 19, however, an editorial in the New York Chinese-language newspaper *Central News* (Zhong bao), criticizing the article's "utilitarian approach and fawning on foreign theories," was relayed back to Beijing. The elders' spokesmen quoted from this editorial to attack not only Ma Ding's economic ideas but also the views expressed in the afterglow of the writers' congress. The atmosphere in late 1985 suddenly seemed as ominous as that in the spring.

Contributing to this darkening scene was a student demonstration at Peking University in September. Initially the authorities allowed the protest, because it was directed against Japanese goods and the homage paid to Japanese soldiers killed in the Sino-Japanese war by Japan's prime minister Yasuhiro Nakasone. But when, on September 18, the fifty-fourth anniversary of Japan's 1931 invasion of China, students began to march to Tiananmen Square and the demonstration spread to the People's and Qinghua universities in the Beijing area and to other cities as well, public security police stopped the demonstrators. The party's quick action was precipitated not only by the demonstration's rapid expansion to other schools and urban areas but by the students' further demands for freedom and democracy. Such developments revealed a network of student activism that must have alarmed the authorities. Hu Qili and others were sent to talk with the students and to persuade them to return to class. Another smaller demonstration of students from Xinjiang studying in Beijing called for an end to nuclear testing in their province. In contrast to the party's harsh response in 1976 and 1979, the party's response to the 1985 demonstrations was relatively moderate and nonviolent. The reform leaders used dialogue and persuasion to defuse the protests, and most students quietly returned to class.

Nevertheless, fearing that such demonstrations would ultimately undermine the party, the elders renewed their efforts to reassert ideological control. At a party conference that same month Chen Yun complained bitterly about the neglect of "spiritual civilization," by which he meant ideology and for which he held Hu Yaobang responsible. Once more he demanded that greater attention be given to ideological indoctrination. He also reiterated his view that China's economic plan ought to play a leading role and the market a subordinate role in the functioning of the economy. At this time Li Peng, the adopted son of Zhou Enlai and Deng Yingchao who had studied at the Moscow Electric Power Institute and was a disciple of the elders, was made a member of the Secretariat. It is within this context that Deng Liqun and Hu Qiaomu were able to organize an attack on the ideas of Ma Ding and, implicitly, on the reform leaders and the members of their think tanks, particularly the Institute for Economic Structural Reform, who held similar views. They arranged for a number of articles critical of Ma Ding's ideas to be published in the national media, including a reprinting of the critical *Central News* editorial by the New China News Agency on March 4, 1986, entitled "Marxist Economics Has Great Vitality."

On this occasion, however, Deng Liqun and Hu Qiaomu were unable to turn their attack into a campaign. If they had limited their criticism to the ideological and literary realms they might have been more effective, but their move into the economic realm, an area of utmost concern to Deng Xiaoping, made it possible for the reform leaders to counterattack, forcing the elders into a quick retreat. On a

Hu Qiaomu critique of Ma Ding, submitted to Zhao Ziyang, Zhao reportedly wrote: "Caution is required in criticizing theoretical liberalism."[90] Perhaps equally important in explaining the elders' retreat were the accusations of blatant corruption leveled at Hu Qiaomu's son at this time. The charges forced Hu Qiaomu into temporary silence, though he continued to appear at official functions. Hu Yaobang took an active role in prosecuting the cases of the children of high party officials charged with corruption, in the belief that party officials, like Confucian officials and their families, must set a high moral standard to be emulated by others. Yu Guangyuan simultaneously took an active role in countering Hu Qiaomu and Deng Liqun. When Hu Qiaomu called for attacks on Ma Ding at a March 2 forum of the Chinese Federation of Economic Societies, Yu retorted by lauding Ma Ding's article and praising the *Workers Daily* for publishing it. He urged that China study Western philosophy and economic theory as well as Western science and technology.

The rebuttal to the elders' critique of the Ma Ding article expanded into a general critique of China's emulation of the Soviet model of economic development. On April 2, Yu Guangyuan reiterated in the *Wenhui News* that Lenin did not provide appropriate methods and solutions for present-day economic problems: "Though Lenin made fairly specific studies of the socialist system after the victory of the revolution, as he lived in the transitional period, he had no contact with the special issues found in the period of socialist construction." Furthermore, Yu complained, while changes in the economy necessitated changes in the political realm, the ideology had not "expanded" to include those changes.[91] Even the *Liberation Army Daily* published an editorial on March 8, 1986, in support of Ma Ding's views, entitled "The Basic Theories of Marxism-Leninism May Be Developed." On April 7 the semiofficial *World Economic Herald* republished Ma Ding's article with an editorial note calling it "a good article, well worth reading,"[92] and on April 21 it ran a long interview with Ma Ding further explaining his views. The Propaganda Department held a forum on April 22, presided over by Zhu Houze, at which Ma Ding was defended and Zhu, echoing his mentor Hu Yaobang, urged bold explorations into ideological questions. Eight days later Hu Qili finally settled the six-month Ma Ding controversy by urging the rejection of ideological ideas that had proved obsolete. The efforts of the elders' spokesmen to launch a campaign had been thwarted.

A Literary Controversy: Liu Zaifu   As the debate over Ma Ding's views waned, another controversy rippled through the literary realm. Differing economic views could be genuinely debated under the Deng regime, but differing literary views more often led to a campaign. Beginning in 1986, however, genuine debates on literary questions also became possible. This change was in part due to the more open attitude of the Propaganda Department under Zhu Houze, with Hu Yaobang's clear support, and in part due to the greater willingness of writers, particularly those associated with the democratic elite, to protest publicly against arbitrary party interference.

Liu Zaifu, the newly elected director of the Institute of Literature, exemplified this boldness. He had been involved in earlier controversies, most recently in the campaign against spiritual pollution, when he, like Liu Binyan, had been criticized behind closed doors. He was attacked for urging writers to express their subjective views as opposed to the party's socialist realist view. In addition, Liu Zaifu had helped to introduce new literary theories from the West, such as semiotics, structuralism, deconstruction, and psychological analysis. Although he had published numerous articles on these subjects, the elders' literary associates directed their criticism at one of his internal speeches, which was attacked in a front-page article in the *Guangming Daily* on February 21, 1986. Liu Zaifu's name was not mentioned, but the article by Lin Mohan implicated Liu in asserting that a writer was "required to be a revolutionary . . . a writer cannot be allowed to be a humanitarian."[93]

This opening charge against Liu was followed by more powerful volleys, particularly from Chen Yong, another former Yan'an writer who continued to attack fellow authors. Although purged as a rightist in 1957, when Chen returned to public life in the Deng era he had become a member of the Secretariat's Policy Research Center under Deng Liqun. He published a 15,000-character critique of Liu Zaifu's ideas in the April 16, 1986, issue of *Red Flag*. A victim of Mao's policies, his thinking had nevertheless been shaped by Mao's ideas. Immediately after Chen's article appeared, *Red Flag* convened a forum specifically to criticize Liu's views. Unlike in the past, however, the proceedings of the forum were not reprinted in journals or newspapers. In addition Liu was defended in journal articles by a variety of people and was himself able to rebut the charges. With Zhu Houze's support, a commentator article in the *People's Daily* on May 12,

1986, "Support Exploration and Encourage Creativity," criticized Chen Yong's article without mentioning his name. On the same day, as if in coordination, Xu Jingchun, an editor of *Workers Daily,* called for an end to the attacks. With virtually the same words that had been used to dampen the criticism of Ma Ding, Xu said: "Prudence must be exercised in criticizing bourgeois liberalization in the theoretical field . . . What we need even more urgently is . . . to protect . . . those who are brave to explore."[94] At a Shanghai conference on cultural development on May 10 attended by both Beijing and Shanghai scholars, Liu Zaifu was warmly received. In his speech at the meeting, Liu explained that his emphasis on the writer's subjective conscience had been shaped by his experience in the Cultural Revolution, when his beloved teacher had been incarcerated in a cow pen and he himself had witnessed many deaths. This traumatic experience, he said, had made him aware of the importance of the individual and the need to reject class struggle.

The controversy over Liu Zaifu's views was more than a generational confrontation or one between an orthodox Marxist-Leninist and a revisionist view of literature. It was another round in the ongoing struggle between the elders and the reform leaders, particularly Hu Yaobang, who was again gaining ascendancy. Those associated with the elders were gradually eclipsed by members of Hu's network. Wu Zuqiang, for example, the younger brother of Wu Zuguang and the president of the Central Conservatory Institute, who was of a similar reformist persuasion, was appointed secretary of the party group in ACFLAC. As Hu Yaobang's network became dominant in the artistic-intellectual sphere in early 1986, the reform leaders moved to encourage wide-ranging public discussion of political reforms.

7

Beyond the Limits
of Discourse

If the first shoots of democracy in the People's Republic emerged in late 1978 and early 1979, then the second sprouting occurred in the spring of 1986. Blossoms appeared in the summer and fall, as public discourse flourished on the reform of political institutions. This blooming was due in part to the congenial political climate created by the reform leaders and in part to seeds the democratic elite had planted earlier. Once again, however, this combination produced a greater variety and brighter colors than the reform leaders anticipated. The flowering environment nurtured large-scale student demonstrations in late 1986, which the elders and their associates then used as an excuse to crack down on Hu Yaobang and members of the democratic elite whom they charged with inciting the demonstrations.

The congenial climate was fostered not only by the ascendancy of Hu Yaobang, his network, and its associates but also by Deng Xiaoping's renewed desire for administrative reform in the spring of 1986. Although the family responsibility system in the countryside had encountered resistance from both local officials and the central bureaucracy, the peasants' enthusiasm for the rural reforms literally overwhelmed the opposition. By contrast, the urban economic reforms, introduced in 1984, had no comparable appeal to the urban population. As China moved to a market economy, the incomes of workers and bureaucrats on relatively fixed salaries could not keep pace with the growing incomes of the burgeoning urban and rural entrepreneurial class. China's bureaucrats, especially those in state industries, either ignored or blocked the reforms and/or used them for their own selfish and corrupt purposes. Despite the rectification of party members that had been under way for nearly three years, there had been little improvement in their work style.

Like Gorbachev in the Soviet Union, the reform leaders thus concluded that party bureaucrats, because of their vested interests and orthodox ideology, were hindering the economic reforms. In April 1986 Deng Xiaoping gave a speech at the National Conference of Provincial Governors in which he reiterated his views of August 1980, calling for reform of the political structure in an effort to eliminate bureaucratic obstruction and corruption. In another speech on June 20 he attributed these "evils" to the political system itself. During the summer of 1986 his August 18, 1980, speech was also republished, this time including the section on reform of the workplace, left out of the 1983 printing. But whereas in 1980 he had focused on the need for fundamental changes in the political system, in 1986 he stressed the need to reduce the bureaucracy and to make it more efficient in carrying out economic reforms. Deng's 1986 emphasis was on separating the party from the government and the economy in order to avoid overlapping and to lessen bureaucratic interference.

Despite the more limited nature of his 1986 concerns, Deng's renewed focus on administrative reform prompted a broad, wide-ranging discussion of political reform. In addition, Hu Yaobang was reported to have called in early 1986 for a more relaxed, tolerant, and generous intellectual atmosphere. Even though Deng and the reform leaders had been urging intellectuals since the late 1970s to provide advice to the leadership, their counsel had been limited to professional and technical questions. But at a cultural strategy meeting in Shanghai in the spring of 1986 Hu Qili called upon writers, social scientists, and scientists to go much further. He encouraged them to conduct systematic studies of major theoretical issues and policies that would help party decision making, and he implied that their advice could be more than technical.

Once more Hu Qili tried to reassure intellectuals that they would not be punished, as they had been in the past, for expressing views that differed from those of the party. He promised: "We will not launch any mass movements, resort to big sticks, stick political labels on people, nor make people the targets of criticism or attack."[1] He quoted Hu Yaobang as having said that the political campaigns of the past against Wang Shiwei, Hu Feng, and the "three-family village" had been counterproductive, concluding: "This kind of abominable behavior should never be repeated."[2] Intellectuals were again portrayed as loving their motherland, even when they were persecuted. Hu Feng, who had been punished for his dissent in 1955 with almost twenty-five years of imprisonment, had finally been rehabilitated in 1982. He was depicted as exemplifying the kind of loyal yet critical intellectual that China needed.

At the same time Hu Yaobang further consolidated his power base, appointing members of his Youth League group to important positions both in the provinces and at the center. In the cultural realm, besides replacing Deng Liqun in July 1985 as director of the Propaganda Department with Zhu Houze, he also appointed a genuine writer, Wang Meng, as minister of culture in June 1986. Wang Meng had been a member of the CYL in 1956 when he had written his controversial story "Newcomer in the Organization Department," which sparked the Hundred Flowers attack on repressive bureaucrats. Though he conformed to the party line during the spiritual pollution campaign, in 1986 Wang expressed views similar to those of Wang Ruowang on the desirability of noninterference in the cultural realm. When asked in an interview about establishing an appropriate atmosphere for artistic creation, Wang Meng responded: "It is best to refrain from making conclusions in the name of the government or party organizations." Party officials could participate in discussions on their own behalf, but should not act as judges. Their role was to provide "an environment and atmosphere so that all those involved may explore the questions with 'fair-play.'"[3]

In addition to putting more open-minded officials into important positions in the cultural hierarchy, Hu Yaobang himself publicly urged learning from the West's "essence" as well as from its "technology," implicitly rejecting the ti–yong dichotomy of his mentor Deng and the elders. On a trip to Western Europe in June 1986 Hu reportedly said to a member of the Italian Communist Party that "outdated" Marxist theories must be rejected and that China must incorporate the latest achievements of all humanity.[4] While in Great Britain he quoted Montesquieu, saying, "Liberty means doing anything permitted by law," and declared elsewhere that "we should not arbitrarily or wantonly regard various opinions and arguments as 'bourgeois liberalization' or 'opposing the four basic principles.'"[5] When he returned to China at the end of June, Hu was quoted as telling the Politburo Standing Committee that China "should act not only by relying on . . . party policies but also according to law."[6] Even before this, in mid-1985 Hu had also been instrumental in organizing a series of seminars on the rule of law for high-level officials and encouraging the general public to learn about law.

Wan Li's closing speech at the National Forum of the State Science and Technology Commission on Research in the Soft Sciences, held in Beijing in late July, gave the biggest impetus to the discussion of political reform. This speech, written by Wu Mingyu, a participant in the theory conference, and others,[7] was the most specific and direct call to date for intellectuals to participate in politics. Born in 1916 in Shandong and a party member since 1936, Wan Li had been persecuted during the Cultural Revolution, but in 1977 he had become first party secretary of Anhui Province, where he carried out the first experiments with the family responsibility system and decollectivization. He was elected to the Central Committee at the Eleventh Party Congress and became a member of the Politburo and the Secretariat at the Twelfth Party Congress. His speech at the forum called for policymaking based on scientific and democratic procedures. He charged that China's previous policymaking procedures were unsound because they were based only on the knowledge, experience, and wishes of the leaders, who had formulated such ill-conceived policies as the Great Leap Forward and the Cultural Revolution. He recommended, therefore, the use of the soft sciences—systems engineering, operations research, information theory, cybernetics, computers, and related technologies—to provide policymakers with feasibility studies, plans, and forecasts about present and emerging problems. Zhao Ziyang's efforts in the early 1980s to establish think tanks and to encourage their staffs to make more scientific analyses and forecasts had been a start in this direction.

Although these "scientific" procedures were not democratic, they revealed that the reform leaders no longer wanted to rely on the arbitrary judgments and outdated experiences of party leaders and cadres. Wan Li complained: "Today, the practice of blind and rash policymaking by some leaders based on their personal experience [is] still quite common and widely accepted."[8] Advisors should be allowed to differ and even to criticize; therefore, "only a high degree of political democracy can encourage people to speak freely, frankly, and vehemently." He thus recommended that China "make use of the legislative means to provide legal protection for policy researchers, so as to gradually turn the policy-making procedure into a rational system."[9] Although Wan Li seemed to be granting freedom of expression guaranteed by law on political matters as well as academic matters, his proposals were intended solely for the intellectual elite, primarily the "policy researchers."

At one point in his speech Wan Li digressed from his prepared text and mentioned that he had read Liu Binyan's "A Second Kind of Loyalty." His reaction was favorable: "Our party requires a 'second type of loyalty' in the present situation of reform."[10] After the speech Wan Li invited Liu Binyan to his office, where he expressed his personal agreement with Liu's view that the party needed "a second kind of loyalty." He also concurred with Liu's view that if the party did not listen to criticism and accept the "masses' supervision," it would fall from power.[11]

In addition to their speeches encouraging criticism and political comment, the reform officials organized groups of younger officials to discuss and explore various methods for implementing reforms. A group within the Secretariat, headed by Hu Qili, assisted by Wang Zhaoguo, another member of the Secretariat; Zhu Houze; and Xiang Nan, previous party secretary of Fujian—all former members of the Youth League and protégés of Hu Yaobang—also explored new political approaches.

The Response of the Democratic Elite

Even before Wan Li had urged intellectuals to become involved with political issues, the democratic elite had already begun to do so in the spring of 1986 at forums celebrating the thirtieth anniversary of the Hundred Flowers. The speeches given at these forums, convened by the institutes of CASS and professional organizations, were published in a steady stream in the party's major newspapers and journals. Members of the democratic elite argued that freedom of expression could not be limited to just professional and scholarly matters, but must be extended to political questions as well. They opposed the party's official policy, as expressed by the editor-in-chief of the *Guangming Daily*, Su Shuangbi, that "academic and political problems belong to different categories, and the overwhelming majority of academic problems can be differentiated from political ones."[12] But as Guo Luoji and Li Shu had stated earlier, the democratic elite retorted that freedom of expression in academia demanded freedom of expression in politics. Because the blooming and contending in Mao's hundred flowers had evoked political repression, they asserted that a genuine hundred flowers in academia was only possible with the establishment of laws and political institutions to protect those who spoke out. Yu Haocheng, for example, explained that the hundred flowers policy was never truly implemented because "there was not enough political democracy." Therefore it was necessary that freedom of creation and academic expression be guaranteed by law.[13] At forums sponsored by organizations associated with the democratic elite this theme was repeated over and over again in 1986.

Even a public forum sponsored by the *Xinhua Daily* made a similar argument. While acknowledging that the spirit of relaxation and tolerance was a form of progress, one of the participants pointed out that "practical experience shows us that a relaxed environment which hinges only on the leaders' tolerant spirit is unstable."[14] But if the exercise of democratic rights is guaranteed by specific laws, then "individual leaders, whether they are tolerant or not, cannot use their powers to impose their personal will on others."[15]

At other forums, participants cited examples of intellectuals in China's recent past whom party leaders had persecuted for offering constructive advice. Those most often mentioned were the late Ma Yinchu, the former president of Peking University, who had warned in the late 1950s of an impending population explosion and had called for birth control measures, and Sun Yefang, an economist, who had advocated the use of material incentives in the early 1960s. If these intellectuals had been legally protected, they might not have been silenced, it was argued, and China might have avoided its huge population increase, the drastic declines in production, and the 30 million deaths of the Great Leap Forward. "Special Commentaries" in the national party newspapers called for new laws to make the rights stipulated in the constitution a reality. They urged the formulation of laws to protect journalists, publishers, inventors, academics, and cultural associations and the establishment of institutions to guarantee that the laws were implemented.[16]

In opposition to the orthodox view of the press as the mouthpiece of the party, the *Workers Daily* exhorted the media to become a forum for debate and criticism.[17] By the summer of 1986, its recommendations were becoming reality. From August 9 to 15, at a forum in Har-

bin of thirty chief editors of provincial newspapers convened by the
Propaganda Department, several editors even suggested the establishment of "civilian" *(minban),* or nonofficial, newspapers that would
exist alongside the official newspapers. Although Teng Teng, a deputy
director of the Propaganda Department, rejected this suggestion, he
declared that editors, and not party committees, should decide on a
newspaper's content. Moreover, despite Teng Teng's rejection, several
other editors at the forum proposed that the All-China Federation of
Trade Unions, the Youth League, the Women's Federation, and the
professional organizations establish their own independent newspapers.[18]

Hu Jiwei's effort to draft a journalism law, which had been suspended in 1985 after Hu Yaobang's orthodox statement on the press,
was revived in mid-1986. His goal was to formulate a legal code that
would protect the rights of journalists and editors. He praised a journal in the Shekou special economic zone for having the courage to
criticize one of the zone's top officials by name. Others praised the
pluralism of the Western media. Challenging the orthodox party view
of Western journalism as monopolized by capitalists, several articles
noted that the Western media were run by myriad interests. Thomas
Jefferson was hailed for demanding that a free press be made a
"fourth power," in addition to the powers of the executive, legislature, and judiciary. Even Marx was quoted as having said that "without freedom of publication, all other freedoms would be just an illusion."[19] In a country where the rule of law had long been held in
contempt, said a former editor, "it seems all the more necessary to
define freedom of the press by special legislation."[20]

Demands for Political and Institutional Reform

The blooming of mid-1986 differed from previous bloomings in its
emphasis on institutional change. Ideological injunctions and rectifi-
cations, it was repeatedly explained, had been unable to curb the
abuse of political power. One journal published by the Marxist-
Leninist Institute observed: "Our several anti-bureaucratism movements in the past were largely ineffective precisely because we failed
to reform the underlying leadership system. Instead, what we usually
did was to oppose bureaucratism with bureaucratic methods."[21] Taking Deng's August 1980 speech as their reference, members of the

democratic elite not only called for the establishment of intraparty democracy as suggested by Su Shaozhi and his disciples, but also called for the establishment of external restraints on the party's power as recommended by Yan Jiaqi and his associates in the Institute of Political Science. The existing political system was described in a social science journal as "a machine without a brake and the machine cannot function properly."[22] The traditional methods of ideological reform, internal supervision through rectification, and disciplinary inspection committees were regarded as ineffective and even counterproductive, because they increased rather than diminished the party's and the bureaucracy's control.

Because the democratic elite believed that democratic institutions could only take root in China by building on existing institutions, they continued to work to strengthen the people's congresses and the National People's Congress in order to limit the overconcentration of power. They proposed extending direct and competitive elections from the local and county levels all the way up to the NPC, as a way of making deputies truly answerable to their constituents. Candidates would conduct political campaigns, present platforms, and provide information on their qualifications. Such methods had already been used in some of the 1980 local elections.

Yan Jiaqi played a pivotal role in the discussions of external restraints. His book *A History of the Ten-Year Cultural Revolution*, written with his wife Gao Gao, a medical doctor at CASS, chronicled the harm caused by unlimited power. After the book had been published, Deng Liqun had prevented it from being distributed until Hu Yaobang gave his approval. Hu commented: "I have not read the book, but everyone has the right to write on the Cultural Revolution." Finally, in December 1986, half a million copies were put into circulation.[23] In addition to reiterating his previous views on limited terms of office and strengthening the people's congresses and the NPC,[24] Yan in 1986 emphasized the need for the "division of powers" and "restricting power with power." These concepts increasingly became articles of faith for Yan.

In several essays and speeches he acknowledged that the use of institutions to check power was contrary to China's traditional culture, because to do so implied that the people running the government, including the ruler, were not necessarily "good" and, indeed, might be "bad." Yan explained: "According to Mencius, 'with an upright ruler in power, national stability is assured' . . . Successive generations of rulers also advocated 'benevolent rule.' All of them pinned their hopes for national prosperity on the emergence of . . . 'honest officials' and 'enlightened monarchs' as if once 'virtuous' rulers came to power they . . . [would] promote their [the people's] welfare and deliver them from danger."[25] But the Cultural Revolution, Yan pointed out, had made the Chinese people realize that they could not rely on their leaders' good intentions. Consequently it was necessary to establish "a web of rules, regulations, institutions, laws, morals, public opinion, and conventions" to check the abuses of officials.[26]

New political concepts as well as new institutions, Yan argued, were needed to prevent the traumas of the past. Indirectly attacking the elders in a speech at a conference in Guangzhou in early September, he compared them to the nineteenth-century self-strengtheners, whose efforts to combine Western technology with the prevailing orthodox ideology had proved unworkable. Those "defending the purity of Marxism," he said, were refurbishing the doctrine of "Chinese learning for the essential principles, Western learning for practical applications."[27] But Yan insisted that there were many valuable Western concepts that came neither from Marx nor from Engels that could help present-day China. He urged a comparative study of political structures in order to adopt the one most suitable for China. In addition to the division of powers, he cited the Western concept of the right to do anything that is allowed by the law, praised by Hu Yaobang while in England.

Yan also referred to relevant concepts from traditional China, such as Mencius' dictum that the people should overthrow any leader who ruled inhumanely. He cautioned, however, that in the past the people "either rose to oppose 'corrupt officials' and 'tyrants' or looked forward to 'honest and upright officials' and 'enlightened monarchs.'"[28] There was nothing in between. Another traditional source of inspiration was the Ming thinker Huang Zongxi, who had criticized the Chinese autocratic political structure and had even suggested some form of institutional reform. But most literati, Yan lamented, emphasized only standards of behavior as a means to limit power abuses. Yet because "supreme power under the traditional political structure was unlimited, the rulers could not possibly voluntarily, conscientiously, and strictly restrain themselves." Therefore Yan insisted that institutions be established to limit the power of political leaders as had been done in the West. He quoted from the *Federalist Papers:* "If men were angels, there would be no need to establish a government."[29]

In an interview a month later, Yan also called for the greater participation of society in the policymaking process, based on "predetermined procedures." He rejected the elders' often-stated belief that the general level of education in China was too low for the people to practice democracy. "If there were people prior to the Cultural Revolution, who discussed political reform, democracy, separation of power and checks and balances," he asserted, "even if the Cultural Revolution did occur, it would not have reached such a tragic extent."[30] Limiting officials' terms of office, stipulated in the 1982 constitution, was a step in the right direction, but this had not been actually carried out. Strengthening the people's congresses so that the people would participate more directly in policymaking was also a way to begin checking power with power, but he complained that the nominating process and elections for deputies had not been fairly implemented. Moreover, "today it is still out of the question for the NPC to be the supreme organ of state power. All power is concentrated in the party's leading stratum. Therefore, before discussing the separation of the three powers, we must first solve the issue of how to make the NPC the supreme power organ."[31] His hope was to convert the National People's Congress into a parliamentary body, as Gorbachev was to do in 1989 with the Supreme Soviet.

While the democratic elite talked about strengthening the National People's Congress, the irony is that under the chairmanship of the elder Peng Zhen, the NPC had actually become much less of a rubber-stamp body than it had been. Peng Zhen's use of the NPC to limit the power of the reform officials who dominated the Politburo Standing Committee and the Secretariat can be seen in the NPC's handling of a bankruptcy law formulated by Cao Siyuan, a former student of Yu Guangyuan and Su Shaozhi. Even though Zhao Ziyang and Hu Yaobang had wanted the law passed at the meeting of the NPC Standing Committee on September 5, 1986, the committee, after heated debate, concluded that the conditions for implementing the law were not yet suitable.[32] Peng Zhen proposed holding off the decision until there were further investigations of its impact. Although Peng Zhen's efforts were meant to counter the reform officials, as an indirect consequence the NPC no longer automatically approved the directives of the party's top leaders.

The democratic elite in 1986 also advocated the formulation of a civil code to protect citizens against official abuses. Yu Haocheng launched a discussion of Western concepts of civil law based on the use of law to protect rather than to punish members of society. He also recommended other radical divergences from both Chinese dynastic and Leninist legal practice. In a *People's Daily* article he observed that the theory of "innocent until proven guilty" was alien to China's criminal procedures and still remained a "forbidden area in legal studies."[33] He also advocated another relatively unknown practice in China: "People should have the right to sue the government if it violates their legal rights." Although he knew that to many cadres this concept was "mind-boggling," he pressed them to "abandon the notion that the purpose of the law is only to limit, control and punish the common people."[34] He called for an independent judiciary, asking, "How can lawyers represent people against the government, or business enterprises against the government, if as 'state cadres' they can only speak for the state?"[35]

In another sharp break from Chinese dynastic tradition, from Leninist practice, and even from the May Fourth definition of democracy as rule by the people, Yu urged that the minority be allowed to continue to state its views publicly even after the majority had made a decision. "When discussing democratic principles in the past, we often mentioned only the minority submitting to the majority, but seldom another important principle, namely, respect for the right of the minority to express and reserve its own views."[36] Paraphrasing Voltaire, Yu declared that a true democratic spirit meant: "I disagree with your view, but I am willing to struggle to the end to defend your right to express it."[37] He and others stressed that the stipulations in the constitution guaranteeing such democratic rights were meaningless, because they had not been accompanied by specific laws for implementation.

In addition to discussing "new" concepts of law and democracy, Yu and his associates began to rethink their own role vis-à-vis the party-state. By 1986 Yu rejected the assumption, both traditional and Leninist, that government leaders, intellectuals, or a small elite knew what the people wanted or could speak in the name of the people. In his view the party slogan "Serving the people" was a "kind of bestowed favor," which was the equivalent of "making decisions for the people" or "taking responsibility for the people." Because of this paternalism, "the people are not placed in the position of being masters of the nation, nor are their democratic rights regarded above all else."[38] Institutions needed to be established that would allow the people to speak for themselves with impunity.

Yu's colleague Li Honglin was one of the few intellectuals, even among the democratic elite, to suggest that the peasants were as deserving as the intellectuals of playing a political role. He observed that although the peasants had been given decision-making powers over production, they also wanted political power to support their economic rights.[39] The political reform leaders and most of the democratic elite, to say nothing of intellectuals in general, favored an "elite democracy," in which only the educated would be qualified to participate. Li Honglin, a few associates, and some former Red Guards, however, called for the full participation of workers and peasants in politics. Such participation would ultimately dispense with the intellectuals' traditional role of political leadership.

Li discussed this issue in the semiofficial *World Economic Herald,* which until 1986 was primarily devoted to articles on economic reform and the writings of members of Zhao Ziyang's think tanks. Qin Benli, its editor-in-chief, had been an early participant in the party underground before 1949, but had spent most of his career during the Mao era in disgrace. He was purged as an editor in 1957 because his newspaper, the Shanghai *Wenhui News,* was specifically criticized by Mao for having a "bourgeois orientation." Qin was then excluded from newspaper work, and during the Cultural Revolution he was persecuted and subjected to two years of solitary confinement. When he was rehabilitated at the beginning of the Deng era, the China World Economic Association and the World Economic Research Institute of the Shanghai CASS asked him to launch a new newspaper.

Qin began the *World Economic Herald* in 1980 from nothing, with some prepaid advertising money, a private contribution from the reformist economist Qian Junrui, and proceeds from the sale of some of his own belongings. He had only enough money to hire seven, mostly retired, veteran newspaper people like himself. He conceived of the *Herald* as an unofficial voice controlled by its editors, journalists, and board, which included the foreign affairs expert Huan Xiang and Yu Guangyuan. By the late 1980s the paper had a staff of one hundred and a circulation of 300,000. Even though the *Herald* was housed in a former French missionary school that belonged to the Shanghai

CASS and was printed under that group's auspices by the *Liberation Daily* for a fee, it was run as a quasi-private paper. It hired and fired personnel and published articles without getting approval from Shanghai's officials or propaganda department. As the paper increased its focus on political issues in the latter part of the 1980s, it came under official scrutiny, especially for its strong defense of Ma Ding and its publication of controversial speeches and articles of the democratic elite.[40] It had a protector, however, in Zhao Ziyang.

In 1986 the *World Economic Herald* became a forum for members of Hu Yaobang's network who emphasized the need for political reforms to accompany economic changes. They argued that to introduce new economic policies while holding on to the old political structure would fail, just as it had in the late Qing dynasty, because the obsolete political structure would obstruct the changing economy. The Marxist belief that the superstructure must correspond with the substructure may have intensified their sense of urgency regarding the need for political reform.

The gradual shift in focus of the democratic elite from revising ideology to reforming institutions and laws is exemplified by Wang Ruoshui's shift in emphasis by 1986. Perhaps because of his own experience as the target of the spiritual pollution campaign, Wang increasingly stressed the need for laws and institutions to protect freedom of speech. A collection of his articles, *In Defense of Humanism,* was finally published in the summer of 1986 after a delay of two years and became an immediate best-seller. In direct contrast to his experience during the Cultural Revolution, Wang found that his victimization now brought him greater status and popularity. He received many speaking invitations and again began writing articles, which expressed his shift in focus, for party newspapers as well as for Hong Kong journals. In an August article, he chastised his colleagues for cheering Hu Qili's promise of freedom of creation at the Fourth Congress of the Writers Association. Wang complained that their cheers proved that the constitution, which already provided for freedom of creation, did not carry as much weight as the words of a leader. He declared: "Freedom of creation is a right of the citizens . . . It is not bestowed and cannot be abolished by any person."[41]

The democratic elite also began to focus on the role of interest groups, although that specific term was not necessarily used. Su Shaozhi in particular stressed their political significance. In an article in the *People's Daily,* he pointed out that "in light of their own interests, different strata, groups, and individuals may hold different views on a certain matter. How can we insist on seeking unity of thinking?"[42] At a forum on political reform in September 1986, he recommended dispensing with the dogma of homogeneity and recognizing that even in a socialist society, different social interests, group interests, and individual interests coexist.

In a statement even more challenging to the Leninist system, Su related the issue of interest groups to politics. He asserted that the existence of interest groups involved the "question of whether or not we acknowledge pluralism in politics and whether or not we need a political system with more than one party."[43] Yet Su remained focused on inner-party democracy, and did not recommend a multiparty system. Few of the democratic elite advocated a multiparty system at this time. As committed Marxists, they still believed that if the party's internal structure were democratized, it would be possible for a one-party state to democratize the political system. In an article in *Reading* (Dushu), Su expressed the view of a number of his colleagues, who yearned for a return to fundamental Marxist ideals. He insisted that the original Marxist vision had never included "democratic centralism"; this concept had been added by Lenin and then distorted to a great degree by Stalin, who emphasized the party's monopolization of power.[44] Su and most of his colleagues were not yet ready to countenance the existence of more than one party, though Yan Jiaqi talked of the emergence of political factions within the party that in time could lead to the development of a multiparty system.

From their younger associates at various forums in 1986 there were calls for some form of multiparty system. Yang Baikui, Yan Jiaqi's colleague in the Institute of Political Science who had run as an unofficial candidate in the 1980 political campaign for the people's congress in the Haidian area, prophesied that intellectuals in the post-Mao period would break with the tradition of the Confucian literati, who "very often became appendages of the imperial power."[45] He envisioned intellectuals' becoming an interest group, joining with other social groups, such as factory workers and entrepreneurs, to form what he called an independent "intermediate strata" that would work for changes in the political structure similar to those suggested by Yan Jiaqi. Yang Baikui was one of the first to suggest publicly that intellectuals join with other social groups in political action. He urged his colleagues to learn from the political reforms going on in Eastern Europe as well as from the West and from the political changes under way among their East Asian brethren.

In the summer of 1986 the small parties, which had the potential to function somewhat like the interest groups that Su Shaozhi had described, suddenly attempted to reassert themselves. After virtually dying out during the Cultural Revolution, they were revived in 1980, not only because their membership of professionals and intellectuals could contribute to policymaking but also because of their links with overseas Chinese, helpful to the economic reforms. In 1985 a political reform leader, Yan Mingfu, was appointed director of the United Front Work Department, the agency in charge of the small parties and of intellectuals in general. In addition to the warming atmosphere, being supervised by a reform official may have helped embolden the small parties in the summer of 1986 to ask for a bigger role. Several of their leaders suggested that the small parties be given organizational independence and that their relationship with the Communist Party be codified into law, so that they would have legal protection to act as a form of "checks and balances" and "feedback" to the party.[46] By helping the party to avoid errors and corruption, they maintained that they would strengthen rather than weaken the CCP.

The saying "Absolute power corrupts absolutely" was frequently quoted by the leaders of the small parties in 1986. Fei Xiaotong, a well-known anthropologist and a vice chairman of the China Democratic League, who accompanied Hu Yaobang on his trip to Western Europe, often cited this dictum of Lord Acton's.[47] Fei also suggested giving the CPPCC, which included members from the small parties, more independence so that it could function like the British House of Lords. In addition, he recommended that the people's congresses be given the right to make inquiries about and even to impeach government officials. But then Fei tempered his proposals, as he had often done ever since being persecuted as a rightist in 1957 for having made similar proposals in the Hundred Flowers period. He pledged that the small parties would not turn into opposition parties.

As important as the myriad of articles published in the mainstream media on the need for political reform were the series of forums on the subject held throughout the nation, beginning with the first one, held April 28–29, 1986, at Taiyuan, Shanxi, sponsored by Yan Jiaqi's Institute of Political Science. Discussions of political reform were not confined to the democratic elite. They were held all over the country, in universities, by youth groups, and even by the Youth League. The most extraordinary of these forums was organized in July 1986 by the graduate students at the Central Party School. Even though Wang Zhen had since 1982 sought to make this training school for high party cadres a center of ideological orthodoxy, its 1986 forum, supported by a number of the school's vice presidents, demonstrated that he had not succeeded. Preparations for it had been under way for over a year, and it was preceded by eight preparatory meetings of the graduate students. The forum used Deng's August 1980 speech on the dangers of an "overconcentration of power" as the basis for its discussion of political reform. Shortly after the forum began, the Propaganda Department director Zhu Houze arrived and took an active part in its deliberations. In addition to urging the participants to revitalize ideology, he advised them to learn from the political reforms under way in Eastern Europe as well as in the West. Just as Marxism had evolved from non-Marxist thinking, he said, so should present revisions of Marxism take advantage of non-Marxist political concepts.[48]

The newly developing democracies evoked much interest among the democratic elite. The Marxist-Leninist Institute held a symposium on the reforms of the East European political systems. The institute's members had been impressed by the president of the Hungarian Academy of Sciences, an activist in Hungary's economic reforms, who on a visit to China in June 1986 had warned the Chinese that their economic reforms could not be successful without basic political reform. At the time in Hungary, Communist Party officials were selected in competitive elections and smaller Hungarian political parties were gaining more independence. The growing opposition parties in Taiwan and South Korea and the shift from military to democratic regimes in Latin America were also discussed at various forums. Deng Weizhi, editor of the Chinese Encyclopedia Publishing House, Shanghai branch, and a sometime associate of the democratic elite, had suggested even earlier that the West European "democratic model of socialism"—a multiparty system that also included different Marxist parties—might be taken as a reference for China. He pointed out that "one-party government control 'too greatly endangers democracy.'"[49] His recommendations provoked vigorous rebuttals, but he continued to express these views throughout 1986.[50]

Nevertheless, despite their interest in East European political reforms, most intellectuals felt that China in 1986 was moving more swiftly and effectively than the Soviet Union in dispensing with both the Leninist structure of democratic centralism and the Stalinist economic system. Mikhail Gorbachev had been in power for just one year, and had yet to embark on his radical political reforms. The foreign affairs expert Huan Xiang observed that China's experience of the Cultural Revolution, "which thoroughly exposed our problems and caused us great pain," had made China "determined not to allow a repetition of such a tragedy as the Cultural Revolution and determined to get rid of the defects brought by it." Consequently, in comparison with the Soviet Union, "our reform can be more thorough and a bit more realistic."[51]

Radical Ideological Views

Even the discussions of Marxism-Leninism at this time were unprecedented. While Deng Weizhi urged a distinction between Marxism and Leninism, Su Shaozhi urged a downgrading of Leninism altogether. Even earlier, Su had referred positively to Rosa Luxemburg's views in her debates with Lenin in which she emphasized inner-party democracy in opposition to Lenin's emphasis on tight discipline. Su used Luxemburg to challenge the undemocratic nature of Leninism and Stalinism. At a theoretical symposium in Shanghai, Zhu Houze, supposedly paraphrasing his mentor Hu Yaobang, described Marxism as at a "low ebb after 1956." Capitalist countries had developed rapidly, but "quite a few socialist countries made mistakes in development."[52] He encouraged the theorists to infuse ideology with new ideas.

Even Hu Sheng, a close associate of Hu Qiaomu and the president of CASS in 1986, declared that it was appropriate for Marxist theorists to discuss schools of political thought that differed from that of the party. Moreover, he acknowledged that non-Marxist research might provide a more accurate understanding of society than Marxist research. "Research not involving conscious application of Marxism is also likely to produce positive results, even greater than research results achieved by the Marxists . . . We must not close ourselves to the different schools of thought abroad and instead, what we should do is to conscientiously discuss, study, and criticize them."[53]

Another unprecedented development was a form of public introspection. For the first time a number of intellectuals asked publicly why they and so many of their countrymen had participated in such despicable acts in the Mao era. They felt that until the population faced up fully to the tragedies of the past and placed blame not only on Mao, the party, the Gang of Four, the system, and Chinese tradition but also on themselves, it would be impossible to prevent such tragedies from recurring.

This public introspection, led by a few literary intellectuals allied with the democratic elite, continued the discussion begun by Ba Jin in his 1979 *Random Thoughts.* An article in *Reading* commented: "Many talk about how they were persecuted during the 'Cultural Revolution,' but few seriously consider what moral and political responsibilities we should share." More people were indifferent and silent to the persecutions before and during the Cultural Revolution and/or were themselves participants. To say that all of society shares in responsibility for such events, the article asserted, "in no way excuses the Gang of Four." But to acknowledge participation means that "we commit ourselves to the obligation of preventing such a tragedy from happening again." To compare the party's role in the Cultural Revolution to "a mother who has wronged her children" as many intellectuals as well as officials were doing, the article insisted, was "more dangerous than useless."[54]

One of the most vocal on this issue was Liu Zaifu, head of the Institute of Literature. Although hitherto he had emphasized the writer's subjective vision, in a speech at a symposium of two hundred writers in September 1986 entitled "Literature in the New Period," Liu urged writers to engage in a form of public introspection. He praised the writers of wounded literature of the late 1970s for paying attention to individual consciousness, but he chastised them and their fellow Chinese for a "lack of the consciousness of repentance by our nation together."[55] He attributed "the lack of self-examination consciousness of 'repenting with the nation'" to China's political culture. "Some scholars," he noted, say that China "has too much 'literature with a sense of happiness,' but lacks 'literature with a sense of guilt.'" Ba Jin's *Random Thoughts,* he pointed out, was the exception. Ba had the "honesty . . . to face the reality of himself and the world."[56] Wounded literature, with its nonidealized heroes, was a beginning, Liu acknowledged, but it did not go far enough because it did not lead to a common sense of repentance.

In an interview given in July 1986, Liu had criticized his fellow intellectuals for their unquestioning allegiance to the dominant political ideology and leadership that had robbed them of their individual conscience, as demonstrated by their participation in the Cultural Revolution. Merely to condemn a handful of people for causing the Cultural Revolution was not enough. "We should also realize our own responsibility. If there had not been a certain national culture and psychological foundation, or if our nation had not had some common weak points, the 'Cultural Revolution' would not have become a fact . . . I feel that we should all have a feeling of repentance and should realize that 'I should also share the responsibility' as a member of this nation for the ten year long national calamity. Otherwise, we may repeat . . . previous mistakes." [57]

Wang Meng echoed Liu Zaifu in the *People's Daily* when he noted that Ba Jin's *Random Thoughts* had been published in Hong Kong, but not in China. Like the survivors of the Holocaust, he declared: "We should never forget the lessons of the 'Great Cultural Revolution' and never forget the painful chapter of the 'Great Cultural Revolution.' Otherwise, the 'Great Cultural Revolution' will repeat itself or there will be 'another reversal.'" [58] Only by remembering the past, he asserted, would it be possible to prevent another tragedy. Wang Ruoshui in an August article criticized not only the party for not preventing the Cultural Revolution, "but also the people[, who] did not have the strength to prevent that disaster . . . they could not and even did not want to stop its development." [59] Liu Binyan, in speeches on university campuses and at the Heilongjiang conference for journalists on September 15, stressed that the party had been able to carry out the Cultural Revolution because the Chinese people had allowed and even welcomed it. He cited the West Germans' confrontation with their own history as an example that would benefit his compatriots.

These calls for a public examination of one's actions in the recent past and for collective repentance evoked very strong reactions. The response of some, especially the elders, was defensive, insisting that they had been the victims rather than the perpetrators. Others tried to explain why so few Chinese had protested against Mao's destructive policies. An article in the *People's Daily,* for example, asked, "When ordinary Chinese, including writers, were deprived of their civil rights and were pushed into a veritable hell on earth, what responsibility should they assume for their sufferings?" To place guilt on everyone allowed those who were genuinely responsible to escape blame. Furthermore, the article continued, the Chinese had "little or no spirit of repentance in a religious sense." Although Chinese writers had written tragedies, they did not necessarily involve repentance. The article cited Qu Yuan's classic poem "Everlasting Regret" (Li sao) as filled with sorrow, but without repentance.[60]

The Reaction of the Elders and Their Theorists

Most of the demands for institutional reform and constitutional rights, the revision of Marxism, and public introspection challenged the political system. Some of the arguments of the democratic elite challenged the elders as well, though they were not mentioned by name. In his article "Modernization and Democracy" Li Honglin, for example, observed that "a few leaders feel frightened when hearing of democracy, especially those leaders who are accustomed to acting as patriarchs who, when hearing of different opinions from people, think that people just want to go against them and make trouble."[61] The virtue of democracy, he explained, was that it was more conducive to stability and unity than the autocratic leadership that had caused so much disruption and division in the past.

By late summer the elders began to marshal their forces for a counterattack. As usual, the earliest signs appeared in the literary realm. Their associate Yu Qiuli, at an inaugural meeting of a new research center, the Institute on Literature and Art Theory, and a new journal, *Literature and Art Theory and Comment* (Wenyi lilun yu piping), announced the need for more guidance from Marxism and Mao Zedong Thought. Both the institute and the journal were established to present the Maoist view of literature and art and to oppose the views of the literary intellectuals associated with the democratic elite. The editor of the journal was Chen Yong, whom Deng Liqun had also appointed as a member of his group in the Secretariat. Chen gathered around him Huang Gang, He Jingzhi, and Yao Xueyin, who had all persecuted writers with political charges since their Yan'an days.

The first target of Chen's new journal was Liu Zaifu's speech calling for public introspection and his subjective, less politicized view of literature. Although Chen and his associates were particularly upset with the encouragement Liu gave writers to experiment with nonrealistic and other styles of literary creation, in rebutting Liu Zaifu's

views, Chen Yong also called for a more pluralistic approach to literature. Feeling themselves eclipsed in 1986 by the democratic elite and
the reform officials' spokesmen, the elders and their theorists found it
necessary to demand a more open intellectual environment so that
they too could be heard. Chen complained: "It is not right that only
a certain type of viewpoint can be expressed everywhere . . . it is not
right that when others put forward different viewpoints, they will be
immediately criticized for 'creating a tense atmosphere.'"[62] Indeed,
with the exception of the literary realm, there was little public rebuttal
to the arguments of the democratic elite and their associates in the
spring and summer. Even *Red Flag* ostensibly joined the demands for
political reform in 1986, though its definition of political reform had
more to do with efficient, more systematic decision making than with
democratic practices.

Suddenly, however, in *Red Flag*'s September 1 issue, rebuttals
appeared. The most sensational was by Wu Jianguo. Originally a
middle-school teacher in Wuxi and later a deputy secretary of the
Suzhou Party Committee, Wu came to the attention of *Red Flag*'s editor Xiong Fu, who had him transferred to Beijing to become a member of his editorial board. His article "'Reflections' on the Question
of Freedom" revived the elders' argument that freedom could only be
relative. Political freedom, he said, could not "be separated from the
existing relations of production and the relation of property ownership,"[63] a reference to class struggle. Without mentioning Wang Ruowang by name, Wu renewed the attacks on him for suggesting that
one should "govern by doing nothing that goes against nature." He
also condemned the Democracy Wall movement and its nonofficial
magazines as examples of what could happen if absolute freedom
were allowed. "If we had allowed the 'Democracy Wall' to continue
and the illegal publications and vulgar tabloids to spread unchecked,
they would have corrupted our people and youth."[64] "Truth is varied
and many-sided," he acknowledged, "but it cannot be regarded as
'pluralistic.' We cannot say that all opinions and views possess the
same truth. In a sense and within a certain range, there is only one
truth."[65]

This article, reworked and edited by Hu Qiaomu[66] and reprinted
all over China, was the first volley in the counterattack against the
democratic elite and their allies. It was also intended to prepare public
opinion for the reemergence of the elders' orthodox view at the Sixth

Plenum, scheduled for the end of September. Wang Zhen in particular became more openly belligerent toward members of the democratic elite and their associates. At the opening ceremonies of the Central Party School in September, he told the students that Deng Xiaoping wanted them to guard against various newly appointed middle-aged and younger cadres in leading positions.[67] His warning could be interpreted as an attack on Hu Yaobang's appointment of younger officials and Yan Jiaqi and Liu Zaifu, who were the youngest directors of CASS institutes.

At the same time Hu Yaobang's intellectual network became increasingly worried about his support. Supposedly Hu Yaobang had praised Wu Jianguo's article and had recommended him for a position in the Propaganda Department.[68] Hu's actions, like his speech urging journalists to be mouthpieces of the party, appeared to be additional attempts to appease the elders, in the hope that they would suspend or at least limit their opposition to political reform. But whereas Hu's appeasement was described by members of his network as "naive,"[69] his mentor Deng Xiaoping's move back toward the stance of his elderly colleagues at this time was influenced not only by their pressure but also by his own underlying concern that the kind of political reforms being proposed threatened the party and himself. His shift was also part of his continuing effort to keep a balance between the elders and the reformers. Reflecting Deng's change in position, an *Outlook* commentator article reversed the priorities that the democratic elite and their allies had stressed in the spring and summer. Instead of emphasizing the need to formulate laws and establish institutions, the author emphasized "education" in spiritual civilization, a euphemism for ideological indoctrination.[70] An *Economic Daily* editorial two weeks later added: "We should not and cannot blindly copy the existing patterns in other countries."[71]

This retreat on political reform, expressed in the national media in late September, had actually begun at the party leadership's August gathering at the summer resort of Beidaihe to prepare for the Sixth Plenum of the Twelfth Congress. At Beidaihe the elders planned to put an end to the balmy climate that had nurtured the wide-ranging discourse on political reform. Deng's close friend and Politburo member Yang Shangkun joined the other elders in demanding that only administrative reforms be allowed. Some of the elders complained about the discussions of a multiparty system and specifically about the articles in the *World Economic Herald*.[72] Shortly after the gathering, when Hu Yaobang welcomed one of Deng's periodic threats to retire, they became even more alarmed, fearing that they would be forced to emulate Deng's example and that Hu would be left in charge. After this episode was reported in the *Shenzhen Youth News* (Shenzhen qingnian bao), Hu ordered that the article not be reprinted elsewhere. But his half-way measures of appeasement once again proved unsuccessful. The elders remained opposed to Hu and were joined by the military elders, who feared that Hu would take over Deng's post as chairman of the Military Affairs Commission and would call for their retirement as well. As survivors of the Long March, the Civil War, and the Cultural Revolution, both groups of elders considered themselves the true defenders of the Communist Revolution. Now they sought to defend it anew by "building a spiritual civilization."

After a fierce debate, in which Hu Qiaomu, Deng Liqun, and Chen Yun insisted on adding a statement against bourgeois liberalization, a compromise resolution for the plenum was worked out at Beidaihe. The elders' call for building spiritual civilization would be given equal importance with the reform leaders' call for political and economic reforms and assimilation of Western culture. Yet despite this compromise, the debate exploded again at the Sixth Plenum meetings in September. The ailing Lu Dingyi, director of the Propaganda Department under Mao and a major victim of the Cultural Revolution, who at Beidaihe had three times urged that the statement against bourgeois liberalization be dropped, again pressed that it be omitted from the resolution. Calling it "absurd and dangerous," he warned that such a statement could give rise to another "leftist" upsurge.[73] Hu Yaobang and Wan Li supported him; Peng Zhen, Wang Zhen, and their allies opposed him.

Finally Deng Xiaoping, again wavering between the two sides, made the decision to include the statement against bourgeois liberalization, reflecting his move back to the side of the elders and away from his supposed successor Hu Yaobang. Deng said: "With regard to the question of opposing bourgeois liberalization, I am the one who has talked about it most often and most insistently . . . Liberalization by itself means antagonism to our current policies and systems and a wish to revise them. In fact, exponents of liberalization want to lead us down the road to capitalism . . . the struggle against liberalization will have to be carried on not only now but for the next ten or twenty years."[74] Deng also criticized "bourgeois scholars" and those in Hong Kong, of whom he said: "Most of them are calling on us to pursue liberalization, and their comments include statements that people have no human rights here."[75] Hu Yaobang subsequently withheld transmission of Deng's Sixth Plenum speech to the lower levels.[76]

Because of the compromise nature of the Sixth Plenum resolution and the initially limited circulation of Deng's speech, which had been published by Wang Zhen at the Central Party School, the democratic elite continued to call for political reform after the plenum. Moreover, although the plenum's resolution reasserted the elders' views, its restatement of the reform leaders' views was sufficient to sustain their side of the debate. The plenum, therefore, instead of resolving the tensions in the top leadership, sharpened them and made them more publicly apparent. Hu's intellectual network continued to press ahead with renewed calls for political reform and ideological revisions. Hu Yaobang himself made few public statements after the plenum, but an indication of his thinking at this time appeared in an interview with Katharine Graham, the publisher of *Newsweek* and the *Washington Post*. There he lamented that the image of socialism had been impaired not only because the economies of socialist countries were no longer developing very quickly but because they were also having problems with "democracy and human rights."[77]

Renewed Political Discourse

Hu Yaobang's position after the plenum appeared to have been weakened. Zhao Ziyang replaced Hu as head of the group preparing proposals for political restructuring, to be presented at the Thirteenth Party Congress in 1987. This group, the Central Research and Discussion Group on Political Structural Reform, was headed by a five-member committee made up of Zhao Ziyang, Hu Qili, Bo Yibo, Tian Jiyun, and Peng Chong and was supervised by Zhao's secretary, Bao Tong. The change in its leadership appeared to shift the control of political reform efforts away from Hu's base of power in the party Secretariat to Zhao's base in the State Council. Nevertheless, some of the participants in Hu's 1979 theory conference, such as Yan Jiaqi, became members of this new group, and Liao Gailong headed its subcommittee on theory.

Despite the crosswinds of the fall, the democratic elite and their associates did not retreat. Rather, the elders' counterattack provoked them to renew their proposals for political reform more directly and with more vigor. Yu Guangyuan, for example, in an article in the *People's Daily,* observed that although the Sixth Plenum resolution opposed the bourgeois view that regarded Marxism as "outmoded," the resolution did not "negate the bourgeois philosophies and social doctrines in a general way," nor did it "advocate a ban on contact with all the bourgeois philosophies and social doctrines." [78] Moreover, in response to the elders' counterattack, a *People's Daily* commentator article warned against repeating the "abnormal criticism we conducted before." [79] It expressed the hope that "leading cadres, at various levels, will reduce their interference in various discussions which do not violate the Constitution and will not use coercive measures to suppress any opinion or make arbitrary conclusions." [80]

The Central Party School continued to be active in the ongoing political discourse. The slight cooling of the atmosphere at the time of the plenum had forced the second forum on political reform sponsored by the Central Party School to be transferred to another location, because Wang Zhen prohibited it from being held at the school. Instead the forum took place at the National Defense University, headed by the relatively moderate General Li Desheng. In the course of the discussion, one postgraduate argued that making policy decisions more scientifically was no substitute for political democracy.[81] A graduate student rejected the idea, often expressed by the leadership, that only when China had developed a pluralist economy could it have democracy. He noted that in the West, political democracy had come before a pluralistic economy. Although pluralistic interests already existed in China, they were not recognized and were "submerged" by the stress on unanimity of interests. He warned that if China waited to introduce political democracy until it achieved "economic democracy," then there would be no economic democracy.[82]

As if anticipating the charge that emulation of Western political practices would be a betrayal of Chinese culture, several articles in the national media pointed out that their Chinese and Confucian brethren in South Korea, Taiwan, and Japan had been successful precisely because they had assimilated Western political ideas and values in addition to carrying out economic reforms. One article in the

Guangming Daily noted that these nations nevertheless still maintained "rather strong characteristics of Oriental culture . . . Therefore, it is unnecessary to worry about the extinction of one's national characteristics when the absorption of Western culture is advocated."[83] A *People's Daily* article added that bourgeois values were not just restricted to the West or the middle class. Western "concepts, ideas, and theories are not only the spiritual wealth of the bourgeoisie, but also part and parcel of the civilization of mankind."[84] And Yu Guangyuan gave an interpretation of "spiritual civilization" that was just the opposite of the elders' interpretation. Instead of limiting it to orthodox ideology, he defined it as opening up to the outside world. He explained that China had developed such a great civilization precisely because since ancient times it had assimilated so much foreign culture. This legacy ought to continue to guide China, because "historical facts have proved that it is impossible for China to make progress or develop when China rejected progressive things from other parts of the world."[85]

Even though the elders, including Deng Xiaoping, had complained at Beidaihe that the discussions on political reform gave too much emphasis to "restraints" on political power, restraints continued to be stressed. A *China Youth News* article defined democracy as institutionalized legal restraints on power. The basic difference between democracy and autocracy, it asserted, was that "democracy is to eliminate the phenomenon of exercising absolute power in political life to keep all power in effective check, and to ensure that the people's rights will not be infringed on by state authority."[86] These checks were to be exercised by the people's congresses, by freedom of speech, and by "the division of the structure and function of state power."[87] Thus even after the Sixth Plenum, in defiance of the elders' publicly expressed opposition to such "Western" institutions, discourse on a system of checks and balances continued.

The Three Intellectuals

Despite the wide-open debates and controversial views on political reform expressed in public forums and articles in the national media in 1986, the party would later charge only three intellectuals publicly—Fang Lizhi, Wang Ruowang, and Liu Binyan—with provoking the student demonstrations that erupted in December 1986. It is difficult to explain why these three men were made the chief targets. Their views were controversial, but not necessarily more so than other views expressed in 1986. In part they were singled out because of Deng Xiaoping's personal dislike of them.

But equally significant, these three intellectuals were popular, charismatic figures who had their own constituencies and had excited and inspired large numbers of people all over the country with their outspokenness and directness in discussing political issues. After the Sixth Plenum they were very active in speaking at universities and forums, where their calls for political reform were greeted with great enthusiasm. Although different in their approaches, the three were similar in that by mid-1986 none of them any longer went through prescribed party channels or used subtle language to express his views. They had ceased remonstrating and pleading with the authorities to modify their ways—actions for which all three had suffered severely in the past. They now began to talk directly to their constituents, primarily in the universities and intellectual circles, and to express views openly in opposition to those of the elders.

Liu Binyan's often-repeated characterization of the Deng reforms as having a very long economic leg and a very short political leg, making it impossible to move forward, must have infuriated Deng, obsessed with economic reforms. In addition, Liu revealed in a number of interviews that his view of political reform had moved beyond his hitherto unsuccessful efforts to persuade the party leadership to live up to Marxist ideals to an emphasis on establishing laws and institutions to protect individuals from the abuse of political authorities. Given that he himself was still having difficulties publishing his own works and was often threatened with lawsuits by local officials whose wrongdoings he had exposed, he was particularly concerned at this time with legal protections for freedom of expression. In an interview with the journal *Democracy and the Legal System* (Minzhu yu fazhi) in Shanghai, he charged that "when a top-ranking party secretary starts a lawsuit against a writer, it is almost a natural law that the former has already half proven his case." [88] He publicized the cases of lawyers for the accused who had been treated as "evildoers" and even arrested. To the authorities, he advised that the best way to prevent him from writing such exposés was to stop the abuses in the first place.

In another challenge, in talks in Heilongjiang, Tianjin, Anhui, Fujian, and Shenzhen from September to December 1986, Liu referred to the press as a "fourth power." His acceptance of this Western view of the press also implied acceptance of a system of checks and balances. In his trips to the Soviet Union during the thaw after Stalin's death, Liu had first learned about investigative reporting, and in his trips to the West, especially to the United States in 1982, he had learned about freedom of the press guaranteed by law as a check on political power. His exposure to the outside world gave him an appreciation of the press as not just a tool for party propaganda but as a forum for the voices of the people. Over the 1980s his concept of the press as the representative of both the party and the people gradually shifted toward a view of the press as primarily expressing the will of the people rather than that of the party.

Wang Ruowang had provoked controversy not only because of his Daoist approach toward literature but also because he had publicly attacked officials by name. As early as 1979 he had criticized by name the top officials connected with the Bohai No. 2 oil-drilling vessel accident, in which several lives were lost. He published articles in the *People's Daily* and the *Guangming Daily* blaming the officials in charge for having "utter disregard for human life" and covering up their actions. Deng, infuriated by Wang's charges, soon ordered him purged in a directive to the Shanghai Party Committee. But the Shanghai party officials considered the punishment excessive, and referred the matter to Hu Yaobang. He too felt it inappropriate to expel Wang merely because of the articles. Considering them "not terribly offensive," Hu ordered the whole matter dropped.[09] Despite Deng's anger, Wang continued to name party officials publicly when he believed that they had acted improperly.

Wang also continued to protest injustices, as he had been doing since the 1930s. When Ba Jin was removed as the head of the Shanghai Federation of Literary and Art Circles in 1984, Wang joined with the playwright Sha Yexin and others to protest. When the campaign against spiritual pollution was launched, he denounced it at Shanghai universities as a "smaller Cultural Revolution." Even though works on the Cultural Revolution had been officially discouraged since 1981, Wang continued to write on the subject. Journals rejected these pieces on orders from higher authorities. Only briefly, around the time of the Fourth Congress of the Writers Association, was he able to publish again. Wang was not initially listed as a deputy of the Shanghai delegation to the congress, but after public pressure he was nominated in a second round of voting and won a position by a wide margin. Shortly after the congress, however, his works were banned again.

Only in mid-1986, at the high point of the discourse on political reform, was Wang able to return to the lecture circuit. He then delivered speeches all over China's east coast and published articles in various newspapers and journals. Several editors suggested he use a pseudonym, but he refused to do so, explaining that his right to publish was guaranteed in the constitution. During the year the Shanghai journal *The Younger Generation* (Qingnian yidai) published his memoirs. In them he describes falling in love with his second wife, Yang Zi, after his first wife died due to the mental anguish she suffered during the persecution of her husband and their children. His cherubic appearance and his spirited speeches, peppered with humorous putdowns of party policies and leaders, were warmly received by various groups. In talks at universities in Shanghai and Hangzhou in late 1986, he even called directly for a multiparty system.

Of all the intellectuals, the astrophysicist Fang Lizhi had the greatest impact on students in talks at numerous prestigious universities in November–December 1986. Born in 1936 to a poor family in Beijing, he began to read and count at the age of two.[90] He entered the Fourth Beijing Middle School, renowned for its academic excellence, at age ten, and the Department of Physics at Peking University in 1952 at age sixteen. Early on he became known for his candor as well as for his brilliance. At a Youth League forum in his department in 1955, Fang interrupted a speech being given by a CYL leader to urge his fellow students to think more independently. In the Hundred Flowers period he and a number of colleagues wrote a letter to the Central Committee requesting that politics and ideology not be allowed to interfere in scientific research, a belief that was to become an article of faith for him. As a result of the letter he was expelled from the party and sent to labor in the countryside.

After being rehabilitated in 1961, Fang married a fellow student in the physics department, Li Shuxian, whose political ideas closely paralleled his. In that same year he began publishing scholarly works in *Physics* (Wuli) and was one of the first Chinese to publish articles on laser physics, a new field in China. During the Cultural Revolution he was put in a cowshed in 1968 and then sent to do manual work in the coal mines of Anhui. The only book he was allowed to take with him was one by the Soviet physicist Lev Landau on the classical theory of fields, which he read over and over again.[91] By the time Fang was able to return to research in the early 1970s he had switched from the field of solid-state physics, which required large-scale equipment, to the field of cosmology, the investigation into the origins of the universe, which required only pencil and paper. Its study was more feasible for one who would undergo long periods of labor reform.

Fang's first published article on cosmology, written with several colleagues in 1972, was also the first article on that subject in China. Cosmology, however, had been decreed a forbidden area of study in 1947 by the Soviet Union's cultural czar, Andrei Zhdanov. The explanation was that the cosmologists, in opposition to Engels's view of an infinite universe, based their work on Einstein's view of the universe as finite, but unbounded, providing arguments for the existence of God. Although the Soviet Union had abandoned this prohibition after Stalin's death in 1953, the Chinese continued to uphold it. Fang was therefore criticized once again, this time by Yao Wenyuan, a member of the Gang of Four, whose writing group launched an attack against him in 1973.

Nevertheless, by the time Fang was again officially rehabilitated in 1978, he had already published numerous articles on cosmology in international scholarly journals as well as in China. His party membership was restored and he became the youngest full professor in China at that time. As he began to be invited to international conferences in Germany, Italy, Japan, England, and the United States and to receive international scientific prizes, he became one of the few Chinese scientists with a world-class reputation. His small group working on cosmology at the University of Science and Technology in Hefei, Anhui (known as Keda, an abbreviation of its Chinese name), where he taught, attracted international attention. On a visit in the spring of 1985, the British astrophysicist Stephen Hawking congratulated Fang on the high level of research in cosmology conducted there.

With the support of the president of Keda, Guan Weiyan, also a prominent physicist, and with the help of Wen Yuankai, an expert in quantum chemistry who in 1979 at the age of thirty-three had become China's youngest associate professor, Fang tried to foster an atmosphere of academic freedom at the university. Despite bureaucratic protests, Fang was appointed vice chancellor of Keda in 1984. His approach to education was in accordance with Hu Yaobang's policy at the time to give certain universities relative autonomy in teaching and research and to allow their administrators, rather than party committees, to determine such matters as curriculum, appointments, and admissions. In the tradition of Cai Yuanpei, the education reformer at Peking University during the May Fourth movement, Fang urged the university to draw on many different cultures and to allow a wide range of ideas to coexist. He compared China's universities to the universities of medieval Europe, which were havens of free thinking, insulated from the theological authorities surrounding them. By mid-1985 Fang began traveling to other universities to talk about Keda's academic reforms. These were also hailed in a series of five articles in the *People's Daily* from October through early November 1986 entitled "Democracy in the Running of Keda." The series depicted Keda's educational reforms as a model for other universities.

Albert Einstein was perhaps the greatest political as well as intellectual influence on Fang. He read Einstein's complete works, translated into Chinese by his close friend, the physicist and historian of science Xu Liangying. As both an outspoken advocate of humanism and social democracy and a great scientist, Einstein became Fang's model. Fang was also inspired by the traditional literati's sense of responsibility to speak out against injustice and abuse of power and by his fellow physicist Andrei Sakharov's unremitting opposition to Soviet repression. These examples, in addition to his frequent travels to Western countries in the 1980s, inspired Fang to challenge his own repressive government.

An equally important impetus for Fang's increasingly forthright demands for democratic procedures were the continuing attacks on his scientific work by the party's chief theorist, Hu Qiaomu. In December 1985 Hu had written a letter to the editorial board of *Science* (Kexue), condemning cosmology as a bourgeois ideology. With Fang's prompting, the board dismissed Hu's letter, explaining that scientific methods had not been used to prove its argument.[92]

The authorities delayed Fang's acceptance of an invitation from the Institute for Advanced Study in Princeton several times, primarily because Fang had denounced by name a vice mayor of Beijing, Zhang Baifa, still a rare act of defiance in China. Fang had criticized Zhang's participation in a scientific delegation to the United States to study synchrotron radiation. He charged that the participation of Zhang and several of his party cronies had denied places to scientists specializing in the subject. Lu Jiaxi and Zhou Guangzhao, the president and vice president of the Academy of Sciences, had urged Fang to apologize, but Fang refused, declaring that he had nothing to apologize for. Fang was finally allowed to go to Princeton in the spring of 1986. On his return home that summer, however, he read an article in the *Beijing Daily* entitled "No Science Can Ever Replace Marxism," reiterating Hu Qiaomu's argument that Marxism must guide science. These rebuffs in his professional life at home, in contrast with the openness he found abroad, impelled Fang to become the first prominent intellectual to denounce Marxism-Leninism publicly and to embrace democratic procedures in order to free scientific research from ideological shackles and to base it on independent norms established by one's peers.

Fang was drawn to members of Hu Yaobang's intellectual network, though most of them were nonscientists, because not only were they being attacked by the same party bureaucrats, but they also agreed with some of his political views. Fang also shared with Hu's group and with Zhao Ziyang's technocrats the elitist and traditional belief that education, training, and professional skills should be the criteria for participation in policymaking and politics. Fang differed from Hu's intellectual associates, however, in his total rejection of Marxism-Leninism. Most of Hu's network had some residual commitment to the ideology, while Fang had none. Moreover, some of them feared that Fang's more radical approach would provoke a reaction that would hurt the reforms as well as themselves.

Fang was outspoken in his rejection of Marxism-Leninism and socialism in his speeches on university campuses after the Sixth Plenum. In a speech at Shanghai's Tongji University on November 18, he declared: "It is an undeniable fact that not a single socialist country has succeeded since the end of the Second World War; the same is also true with China's socialism of thirty years . . . socialism has failed, from Marx, Lenin, Stalin, and all the way to Mao." He explained that democracy's success was due to its recognition of the "basic rights of the people, or human rights."[93] One right he often cited was freedom from fear and unlawful suspicion. The Chinese people, unfortunately, still had to live with such fears, and as long as they existed, there would be "no democracy."[94] Fang's fearlessness and directness in challenging the party's orthodoxies and in expressing views others held but were afraid to utter publicly had a tremendous appeal to students. They called him "China's Sakharov," and adopted him as their role model and inspirational leader.

Fang's listeners recorded and transcribed his speeches and sent them to fellow students around the country. The most famous and most defiant was the talk he gave at Shanghai's Jiaotong University on November 15, in which he emphatically repudiated the Marxist guidance of academic work. In the sciences, he asserted, Marxism had been "100 percent wrong." Perhaps even more disturbing to the leadership was his advice to students to assume responsibility for their own rights and political acts. "If the democracy we are striving for remains one that is granted only from the top, then the democracy that is practiced in our society is not the true democracy." He articulated the Western concept of inalienable rights, saying that "democracy itself embodies recognition of individual rights . . . which are not granted from above. Rather men are born with rights." When the party granted "democracy" from above, Fang asserted, that was not democracy but only "relaxation of control." Although the "ropes" were loosened a bit, they were still controlled by the top leaders, not the individual. Therefore, in contrast to their predecessors, "the obedient" intellectuals of the 1950s, he urged present-day students and intellectuals "to strive for what is one's due," declaring: "It is up to the intellectuals as a class, with their sense of social responsibility, their consciousness about democracy and their initiative to strive for their rights." He summoned them to "show the power they possess."[95]

Just as challenging to the elders was Fang's joining with Liu Binyan and Xu Liangying to organize a commemoration of the thirtieth anniversary of the anti-rightist campaign, of which the three had been victims and in which most of the elders, led by Deng Xiaoping, had actively participated. In October 1986 the three sent a letter to a wide spectrum of intellectuals who had suffered in the campaign. They invited them to attend a conference to be held in February 1987, at which prominent former rightists would talk about their persecution, provide oral histories, and openly discuss the campaign. The proceedings were then to be published in literary journals and books. Such an event would make graphically clear that the traumas of the Cultural Revolution were due not to an aberration of Mao and the Gang but to a political system that gave unlimited power to its leaders, including the present ones, who used their power without restraint.

Xu Liangying, who was the prime organizer of the commemoration, explained: "Those who went through the anti-rightist campaign have the responsibility to bring up this part of history and cause people to see it as a lesson in order not to repeat it."[96] At the start of the anti-rightist campaign in mid-1957, Xu, then a professor of physics at Zhejiang University, was virtually the only protester against the party's branding his students and colleagues as "rightists," an act for which he and his family were to suffer twenty years of labor reform in rural Zhejiang. Anyone even associated with Xu suffered a similar fate as well.

It was while in exile in the countryside that Xu translated Einstein's works. Like Fang, Xu has a poster of Einstein's soulful gaze on his living room wall with a quotation underneath: "Great spirits have always encountered opposition from mediocre minds." Xu's translation of Einstein had a transformative impact on his life. He learned from Einstein that scientists need more than the proper scientific equipment to carry out their work. They need an "atmosphere of freedom," based on legal safeguards and a democratic political system. The party's "mass line" and "democratic work-style," Xu declared, were not democratic because they meant "making decisions for the people."[97] They also harked back to the traditional system, under which the masses were passive and "at most, were allowed to offer suggestions but not to make decisions in accordance with their will."[98] By contrast, Xu asserted, democracy means that "legally and as individuals the people are equal and have inviolable human rights (including personal freedom and freedom of speech)." These rights allow people to make decisions on their own."[99] Xu's view of democracy greatly influenced his younger colleague, Fang Lizhi, who in turn influenced China's students.

That the student demonstrations of late 1986 began first at Keda in Anhui Province is not surprising. Fang's university was an obvious center, and the province was relatively progressive, the first to allow the family responsibility system to develop and one in which the media had published a variety of views on political reforms. The protests spread quickly to the campuses where Fang had given speeches. The students' slogans, such as "Democratic rights are not bestowed as a favor" and "Only the rights won by ourselves are dependable," echoed Fang's ideas.

Just as informal student debates and political discussion groups had launched the demonstrations in 1985 against Japanese goods, so did they also launch the movement in late November 1986. On November 30 Anhui's former party secretary, Wan Li, traveled to Hefei to urge the local university heads to tighten control over their student bodies. He was reported to have cautioned them that "democracy without centralism and freedom without discipline are both against the essence of the [party]."[100] In a meeting with Keda's president, Guan Weiyan, and Fang Lizhi, Wan Li was quoted as saying: "I have already granted you enough freedom and democracy." It is said that Fang responded: "It's not up to any single person to hand out democracy."[101] Whether or not these quotes, reported in the international press, are accurate, Wan Li's message revealed that even a reformist official like himself had little understanding of democracy.

When a thousand students staged another demonstration on December 5 to protest the selection of deputies to the local people's congress by the party leaders rather than by their constituents in competitive elections, Guan and Fang did not restrain them. Critical of the local party press for only presenting the party's side, some of the demonstrators marched to the Anhui provincial party headquarters to demand freedom of the press. Although Fang had tried to moderate their protests, the students were fighting for their rights, as Fang had earlier urged them to do. The local authorities yielded to the students' demands and delayed the election for the local people's congress until December 29, so that the students could nominate their own candidates on a newly expanded slate. Fang Lizhi and several student candidates were subsequently elected.

The success of the students in Anhui inspired demonstrations by students in other cities. By the second week in December student demonstrations had occurred in Wuhan and then in Xi'an, Tianjin, Nanjing, and Shanghai, where the turnout was in the tens of thousands. By late December protests had spread to 150 campuses in at least seventeen cities.[102] As in Anhui, several demonstrations also protested the unrepresentativeness of the party's selected delegates to local people's congresses. Although the State Education Commission later pointed out that fewer than 2 percent of China's students participated in the protests,[103] those who did came from China's most prestigious and most competitive universities.

The methods and even the slogans used in the 1986 demonstrations established precedents that were later followed in the 1989 Tiananmen Square demonstrations. Unlike in the Cultural Revolution, the

demonstrations began spontaneously but were then quickly coordinated and organized as if the procedures and slogans had been
planned well in advance, waiting only for an occasion. The activists
were usually leaders of informal discussion clubs established on most
campuses in the early 1980s. They visited, telephoned, and telexed
their friends and colleagues at other universities within their own
cities and then in other cities. Some of the slogans in 1986, such as
"Give me liberty or give me death," and the repeated singing of the
"Internationale" would also be heard in the 1989 demonstrations.
Even the form of organization was similar, with student demonstrators
organized into groups of thirty under a student leader. Voice of America
(VOA) and the BBC broadcast reports of these demonstrations, which
spread news of them beyond the local area. Because China's own media and newspapers did not cover the demonstrations until a week or
more after they had begun, and then in a distorted way, VOA and the
BBC became the main sources of information for the students. The
1986 student protesters were also influenced by the methods and slogans of the numerous student demonstrations in South Korea and the
February 1986 Philippine demonstrations against Ferdinand Marcos,
which they had seen on Chinese television.[104]

The largest student demonstrations took place in Shanghai, where
Fang had voiced his strongest criticisms of the party before his largest
audience. On December 19 students from virtually all the major universities in Shanghai, including Jiaotong, Tongji, and Fudan, marched
down the city's main streets to the Bund along the waterfront. With
demands similar to those that would initially be made in the 1989
demonstrations, the posters, slogans, and chants called for more independent student unions and more control over student newspapers,
in addition to more general demands for democracy, human rights,
and freedom of the press.[105]

In accordance with Hu Yaobang's instructions, Jiang Zemin, who
was then mayor of Shanghai, responded to these demonstrations by
talking with and trying to persuade the students to return to their
campuses. He went to Jiaotong University on the eve of the first protest, where he encountered 3,000 students, protesting the lack of press
freedom. He tried to persuade them to cancel their march, but was
booed and hissed. After four days of protests Shanghai's municipal
government issued a ban on demonstrations, noting that the Chinese
constitution had already eliminated the four big freedoms. But as the

demonstrations died down in Shanghai they moved to Beijing, where thousands of students from Peking University, People's University, Qinghua, and other academic institutions marched to Tiananmen Square on December 24. In addition to calling for better campus living conditions, they echoed their Shanghai brethren's calls for freedom, democracy, and inalienable rights.

Although Beijing's municipal party leaders, Chen Xitong and Xu Weicheng, were even less responsive than Shanghai's leaders to the students' demands, the presidents of the universities were more forthcoming. The president of Peking University, the mathematician Ding Shisun, expressed sympathy with the students. When 2,000 students gathered outside his home on New Year's Day at nine P.M. calling for the release of student leaders who had already been detained, Ding promised to gain their release and sent cars to return them to campus. The president of Jiaotong University had similarly acted as a mediator between the demonstrators and the Shanghai municipal authorities. Paraphrasing Voltaire, he told them: "I don't agree with your decision to march, but I support your right to march."[106] By contrast, the Beijing party newspaper *Beijing Daily* (Beijing ribao) continued to denounce the demonstrators, provoking the students to burn copies of the paper on their campuses. Nevertheless, when Deng Xiaoping ordered the students to return to their classes in early January, they quietly did.

Unlike the September 1985 student demonstrations against Japanese goods, which can be interpreted as unfavorable to the reform leaders, who advocated trade with Japan, the 1986 protests can be seen as supportive of the reform leaders. The students' demands for better food and dorms and even their demands for more independent student organizations and student newspapers and representation in local party congresses were common complaints on university campuses. But the students' calls for freedom of speech and democratic reforms were meant to hasten along the political reforms supported by Hu Yaobang. After the Sixth Plenum the students were very much aware of the elders' increasing opposition to any political reform. Their protests were in support of the reform leaders and their intellectual network in the struggle with the elders. As the demonstrations moved from campus to campus and from city to city across the country, they became a coherent movement on the side of political reform and the reform party leaders. Their slogans calling for democracy, however, were general and vague. They did not go as far as some members of the democratic elite and their associates, who in their talks and articles called for a system of checks and balances, institutional restraints on power, and even a multiparty system.

There were major differences between the 1986 demonstrations and the 1989 Tiananmen Square demonstrations. The 1986 demonstrations did not gain support from the urban residents and workers, who showed some curiosity but did not participate to any degree. Equally important, the students themselves purposely kept the workers at arm's length for strategic reasons. They knew that the party leadership greatly feared any cooperation between workers and students or intellectuals as had occurred in Eastern Europe, particularly in Poland. In 1986, China's inflation was not as high nor its corruption as blatant as they were to become in 1989. These were to be the major factors inciting workers and urban residents to participate in the 1989 demonstrations. The small number of workers who did join the 1986 movement were punished by the party much more harshly than were the students, which would happen again in 1989. The workers were arrested and given indeterminate sentences. By contrast, although scores of students were reported to have been arrested, most student protesters suffered merely a reprimand. Moreover, unlike in 1989, Deng Xiaoping's order for the students to return to class was sufficient to cause their peaceful dispersal in 1986. They were subjected to long sessions of political education at their universities, and during their summer vacations they were sent to farms and factories for reeducation. A small number were even forced to undergo military training, as would happen in 1989 as well.

The elders' reaction to the 1986 demonstrations presaged their reaction in 1989. They regarded the demonstrations as an expression of opposition to the party and hence to themselves. As would happen in 1989, the 1986 demonstrations ultimately evoked a response exactly opposite to what the students had intended. They provided the elders with the opportunity they had been waiting for to win Deng Xiaoping's acquiescence to a crackdown, not only on the student demonstrators, but also on their supposed patrons, Hu Yaobang and his intellectual network. In early January 1987 a cold blast froze the intellectual atmosphere and withered the blossoms of democracy that had bloomed so brightly the preceding summer and fall.

8

The Campaign against Bourgeois Liberalization

The student demonstrations brought the power struggle that had been building between the elders and Hu Yaobang since the Third Plenum to a climax. Deng Xiaoping's shift of support away from Hu and back to the elders played a critical role in the showdown. When the demonstrations first began in early December, Deng urged Hu at a meeting of the Military Affairs Commission to stop them from escalating, but Hu, in a rare act of defiance, did not crack down on the demonstrators. Following his lead, his propaganda director, Zhu Houze, restrained the propaganda apparatus and his public security head, Ruan Chongwu, restrained the public security forces. Afterward, therefore, when the elders criticized Hu for his lack of leadership in ideology, for protecting the intellectuals who spread liberalization, and for creating the conditions that led to demonstrations, Deng was receptive.

By late December the student demonstrations had spread to Beijing. Rumors were rife of a larger demonstration, planned at Peking University, to take place on New Year's Day in Tiananmen Square, China's symbolic political center. Deng expressed his displeasure at a meeting on December 30 with Hu, Zhao Ziyang, Wan Li, and Li Peng, blaming those in charge: "When a disturbance breaks out in a place, it's because the leaders there didn't take a firm, clear-cut stand."[1] He again instructed Hu to deal firmly with the student unrest. He also expressed his admiration for Polish President Wojciech Jaruzelski, for his imposition of martial law during the birth of the Solidarity movement in 1980. Even though few workers in China were joining the 1986 demonstrations, Deng's worries about worker unrest and his desire to take strong action before the protests spread were not totally unfounded. There were reports of worker strikes, one of them at the Luoyang Tractor Factory in Henan Province, where 20,000 workers demanding higher wages had gone on strike for two days in late December. The continuing fear that worker and other groups might join the demonstrations was another factor pushing Deng to join the elders in advocating stronger measures against the demonstrators.

Deng's anger with Hu Yaobang had been growing since the Sixth Plenum, when Hu had welcomed Deng's threat to resign and had not disseminated Deng's statement against bourgeois liberalization to the lower-level cadres. Deng was also upset because Hu had not yet purged Fang Lizhi and Wang Ruowang from the party as he had earlier been ordered to do. In the December 30 meeting, Deng said, "I have read Fang Lizhi's speeches. He does not sound like a Communist Party member at all. Why do we keep people like him in the Party? He should be expelled, not just persuaded to quit . . . Wang Ruowang in Shanghai is very presumptuous. He should have been expelled from the Party long ago—why this delay?" Of the student demonstrations, Deng complained: "We have to admit that on the ideological and theoretical front both central and local authorities have been weak and have lost ground. They have taken a laissez-faire attitude towards bourgeois liberalization, so that good people find no support while bad people go wild."[2]

In contrast to his repudiation of Fang and Wang, Deng praised the leaders of the small parties. These included Zhou Gucheng, chairman of the Chinese Peasants and Workers Democratic Party, and Fei Xiaotong and Qian Weichang, vice chairmen of the China Democratic League, who Deng said had taken a "correct position."[3] As usual, the leaders of the small parties went along with the switch in party line, but now their support was not quite as unanimous or as obedient as in the past. Lei Jieqiong, a legal expert and a vice chairman of the CPPCC national committee, for example, refused to denounce the 1986 student demonstrations categorically. She declared: "For young students who are concerned about state politics to voice their views through demonstrations is in line with the Constitution . . . If it is just a demonstration, then it cannot be considered illegal."[4] Nevertheless, she agreed with the elders' belief that "so long as our people are still suffering from poverty and ignorance, democracy can hardly be realized. Since it has taken Western countries a long time to establish democracy, we cannot on our part accomplish a high degree of socialist democracy in one move, nor can we reach our goal by simply shouting slogans and demonstrating."[5] Her arguments were persuasive to perhaps the majority of intellectuals at the time.

Fei Xiaotong, after being branded a rightist in 1957, had gone along with every shift in the party line thereafter. In fact, he and his fellow vice chairman Qian Weichang had informed Zhao Ziyang about the planned memorial for former rightists. Zhao told Deng about the memorial at the December 30 meeting and said it had been instigated by Liu Binyan. Consequently Deng may have then lumped Liu with Fang Lizhi and Wang Ruowang as the three intellectuals responsible for the demonstrations.[6]

At that meeting, Deng also belittled any fears about the impact a crackdown might have on world opinion. Yet unlike Mao, who was unconcerned with external pressure, Deng's repeated references to the outside world revealed his real concern with other countries' perceptions of China. He cited the example of the arrest of Wei Jingsheng in 1979: "A few years ago we punished according to law some exponents of liberalization who broke the law. Did that bring discredit on us? No, China's image was not damaged. On the contrary, the prestige of our country is steadily growing."[7] Because of the outside world's relative silence at the time of the arrest of the Democracy Wall activists, Deng maintained that the regime could again repress dissidents without incurring censure from abroad. He even threatened an effort similar to the anti-rightist campaign. "The struggle against the bourgeois rightists in 1957 was carried somewhat too far, and the mistakes made should be corrected. But that doesn't mean that we have negated this struggle as a whole. The struggle against bourgeois liberalization is also indispensable. We should not be afraid that it will damage our reputation abroad."[8]

Deng also rejected the kinds of political reforms proposed in 1986, such as a system of checks and balances, as inappropriate for China. Democracy, he insisted, could only be carried out under party leadership and in an environment of stability and unity. He warned: "Bourgeois liberalization would plunge the country into turmoil once more. Bourgeois liberalization means rejection of the Party's leadership; there would be nothing to unite over 1 billion people, and the Party itself would lose all power to fight."[9] In an indirect criticism of Hu Yaobang's restraint, Deng praised Hu's disciple, the mayor of Tianjin Li Ruihuan, who had acted firmly in putting down the student demonstrations there. "That the leading cadres take an unequivocal stand encourages those who are firmly opposed to disturbances and helps to persuade those who are undecided on the matter. Disturbance can be checked if the leaders take a strong stand." [10]

Deng's consistent opposition to any kind of public protest was reinforced by "special reports" he received from his old comrades Wang Zhen, Bo Yibo, and the Beijing municipal party officials. Xu Weicheng, who had served under Jiang Qing during the Cultural Revolution and was head of propaganda in Beijing, was responsible for the Cultural Revolution rhetoric against the demonstrators in the *Beijing Daily* that provoked students into burning a pile of its newspapers in protest.

When on January 2 student demonstrators were about to march on Tiananmen Square and once again Hu Yaobang disobeyed Deng's orders to arrest them, Deng finally supported a crackdown and the purge of his supposed successor. He lost patience with Hu's efforts to persuade students to return to their classes through dialogue rather than by threatening to use force. [11] On January 16, 1987, at an enlarged meeting of the Politburo, Hu Yaobang was forced to resign as party general secretary. The enlarged meeting included members of the Central Advisory Commission, the Central Discipline Inspection Commission, and other outsiders, who were granted the right to vote despite the provision in the party constitution that the general secretary could be appointed or dismissed only by a Central Committee plenum.

Hu's removal revealed not only the continuing use of illegal measures to resolve political conflict but also the persistent power of a group of elderly leaders. The Central Advisory Commission, which Deng had established as an ad hoc committee with ambiguous duties to which the senior leaders retired, had ironically become a "shadow cabinet," with real power that could be exerted when the elders felt that their or the party's authority was being threatened. Their power also derived from the support of veteran military leaders, who likewise opposed Hu and the demonstrations. They were angry with Hu for forcing the retirement of older military officers as well as party cadres and for cutting the military budget and reducing the size of the military by one quarter. Although Deng Xiaoping had actually masterminded these reductions, the military held Hu, not Deng, responsible. As was to happen again in 1989, the army played a major role in the 1986 crackdown, but this time it participated through pressure and propaganda rather than through force. Like the elders, the military used the occasion to reassert itself. The *Liberation Army Daily* set the tone by once again resurrecting the ordinary soldier Lei Feng, the "untiring screw" in the party machine, as the symbol with which to educate and reunite the whole population.[12]

The elders were also angry with Hu for very personal reasons. Hu's anti-corruption campaign launched in early 1986 had implicated several children of the top leadership, among them Peng Zhen's daughter as well as Hu Qiaomu's son. In addition, Hu's efforts to retire older political appointees in favor of younger, better-educated officials, particularly in the provinces, threatened the elders' political machines. Many of Hu's appointments had come from the Youth League, his political machine. The struggle was thus between political organizations as well as between ideological views and personal networks. The elders sought to retire Hu before he retired them.

The Symbolism of Hu Yaobang

As the 1986 demonstrations led to results opposite to those that were intended, so too did the party's removal of Hu Yaobang. Hu came to the meetings, held from January 10 to 15, prepared to defend himself, until he discovered that his supposed ally in reform, Zhao Ziyang, not only did not support him but in fact was against him. Although Zhao had joined with Hu to stop the campaign against spiritual pollution in 1983, after that he increasingly resented Hu's pronouncements on economic reform, the area he considered to be his bailiwick. As early as 1984, he wrote a letter to Deng and Chen Yun, calling for Hu's dismissal. Hu's protégé Hu Qili also joined in the attacks against him. For five hours, moreover, Deng Liqun lambasted Hu for his actions since the theory conference.[13] Alone, deserted by his allies and surrounded by opponents, Hu made a self-criticism. Wang Zhen and Bo Yibo were the most vehement in their denunciations, and they rejected Hu's first self-criticism as "too narrow." Under great pressure Hu wrote another, which circulated to the elders and others. It even included a criticism of Liu Binyan, calling him a "rightist" who had not sufficiently reformed. This self-criticism became a Central Committee document.

If the elders had expected to diminish Hu's popularity among intellectuals by forcing him to make such a self-criticism, they were not successful. Even Liu Binyan forgave Hu, explaining that Hu had been close to a nervous breakdown. Later Liu Binyan was informed that Hu regretted his words about him; Hu had tried to delete them from the public release of his self-criticism, but Deng Liqun kept them in.[14] Most intellectuals were aware that unlike the other elders, Hu had never singled out others for attack and had tried to protect and resist Deng's orders not only to crack down on the demonstrations but also to expel the three intellectuals from the party.

Bo Yibo's list of specific charges against Hu at the enlarged Politburo meeting became Central Document no. 3 of 1987. The document criticized Hu for advocating consumption over production and for making unauthorized statements and taking unauthorized actions regarding foreign policy, such as inviting 3,000 young Japanese to visit China. Hu's major "crimes," however, were his opposition to the campaigns against spiritual pollution and bourgeois liberalization, his repudiation of the left but not the right, his tolerance of dissident intellectuals, and his failure to adhere to the four basic principles. In addition he had failed to obey the collective decisions of the leadership on major issues, and had acted and spoken without appropriate consultation with other leaders. The document also revealed that Hu had been reprimanded several times earlier by the elders. Bo Yibo and Wang Zhen had reprimanded him at the end of 1983; the military leaders, including Yang Shangkun and Yu Qiuli, had done so in 1986; and Deng himself had criticized him on four occasions.[15] Hu had supposedly been unresponsive to their reprimands.

Bo Yibo's report concluded that the authority of the general secretary must be limited in order to prevent whoever held the post from acting arbitrarily. Although the elders refused to accept any restrictions on their actions, they appear to have accepted at least theoretically the need to restrain the general secretary, not only because of Hu but because of their own persecution by Mao during the Cultural Revolution. When they themselves felt threatened, they became advocates of such limitations on power.

Central Document no. 8, distributed only to the top levels of the party and army, added further charges against Hu.[16] In addition to his sponsorship of the theory conference, it listed his efforts to stop the campaign against Bai Hua and the Fourth Congress of the Chinese Writers Association in December 1984, where Hu had allowed open elections with multiple candidates. He was also rebuked for his support of Lu Dingyi's objection to inserting "oppose bourgeois liberalization" into the Sixth Plenum resolution in September 1986 and for protecting many scholars, theorists, writers, and intellectuals who had called for political change. He was further upbraided for his interview with the Hong Kong editor Lu Keng in 1985, when he was said to have criticized several members of the Politburo. In that interview Hu had actually defended Deng Liqun against Lu Keng's criticisms. The only specific criticism he made was of Hu Qiaomu, which he qualified by saying that he himself had some of the same shortcomings. Finally, Hu was accused of revealing state secrets, because he had told Lu Keng: "With comrade Deng Xiaoping taking charge, one sentence from him is sufficient, where we have to say five sentences."[17] This remark supposedly revealed that Deng was the paramount leader.

Although Hu Yaobang's removal made possible the return to center stage of Peng Zhen, Bo Yibo, Wang Zhen, Chen Yun, and their spokesmen, all somewhat eclipsed since the end of the spiritual pollution campaign, it also made Hu into a popular symbol of reform. Before his purge, Hu was regarded as well intentioned but a bit of a bumbler, without the reserve and air of an official. Afterward, he rose in the estimation of not only intellectuals but officials as well, dismayed by the arbitrary way in which he had been dismissed. Provincial officials in Gansu, Qinghai, Guizhou, and Sichuan, in a joint statement to the Central Committee, questioned whether Hu had really committed any major mistakes.[18] Whether because of such resistance or because Deng was unwilling to use the draconian methods of his predecessor, Hu was not imprisoned or even made into a nonperson as had happened to those Mao purged from the Politburo. As in the Khrushchev era in the Soviet Union, the purged leader no longer suffered purgatory. Hu, like Hua Guofeng, was allowed to retire peacefully from the scene, politically neutralized. But unlike Hua, Hu increasingly came to be held in great esteem by the populace, which regarded him as an honest, genuine reformer who had been treated unfairly.

The Return of the Elders' Spokesmen

With Hu Yaobang out of the way, the ideological realm was again taken over by the elders' spokesmen. Their headquarters was the Secretariat's Policy Research Center, headed by Deng Liqun, which provided the materials and strategies from which the leaders made major policy decisions. The center had a staff of one hundred, including specialists in various fields. Ironically, some members, like the democratic elite, had also called in 1986 for a more pluralistic atmosphere. Despite the elders' control of *Red Flag* and sometimes of the *Guangming Daily,* they charged that they had been unable to get their more orthodox views into the major newspapers, journals, and meetings because these forums were dominated by advocates of bourgeois liberalization.

Red Flag's editor Xiong Fu cited his young disciple Wu Jianguo's article "Reflections on the Question of Freedom," which Wu had first unsuccessfully tried to publish in *Philosophy Research.* Even his own journal *Red Flag,* Xiong said, had been unable to criticize bourgeois liberalization directly for most of 1986. Instead, "we commented on the Western bourgeois trends of thought but said nothing of their spread and influence in China." [19] Even the controversial literary work *Half of Man Is Woman* by Zhang Xianliang was not criticized in *Red Flag.* The elders' spokesmen called the 1986 political debates "false pluralism," imposed by an "intellectual elite." At a forum convened by the *Red Flag* editorial department, twenty orthodox theorists complained that they had not experienced "relaxation" and "leniency" in 1986; on the contrary, they had been "tied up and gagged." [20] Yet, unlike 1986, those attacked in the campaign against bourgeois liberalization launched in January 1987 were unable to respond to their critics in any way.

The elders and their spokesmen revived Mao's ideological methods, honed from their Yan'an days—unanimous media attacks on specific intellectuals, criticism and self-criticism sessions, denunciation by one's peers, and public confessions—which had gone into disuse under Hu Yaobang. Some of Mao's ideas were revived as well. Peng Zhen, who in November 1986 became honorary president of the Yan'an Literary and Art Society, met with veteran writers from the Yan'an period and praised the Yan'an Talks as "still applicable . . . In the Yan'an period, we had the same thinking and acted in step with one another." [21] Yan'an writers, such as Liu Baiyu and Lin Mohan, hailed the contemporary significance of the Yan'an Talks. Forums of older revolutionaries were held at which they described the glory days of the revolutionary movement, when they had discovered that only the party could save China.

While reviving Mao's Yan'an practices and ideas, the elders rejected

Mao's Cultural Revolution policies by comparing the 1986 student demonstrators to the Red Guards. Both groups were characterized as disrupting the unity and stability necessary for economic modernization. A commentator article in *China Youth News* noted: "The Great Proletarian Cultural Revolution has taught us the lesson that turmoil must not be permitted to wreak havoc but must be repulsed."[22] Two days later, a *China Youth News* front-page editorial declared: "The practice of great democracy that attempts to deviate from party leadership . . . can only bring about chaos and retrogression."[23] Despite these comparisons, however, there were few similarities between the spontaneous 1986 student demonstrations calling for political reform and the manipulated Red Guard demonstrations seeking to overthrow specific leaders whom Mao disliked.

In the early months of 1987 one ideology, Marxism-Leninism, held sway over the intellectual community. In contrast to his 1986 statements, the president of CASS, Hu Sheng, decreed that Marxism was no longer to be treated as one school of thought among many but was to be the supreme guiding authority in academic endeavors. As for the universities, *Red Flag* declared: "We should not give rein to all schools of thought and let students choose them at will, nor should we end the study of Marxism in the classroom."[24] Acknowledging that Marxism was not spontaneously accepted by students, it asserted that "we must therefore guide them to conscientiously read the works of Marx and Lenin."[25]

Bourgeois liberalization became any Western ideas that the elders found distasteful. Among these was the statement of the former U.S. secretary of state, John Foster Dulles, who in 1956 had said: "The U.S. policy is to bring about liberalization (that is, capitalism) in the Soviet Union and East European countries; whether China will realize Western liberalization remains to be seen."[26] From this threat, the elders supposedly derived the phrases "bourgeois liberalization" and, later, "peaceful evolution" to characterize the subversive nature of Western ideas. As in 1983, Western technology, economic practices, and capital were still welcome, but Western political and humanistic ideas were condemned. Once more Freud was attacked for his stress on the unconscious, sexual desire, and the nonrational, and Sartre for his existentialism, with its stress on individual freedom of choice.

Western modernism was again criticized for creating extreme individualism, irrationalism, decadence, mysticism, and sexual indulgence.[27] Zhao Fusan, a vice president of CASS, used the West's own criticisms to highlight the decadence of Western culture. He cited *Habits of the Heart,* a work by Robert Bellah and four others based on two hundred interviews with members of the American middle class. It showed, according to Zhao, that "the ideology of individualism only corrodes social ethics and morality . . . and will eventually and surely develop to the extent that people become selfish."[28] Friendship and family are put in a secondary position to one's status and profession. "The pursuit of individual freedom," Zhao declared, "has brought about the individual's spiritual loneliness."[29] The writer Li Zhun blamed China's Cultural Revolution for inducing a sense of solitude in certain people, but he warned that "this modern sense of solitude, which is estranged from, fearful of, and hostile to the entire relations of reality, must be totally negated and combated since it directs its spearhead of criticism at the socialist system."[30]

To counter the intellectuals' interest in Western culture and values, the elders increasingly extolled traditional Chinese culture and nationalism. Wang Zhen was in the forefront of this effort. "Our nation has a rich and valuable cultural heritage," but, he complained, "some people go in for national nihilism."[31] Bo Yibo and even Zhao Ziyang stressed that China had not only a rich humanistic culture but also a rich record of scientific achievement that some Westerners, such as the English historian of science Joseph Needham, had praised very highly. Citing Needham, the elders pointed out that when Europe was still in the Dark Ages, China was making brilliant contributions to the development of science and only in the modern times had fallen behind. In March 1987, when the Institute of Physics of CAS and the Physics Department of Peking University made a breakthrough in the development of a supercomputer, Zhao Ziyang hailed it as proof that China could now finally stand on its own among modern nations.

The most concerted attacks, however, were made against the Western democratic practices that had been praised in 1986. At a forum sponsored by the military, the idea of a multiparty system for China was rejected because "under socialist conditions, no conflicts of basic interests exist."[32] A *Guangming Daily* article charged that Western political parties created the illusion of representing the interests of all social classes, but in reality only represented the bourgeois class.[33] China's present system of multiparty cooperation under party leadership, therefore, was more appropriate for China. The media was particularly vituperative in its denunciation of the Western system of separation of powers, which Deng himself considered to be disruptive and enfeebling. Because the National People's Congress exercised legislative power, the State Council executive power, and the courts judicial power, another *Guangming Daily* article noted, "some comrades assert categorically that our country is now implementing the system of the 'separation of the three powers.'"[34]

Indeed Peng Zhen, as head of the NPC, had continued to give the body a bit more autonomy than it had had under Mao. In addition to delaying and then watering down the bankruptcy law, Peng Zhen in March 1987 postponed consideration of an enterprise management reform proposed by the reform officials because it restricted party bureaucrats from interfering in management of state factories.[35] Even though Peng's purpose in giving the NPC more autonomy was not to use the NPC to check the leadership, but to limit the reformers in the leadership, nevertheless, some genuine reforms did pass the NPC under Peng Zhen's leadership. In December 1986, for example, the NPC approved direct election to the people's congresses at the county level and stipulated that the number of candidates for village, district, and county people's congresses must exceed the number of positions by 30 to 100 percent. Furthermore, any group of ten could nominate candidates, to allow more choice. Even though these local congresses had very little power and often anyone elected whom the party disliked was unable to take his or her seat, these reforms permitted some practice in democratic procedures at the grass-roots level. Equally important, these experiences gave members a sense of the potential power the NPC might be able to wield. Whether supportive or unsupportive of reform, the NPC had acquired more power than it had in the Mao era.

The Targets of the Campaign

The principal targets of the campaign against bourgeois liberalization—Fang Lizhi, Liu Binyan, and Wang Ruowang—were pilloried for advocating Western political values and institutions. Even though Fang Lizhi's concept of democracy differed from the Western view in being based on the rule of an educated elite, the party media charged Fang with wanting the complete Westernization of China. Party bureaucrats felt personally threatened, as well, by his demand that an intellectual elite should replace the party elite. Fang's view that science required a pluralistic environment and complete openness, however, upset the elders less than his outright rejection of Marxism-Leninism as irrelevant to present-day China. Also disturbing was his willingness to denounce the elders by name, something normally not done by anyone other than another top official. Fang's public ridicule of Hu Qiaomu's ignorance of the workings of modern science[36] was particularly infuriating. Such a criticism could easily be applied to all the elders who, in the name of the party, believed that they had the right to dictate to scientists as well as to everyone else.

Even though Liu Binyan had never rejected the party as Fang had, the elders found his work just as threatening. He was attacked for his "negative" portrayals of China in his investigative reporting. At a forum of the All-China Federation of Journalists, one of the many forums to denounce him, his critics explained why he upset the elders: "What he revealed was not this or that corrupt practice but the root, or soil of these malpractices; in other words, that 'the CCP is corrupt.'"[37] Elsewhere Liu's criticisms of party officials and policies were described as attacks on the Chinese nation, which the party supposedly represented. "A Second Kind of Loyalty," which implied that one who criticized the party was a more loyal citizen than one who obeyed the party unquestioningly, made it appear, the party charged, that Liu, rather than the party, expressed the views of the nation. A People's Daily article complained: "Only he himself is the defender of truth and the representative of the people's interests."[38] The elders resented intellectuals who dared to speak on behalf of the people and castigated them for being part of an "elite."

Wang Ruowang was also chastised for his temerity in criticizing high officials, including Deng Xiaoping, by name. Wang's criticisms of Deng and his policies had been compiled and shown to Deng. In addition, Wang was attacked for publishing in Hong Kong journals. He did so primarily because he had been prevented off and on from publishing in his own country. He had tried to found his own magazine, Great Pleasure (Kuaizai), and had placed an announcement about its forthcoming publication in various newspapers and journals. He had edited articles for it and planned for its inaugural issue in summer of 1985, but the authorities prevented it from appearing.

With Hu Yaobang's dismissal, no one dared to protect these three intellectuals from the wrath of Deng and the elders. As in 1957, the three were again purged from the party. The impact of the campaign against them in 1987, however, was radically different from that of the Mao era. When Liu was denounced in the anti-rightist campaign, only his wife, Zhu Hong, and his family stood by him. In 1987 Liu received visitors, letters, and even gifts from hundreds of people he did not know. Whereas in 1957 his colleagues eagerly criticized him, in 1987 most of his colleagues remained conspicuously silent. Well-known intellectuals had to be offered payment—as much as 90 yuan per thousand characters—to write articles against Liu, and still few responded. Not only did they fear that renewed attacks on intellectuals might lead to another Cultural Revolution, but they also did not want to be ostracized by their colleagues, many of whom had sworn never again to criticize others for political reasons. There were some important exceptions. The philosophers Ru Xin and Xing Bensi, who had turned against Wang Ruoshui in the spiritual pollution campaign, spoke out against the three intellectuals in the anti–bourgeois liberalization campaign. Although they were repaid with movement up the bureaucratic ladder, they were shunned by their scholarly colleagues.

The public attacks were limited to only these three targets. Most of the criticisms were written by party functionaries, and even most of these used pen names. As minister of culture Wang Meng was expected to criticize the three intellectuals, but this time he and others, among them Ai Qing, engaged in passive resistance, unlike their participation in the spiritual pollution campaign. Others, such as Liu Zaifu, editor of the journal *Literary Commentary* (Wenxue pinglun), carried out active resistance. A Liu Binyan article that was to be published in *Literary Commentary* in January 1987 was ordered deleted, but the English-language table of contents in the issue retained the title of Liu's article covered over ineffectively in black ink, to the authorities' great displeasure. Liu Zaifu offered his resignation from the journal, but his like-minded deputy editor He Xilai then assumed his post. Another form of resistance was demonstrated by Zhou Guangzhao, a highly regarded nuclear physicist trained in the Soviet Union. He took over as the new president of the Academy of Sciences from the deposed president Lu Jiaxi and vice president Yan Dongsheng, who had been dismissed because of their support for Fang Lizhi. Zhou praised his two predecessors for their promotion of scientific research. He also pledged to continue their practice of having the directors of the academy's institutes elected by their peers rather than appointed by the party and of giving the directors direct responsibility over research.

Another difference in the Deng era was the international pressure mobilized in support of the three targeted intellectuals. Because of China's opening to the outside world, Fang, Liu, and Wang had friends, colleagues, and kindred spirits abroad who rushed to their defense. Western scholars, some of them Nobel laureates, and Chinese students and friends studying overseas sent statements to the Politburo Standing Committee calling for a cessation of the attacks on the three, whom they described as patriotic individuals, devoted to their country. A public statement signed by Chinese students abroad also protested the treatment of Hu Yaobang. About half of the almost one thousand student signatories signed their real names, another unprecedented act in the People's Republic.

Although the three were not sent away to prison or labor reform, they were put under surveillance by plainclothes policemen, had their phones tapped, and their works banned. Wang Ruowang's house was searched on January 15 and many manuscripts and letters were confiscated, but he did not disappear from the scene as he had under Mao. Fang Lizhi delivered a scholarly report at the Fourth National Congress of the Chinese Physics Society on February 28, 1987, which was chaired by his colleague Guan Weiyan, though Guan had been dismissed from his post as president when Fang was dismissed as vice chancellor of Keda. Fang continued to be a member of CAS and a vice chairman of the Academic Committee of the Institute of Physics, to which he was transferred. Fang was given a new apartment, moreover, and in spring 1987 his wife Li Shuxian was allowed to run for election to the people's congress in the Haidian university district, a post she won by a landslide.

Liu Binyan and Wang Ruowang remained members of the Writers Association, and Liu retained his post as a vice chairman of the association, though he was forced to retire from the journalists' federation. Both men appeared at gatherings of literary circles in Beijing and Shanghai at the time of the 1987 Spring Festival. But Liu, feeling that his reappearance was being used to show the outside world that little had changed, shortly thereafter declined to attend public gatherings. He did not want others to think his life had returned to normal. Nonetheless, that the three intellectuals did not become nonpersons suggests that the Deng regime was concerned with not antagonizing either the international community or China's intellectual community. The elders' own experience of persecution in the Cultural Revolution may also have restrained them from pushing this movement too far, for fear of sparking another upheaval.

When compared with the Mao era, the treatment of the three intellectuals was thus relatively lenient. Although they were criticized within their units, they did not have to endure mass criticism sessions. They were asked to write self-criticisms, but when they refused, they were not forced to do so. Perhaps the most unanticipated result of the campaign against the three was the way in which attacks on them spread their ideas beyond elite intellectual circles. As the urban population in particular read excerpts of their speeches, quoted at length in the criticisms in the media and in official compilations, those outside the intellectual community became acquainted with their thinking. Instead of leading to a rejection of their ideas, the campaign created an atmosphere more receptive to their acceptance.

Others Targeted behind Closed Doors

Other targets were not publicly attacked in the media but came under great pressure in 1987. Most of these individuals had participated in the practice criterion discussion and the theory conference and had helped create a pluralistic ideological environment more appropriate for reform than the restrictive environment of orthodox Marxism-Leninism. In the process of revising the ideology, they had become more knowledgeable about Western Marxism and Western political ideas and practices, which led them to question even more the orthodox ideology and Leninist political structure. Equally important in explaining their censure in 1987 was that most of them—Su Shaozhi, Wang Ruoshui, Sun Changjiang, Zhang Xianyang, Yu Haocheng, Li Honglin, Yan Jiaqi, Tong Dalin, Yu Guangyuan, and Wu Mingyu— had been associated at one time or another with Hu Yaobang.

A few of Hu's associates, such as Ruan Ming, had already been dismissed from the party before the 1987 campaign. When Wang Zhen became president of the Central Party School in 1982, he not only purged Ruan but persisted in a personal vendetta against him until Ruan sought exile abroad in 1988, an option that had not been open in the Mao era. Sun Changjiang was also dismissed from the school, but with the help of Hu Yaobang he became a deputy editor of the *Science and Technology Daily* (Keji ribao).

Other elders also used the campaign to carry out their own personal vendettas. Hu Qiaomu felt a personal animus toward Yu Guangyuan, who had been a major link between Hu Yaobang and the theorists. Hu Qiaomu convened ten criticism sessions against Yu, whose open views and emphasis on a market economy were characterized as political opposition to the party. Yu was allowed only fifteen minutes to respond, and when he later wrote a written response, it was not distributed. Despite the campaign's insistence that China would continue to adopt Western economic practices, the attacks on Yu indicated that some of the elders were interested in repudiating not only Western political ideas but also Western economic ideas.

Yan Jiaqi and his wife Gao Gao's book, *A History of the Ten-Year Cultural Revolution*, finally published in December 1986, was banned early in 1987. Yan stopped attending and then withdrew from the political reform group, though Zhao Ziyang and Bao Tong, who had created the group, were still very much in power. Even Hu Yaobang's associates in the supposedly untouchable areas of science and technology were affected. Wu Mingyu, a vice minister of the State Science and Technology Commission and for many years a bridge partner of Deng Xiaoping's, was retired. He was the first ministerial-level official to be dismissed in the 1987 campaign. Wu had participated in the theory conference and had tried to shield Fang Lizhi and then Sun Changjiang from attack.

Hu Qiaomu, Deng Liqun, and their associates compiled a booklet of excerpts of articles and speeches by Hu Yaobang's network as well as by the three publicly targeted intellectuals and Fang Lizhi's close colleague, Xu Liangying. Alongside the excerpts they printed the slogans used by students in the 1986 demonstrations. In making the compilation, they sought to show the similarities between the two views in order to prove that those connected with Hu Yaobang were responsible for the student protests. The excerpts, culled from a variety of different sources and speeches given all over the country, revealed an in-depth surveillance of Hu's associates. Deng Liqun and Hu Qiaomu also organized writing groups to critique members of Hu's network and paid them 100 yuan per thousand characters for their efforts. Most of the articles were tedious and unconvincing.

Again, the impact of the compilation and the dull critiques was the opposite of what the authorities intended. Instead of defaming Hu's associates, the attacks on them, like those against Hu Yaobang and the three intellectuals, made their views more well known and accessible to the literate population.

While Hu's intellectual network was attacked behind closed doors, his protégés Zhu Houze, director of the Propaganda Department, and Ruan Chongwu, the minister of public security, were dismissed. Zhu, who had been involved in rural reform as well as in ideological revisions, and Ruan, who had been a scientific researcher and a Shanghai party official, were examples of the kind of younger, educated administrators Hu had tried to place in important positions. Both were blamed for being too soft on the student demonstrators and were replaced by others associated with the elders. A professional security official of long standing, Wang Fang, became the minister of public security, and Wang Renzhi, a close associate of Deng Liqun and a former deputy editor of *Red Flag,* became the director of the Propaganda Department. Other reform officials associated with Hu Yaobang, such as Wan Li and Hu Qili, had made self-criticisms and had thereby held on to their positions, but Ruan and Zhu had refused. Instead of being purged or worse for their "insolence," however, Ruan was appointed a vice minister of the State Science and Technology Commission and Zhu Houze became a deputy director of the China Rural Development Research Institute.

Like the campaigns of the Mao era, the 1987 campaign was also directed against nonconformist writers. Wu Zuguang was attacked because in addition to calling for an end to censorship he, like Fang Lizhi, had dared to criticize Hu Qiaomu publicly. Zhang Xianliang was criticized for his "sensational" literary works, primarily his novel *Half of Man Is Woman.* In April he was brought out for a press conference with two other writers to demonstrate to the world that all was normal. But in contrast to a 1986 press conference, when Zhang had talked volubly, he was now very cautious and admitted that the attacks on his works had depressed him. Acknowledging that he still had "not realized where my serious mistakes are,"[39] he insisted that the impulse for his work came only from his love of his country and his desire to correct some of its unhealthy practices.

Liu Xinwu, who in November 1977 had published "The Schoolmaster," the first work of the wounded literature writers, and had taken over the editorship of *People's Literature* from Wang Meng when Wang became minister of culture, was suspended from his position. He was charged with publishing in the January 1987 issue a story by Ma Jian, "Show Your Tongue Coating," which supposedly ridiculed Tibetan social customs. A more important reason for his dismissal, however, was that he too had offended Hu Qiaomu and Deng Liqun. Like Liu Zaifu, he had urged his compatriots to reflect on their own guilt in the Cultural Revolution, a guilt he felt keenly for his own inaction when confronted by a fatal beating being administered by Red Guards. But now public discussion of a Ba Jin proposal to establish a museum on the Cultural Revolution was banned, and those who had continued to denounce the Cultural Revolution were criticized.

The young directors of the "fifth generation," or Cultural Revolution generation, of filmmakers, such as Chen Kaige, Tian Zhuangzhuang, Zhang Yimou, and Wu Xiaomu, known for their innovative styles and symbolic criticism of the political system, were also criticized. But attacks were not limited to the young. Even an older and prestigious figure such as the playwright Xia Yan was censured. He had taken positions similar to those of his longtime friend and colleague Zhou Yang, and he was also held responsible for suggesting to Hu Yaobang that members of the Writers Association be allowed to elect their own officials rather than have them imposed by the party.

The obscure poets, who had been targets in the 1983 campaign, were left relatively alone in 1987. Still, Bei Dao resigned from the Writers Association in protest over the closure of *China* (Zhongguo), a journal he had helped establish under the patronage of Ding Ling, who had died in 1985. To resign from one's unit *(danwei)* was a strong form of protest. Hitherto virtually everyone in China belonged to a unit, the source of one's wages, housing, medical care, and education for one's children and also the means by which the party controlled its members. To withdraw was to assert one's independence from the party spiritually as well as materially.

Apart from the criticism of the three intellectuals, the harshest words of the 1987 campaign were directed at the press. Although the relatively free-wheeling economy of the Shenzhen special economic zone remained almost untouched, its newspapers and magazines were attacked. Looking for a more open place in which to publish their articles, intellectuals from all over China, among them Liu Binyan and

Wang Ruoshui, had published in the Shenzhen media. The editor of *Shenzhen Youth News,* which had published an article recommending Deng's retirement, was relieved of his post and forced to make a self-criticism. Other papers, such as the *Shenzhen Worker News* and *Shenzhen Literature,* were also suspended. Even scientific journals, especially those associated with Fang Lizhi, such as the *Anhui Science Journal* and *Anhui Journal of Science News,* were closed down in early 1987.

A number of semi-independent papers were closed as well. *Modern People's News* (Xiandairen bao) in Guangzhou and *Society News* (Shehui bao) in Shanghai, small outspoken weeklies, unattached to any party unit and supposedly supported by independent financial sources in Hong Kong as well as in China, were shut down. They had criticized Hu Qiaomu and Deng Liqun for their attacks on Ma Ding. The *World Economic Herald,* also relatively independent financially and underwritten by nonparty financial sources, came under pressure at this time because of the Ma Ding affair, but was not closed; it was supposedly shielded by Zhao Ziyang. *Youth Forum* (Qingnian luntan), a relatively liberal bimonthly on political issues, had been founded in 1984 with the support of Hu Yaobang's son Hu Deping. The journal had reprinted Hu Ping's talk "On Freedom of Speech" in its July–September 1986 issue, and had also published articles calling for limits on government. It too was ordered shut down by Deng Liqun. By contrast, the journal under the aegis of Deng Xiaoping's son Deng Pufang, *March Wind* (Sanyue feng), remained in operation.

In late 1987 the elders increased their control over the media by setting up the State Media and Publications Office, headed by one of their spokesmen, Du Daozheng, with a staff of several hundred. Du had worked in the army, had been a Xinhua reporter, and most recently had been editor-in-chief of the *Guangming Daily.* He was a Deng Liqun associate and lived in the same building complex in Beijing as several of the others put in charge of the media at this time. While at the *Guangming Daily,* Du had published editorials written by Hu Qiaomu and Deng Liqun attacking bourgeois liberalization. Under great pressure, the *People's Daily* criticized itself for its series praising Fang Lizhi's innovative educational reforms at Keda and for organizing forums on political reform in 1986. By contrast, *Red Flag,* the *Guangming Daily,* and *Literature and Art Theory and Comment* were lauded as model papers that others should emulate. Not surprisingly, Hu Yaobang was charged with allowing editors and journalists too much freedom.

The mandate of the State Media and Publications Office was not only to censor all newspapers, magazines, and books but also to reduce the number of "illegal" publications, that is, the nonofficial press, which had exploded in the mid-1980s. As the government had cut back its subsidies and ordered government enterprises to use market forces, nonofficial publications printed by official publishing houses had become lucrative sources of income. It was estimated that by 1987 there were more than 25,000 printing houses and hundreds of collective and individual bookstores and book peddlers selling nonofficial publications.[40] Most of these were tabloids filled with stories of romance, adventure, crime, folktales, and pornography; a smaller number discussed political issues. The effort to crack down on these nonofficial publications, however, was relatively ineffective. The market for them was huge, and they were a great source of income for the party officials running the official printing houses where most of them were published as supplements. This section of the media had attained a certain degree of autonomy owing to unclear lines of authority, economic incentives, and a loosening of controls. To regain control over it proved virtually impossible.

There was also active as well as passive resistance to the effort to censor the official press. When Du Daozheng sent a work group to Shanghai to reorganize the *Wenhui News,* the Shanghai Party Committee refused to carry out its bidding. While Du's office was drafting a law to restrict journalists, Hu Jiwei continued to work on a law to give journalists more freedom. Both the contradictory nature of this most intense and widespread campaign of the Deng era and the resistance to it produced results quite the opposite of those of the Mao period. Instead of stigmatizing the victims, the campaign enhanced their stature. The more one was criticized, the more prominent one became; the more one's works and ideas were singled out and quoted for criticism, the more they became known and were found appealing. The attacks on Hu Yaobang, the publicly targeted three intellectuals, the theorists, and the nonconformist writers and journalists made them heroes, rather than villains.

Restraints on the Campaign

Divergence in the leadership of the campaign began to appear early on. The strategy of Deng Xiaoping and Zhao Ziyang was to let the elders and their associates dominate the ideological front, while they continued to encourage economic reforms. Zhao, a shrewd administrator, tapped the talents of younger economists, social scientists, and technocrats. Unlike Deng, he was not completely uninterested in political structural reform, as demonstrated by his sponsorship of the political reform group established in the fall of 1986 under the direction of his secretary Bao Tong. Although, unlike Hu Yaobang, Zhao was disinterested in ideological issues, the effect was similar. Editors, publishers, and the public in general had more leeway to make their own judgments. Like his mentor Deng, however, Zhao's main focus was on economic reform. In the first three months of 1987 Deng and Zhao were very much on the defensive, as they tried to limit the campaign. Zhao was behind Central Document no. 4, issued on January 28, 1987, which sought to ensure that the campaign would not be extended to the economic realm, the countryside, or the areas of science and technology.

Nevertheless, except for the cessation of attacks on Western lifestyles, Zhao's and Deng's efforts from late January until early May to limit the campaign were effectively blocked. Zhao found himself in conflict with the elders he had joined to oust Hu Yaobang, but who now opposed his efforts to limit the campaign. Once more, intellectuals feared another anti-rightist campaign or even a Cultural Revolution. The campaign did not even leave the economic realm altogether alone, as Zhao and Deng wanted. There were denunciations not only of capitalism but also of Western economic methods, the same target in the 1985 criticism of Ma Ding. The media in the early months of 1987 issued mixed messages on the economy. While articles in the *People's Daily* continued to promote a market form of socialism advocated by Zhao,[41] a *Guangming Daily* article reiterated: "It is still Marxist economics that can save China, for it is an economics that criticizes capitalism and builds socialism."[42] Various articles again rejected Western statistical and quantitative methods in favor of Marxist economic theory.[43]

Zhao repeatedly tried to bring the campaign to an end. At a mid-March meeting of the CPPCC, he announced that "the 'general atmosphere' has changed," quoting Deng to the effect that "the 'trouble' is over."[44] At another meeting, this one at the Academy of Sciences, Zhao declared: "We must absolutely not oppose bourgeois liberalization at the expense of democratization."[45] He assured intellectuals that the channels were still open for them to express their views and to assimilate foreign culture that was useful to China.

Zhao and Deng were especially concerned with China's image in the international community. Zhao, in particular, feared that the campaign might allow the reforms under way in Eastern Europe and just beginning in the Soviet Union to overtake China's efforts.[46] China was also engaged in another form of competition with Taiwan, which was enhancing its image abroad by its galloping economic growth, its moves to end martial law, and its recognition of opposition parties in the first steps of political reform. The concern expressed by foreign businesses as well as by foreign scholars and Chinese students studying abroad was another factor influencing Zhao and Deng to moderate the campaign. Hu Yaobang was presented at the Fifth Session of the Sixth National People's Congress in March to reinforce the regime's claim that the situation had returned to normal. But Hu's appearance—grim, downcast, and without his usual buoyancy—told a different story. When he was greeted with sustained, warm applause from the 2,000 delegates, press units were immediately told that nothing about the enthusiasm of the delegates was to be reported, and all pictures of it were banned. Well aware that their ouster of Hu had been generally unpopular, the leadership sought to suppress any public outcry.

The Zhuozhou Conference

Just as Zhao seemed to be regaining the offensive, a conference was convened on April 6–12 at Zhuozhou in Hebei, sponsored by *Red Flag,* the literary and art section of the *Guangming Daily, Literature and Art Theory and Comment,* and the Propaganda Department in an effort to reenergize the campaign and solicit more articles against bourgeois liberalization. The meeting was attended by 120 scholars, editors, writers, theorists, and propaganda officials and excluded representatives from the *People's Daily,* the *Literary Gazette,* and the Ministry of Culture, all supposedly organs of the reform officials. The spokesmen for the elders—Xiong Fu, He Jingzhi, Lin Mohan, Liu

Baiyu, Chen Yong, Li Xifan, and Yao Xueyin—reemerged at the gathering with a vengeance. They refused to accept Deng's pronouncement that the "trouble" was "over," and they reminded their listeners once more of the evils of bourgeois liberalization.

Deng Liqun's keynote address not only repeated the slogans of the campaign but gave vent to the anger the elders and their spokesmen felt at having been denied access to the media by reform officials and their intellectual network. Many speakers rehashed past controversies. Condemned once more were the theory conference for repudiating Mao, Marxism-Leninism, and even socialism; Liu Zaifu's humanistic, subjective view of literature; and the purge of the elders' supporters at the Fourth Congress of the Writers Association. This last event was again blamed on Hu Yaobang, whom they quoted as having said prior to the congress: "During mass [group] elections, what is there for you [CCP committees] to control! Let them elect whomever they want." Hu's order, they charged, had deprived He Jingzhi and Liu Baiyu, who had been approved by the party committee, of their positions as vice chairmen, and instead those who had defied the party committee, such as Liu Binyan, Bai Hua, and Wang Ruowang, were elected to the presidium and council of the association. The elders' spokesmen claimed that the Fourth Congress had been a concerted effort to eliminate the party's leadership over literature and art and to "kick out of positions of leadership in the [association] many fine comrades who upheld the four basic principles, and who took a clear-cut stand against bourgeois liberalism."[47] Over two hundred articles, to be published in major newspapers and journals, were commissioned at the conference. One hundred and fifty yuan were to be paid for every thousand characters of criticism. The amount paid for such commissioned condemnations continued to increase.

When the *Guangming Daily* carried a report on the conference a few days later, Bao Tong sent an assistant to retrieve the recordings of the speeches made at the meeting.[48] Excerpts were typed up and shown to Deng Xiaoping, who was reported to have reacted angrily. Subsequently the commissioned condemnations were banned from publication. The elders and their spokesmen had gone beyond the limits set by Deng, provoking him to switch his support back to the reform officials. Although the Zhuozhou conference may have been the catalyst for this reversal, both Deng and Zhao were even more disturbed by the elders' attacks on market practices and their efforts to make the economy conform to orthodox Marxism-Leninism. Zhao was particularly upset by rumors charging that while Hu Yaobang only talked about capitalism, Zhao Ziyang practiced it. With Hu gone, there was no one else of his stature able to deflect the elders' attacks on the reforms, and Zhao was now blamed for the policies that they opposed.

The Return to Relaxation

With Deng's approval, Zhao abruptly concluded the campaign against bourgeois liberalization with a speech on May 13 to propaganda, theoretical, press, and Central Party School cadres. His message was written by the political reform group under Bao Tong, which had taken over from Hu Yaobang's group the drafting of political reform proposals to be presented at the Thirteenth Party Congress in the fall. Under Mao, Bao Tong had been director of research in the party's Organization Department. During the Cultural Revolution, he was sent to Henan to do labor reform, but returned to Beijing soon after Mao's death to become a deputy director of the State Science and Technology Commission. One of his first tasks had been to help draft Deng Xiaoping's 1977 speech on science and technology, in which Deng had elevated intellectuals from the bourgeoisie to the working class and called them a leading force in the party's modernization. Bao had also attended the theory conference and, like the democratic elite, had become embroiled in ideological debates with Hu Qiaomu.

A member of Bao Tong's political reform group, Wu Guoguang, who wrote the important commentator articles in the *People's Daily* expressing Zhao's views, has described the activities of the group.[49] It convened a series of symposia, read huge stacks of relevant materials, and met frequently. Subgroups worked on specific political issues. Its first meeting was held on October 7, 1986, at the guesthouse used for provincial officials. Ironically, Hu Qiaomu and Deng Liqun gathered their advisors and writers a few months later in the same guesthouse, though on different floors, to organize the campaign against bourgeois liberalization. Although members of both groups had known each other for a long time, Wu Guoguang noted that when they met in the corridors, they did not speak. In terms of age and education, most of Bao Tong's group were between thirty and forty and had entered universities after the Cultural Revolution. Most of Deng Liqun's group was between fifty and sixty or even older and had entered universities before the Cultural Revolution. Bao Tong's group was drawn from a wide spectrum of organizations, including research institutes, universities, the *People's Daily,* and Zhao's think tanks, especially the Institute of Economic Structural Reform under Chen Yizi; most of Deng Liqun's group were from the party and army propaganda departments and nearly all were middle- or slightly higher-ranking officials.

Deng Liqun's group set the tone for the anti–bourgeois liberalization campaign; Bao Tong's group set the tone for the countermovement. Although Zhao's May 13 speech was not made available as Central Document no. 16 until two months later, its contents became known almost immediately. Zhao repudiated the views of the elders and their spokesmen, though without mentioning them by name. He characterized the elders' spokesmen as being "good at writing articles for 'mass criticism' but not good at conducting positive education or writing articles which will [take] root in people's minds."[50] He charged them with regarding political reforms as subversive to party leadership.[51] Most disturbing to Zhao were their "slurs" against the economic reforms: "'To oppose political liberalization,' it is imperative to oppose economic liberalization"; "the deepest cause of bourgeois liberalization can be found in the economic sphere"; and the enterprise contract and leasing system were regarded as "promoting private ownership."[52] He charged that some had even sought to "restrict" Central Document no. 4, which opposed extending the campaign to the economic sphere. This action, Zhao asserted, was against party discipline. He concluded: "Today, outmoded, stagnant, and ossified viewpoints that are divorced from actual work and life are still quite a serious problem in economic theoretical study. These views restrict the minds of some comrades."[53]

Zhao's May 13 speech was followed by scores of articles reaffirming the economic reforms and denouncing their critics. The voices of the elders' spokesmen slowly faded away. Deng Liqun was forbidden from involvement in propaganda; Hu Qili headed a five-person group, which included Bao Tong, to take over the propaganda portfolio. Because of his self-criticism and his attack on his mentor Hu Yaobang, Hu Qili remained a member of the powerful Secretariat. By mid-August, Zhao had removed Deng Liqun's group in the Policy Research Office. Even the Central Discipline Inspection Commission, the elders' haven, was publicly attacked for its doctrinairism by Li Chang, a former member of the commission, who had been compelled to retire because he had opposed its purge of a number of reformist theorists.

The idea that China was moving to the primary stage of socialism, initially suggested by Su Shaozhi and Feng Lanrui in a slightly different formulation at the 1979 theory conference, was revived in spring 1987. The concept was used as the theoretical basis for China's move toward a diversified economy, including individual economic activity, and was widely discussed in the media in order to counter some of the elders' opposition to a market economy. Su and Feng were not given credit for the idea; it was attributed to the "Resolution on Party History" of June 1981. Nevertheless, their associate Yu Guangyuan reemerged to champion the concept, and reformist economists expounded on it in universities and research centers. Among its advocates was the economist and Peking University professor Li Yining, then just becoming known. He spoke to packed audiences about the initial stage of socialism, which, he said, should also include a shareholding system in state industries.

Although the campaign finally appeared to be ending, and party leaders for the first time in their history welcomed, amid great publicity, a group of intellectuals, primarily scientists, to their retreat at Beidaihe, the party was planning another purge of the Hu Yaobang network. In order to gain the elders' cooperation in continuing the economic reforms, Deng Xiaoping and Zhao Ziyang gave in to the elders' demands to purge the individuals whose views had most enraged them. At the beginning of the campaign against bourgeois liberalization, Hu Qiaomu and Deng Liqun, with the assistance of Xu Weicheng of the Beijing Party Committee, had drawn up a list of ten or so intellectuals to be purged and had given it to Zhao.[54] Zhao procrastinated until the summer, and then only five were punished. Of the five, four had been closely identified with Hu when he headed the Central Party School, had attended Hu's theory conference, and were Marxists who dissented from the orthodox interpretation.

One of these individuals, Zhang Xianyang, a member of the Marxist-Leninist Institute, had continued to criticize Mao in numerous articles after the theory conference. In the fall 1980 *Newsletter of the Society of Marxism-Leninism,* he repudiated Mao's characterization of peasants as "poor and blank" as having nothing in common with true socialism. At a seminar sponsored by the editorial department of the *Guangming Daily* in October of the same year, Zhang also questioned the Leninist political system by calling for a reexamination of the concept of democratic centralism. He charged that "democracy under centralized guidance" was not really democratic, because one only endorsed the candidate chosen by the leadership.[55] Zhang had further infuriated Hu Qiaomu by dubbing him "antihumanitarian." Hu then attempted to ban Zhang from various conferences, but was unsuccessful because Zhang was protected by other members of the Hu Yaobang network. Nevertheless, when Deng Liqun became the propaganda head in 1982, Zhang was forced to step down as the director of the Marx-Engels Research Office in the Marxist-Leninist Institute. He subsequently withdrew from direct political engagement and joined with Yu Guangyuan, Su Shaozhi, and others in editing ideological materials on socialism.

As Hu Yaobang began to regain ascendancy in the fall of 1985, however, Zhang was allowed to reregister as a party member, was given the title of research associate, and was restored to his former administrative position. He was also made deputy editor of *Marxist Studies,* published by his institute. Zhang resumed his more public activities and began publishing articles in the *People's Daily* again. He attacked Maoist slogans such as "Continuing the class struggle in the ideological arena," still being pushed by Deng Liqun and Hu Qiaomu. At a conference sponsored by the *Science and Technology Daily,* he called such views "ultraleft." For these reasons as well as others, he was on the list to be purged.

The elders also included Zhang's close associate Su Shaozhi on their list. His purging, ironically, took place at the same time that the concept of the "initial stage of socialism," about which Su was the first to theorize, was to be formalized at the Thirteenth Party Congress. Yet he too was tainted by his participation in the theory conference and his efforts to revise the orthodox ideology. Some of the elders also opposed the "initial stage" concept because it implied that capitalist methods were appropriate for China. Wang Ruoshui, also at the theory conference and involved in the effort to humanize Marxism, was similarly slated for purging.

Sun Changjiang, who had been most active in editing the practice

criterion article for publication, was another member of Hu Yaobang's network asked to resign from the party. Sun, like Zhang Xianyang, had continued to criticize Mao's thought and policies. Both were
also censored for their violent activities in the Cultural Revolution. Sun was attacked because he had been a member of the "combat
team" at People's University, even though the members of the Beijing
Party Committee, particularly Xu Weicheng and Chen Xitong, who
were most vehement in making the charges, had themselves been associated with the Gang of Four. Thanks to connections with the old
army general Nie Rongzhen, in charge of science and technology in
the defense establishment, and with the consent of Chen Yun, Sun
escaped expulsion from the party and remained deputy editor of *Science and Technology Daily.*[56] Su Shaozhi's connections with Zhao Ziyang also helped him to retain his party membership. Although he
was deprived of his position as head of the Marxist-Leninist Institute,
he remained a research fellow there. Those reported to be on the
longer list were Li Honglin, Yu Guangyuan, Yu Haocheng, Yan Jiaqi,
and Ge Yang, the editor of the *New Observer.* They were reprimanded, rather than removed from the party.[57] Though not purged,
they were in effect silenced.

The playwright Wu Zuguang was the only one on the short list
slated for purging who had not participated in the theory conference.
His public criticism of the spiritual pollution campaign and of Hu
Qiaomu by name at the Fourth Congress of the Writers Association
had infuriated the elders. His selection suggests that the settling of
personal scores was as important as ideological dissent in the choice
of targets. In a letter to the Central Discipline Inspection Commission
to protest the improper procedures used in dismissing him from the
party, Wu sarcastically described how "poor and old Hu Qiaomu,"
climbing four flights of stairs, "huffing and puffing," asked him to
resign from the party. Wu, who had little regard for ideology or the
party in the first place, said he readily assented to Hu's request because
of respect for Hu's "old age."[58] Wu was then seventy; Hu was seventy-
five. Moreover, Wu added, since he knew nothing about Marxism, he
should not have been asked to join the party in the first place. His
ridicule of Hu Qiaomu and the party further enraged the elders.

Whereas Wu Zuguang treated the party with sarcasm, Wang Ruoshui treated the party with passive resistance. He refused to confess
any wrongdoings, making it necessary for the Central Discipline In-

spection Commission to remove him. In the Mao years, Wang would have been forced by the threat of violence to make a self-criticism, and neither man would have been allowed to treat the party with such disrespect.

The Thirteenth Party Congress

At the same time that the intellectuals who had championed political and ideological reforms were targeted to be purged, Zhao Ziyang and his associates prepared to introduce political reforms at the Thirteenth Party Congress. Throughout the summer and fall of 1987 public opinion polls were published showing that the majority of the population wanted political change. It was significant that China's population was being asked its views on political matters.[59] Only five years earlier, public opinion polling had been characterized as bourgeois and inappropriate in a socialist country. But when Chen Yizi, head of the Institute of Economic Structural Reform, established a polling bureau in 1984 to find out opinions on price reforms, other polling agencies mushroomed at universities and research institutes. Even if these polls, such as the one indicating that 93.8 percent of the people questioned believed that such reforms were necessary,[60] were manipulated, they helped Zhao mobilize popular support for political reforms to be proposed at the Thirteenth Party Congress.

Zhao's report to the congress, drafted under Bao Tong's direction, went through several revisions in accordance with recommendations from party leaders. Each time a new draft was produced, Zhao Ziyang presided over its discussion. At the July leadership meeting at Beidaihe further revisions were suggested, and again the draft was rewritten and circulated to more officials in the party. In August an "Opinion-Seeking Draft," in book form, was distributed to about five thousand party cadres and leaders of the small parties, mass organizations, religious circles, and various nationalities to solicit more opinions. In early September Zhao presided over the meeting of the Secretariat to hear reports on the various discussions of the report, and on September 30 the Politburo held meetings to discuss the fifth draft.[61]

As described by Wu Guoguang, who took notes on Zhao's talks with the original drafting body, the political reform group, the final report was a much more limited program of political reform than the one Zhao had earlier discussed. At a seminar of the group on November 7, 1986, Zhao had emphasized a division of authority, which was suggested in the first draft's recommendation that power be dispersed to many different organizations, people's congresses, and social groups. At another seminar on January 4, 1987, Wu reported that Zhao blamed the rigged local elections in 1986 for the student demonstrations and called for genuinely competitive elections with more nominees than positions. At a seminar on February 4, 1987, Zhao urged making the government's labor union more representative of workers' interests. Shortly thereafter, Zhu Houze, who when deposed as propaganda head had initially worked on rural reform, was appointed first secretary of the All-China Federation of Trade Unions. His appointment demonstrated Zhao's desire to reform the labor unions.[62] But when Deng saw the draft in May 1987, Wu reported that he denounced it as based on the U.S. division of powers and insisted that the overall criterion for political reform be efficiency.

A participant in one of the subcommittees of the political reform group described the discussions within the committees as "wide-ranging." Radical proposals were considered. One was to end the one-party government by reviving the one-third system of the party's guerrilla days—United Front bodies made up of one-third party members, one-third leftists, and one-third middle class and gentry. A few participants even proposed taking the army out of politics and treating it as a defense force to be used only against external enemies. Such ideas, discussed behind closed doors, did not appear anywhere in Zhao's report to the Thirteenth Party Congress or even in the public discussion by the participants.[63]

Zhao was careful not to upset his mentor Deng. Although the descriptions by Wu Guoguang and others of the report's drafting may have overstated Zhao's democratic inclinations in order to gain support for Zhao abroad, Zhao was nevertheless more open to political reform than Deng. But because he served at Deng's will and had no independent political base, he could not go very far beyond his mentor. He also had to remain attuned to the wishes of the elders, who could put pressure on Deng to oust him just as they had ousted Hu Yaobang.

Despite the extended process of revision and the removal of the more radical proposals, Zhao's report, presented on October 25, 1987, at the Thirteenth Party Congress, did express some of the concerns about the party's concentration of power that Deng had stressed in his August 1980 speech. Several of the proposals, such as the establishment of a professional civil service based on competence rather than on political orthodoxy, had been consistently favored by the political reform leaders. Although the report claimed that the idea was based on the French school of public administration, in reality the proposal for a civil service was a return to China's own tradition, borrowed by the French from the Chinese in the eighteenth century. The report's call for more dialogue between officials and ordinary people was a restatement of the mass line; the people were to be consulted, but not to decide important issues.

Zhao's report, nevertheless, also expressed some of the ideas that the democratic elite had been suggesting for almost ten years. Zhao concurred with their view that the reform of the economic structure could not be achieved without political reform, but his emphasis, like that of Deng, was on reform of the administrative rather than the political structure. He repeated Deng's dictum that China would never introduce the separation of powers and the multiparty system used in Western-style democracies. Like Deng in 1980, he called for the separation of party and government activities and even suggested the elimination of party cells *(dangzu)* in government and academic institutions. This proposal implied a shift away from the party's exclusive control over political power. Here, however, Zhao talked about the separation of party and government, not at the top levels, but primarily at the county and enterprise level, where the party organization's supervision would gradually give way to management by government officials or directors. The separation, he explained, was to give more initiative to the people. "This devolution of power has proved effective in rural reform and should be carried out in all other fields . . . so that the people will handle their own affairs." [64]

Perhaps the most radical aspect of Zhao's report was its acknowledgment that China was a pluralistic society. Zhao noted the emergence of different social groups and urged the establishment of mechanisms so that they could express their legitimate interests. "There should be channels through which the voices and demands of the people can be easily and frequently transmitted to the leading bodies, and there should be places where the people can offer suggestions or pour out any grievances . . . Different groups of people may have different interests and views, and they too need opportunities and channels for the exchange of ideas." At the same time, Zhao urged that the government become more open to scrutiny by the public. "We should provide wider coverage of the activities of the government and Party through all forms of modern mass media, to give scope to the supervisory role of public opinion, to support the masses in their criticism of shortcomings and mistakes in work." These views had been voiced at various times by Hu Jiwei and Liu Binyan. And virtually in the words of Li Honglin or Wang Ruoshui, Zhao stated: "The essence of socialist democracy is that the people are masters of the country, genuinely enjoying all citizens' rights."[65] Zhao also proposed that the CPPCC, the united front organization of outstanding individuals and intellectuals, become a forum where important policies and major issues could be genuinely debated. Most important, as Liao Gailong had proposed in 1980, Zhao recommended that trade unions and organizations such as the Youth League, the Women's Federation, and other mass organizations "carry out their work independently in light of their own characteristics."[66]

Like the democratic elite, Zhao recommended ways to strengthen the people's congresses and the National People's Congress. Members of the NPC should be able, for example, to serve full-time and, as Yan Jiaqi had been suggesting since the mid-1980s, they "should improve their rules for discussion and their working procedures, so that they will have adequate rules and regulations to abide by." Furthermore, Zhao called for continuing "the practice of holding elections with more candidates than posts, as prescribed by law, and improve procedures for nominating candidates and methods of publicizing them." He also urged that the small parties resume the role they had before the anti-rightist campaign, when the officials in these parties were appointed to positions as high as the vice-ministerial level. Admitting that the rights of Chinese citizens had been encroached upon, Zhao called for "establish[ing] a people's appeals system, so as to guarantee the citizens' rights and freedom as stipulated by the Constitution."[67] Moreover, he urged the "judicial organs to exercise independent authority as prescribed by law, and enhance the citizens' awareness of law."[68] These too were recommendations that Yu Haocheng had repeatedly proposed.

Finally Zhao declared that China must remain open. "We can never go back to the closed society of the past, when people were forbidden contact with ideological trends of different sorts."[69] Such an open ideological approach echoed Hu Yaobang and his intellectual network. Another echo was heard in the report's official confirmation that China was in the initial stage of socialism, the concept developed by Su Shaozhi, Feng Lanrui, and Yu Guangyuan.

Despite Zhao's relatively radical political proposals, the changes in the leadership configuration at the Thirteenth Party Congress were not so far-reaching. Deng Xiaoping set an example for the elders by resigning from his positions on the Central Committee and the powerful Politburo Standing Committee, but he continued to hold on to his power as the chairman of the Military Affairs Commission, which controlled the army. Changes were made in the constitution so that he could remain as head of the commission despite his resignation as a Central Committee member, revealing once again that China's constitutions were products of political expediency. Deng was the first Communist Party leader to yield his high party position voluntarily, but in reality he retained ultimate power as chairman of the Military Affairs Commission. His old friend Yang Shangkun was made the permanent vice chairman of the Military Affairs Commission. Zhao Ziyang was made a vice chairman of the commission, but he had little support in the military because he had spent most of his life in administrative positions and had joined the party after the Long March. Peng Zhen retired as chairman of the NPC and Li Xiannian as president of the People's Republic. Although their only other positions were in the Central Advisory Commission, supposedly an organization without any formal power, the elders' active role in Hu Yaobang's purge demonstrated that this commission, with Chen Yun as its chairman and Bo Yibo and Song Renqiong as acting chairmen, still had the potential to wield great power informally.

Nevertheless, the elders' power in the formal political structure was weakened. The congress brought about the departure of 96 full members of the 209 members of the Central Committee and the election of new and younger members. Excluded were most of those in their eighties who had dominated the party for over five decades. In addition, the military's influence in the Central Committee was further whittled away with the departure of several high military officials. Even more significant, for the first time there were 5 percent more candidates than positions in the elections to the Central Committee. Stuart Schram has characterized the procedures at the congress as a form of "negative democracy": its members may not have been able to elect anyone they wished to a leading position, but they were able to get rid of those whom they did not want in power.[70] Those who had figured prominently in the downfall of Hu Yaobang and the campaign against bourgeois liberalization were virtually voted out of office. Deng Liqun and Hu Qiaomu failed to get enough votes to be elected to the Central Committee. Chen Yun then proposed that they be elected to the Central Advisory Commission. Even though they again came in near the bottom of the election list, along with their ally Wang Renzhi, they were made members of the commission and continued to be in charge of party history, documents, and decrees on ideological matters.

At the same time, even though Hu Yaobang remained on the Politburo, his position was titular. The eight newly appointed members to the Politburo were identified with Zhao's pragmatic approach, but the Politburo's Standing Committee, where the real power lay, represented a more even balance of political forces, with Zhao Ziyang and Hu Qili representing the reformers and Yao Yilin and Li Peng representing the elders, particularly Chen Yun. The fifth member, Qiao Shi, who had been brought to power by Hu Yaobang, straddled a middle position between the reformers and the elders in this period. Finally, Li Peng became the premier shortly after Zhao Ziyang assumed Hu Yaobang's position as party general secretary in 1987. The reform officials appeared to have prevailed, but in reality the situation was much more ambiguous. The elders and their spokesmen withdrew somewhat from political action, but they were poised to reassert themselves at the next opportunity.

9

The Return
of the
Democratic Elite

With the revival of discourse on political reform and the reform officials' reassertion of their authority at the Thirteenth Party Congress,
the elders' spokesmen were again eclipsed. In addition to Hu Qiaomu
and Deng Liqun, Xiong Fu was also not reelected to the Central Committee at the congress, and he was retired as editor-in-chief of *Red
Flag*. Even more significant was Zhao Ziyang's announcement in mid-
December of the closure of *Red Flag*, the most prominent opposition
to the reforms within the media. Because of the elders' intense lobbying, however, it did not actually cease publication until June 1988.
This six-month grace period indicated the power that the elders could
still wield on occasion. Nevertheless, until its demise, *Red Flag*, along
with the other media controlled by the elders, ostensibly complied
with the reformist line set out by Zhao at the congress. The elders
could express their views in subtle ways, but there was some substance to their earlier charge that when the reform leaders were in the
ascendancy, they had difficulty getting a hearing. The reform leaders
too had little understanding that freedom of expression involved tolerance of opposing views.

With the elders on the defensive, the three publicized targets of the
anti–bourgeois liberalization campaign resurfaced and restated with
even more directness the views for which they had been attacked. In
the year since Fang Lizhi had been purged, moreover, he had produced
five new papers on cosmology, three of which were published in
American scholarly journals. He continued to train postgraduate students from Keda. When Fang was allowed to revisit Keda in Novem-

ber 1987 on the condition that he lecture only on nonpolitical subjects, he was enthusiastically greeted by 5,000 students. He was permitted to go to Australia in the summer of 1988 to attend a scientific conference, and while passing through Hong Kong he gave interviews in which he openly discussed his disillusionment with the party. He contrasted his feelings of sadness when he was expelled from the party in 1957, still believing in the party and socialism, with his lack of regret when he was expelled in 1987. He revealed that he questioned Marxism, especially its view of the universe as infinite, since the early 1960s. Now believing that "Marxism is by no means an eternal truth," he vowed never again to rejoin the party even if invited.[1]

Liu Binyan was also allowed to publish again at the end of 1987 and to give interviews to the foreign press. In one of these he stated, as he had many times before, that freedom of the press was "the first step toward true political reform." He added that the Soviet press, even under Brezhnev, had greater freedom than the Chinese press, because at least in the Soviet Union there was the samizdat, a clandestine press, which Liu claimed had not existed in China since the end of the Democracy Wall movement. On his expulsion from the party, he said that "it was not the first time that the Central Committee had made a wrong decision."[2] His colleague, the poet and literary critic Shao Yanxiang, called for a reversal of the verdict against Liu at a meeting of the Writers Association, of which Shao was a vice chairman. Except in the Hundred Flowers period and briefly after Mao's death, to call publicly for a reversal of a party verdict was rare. In March 1988 Liu was allowed to go to the United States to teach and to become a Nieman Fellow at Harvard for the next year.

Of the three only Wang Ruowang was still not yet allowed to go abroad, but in 1988 he was able to meet and speak with foreigners and publish once again. His more politically oriented articles, however, continued to be published only in Hong Kong. Other members of the democratic elite, such as Yu Guangyuan, Liu Zaifu, Yan Jiaqi, Li Honglin, Su Shaozhi, and Yu Haocheng, reappeared in late 1987 at forums, in the press, and in university lecture halls. Despite their virtual silencing a year earlier, they and kindred spirits voiced their views with even more force and daring. The anti-bourgeois liberalization campaign had perhaps made political reform seem all the more urgent.

Institutional and Procedural Restraints

Although most of the democratic elite still referred to themselves as Marxists, they continued to call for both institutional reforms and an infusion of non-Marxist ideas. Again, as in the past, their views and increasingly their actions in 1988 went beyond the parameters set forth by Zhao in the Thirteenth Party Congress report. They repeatedly pointed out that the reforms it recommended, such as delegating power to lower levels, streamlining the administration, establishing a civil service system, and separating government and party were more administrative reform than democratic politics.

Even some of the intellectuals associated with Zhao, such as Wu Guoguang and Gao Shan, an assistant to Bao Tong who also had been involved in drafting the report, stressed the need to "institutionalize political activity and provide effective legal guarantees." The People's Republic had formulated four constitutions and many laws, but they noted that "although our country's Constitution acknowledges that citizens enjoy wide rights, there is a great lack of appropriately specific laws to guarantee these. This even leads to illegal violations of citizen's lawful rights and there is generally no way one can complain to a specified legal organ through specified procedures."[3] They feared that "if there are not generally accepted norms, democratic life can easily be damaged by the will of a number of people or even specific individuals."[4] They concluded that "promoting the institutionalization of our country's socialist democratic politics is a basic guarantee that the tragedy of the 'Cultural Revolution' will not be replayed."[5]

Yet it was the members of Hu Yaobang's intellectual network who made the most radical interpretations of Zhao's report. Since the theory conference, Yan Jiaqi had defined democracy as a process of establishing procedures.[6] He lived by his beliefs. In accordance with his often-stated recommendation that officials serve only two terms in office, he announced at a meeting of the Institute of Political Science in April 1988 that he would not continue as its director when his second term expired at the end of the year. He also criticized the appointment of CASS institute directors by party officials rather than by direct election of their peers. Although Yan's institute, the Institute of Literature, and the Marxist-Leninist Institute had elected their own directors, this was not the norm.[7]

In contrast to the precedent of a two-term limit and election by one's peers that he set in his own institute, Yan pointed out that in both China's dynastic system and its prevailing political system "the exercise and succession of power followed no established procedures."[8] Furthermore, he complained, "the principle of official 'omnipotence' has yet to be powerfully challenged. Party and state organs are still free to intervene in all facets of social life as they please." Democracy "recognizes that human nature is imperfect and that man makes mistakes." Consequently, it contains the concept of "restraining man with institutions." Unless China adopted set procedures or rules, he warned that it would continue to endure internal party struggles.[9] In opposition to Deng's dismissal of Western democratic practices as inappropriate for China, Yan insisted that they were necessary in order to prevent a relapse into the arbitrariness of the past.

Yan's most controversial statement on limiting political power was his famous article "China Is No Longer a Dragon." The image of China as a dragon, symbolizing "imperial authority or unrestricted power," Yan asserted, was inappropriate for a nation seeking to be a democracy.[10] This "symbol of personal authority that reigns supreme, and is all powerful" was harmful to a modern society that needed "the authority of law to replace the symbol of authority." He maintained that "we want to change the concept of the worship of authority represented by 'dragon culture,' so that governments at all levels, various enterprises, and every individual . . . can make their own decisions under conditions permitted by the 'optional norm' in the law."[11] A stable political system, he observed, was one in which man is "not a god" and where the leader is restrained.[12] In an interview in Hong Kong, Yan acknowledged that "democracy cannot ensure a decision is absolutely correct," but, he insisted, "it ensures an erroneous policy will be amended through a set procedure."[13]

Yan's suggestion that leaders, even good leaders, could not be trusted was alien to the Confucian emphasis on moral, competent leaders and contrary to accepted wisdom in China. Yet in 1988 several other prominent intellectuals also questioned whether a good leader could solve China's problems. This skepticism may have reflected increasing disappointment with the Deng-Zhao leadership since the purge of Hu Yaobang. One of the authors of the controversial television series "River Elegy" *(He shang)* broadcast in the summer of 1988, Yuan Zhiming, praised traditional paragons of virtue, such as Judge Bao of the Song Dynasty, for their sense of justice and conscience, but he cautioned that history "shows that this power system is defective because it . . . cannot limit, restrict, and transform individual moral character, because it unexpectedly cannot rely on its own strength to protect the legitimate rights and interests of the people but can only rely on the conscience and awareness of individual cadres."[14]

As if competing with Gorbachev's call for *glasnost* in the Soviet Union, Zhao's report had called for "transparency" *(toumingdu)*. One sign of transparency was the announcement of the New China News Agency in November 1988 that it would regularly publish collections of government regulations, including those that might not appear in the media.[15] Because Zhao used "transparency" to emphasize the need to open up the government to wider media coverage more than the need to use the media to scrutinize the government's activities, his term was not as radical as that of Gorbachev. Nevertheless, his championing of transparency unleashed a flood of articles and seminars on freedom of the press and information that went far beyond his limited concept.

Despite the insistence of the Media and Publications Office, the elders' bailiwick, that criticisms of leading officials be printed only in the internal media, restricted to high party officials, the articles called for public exposure of official wrongdoing. The economist Qian Junrui, who had used his own funds to help establish the *World Economic Herald,* charged that "some leaders are not afraid of unpublished criticism but are afraid of open criticism published in newspapers."[16] Similarly, a commentator article in *People's Daily* reiterated that open criticism in the media was the most effective way of exposing official corruption.[17] But without any legal protections, as Hu Jiwei and others observed, open criticism could be very dangerous for the critics. A seminar sponsored by *Legal News* (Fazhi ribao), attended by academics, judicial officials, and journalists, became a forum to decry the increasing attacks on reporters investigating official abuses. Some participants insisted that the law, rather than government, must be used to resolve the disputes arising from investigative reports.[18]

Although Hu Jiwei was no longer formally in charge of formulating the press law, he still held important posts as a vice chairman of the NPC Education, Science, Culture, and Public Health Committee and as a member of the NPC Standing Committee. In 1988 he increasingly urged that the media be run by a variety of sources. In addition to party and government ownership, he advocated nonofficial individual- and collective-run media. His recommendation was supported by several professors of journalism at People's University. One of them wrote in the *World Economic Herald* that "press freedom will not exist as long as the press is under the control of party committees,"[19] a condition that prevented the press from criticizing the party. Another *Herald* article recommended that the media, not the party, determine editorial policy. Because the party only hears and reads its own words, the article asserted, "it fools itself into believing that it is the voice of the people." This form of party "self-deception" had led to such disastrous policies as the Great Leap Forward and the Cultural Revolution. In the past few years some "truthful things" had been stated in the media, but the article cautioned that they were the result of the personal influence of individuals or particular leaders, not because the media had become responsible for its own actions.[20]

As the anti–bourgeois liberalization campaign waned, private and semiprivate tabloids and supplements reemerged. In addition, bourgeois interest groups with independent sources of income, particularly the private entrepreneurs *(geti hu),* were also able to fund periodicals. One example was the *Shenzhen Commercial Daily* (Shenzhen shangbao), introduced in April 1988, sponsored by several enterprises in the area, which chose their own editor and board of directors. The party's tight control over the media, however, had been weakened by economic factors rather than by legal and institutional restraints.

In January 1988 Zhao Ziyang directed that a document be drafted prohibiting arbitrary interference in the creative and performing arts. The drafting group held twenty forums, consulting with well-known cultural figures, from February to mid-March. On June 4 the Politburo's Standing Committee approved the sixth draft, whose message was that a creative work should be judged by its audience, the author's peers, and history; the opinions of political leaders should carry no more weight than those of ordinary members of the audience.[21] Wang Meng, minister of culture, declared that only a small number of plays involving important historical and diplomatic questions and issues of nationhood and religion would be censored.

As Hu Jiwei had for the press, Wang Meng called for nonofficial literary and art enterprises. The major national cultural institutions, such as the Philharmonic Orchestra, the Central Opera, and the

Beijing Ballet, would still be run by the state with state financial support, but all other cultural enterprises, Wang Meng proposed, could be run by individual or collective units. Such a change, he explained, would not only lighten the government's financial burden but also produce a "more colorful cultural market." As long as literary and art works did not politically oppose party leadership and socialism, he asserted, the party should not interfere with their subject matter, school of thought, or style. Moreover, if problems should arise, they would no longer be dealt with by administrative procedures, but by legal procedures.[22]

Wang Meng was one of the few highly placed intellectuals to speak out favorably on popular culture. He even praised the mushrooming of private bookstores, video centers, and ballrooms, which most officials condemned and blamed on decadent Western influence. He commented that the "craze for pop culture is not a bad thing; even the pounding of Hong Kong and Macao culture cannot be said to lack any positive meaning."[23] A *Guangming Daily* commentator article explained that the market forces in the cultural arena "to a considerable degree, represent public choice." In contrast to the traditional and Communist emphasis on the educational purposes of culture, the article stressed that "socialist culture and art creation should serve only one purpose, that is, to satisfy the increasing needs of the people in their cultural lives." Consequently the "market mechanism," rather than administrative decision making, was regarded as more appropriate[24] to the cultural realm. The emergence of the market and popular culture may have inadvertently been more effective in weakening the party's overall control over society than the efforts of the democratic elite to limit the party's power—a fact that few in the democratic elite openly acknowledged.

Further Revisions of Marxism-Leninism

Although Su Shaozhi had been purged as head of the Marxism-Leninism Institute shortly before the Thirteenth Party Congress, after the congress he again engaged actively in political debate. His reappearance in party newspapers and forums so soon after his purge was another departure from Maoist and even previous Dengist practices. This lenient treatment was in part attributable to the more relaxed atmosphere in 1988 but also stemmed from Su and his collaborator

Feng Lanrui's status as the first theorists to discuss publicly the concept of the initial stage of socialism, a version of which became party policy at the congress. A *People's Daily* commentary article even used virtually the same argument that Su and Feng had made at the 1979 theory conference—that the party had overestimated China's readiness for socialism. "During a certain period in the past, the call for communism was deafening. Although the call was loud, it was regrettably far from reality. It made the masses suffer and really discouraged them." Therefore, the commentary cautioned, "we should not forget historic lessons in this connection," and predicted that the initial stage might last at least one hundred years.[25]

Su Shaozhi and other associates from the theory conference took the official acceptance of the "initial stage" as an opportunity to discuss other ideological concepts that had not been officially approved. Yu Guangyuan, in the journal *Economic Research,* stressed that the historical limitations of Marx and Engels rendered them unable to recognize the need for a socialist commodity economy, an ideological euphemism for the market, as "the foundation and center of the whole socialist social-economic structure."[26] Su and his disciple Wang Yizhou added a political reason for expanding the market economy: to restrain the power and privileges of the party.[27] Similar suggestions were voiced and written about by colleagues in the institutes of political science and economics of CASS. Their justification was that only a variety of socialist practices and ideological views could reinvigorate and relegitimize Marxism.

Su Shaozhi and other ideological "revisionists" may have been given such wide coverage in the press and so many opportunities to speak at forums in order to rebut those who opposed the concept of the initial stage. *Outlook* magazine pointed out that a "small number of comrades find [it] 'hard to accept'" and do not understand the need to develop an individual and private economy. They regard policies and principles based on this theory as "retrogression." But earlier attempts to skip over the initial stage of socialism and the anti-Marxist "theory of the unique importance of will," a reference to Mao's policies, had led the "economy to the brink of collapse."[28]

"Revisionists" were uncharacteristically portrayed in a positive light. Su Shaozhi was depicted in an interview as busily writing and receiving visitors in his "elegantly decorated small parlor."[29] He was described as guiding graduate students, writing articles for many newspapers and journals, and preparing to publish a major book, *Democratic Reform and Development*. The interview concluded with a restatement of Su's belief that China must "drop the utopian, outdated, dogmatic, ossified" aspects of Marxism-Leninism, an undisguised critique of ideological orthodoxy and its elderly adherents.[30]

In addition to the democratic elite, even the reform official Hu Qili, in an address to a conference of directors of propaganda departments, urged them to "dare to break with dogmatic interpretations of Marxism."[31] A meeting on Mao's thought in his later years, organized by the Central Party History Research Institute, revived criticism of Mao. Some participants even suggested that his "ultra-leftist utopian socialism" began before the Great Leap Forward. The party historian and a theory conference participant, Gong Yuzhi, even traced it back to the idealized guerrilla days in Yan'an, a critique that could be interpreted as a virtual rejection of the Mao era.

All the "great" Communist leaders were repudiated in one way or another. A *Guangming Daily* commentator article pointed out that Lenin died too soon after the Russian Revolution to be helpful on the practice of socialism. As for Stalin's and Mao's interpretations of socialism, they "committed many mistakes, for which high prices had been paid."[32] Furthermore, some pointed out that the prediction of Marx and Engels as well as Lenin that the contradictions between the bourgeoisie and the proletariat would worsen had not occurred. Instead, these contradictions had "mitigated to a certain degree" since World War II.

Positive appraisals of noneconomic aspects of capitalist societies appeared in mainstream newspapers. A *Guangming Daily* article commented that "some reasonable and useful things in ideological and cultural fields in the capitalist society have transcended the limits of time and space and the differences in social systems of various countries."[33] Various symposiums on "restudying capitalism" noted that the pauperization of the proletariat predicted by Marx did not take place. On the contrary, workers participated in the management of some enterprises and benefited from social welfare programs. These positive achievements of capitalist society, it was suggested, could also be adopted by socialist societies.[34] At a symposium held in Shenzhen, the participants specifically recommended emulation of the West's political achievements, explaining that China had little experience in building a modern political structure.[35]

Equally challenging to the party leadership's view was criticism of the belief that Western science and technology would solve all of China's problems, a dogma introduced in the May Fourth period and reinforced by the Deng regime. At a symposium held by the Society of Research in the Dialectics of Nature and the Institute of History of China's Natural Science, under Xu Liangying's leadership, the argument was made that before the "miraculous" cures of science and technology could work, other changes in society, culture, economy, and politics would be necessary.[36] The *Science and Technology Daily,* where Sun Changjiang was deputy editor, made the same argument. One of its special commentary articles, reprinted in the *People's Daily* (overseas edition), noted that the view that modern science could save the nation "had its limitations," because "it only saw the role of science and technology" and did not grasp the "social prerequisite for social development."[37] Li Honglin, who had resigned as the president of the Fujian Academy of Social Sciences, had been engaged in a comparative study of socialist and capitalist systems since 1987. He acknowledged that current economic and technological reforms were correcting some of the mistakes of the past, but he lamented that "our ideology, theory, and political tendency are moving along another course or still sticking to the leftist errors. The two movements contradict each other and are incongruous." Using an analogy similar to Liu Binyan's long leg of economic reform and short leg of political reform, Li warned that the two uneven movements were like a "train advancing on this pair of unparallel rails," which would be derailed sooner or later.[38]

Another criticism of the leadership's selective adoption of Western culture was its tendency "to introduce theories which placed lopsided emphasis on the whole and neglected the individual," particularly Soviet theories. The compliant Lei Feng, for example, the screw in the machine, was criticized as a model for the nation.[39] Repudiation of Lei Feng in 1988 became another form of protest, similar to Bai Hua's "Unrequited Love" and Liu Binyan's "A Second Kind of Loyalty," against the elders' definition of patriotism as unquestioning loyalty to the party. Contrary to the elders' definition, a *Literary Gazette* article, reprinted in the *People's Daily,* defined patriotism as "inseparable from a deep and broad devotion to the land on which we were born, brought up, and are growing old, as well as to our history characterized by calamities and disasters." This kind of patriotism, the article declared, might "contain some bitterness as well as fiery self-examination and criticism, but not . . . the silliness of cracking oneself up for one's blind loyalty."[40]

Discourse on Society and the Party-State

In 1988 the members of the democratic elite, influenced by their own experiences under Deng as well as Mao and by the civil societies breaking away from state control in the Soviet Union and Eastern Europe, talked increasingly about giving society priority over the state. Some called this phenomenon "new socialism" and defined it as the "switch from 'state socialism' with the state as the center, to 'citizen socialism,' with the citizens as the center." In "new socialism," decisions on political matters were made by means of democratic procedures rather than by "strongman politics," and society was moving away from "unity of thinking and principles dictated by the state to freedom of thinking by the citizens."[41]

Unlike their East European counterparts, however, China's intellectuals saw state and society not as separate entities, but as inextricably connected. Nevertheless, some of them argued that China's troubles were related to the omnipotent role of the state. Even though most articles on the subject traced the state's omnipotence back to the centralized, autocratic rule of traditional China, they also blamed the Western challenge in the twentieth century, which compelled China to build a strong state in order to save the nation. This challenge, one article complained, "constrained the development of democratic politics." And since 1949, the state had become the "organizer and manager of all social life." The people needed only to "closely follow" the state's lead. Consequently "our economic and political systems and even our ideology and culture were then completely imprinted with the seal of statism." As a result, "the state overrode the entire society."[42]

The *World Economic Herald* became the major forum for discourse on the relationship of society to the state in 1988. One discussion pointed out that China's "highly centralized political and economic systems" had "consigned the people to a subordinate status . . . [and] cut the people off from political power." Government bodies, filled with unelected officials, did not truly represent the people. By contrast, in democratic countries administrative organs were held accountable to freely elected representative bodies. Though not mentioning Deng Xiaoping by name, the article refuted Deng's argument that the separation of powers meant division of sovereignty. Rather, it explained, the division meant that administrative organs were checked by organs that represent the people. Although "we talk of the supremacy of representative organs and the subordinate status of administrative ones," the reality was that "representative organs" could not supervise and restrict the administrative organs because China had no true separation of powers.[43]

Another *Herald* article further explained that "during the 'Great Cultural Revolution' in China, the interests of the 'gang of four' were considered state interests," causing incalculable damage. From this experience China had learned that "we must not continue to stress that 'the state comes first.'" The author also pointed out that whereas in China "people gain socioeconomic rights before they gradually earn political rights," in the West the establishment of democracy "is based on the concept of 'citizens.' The people start with the right of political freedom and gain some socioeconomic rights through political struggle."[44]

Yu Guangyuan's and Su Shaozhi's former student Cao Siyuan, who in 1988 became head of a think tank established by China's largest private computer company, the Stone Group, ridiculed Mao's practice of "letting people speak out" as having nothing to do with representative government. Mao wanted people to speak only within the limits determined by the leadership. Such a practice, Cao asserted, had led to disastrous results, such as the purge of Peng Dehuai in 1959 merely for exercising his right to criticize the Great Leap Forward at a Central Committee meeting. While Cao rejected this controlled kind of "democracy serving as a tool of the leader," he also rejected the "anarchic democracy" of the Cultural Revolution. Only through regular procedures and a truly representative legislature, he said, could democracy serve the people.[45]

Like other members of the democratic elite, such as his former teacher Su Shaozhi, Cao did not yet accept a multiparty system, which he described as "various parties rule in turn." As if acknowledging the existing political reality, he admitted that the "one-party rule of the Communist Party cannot be easily abolished." But like most members of the democratic elite by the late 1980s, he vigorously advocated a system of checks and balances, with the primary emphasis on making the people's congresses and the National People's Congress stronger and more independent through competitive elections and institutional protections: "We must truly establish a system which will guarantee that the people can truly exercise state power through parliament."[46] At a forum in Beijing titled "Emancipation of the Mind," jointly sponsored by the Stone think tank, the *World Economic Herald,* and *Seek Truth from Facts* (Qiushi), the replacement for *Red Flag,* Wu Guoguang observed that in the past hundred years China had had many rounds of reform, but none had succeeded because they did not transcend the emphasis on "'state values' and 'national values.'" He urged that emphasis be transferred to "'individual values' and 'civil rights values'" in order to transform the whole society and state.[47]

Wang Ruoshui became another strong advocate of citizens' rights in 1988. No longer bound by party rules, Wang published and spoke out at forums in 1988 more boldly than at any other time since the theory conference, although his most daring works appeared in the Hong Kong media. Still agonizing over the same question that had obsessed Ba Jin and Liu Zaifu since the late 1970s, Wang asked: "Why was it that the whole nation voluntarily entrusted its fate to one man and this man bears nothing for their fate?"[48] He answered that question by asking another: "Why could such a situation of an individual reigning above the law, his authority crushing everything[,] happen in the Soviet Union and again in China, but could not happen in countries like England, France and the United States?" Holding the political system responsible, Wang again criticized Hu Qiaomu for attributing a leader's absolute power to the cult of the personality, which Wang insisted was an insufficient answer. Rather, Wang explained, the Leninist-Stalinist political system was "not only powerless to prevent the cult of the individual, but it also nurture[d] negative phenomena."[49] In addition to one-man rule, it encouraged bureaucratic power, special privileges, and the suppression of "people's rights." He concluded that "systems change people," but then added, "they also have to be changed by people."[50]

Zhao Ziyang's recognition of interest groups in his report also unleashed demands for limiting the party-state's authority by allowing more social autonomy. Although Zhao primarily acknowledged the existence of different economic, generational, educational, and geographic interest groups, a *People's Daily* article called on interest groups not to "become mere administrative institutions," but to assert a degree of independence from the party and to express their aspirations in an organized way in order to influence policymaking. It also advised them to safeguard their own interests by means of legislation; otherwise "many social groups fail to carry out their work independently in the full sense and they are far from performing their functions fully."[51] Organizations such as the Youth League, the All-China Federation of Trade Unions, and the Women's Federation were criticized in a *New Observer* article for not representing the true interests of their constituents and for acting merely as the party's tool. It urged them to seek more independence so that they could "exercise a certain supervisory role over party and government work, thereby restraining any tendency toward an inflation of power or misuse of power."[52]

That the intellectuals in the People's Republic, owing to persecution, had been unable to carry on the role of their literati ancestors as critics of the government and mediators between the rulers and the ruled was frankly acknowledged. Rong Jian, a doctoral student in the philosophy department at the People's University, who was to figure prominently in the debates over neo-authoritarianism in late 1988, believed that "Chinese intellectuals were spiritually destroyed . . . by the transformation of the world outlook that went on for years . . . As a result, they came to believe that they [were] not critics, but somebody to be criticized."[53] They had lost their role not only as critics of the government but also as spokesmen for the people.

Su Shaozhi became one of the major advocates of greater autonomy for interest groups. Like Hu Jiwei, he favored the establishment of a variety of newspapers and journals to express different interests. He even recognized that interest groups had the potential to lead to political pluralism. Once interests were recognized, he explained, then "we must recognize political pluralism . . . and the next logical step would be to address the question of a multiparty system." Yet Su did not take this "next logical step." Like Cao, he acknowledged that "due to historical reasons and China's contemporary conditions, a multiparty system is impossible and unnecessary."[54] Nevertheless, with his collaborator Wang Yizhou, Su insisted that "democratic politics" meant respect of people's "civil rights" and restraints on the "omnipotent" state.[55]

Implementation of Political Reforms

While the members of the democratic elite and their associates talked about a more limited, more truly representative government, there were some small but by no means trivial moves in that direction in the people's congresses and in local elections. In various provincial congresses in 1988, some officials were elected by means of competitive elections.

As in the Central Committee, competitive elections at the local level were a form of negative democracy. The Guangdong Provincial People's Congress, for example, initially failed to elect a president of the People's High Court. Because the candidates were regarded as lacking professional requirements,[56] neither of the party's two nominees received more than half of the votes. New nominees were therefore listed for the next round of voting. Supposedly this method of voting nonconfidence had been used in the guerrilla areas in the 1940s, and the requirement that a nominee must have 50 percent of the vote to be elected was used in Soviet elections in the late 1980s. This negative form of democracy has one advantage over the more positive Western approach, in that the voter is not forced to select the lesser of two evils.

Even in the elections for the relatively orthodox Beijing Party Committee on December 17, 1987, Chen Yuan, son of Chen Yun, lost his position as a standing committee member. Xu Weicheng, who had been in charge of Beijing propaganda during the 1986 student demonstrations, won the fewest number of votes, finishing last among the fifty new members of the Beijing Party Committee. For the first time, the All-China Federation of Trade Unions also used a form of competitive elections in selecting its highest executive body. Zhu Houze, dismissed as propaganda head at the time of the purge of his mentor Hu Yaobang, became a vice chairman of the federation and secretary of the federation's Secretariat.[57]

In a competitive election in the Henan Provincial People's Congress in January 1988, a vice mayor of Zhengzhou, Liu Yuan, was elected a vice governor, although he was not the party's official candidate.[58] Liu was the son of China's persecuted late president Liu Shaoqi, who had died during the Cultural Revolution and had only been posthumously rehabilitated in 1980. Liu Yuan had been sent to the countryside when his parents were imprisoned. Instead of returning to Beijing, however, as many of his peers did after the Cultural Revolution, he became active in local politics and township enterprises.

When given a choice at the grass-roots level, voters seemed to use it to rid themselves of officials they found abusive and incompetent and to vote for those who might be more responsive. In the preliminary round of the elections for leadership positions in the township and county congresses, it was reported that of the 593 candidates recommended by the local party committees, 499 were elected, and of those not elected, 26 had originally held positions of vice governor or above. In the second round, of the 99 people nominated by the local party committees, 12 were elected.[59] Although even the nonparty candidates had to be approved by the party, the process of competitive elections nevertheless gave the local population some practice in choosing among candidates.

A reporter who observed a local election in Dingxiang County, Shanxi, admitted that before the election he had always felt that peasants were disinterested in voting, but he discovered that when given a choice, the Dingxiang peasants voted three village heads and ten assistant village heads out of office.[60] A *People's Daily* commentator article observed that the "public's understanding of democracy is by no means weak or thin."[61] These procedures fit in with the approach of Deng Xiaoping as well as Zhao Ziyang to replace older, entrenched political cadres with younger, better-educated officials at the local level.

Competitive local elections, however, were held erratically. A work report of the NPC's Standing Committee criticized some cadres and localities for not implementing democratic processes or, if they did, for not abiding by their results.[62] A *People's Daily* (overseas edition) article complained that the newspapers talked about political democracy, but in actual fact it was rarely seen because "many citizens still cannot exercise this right." Nor did they have the right to criticize. The article cited a meeting of a county people's congress at which a local deputy's criticisms were interpreted as "anti-party," and he was immediately investigated by the county party committee.[63] The practice of nominating more candidates than positions still must have taken place in a sufficient number of local areas, however, to prompt the *People's Daily* to advise those who lost in the elections not to despair or to blame the masses for their defeats.

Some of the proposals to strengthen the NPC also appeared to be bearing fruit in 1988. The debate of the bankruptcy law at the Sixth NPC had set a precedent for questioning decrees sent down by the party leadership. As a result before the Seventh NPC was held in March 1988, new demands were heard for the government's work report to be distributed ahead of time, so that the deputies could be better equipped to discuss it. Wang Houde, a deputy secretary general of the NPC Standing Committee, also urged the press to give full coverage to the criticisms and suggestions made by the delegates.[64] Although the party continued to nominate the top officials for election to the standing committees of the Seventh NPC and the Seventh CPPCC, another precedent was set in its nomination of more candidates than positions. One hundred forty-four candidates were nominated for the 135 positions on the standing committee, nine more candidates than positions.[65] Age again seemed to be a primary criterion in the election; of the nine candidates who lost, seven were over seventy years old.[66]

Only one candidate was nominated for each of the top government positions, but instead of the usual unanimous showing of hands, for the first time the NPC provided a secret ballot. This vote could also be characterized as a negative form of democracy. One hundred twenty-four votes were cast against Yang Shangkun, who became the new president, and 212 votes were cast against Wang Zhen, who became vice president, the largest number of negative votes for any top leader. By contrast, the reform leader Wan Li, who took over as chairman of the NPC, had only 64 votes cast against him, and Deng Xiaoping, as the head of the State Military Commission, had only 25 votes against him.[67] Although these negative votes were only a tiny proportion of the almost 3,000 votes cast, the secret ballot became another channel for expressing dissatisfaction.

At the Seventh NPC the congress also became a public forum for articulating popular discontent for the first time. Several deputies openly criticized the meager allocation of funds for education and intellectuals' salaries; other deputies complained about price hikes and official corruption. These discussions were given full coverage in the press, and delegates continued to express these criticisms in radio, television, and newspaper interviews. Suggestions were also made that a public gallery be established in the NPC so that constituents could observe their deputies in action and evaluate their competence and views. The first public opinion survey of the views of all the NPC deputies was made in April 1988 by Chen Ziming's nongovernmental think tank, the Social and Economic Research Institute (SERI). Although the survey revealed that 41.5 percent of the deputies still believed in the Leninist concept of democratic centralism, it also showed that 62.6 percent believed that the NPC should supervise the government on behalf of the citizens[68] and that 85.2 percent acknowledged that freedom of speech had increased.[69] The deputies also expressed support for other civil rights, such as the right to be elected, personal freedom, and freedom of work. Despite their substantial support for democratic centralism, they also listed independent judgment as a qualification for NPC delegates.

Even the CPPCC no longer acted as a rubber stamp. Preceding its 1988 meeting an article in the *Unity Journal,* a newspaper of one of the small parties, the Revolutionary Committee of the Guomindang, urged that legislation be introduced that defined exactly what the deputies could and could not do. Without such safeguards, the article declared, it was very difficult to advise leaders on policy decisions and discuss political affairs.[70] At the meeting itself, a number of deputies complained about their nominal role. One of them, a woman announcer at the Central Broadcasting Station, characterized a CPPCC deputy as "indeed an ornamental vase." Another chastised the top leaders for not engaging CPPCC deputies in a dialogue.[71] The appointment of the eighty-nine-year-old Zhou Gucheng, who in the post-Mao era had moved closer to the elders than to the reform officials, as the chairman of the CPPCC Education, Science, Culture, and Public Health Committee, was criticized because he was too old to hold the post for a five-year term.[72]

Yet while these events indicated that the CPPCC might become a more open forum for the expression of differing views, the treatment of the playwright Wu Zuguang, who had been a member of the CPPCC's National Committee for three terms since 1979, indicated that much remained the same. Wu was not allowed to address the deputies, because the literary and art group to which he belonged had delayed approval of his speech and then, on orders from higher authorities, told him there was not enough time for him to deliver it. His speech, entitled "Trust the Intellectuals" and charging the party with repeatedly trampling on the dignity of China's intellectuals, displeased those at the top. He accused a "small group of leftist extremists in positions of power" of ousting him from the party, which he again insisted had been done illegally.[73] He did not name names, but he was clearly referring to his old nemeses Hu Qiaomu and Deng Liqun, who had been hounding him since 1983. Although some things had changed, much still remained the same.

10

The Beginning of Organized Opposition

From late 1988 into the spring of 1989, the members of the democratic elite began to organize themselves into a political force outside the official system for the first time and launched an accelerating series of public challenges to the party leadership. Their emboldened stance sprang in part from their increasing disillusionment with the party leadership and in part from the party's relatively restrained response to their earlier ideological challenges. After the experience of revising ideology in the late 1970s and of wide-ranging political and ideological discourse in 1986, intellectuals were ready for an even more fundamental reevaluation of the Leninist party-state.

The Tenth Anniversary of the Practice Criterion

Members of Hu Yaobang's intellectual network used the occasion of the tenth anniversary of the practice criterion discussion to recriticize not only the "two whatevers" faction but also the ideas of the elders. Numerous forums were held in the spring of 1988 to celebrate the practice criterion. One, convened by the *Guangming Daily*, invited the original participants. Those who did not attend submitted written speeches. Nearly all praised the major figures of the movement, Deng Xiaoping, Luo Ruiqing, and most significant, Hu Yaobang. The participants in the original conference were praised for having taken "great risks and political and theoretical courage to publish articles on such a topic" at that time.[1] Yu Guangyuan explained that the practice criterion was meant to extend "far wider" than the economic realm.[2] Yang Xiguang, the former editor-in-chief of the *Guangming Daily*, related the practice criterion to the present in stating that "whether we should respect practice or respect dogmas is still a problem of ideological line in the course of reform."[3] He complained: "Our thinking has long since been trammeled by dogmatism."[4] And Wu Jiang, in an interview in the *Guangming Daily*, observed that the experience of the past ten years had proved that "it is no easy job to regard social practice as the criterion of truth."[5]

Although *Red Flag* articles gave Deng Xiaoping complete credit for introducing the practice criterion and did not mention Hu Yaobang's role,[6] other journals praised Hu's leadership in this effort. *Outlook*'s editorial board held a forum in which the whole discussion was described in detail, starting with Hu's asking *Theoretical Trends* to refute the "two whatevers."[7] The effect of these celebratory articles and forums was to revitalize Hu Yaobang's network and to put the elders and their spokesmen on the defensive once again.

Conflict over "River Elegy"

In the spring of 1988 the television series "River Elegy" *(He shang)*, produced by former Red Guards, was aired. It condemned China's traditional civilization, represented by the Yellow River, the Great Wall, the dragon, and other symbols, as hindering the nation's modernization. Visually, the series conveyed the sense that the once-flowing Yellow River civilization had dried up because of China's emphasis since the seventeenth century on stability, isolation, and conservatism. With vivid cinematography, it compared China's civilization with the extinct cultures of the Middle East, South America, and Africa, warning that if China did not open itself to the outside world, symbolized by the blue ocean leading to the West, it too might become extinct. China had once been in the forefront of world civilization, but its withdrawal into itself, as symbolized by the dried-up Yellow River, had created a stultifying atmosphere in contrast to the dynamic, developing, and open cultures of the West and of Japan.[8]

"River Elegy" was the climax of an ongoing discussion on the nature of China's culture known as "cultural fever,"[9] under way in China since the mid-1980s. Controversial intellectuals involved in the television series included: Jin Guantao, the chief editor of the book series "Toward the Future," which published works of and about Western social science; Li Yining, the Peking University economist who advocated shareholding; Li Zehou of the Philosophy Institute of CASS, who held that democracy had not developed in China because of the concern for national survival; and Wang Juntao, the associate editor of the nonofficial journal *Economic Weekly* (Jingjixue zhoubao) associated with SERI. The series' director, producers, and chief creators, Su Xiaokang and Wang Luxiang, were in their late thirties and early forties; most of them had been in and out of political trouble since the Cultural Revolution.

While the elders emphasized the authoritarian elements of traditional culture in their efforts to block Western ideas, many intellectuals blamed these same aspects of the tradition for the stagnation of Chinese civilization. Yet it was not until the "cultural fever" discussion moved beyond intellectual circles to reach an audience of millions through the "River Elegy" series that these views caught the attention of the elders. As long as the discussions of culture were confined to talks at academic forums and the printed pages of journals and scholarly books, they were allowed to continue, unfettered by official interference. But as soon as the series was televised in June 1988, and then with Zhao Ziyang's permission was run again in August, it evoked strong reactions, both positive and negative. Excerpts and articles praising it were printed in not only reformist journals such as the *China Youth News, Economic Daily, Wenhui News,* and *People's Daily* but also in the *Guangming Daily.* In July a printed scenario was compiled and sold in the myriad nonofficial bookstores in Beijing and elsewhere.

Zhao Ziyang, depicted positively in "River Elegy" because of his efforts to open China to the outside world, was supportive of the series and presented a videocassette recording of the television series to Prime Minister Lee Kuan Yew of Singapore as a gift. In contrast, the reaction of most of the elders was angry and condemnatory. They attacked the series as a "betrayal of the nation"; they were upset not so much by its criticisms of Chinese tradition, of which they knew little, as with its praise of Zhao's reform policies. Moreover, the series contained film clips of the repression during the anti-rightist campaign and the Great Leap Forward as well as during the Cultural Revolution, in which the elders themselves had played either active or acquiescent roles. The series also criticized the intellectuals' inability to achieve a degree of independence from the state. By implication, therefore, the work was an attack on the party's efforts to maintain ideological control and to isolate China from Western culture. More directly, the elders regarded "River Elegy" as a challenge both to themselves and to the party.

As in the past, the elders used this supposed threat as an opportunity to reassert their authority. Particularly incensed was Vice President Wang Zhen, who, along with Peng Zhen and Bo Yibo, took the lead in denouncing the series. Wang Zhen summoned the chief editor of the *People's Daily*, Tan Wenrui, and other editors to his home in the summer of 1988 for a two-hour harangue in which he angrily criticized the paper for praising the series. Although he ordered that critiques of "River Elegy" be written and published, the *Guangming Daily* and the *People's Daily* both refused. Wang then used the thirtieth anniversary celebration of the Hui Autonomous Region in Ningxia, where he had fought in the civil war, to criticize the series for vilifying the Chinese people. His attack was published in the *Ningxia Daily*,[10] but unlike most important statements of high leaders, it was not reprinted in other newspapers across the country. He then ordered that an open letter to Deng Xiaoping, critical of the series, be sent to the *People's Daily*, signed by a "peasant." Again the *People's Daily* refused to publish it.[11] At the closing session of the Third Plenum of the Thirteenth Central Committee in mid-September, Wang exploded: "I fought for so many years to rule this country, yet now I run into this band of press and graduate students . . . I have never been so angry in my life. Intellectuals are dangerous."[12] Wang's fulminations finally pushed others to echo his denunciation.

Unlike in the past, however, the elders' attacks did not lead to a campaign. Zhao was more successful in blocking their attacks than Hu Yaobang had been in blocking their criticism of "Unrequited Love," perhaps because he had more support from Deng Xiaoping. Zhao's cultural policy of noninterference in specific works, moreover, provided the rationale for the *People's Daily's* refusal to print Wang Zhen's commissioned critiques. But despite Zhao's policy, its supposed implementer, Hu Qili, on the defensive since the purge of Hu Yaobang, tried to suspend the series temporarily and to ban its distribution in China as well as abroad. When this proved impossible, he then worked to stop discussion about it in the media so as not to provoke the elders to further action.

Although the dispute over "River Elegy" was intertwined with the ongoing power struggle at the top, it also stimulated further discussion of Chinese culture. Some intellectuals agreed with Wang Zhen's criticism of the series as a rejection of Chinese tradition, but their views were more sophisticated and balanced. An article in the *People's Daily* observed that "a nation which lives only in the past has no future. But there can be no future either for a nation that denies its own heritage. We should be proud of our 5,000 year old Yellow Earth."[13] Kuang Yaming, the former president of Nanjing University, criticized a nihilist view of Chinese civilization, cautioning that China's present culture must be built on its past.[14] Others argued that it was inaccurate to present China's traditional culture as less civilized and humane than that of the West, noting that some aspects of the traditional culture were worth retaining. While some used the debate over "River Elegy" to focus attention away from the immediate political situation and onto the past, others used it to awaken people's consciousness to current ills, which they blamed not on China's traditional culture but on its emulation of the Soviet model and on Maoist policies.

A Cloud over the ACFLAC Meeting

Even though the controversy over "River Elegy" did not spark a campaign, the elders' attacks cast a shadow on the Fifth Congress of ACFLAC, held November 8–12, 1988. The meeting was only the second ACFLAC congress to be held in the Deng era; the first had taken place in 1979. The congress that was to have been convened in 1985 had been postponed because the leadership feared that the delegates would usurp the proceedings as had happened at the Fourth Congress of the Writers Association in December 1984. To prevent such an occurrence in 1988, two enlarged meetings of the Politburo were held beforehand to stress the need for tight discipline and to advise against any reevaluation of the spiritual pollution and anti–bourgeois liberalization campaigns.[15] Hu Qiaomu, who had not been active in public meetings for some time, reappeared to publicize his usual theme of the need for stability and unity.

The party leadership was also worried about the preparatory group in charge of the congress. The group's co-leaders were the composer Wu Zuqiang and the eighty-eight-year-old playwright Xia Yan.[16] The leadership did not trust either Wu, who was the brother of Wu Zuguang, or Xia, who, like his close associate Zhou Yang, no longer complied with party discipline. Only Lin Mohan, the deputy leader, was firmly in the elders' camp. With Wang Meng in tow, Hu Qili visited the elderly Xia Yan to make sure that he understood party orders about the congress. Afterward Xia was reported to have told a friend: "I had no alternative but to endure abuse and say something contrary to my thoughts."[17] Nevertheless, in interviews before the conference, Xia Yan expressed his own opinions. In one he criticized those who discouraged the use of the term "humane," and described the campaigns against spiritual pollution, bourgeois liberalization, and humanism as "reverses." He also praised Gorbachev's *glasnost* as much more open than China's "transparency" and the Soviet press as more critical of Stalin than China had been of its past leaders.[18]

At the congress, despite the party's precautions, Xia Yan expressed views that differed from those of Lin Mohan. Whereas Lin stressed Mao's Yan'an principle that the arts must "serve the masses," Xia countered that more harm than good had come from subordinating the arts to politics. Although in the Mao era Xia had obediently echoed Mao's doctrine, his speech at this congress protested against the use of literature and art for political purposes. He praised the intellectuals for their "sense of responsibility for the rise and fall of the nation," but he insisted that "the tradition of 'using poems to express one's aspirations' and 'using articles to publicize morals' is not so narrowly defined, and it does not exclude poems that depict the beauty of nature." The subordination of literature to politics, he complained, had "suffocated the originality and the initiative of writers and artists . . . This is indeed a bitter lesson."[19] His speech so moved Mei Zhi, the widow of Hu Feng, whom Xia and his colleagues had mercilessly persecuted in 1955 for having expressed similar views, that she lamented that her husband, who had died in 1985, had not lived long enough to hear it.

Xia's speech was greeted with warm applause, and the atmosphere of the congress became less tense after he had spoken. But unlike the first ACFLAC congress in 1979, no one except the officially designated speakers with their officially approved texts was allowed to speak. Nor were journalists allowed to report on the speeches. There were no competitive elections for the leadership positions as there had been at the 1984 writers' congress, the Thirteenth Party Congress in 1987, and the trade union and small parties' congresses held in 1988. With no more nominees than positions, election procedures reverted to the practice of the Mao era. Some of those attending protested verbally, others by passive resistance. The representatives of the Chinese Dramatists Association, a component of the federation, for example, refused to participate in the noncompetitive elections, and only half of the representatives from the Writers Association attended the discussions.[20]

An editorial in the *Guangming Daily* on November 8, 1988, the opening day of the congress, urged the federation's various component associations truly to represent their professions and protect their members' legitimate rights and interests,[21] but nothing like this occurred. As at the Fourth Writers Association Congress, Hu Qili presented a message on behalf of the Central Committee, but this time his message did not promise the participants freedom of creation as it had in December 1984. While Hu again echoed Zhao Ziyang's cultural line about noninterference in creative works, the major emphasis of the congress and of Hu's address was not on writers' and artists' freedom, but on their responsibilities. These were defined in Lin Mohan's closing address, which exhorted them to produce more wholesome and inspiring works to boost the nation's morale.

The Tenth Anniversary of the Third Plenum and the Theory Conference

The elders' greatest effort to reassert their power occurred at the tenth anniversary celebration of the Third Plenum of the Eleventh Central Committee and the theory conference, but the event also became an equally strong effort on the part of Hu's network to repulse the elders' offensive and to launch an offensive of its own. In contrast to the original theory conference, over which Hu Yaobang had presided and which had been dominated at least during its first half by the democratic elite, the anniversary was organized by the elders' spokesman Wang Renzhi, director of the Propaganda Department, with advice from Hu Qiaomu's close associate Hu Sheng and from Hu Qili, who, because of his past relationship with Hu Yaobang, feared doing anything to antagonize the elders.

With one important exception, the official anniversary celebration bore little resemblance to the path-breaking conference it was honoring. Most of the members of Hu's network who had attended the original conference were put on a list of "special invitees." Those on the list were characterized as having "erred" and were advised not to bring up any misgivings about the past, particularly concerning the spiritual pollution and anti–bourgeois liberalization campaigns, the same admonition given to the participants in the ACFLAC congress. Among the "special invitees" were Yu Guangyuan, Li Shu, Wang Ruoshui, Tong Dalin, and Yan Jiaqi, who protested by not attending. Li Shu had died just before the conference, but this did not prevent repeated criticisms of his ideas, especially his contention that the Maoist concept of the masses as creators of history had no foundation in classical Marxism-Leninism. Others who attended the original conference, such as the theorists Sun Changjiang, Zhang Xianyang, Yu Haocheng, and Li Honglin, were not invited at all.

The one event of the anniversary in keeping with the previous conference was Su Shaozhi's speech. Ding Weizhi, a vice president of CASS and an organizer of the anniversary, had asked Su to write an essay for the occasion, which Su did, outlining the changes that had occurred in Marxism since the Third Plenum. The drafting group for the anniversary apparently was so impressed by Su's essay that it incorporated many of his ideas into their own report. Su was then asked to participate in the proceedings. Just back from a semester at Oxford University, Su was a bit out of touch with the Chinese scene; he was somewhat surprised to learn just before the conference that Wang Renzhi had changed the report of the drafting group to reflect more of the elders' views.[22]

Nevertheless, in his speech to one of the fourteen group sessions at the anniversary, Su disregarded the admonition "not to quibble over the past."[23] On the contrary, Su condemned the party's campaigns against spiritual pollution and bourgeois liberalization and defended his colleagues who had been the targets. He charged that Li Shu, Yu Guangyuan, and Wang Ruoshui had "suffered from unfair treatment in these campaigns."[24] Moreover, "their only mistake was that their views did not suit the taste of the leading people in theoretical circles at that time. Even if their academic views were wrong, their being punished because of their different academic and theoretical views was in itself a violation of the provisions of academic freedom laid down in the Constitution."[25]

Su then criticized the use of campaigns altogether, including the supposed "noncampaigns" of the Deng era: "Campaigns which are not called campaigns, or academic mass criticism which was not called academic mass criticism, still happened."[26] He also criticized the elders' spokesmen: "A small number of leaders in the theoretical field regarded themselves as the embodiment of the party and proclaimed themselves fighters defending the purity of Marxism."[27] He even took the rare step of singling out Hu Qiaomu by name for making Wang Ruoshui and his views on humanism and alienation the target: Hu Qiaomu had "announced that academic discussion on the above-mentioned two issues was a forbidden zone, and regarded Wang Ruoshui's problem as a political one and punished him repeatedly." Furthermore, Su complained, Yu Guangyuan had to endure "ten meetings of so-called criticism and self-criticism," organized by the Central Advisory Commission.[28] Treating the academic and theoretical views of Wang, Yu, and Li Shu as political crimes, he said, resonated with the practices of the Mao era.

Su also challenged the elders' orthodox ideological views. He urged his fellow theorists to "frankly admit that at present Marxism is in crisis." Because Marxism had been made into a dogma and used as a tool in the struggle for power, it lagged "behind the reality of modern capitalism and socialism and also behind the reality of reform in China." This dogmatic form of Marxism, which had begun with Stalin and had intensified over the last twenty years, not only diverted China from confronting new and real problems but "greatly corrupted [its] prestige."[29] One way to revitalize Marxism, he suggested, was to "recognize that there are various schools of thought inside Marxism and that apart from Marxism, there are other schools of thought in academic circles. Therefore, it is wrong to force scholars to accept Marxism."[30] Su concluded that it was not the academic and theoretical differences in themselves, but the theoretical leaders who "proclaimed themselves Marxists, discriminated against those cadres who held views which were not commensurate with theirs, raised academic and theoretical differences to the higher plane of politics" who had "impaired stability and unity."[31]

Even more wary of this anniversary meeting than of the ACFLAC congress, the elders allowed only Xinhua to report on its proceedings. Not only were the semiofficial papers such as the *World Economic Herald* and nonofficial journals such as *Economic Weekly* not permitted to cover the meeting, but even the *People's Daily* was not allowed to issue its own news release on it. Despite these precautions, however, the *World Economic Herald* published an excerpted text of Su's talk on December 26, 1988, which a *Wenhui News* reporter had given to one of the *Herald* editors. Xinhua had not published a word of the speech. Although the *Herald* was nearly closed down in early 1987 at the time of the anti–bourgeois liberalization campaign, it had become increasingly more outspoken and daring. Hu Qili and Wang Renzhi now reacted by ordering that Su's speech not be reprinted anywhere else. They summoned the *Herald*'s editor, Qin Benli, to Beijing, where he was reprimanded for publishing it, particularly the portions defending the targets of the campaigns and revealing internal party matters to the public. Su's direct attack on Hu Qiaomu had been cut out of the *Herald*'s published version. Bo Yibo showed Deng Xiaoping the full text, urging him to censure Su, but Deng declined, explaining that it was not necessary to take action against different views expressed by intellectuals.[32]

Less than a week after the official anniversary meeting, members of Hu's network who had participated in the original 1979 conference convened their own anniversary gathering. Among those attending were Yu Guangyuan, Su Shaozhi, Sun Changjiang, Zhang Xianyang, Wu Mingyu, plus some of their associates, including Zhu Houze, Li Rui, and Shao Yanxiang. In addition Hu Jiwei and Yu Guangyuan edited a collection of essays by some of the original participants entitled *The Moment of Awakening* (Mengxing de shike). The edited volume was part of the "Democratic Studies" series, whose editor-in-chief was Hu Jiwei and deputy editors were Yu Haocheng, Wang Ruoshui, and Li Honglin, all participants in the original theory conference. The book was subtitled "A special edition commemorating the tenth anniversary of the Third Plenum." As explained by the editors: "This plenum, the other central work conferences before the plenum, and the theoretical preparatory conference after it made a timely contribution in liberating thought, setting things straight, and beginning the reform."[33]

In addition to articles by the editors there were essays by the theory conference participants, including the disgraced Guo Luoji. Several praised Hu Yaobang for leading the effort to liberate thought. In the preface Hu Jiwei explained that since the original conference, "to establish a theory on democracy and promote democratic politics has been our aspiration for many years."[34] A former deputy editor of the *Guangming Daily,* Ma Peiwen, without specifying names, excerpted long portions of the speeches given at the original conference in his essay. Ruan Ming, in his essay "On the New Enlightenment," explained that because he had been rather "obedient" in the past, when the party had committed mistakes, he too had committed mistakes. Only when the discussion on the practice criterion developed in May 1978, he confessed, did he finally awaken and begin to "disobey" erroneous party policies.[35] Hu Jiwei, in his article "Obey or Disobey," similarly acknowledged that only after the Cultural Revolution and the attack on the "two whatevers" did he realize that if one "obeyed" the leadership one would commit mistakes and hurt one's "comrades"; if one "disobeyed," then one made fewer mistakes.[36] The authors' acknowledged willingness to disobey authority when it conflicted with their own conscience was not only a challenge to the elders and the party leadership. The position these intellectuals were taking reasserted an intellectual and moral independence harking back to neo-Confucian values.

The Democratic Elite Takes the Offensive

By the fall of 1988, owing to pressure from the elders and the bureaucrats in state industry, a retreat was under way in economic as well as in political and intellectual reform. The efforts of Zhao Ziyang and Deng Xiaoping to carry out price reforms in June 1988 had led by late summer to sharply increased prices. Officially the inflation was said to be 19 percent; unofficially it was double that in China's major cities. The sudden jump in prices provoked the elders, through Li Peng, to try to recentralize control over the economy, tighten the money supply, and delay further reform in order to decrease the inflation.

   Even though it was Deng, not Zhao, who had insisted on the price reforms, Zhao was blamed for the sharp increases in prices. At the summer Beidaihe meetings preceding the Third Plenum of the Thirteenth Central Committee, Zhao was compelled to make a self-criticism for the overheating of the economy and the concentration of economic development in the coastal areas. The elders' criticism of Zhao's economic and administrative reforms was in tune with the increasing disillusionment of the urban population at this time. Although its standard of living had risen overall, the urban population's expectations had risen even faster. When inflation took off in the summer of 1988, there was a run on the banks as well as panic buying at the stores, as customers rushed to hoard goods before more price increases. Fears of hyperinflation as in the last days of the Guomindang still lingered. Furthermore, much of the urban population blamed the economic reforms for giving party officials and their families opportunities to use their positions and control over resources to become involved in all kinds of corrupt money-making schemes.

Despite the fact that Zhao had assumed Hu Yaobang's former role as the protector of the intellectuals, members of the democratic elite took advantage of the increasing conflicts between Zhao and his technocratic allies on the one hand and the elders and a sizable portion of the bureaucracy on the other to insert their own ideas into the controversy. They did this at a series of symposiums on reform, excerpted in the *Economic Weekly, New Observer,* and *World Economic Herald.* At a symposium entitled "Enterprise Culture" convened on November 16, a dialogue between Yan Jiaqi and Wen Yuankai, the professor of applied chemistry at Keda who had supported Fang Lizhi's efforts in 1986 to liberalize the educational curriculum, expressed views that differed radically from those of both the technocrats and the elders. Wen traced China's current retreat on reform to a reluctance to face its Cultural Revolution past; Yan saw it as an unwillingness to change the decision-making mechanisms of the political system. Both men believed "an all-around reform, including political reform," was necessary.[37] They contrasted China's current retrenchment with the dramatic political reforms under way in the Soviet Union. Again Yan stressed the need to make China's political system conform to its constitution, particularly the stipulation that the National People's Congress be the supreme organ of power. He and Wen also wanted to insert a new stipulation in the constitution guaranteeing the right of private property as well as other civil rights. Like Liu Binyan, Yan cautioned that since China still had the same political system that it had during the Cultural Revolution, "a repeat of the Cultural Revolution is possible,"[38] and Wen warned of the possibility of "completely irrational behavior."[39]

Other members of the democratic elite also sought to avoid a replay of history by becoming more outspoken in the demand for human rights. They used the fortieth anniversary of the United Nations Declaration on Human Rights, which China officially commemorated for the first time, to present a view of human rights very different from the one promulgated by the party. At an official forum to celebrate the occasion, most of the speakers praised the provisions of the declaration that conformed to the party's emphasis on national self-determination and on economic rights provided by one's government. By contrast, members of the democratic elite published articles in the official media praising the declaration's emphasis on individual and political rights and its affirmation of human rights as natural rights. They asserted that the bourgeois view of human rights was also appropriate for socialist societies.

Yu Haocheng articulated the strongest and most direct statement of this view in a long article in which he defined human rights as inalienable and as guaranteeing the rights of speech, publication, assembly, association, march, demonstration, religious belief, scientific research, and literary and art creation. He complained, however, that this definition had been "almost totally off limits in China" since the 1950s.[40] In the Deng period too, he said, human rights were regarded only as a bourgeois slogan, not shared by the working people, and in 1983 even the very concept of "humanism" was criticized, greatly hindering China's development of democracy. He counseled his government: "The practice of using outside interference in one's own internal affairs as an excuse to refuse to discuss human rights conditions in one's own country is no longer credible."[41] Human rights were no longer an internal affair, he pointed out, as could be seen in the condemnation of South Africa for racial discrimination by the international community, including China.

Yu blamed the "human rights outrages that occurred during the Cultural Revolution and some of the infringement that still persists" not on the socialist system per se but on what he believed were distortions of the socialist system in practice.[42] In addition to referring to the distortions caused by Stalin's many injustices and the Cultural Revolution, he specifically cited Mao's argument, made in his Yan'an Talks, that there was no such thing as human nature transcending class nature. Although the concept of universal human rights or a universal human nature had first been raised by the bourgeoisie in its struggle against feudalism, Yu argued that the concept applied to all people and had now gained worldwide acceptance, especially after the atrocities committed during World War II. He urged the Chinese people not to "hand the slogan [of human rights] over to the bourgeoisie on a silver platter, and let that class treat human rights as its monopoly." Quoting Lenin, he ironically asserted that "socialism cannot be achieved if these rights are not proclaimed, if one does not fight for them, and if this fight is not used to educate the masses."[43] Like Fang Lizhi, he concluded that the only way to have human rights was to fight for them.

The democratic elite's pleas for democratic procedures took on a greater urgency in late 1988 as members of the elite saw them as an outlet for the widespread public discontent over inflation and corruption. They pressed for immediate political reforms in order to prevent what they felt was an impending social explosion. In a *World Economic Herald* article, Cao Siyuan of the Stone think tank called for a political system in which citizens "peacefully replace their government through parliaments and the government can only impose restrictions on citizens through legislation and law enforcement, so this avoids, to the largest extent, violent confrontation."[44] In response to the view of not only the elders but most officials and intellectuals that China's lack of democratic traditions and experience made it impossible to introduce a parliamentary system, Cao asked: "Where then should we carry out the democratic training? Should we carry it out in the streets or learn our lesson at the halls of the people's congresses?" He answered that the "ideal venue for our lesson on democracy is at the meetings of people's congresses," where deputies elected in multicandidate elections seriously debated political issues. He urged that these debates be carried on national television, and he cited the positive impact of televising the heated debates on the bankruptcy law in the NPC, which had provoked further discussion among the citizenry and had increased awareness of the issue.[45]

While granting that countries with parliamentary democracies also experienced popular disturbances, Cao explained that their overall social order was so stable that the government continued its work as usual and in an orderly manner. In China, however, "when the masses of a particular locality chant democratic slogans, it indicates that the social order of that particular locality has become chaotic and the government cannot function well." He suggested that one way to prevent direct clashes between the government and the people was to use the people's congresses as regularized venues for airing popular discontent. Providing "regularized venues," where citizens can express their grievances, "prevents the government and masses from being directly involved in a tense and hostile situation, and the normal work and efficiency of the government are thus maintained."[46]

Cao also suggested further strengthening the NPC by having its standing committee meet full-time rather than just once a month. In addition, he proposed the use of lobbying and election campaigns for candidates to the congress, practices that had been used in the 1980 local elections. Such practices, Cao pointed out, informed the delegates about their voters and informed the voters about their delegates. He also recommended a system of hearings and fact-finding committees that could discuss issues with experts and could question members of the executive branch. Others proposed reducing the more than three million deputies in the local people's congress to a small number of professional deputies who worked full-time rather than only a few weeks a year.

The role of a free press as a deterrent against instability was stressed. A *New Observer* article suggested that the press provide a channel for expressing popular discontent, warning: "If it [discontent] has no channel to express itself, it will smoulder in secrecy, and will become an unpredictable political element."[47] An article in the *World Economic Herald* explained that "if the media is free then it can discuss and test various policy options before they are carried out[;] in that way it can prevent misguided policies from being carried out or correct them before they cause damage."[48] Numerous articles viewed democratic forums as pressure valves that could reduce or even prevent a social explosion. Party leaders however, did not heed such advice, and later that spring they would be confronted in Tiananmen Square by the "unpredictable political element" forecast by the *New Observer.*

If the media was to be an outlet for discontent, then the need for a press law was all the more urgent. In the first half of 1988, two hundred lawsuits were brought against the press, primarily by officials, in which editors and journalists were almost invariably deprived of their rights for at least one year. The case of Zeng Zhaoren, deputy editor of the *Asian Pacific Economic Times,* published by the Guangdong Academy of Social Sciences, exemplified what happened to editors who dared to criticize party policies. The paper had a relatively small circulation of 40,000, but it was a prominent semi-independent newspaper. Its income came mainly from advertisements and subscriptions. Nevertheless, when Zeng criticized Li Peng's austerity program for cutting credit to some enterprises, he was demoted from his job as deputy editor to selling advertisements.[49] Even in Guangdong, whose leaders were supposedly more independent and more enterprising than elsewhere, a relatively independent editor had no protection. The *China Youth News* had been warned that it would be "reorganized" if it continued to run stories exposing the corruption of high officials and their children.[50]

Even a majority of the NPC deputies believed that the press should express the views of the government. Only a little over one third, 35.3 percent, agreed that freedom of the press meant that ordinary citizens could also publish newspapers or journals; 60.1 percent believed that only the party and its affiliated organizations should run the media.[51] While urging that specific interests of different groups be expressed in the media, the "Monthly Commentary" in the *Chinese Journalist* (Zhongguo jizhe) cautioned that "journalists should first maintain political uniformity with the party Central Committee. If they have different opinions in regarding the party's policy and stand, they are absolutely free to discuss them with the party . . . However, in news reporting and speeches, they should do propaganda as required by the Central Committee, and avoid bringing personal bias and dissenting views into news reporting."[52]

Hu Jiwei, who had worked in vain for a journalism law for several years, concluded by late 1988 that the only way in which freedom of the press could be achieved was through political reform. In the preface to *On Democracy*, written with Chang Dalin and the first volume in the "Democratic Study" series, Hu asserted that in order to guarantee citizens' freedom of speech and publication by law, it was first necessary to have overall political reform. By the late 1980s this was the view of most of the democratic elite. The differences among them concerned the ideological basis for the political reform. Hu Jiwei urged his colleagues to look for inspiration not only in the Western democracies but also in their traditional culture: "We should understand that the traditional Chinese culture contains both the pernicious influence of the feudal autocracy, which is detrimental to the building and development of Chinese democracy, and the rational factors which are conducive to the formation and development of Chinese democracy."[53] He completely rejected any guidance from Marxism-Leninism, at least as it had been interpreted in China: "We must renounce our past rigid and dogmatic attitude toward Marxism."[54]

The hitherto sacrosanct system of democratic centralism was implicitly questioned. At a national seminar on modernization theories in late 1988, the "Montesquieu concept" of democracy, which restricts power with power and allows the minority to have a voice, was treated more favorably than the Rousseauist concept, in which the minority is subordinate to the majority, a position more akin to the views of the May Fourth movement and democratic centralism. The concept of democracy as based on class was also rejected. A *Guangming Daily* article commented that "the degree of realization of the democratic principles does not bear any class characteristic." Democracy should be judged by the degree of the people's actual role in determining the life of the nation. In fact, "under an imperfect proletarian democracy, the degree of the democracy may be lower than that of a bourgeois democracy."[55]

Some admitted that their understanding of democracy had been inadequate until now. Several members of the democratic elite acknowledged that democracy did not mean the rule of intellectuals. Increasingly they talked of a middle class and a pluralistic social base as necessary for a functioning democracy.[56] Although Fang Lizhi had previously talked about democracy as being understood and practiced only by an educated elite, by early 1989 he had come to believe that in order for democracy to take root, other groups and classes must also participate in the political process. He spoke of the participation of professions and trades "at all levels of Chinese society" and the emergence of "unofficial clubs, associations, discussion groups, and other informal gatherings that have begun, in various degrees, to wield influence as pressure groups."[57] An example of what Fang was referring to was a series of symposiums held in early 1989 under the auspices of members of Hu Yaobang's network, to which they invited not only literary intellectuals, academics, members of the nonofficial think tanks, such as Wang Juntao and Chen Ziming of SERI and Cao Siyuan from the Stone think tank, and associates of Fang Lizhi such as Xu Liangying and Wen Yuankai, but also a number of the newly emerging urban and rural entrepreneurs.

Some of the seminar topics had never been publicly discussed before. At one symposium on the crisis of the state ownership system, Wang Ruoshui asserted that there was more monopoly in socialist countries than in Western countries, where there was competition. Zhang Xianyang admitted that "in the past, we wrongly regarded the state ownership system as the essence of socialism," and Wang Yizhou, a collaborator of Su Shaozhi's, declared that the state ownership system, and its monopolization of all resources, was the root cause of the corruption in a society moving toward the market. With their demands for an independent judiciary, a strong NPC, and freedom of the press, therefore, some members of the democratic elite recommended the introduction of private property and private enterprise as another way to lessen corruption. Wang Yizhou noted: "The privileged treatment for those vested beneficiaries does not come from party membership dues, but from the monopoly of the state ownership system." [58]

Zhang Xianyang even repudiated basic elements of Marxism. In addition to rejecting the concepts of class struggle, dictatorship, and a centrally planned economy that had distorted classical Marxism, Zhang rejected the excessive emphasis on rationality in classical Marxism. Influenced by Western Marxists' critiques of Marxism-Leninism, he asserted that "Such extreme rationalism and mechanical historical determinism led to Marx's simplification of the analyses of the whole human society and the capitalist society." [59] Marx's solution for society's problems, he said, could be summed up "with one sentence: Eliminate private property," [60] as if that were the answer to all of life's problems. Even though some members of the democratic elite remained faithful to a form of public ownership, most accepted the need to expand the market economy and to introduce private property.

Yet it was not so much Hu Yaobang's network, whose members were perhaps still unconsciously tied to their Marxist beliefs, as the relatively more cautious members of the small parties who most actively advocated a multiparty system at this time. They were given an opening by Zhao Ziyang's Thirteenth Party Congress speech, in which Zhao had rejected the concept of an opposition party, but sought to formalize and legalize the participation of the various small parties in political affairs, albeit under Communist Party leadership. Although the membership in the small parties had grown from 80,000 in 1979 to 290,000 in 1988, [61] it was not their increased numbers to which Zhao was responding. They could not rival the party's forty-four million members. His attention to the small parties was now prompted not only by their professional constituencies and their contacts with overseas Chinese but by external pressure from the recent establishment of new multiparty systems all over the world. These especially included China's ideological siblings in Eastern Europe and ethnic siblings in Taiwan, where the Guomindang one-party state had acquiesced to the establishment of the Democratic Progressive Party in 1986 and in 1989 officially recognized other political parties.

Nevertheless, Zhao sought to use the small parties primarily as window dressing. In late 1988, however, the small parties began to ask for some substance behind the façade. They were increasingly bold in their demands for a role in government. In 1988 they used the method of direct election for officials in their own parties for the first time. A newly elected vice chairman of the Association for the Promotion of Democracy, Deng Weizhi, also a vice president of the Shanghai Sociology Association, expressed dismay at the slow pace of the process of separating the party from the government and suggested that greater participation of the small parties in government would speed up that separation. He asserted: "Trying to restrict the government to one party is not only harmful; it's becoming impossible." He also urged that the role of the small parties be protected by laws. He observed: "Too many of our laws are about control, control, control. They should protect us, not control us."[62]

Another small party, the Party for the Public Interest (Zhi Gong Dang), with only 800 members in 1988 as compared, for example, with 80,000 in the China Democratic League, decided to dispense with Communist Party support altogether. Made up of returned students, it was better able to become financially independent than the other small parties. One of its members explained: "Democratic parties cannot get political independence unless we are independent economically." In addition, it planned to delete the stipulation from its charter that it was "under the leadership of the Chinese Communist Party."[63] Such an assertion of independence was new in the PRC.

Several of the leaders of the small parties publicly chafed at their subordination to the Communist Party. The economist Qian Jiaju, a vice chairman of the China Democratic League, complained that "their very existence depends on the wishes of the Communist Party leadership."[64] The physicist Li Xinzhou of the Jiusan Society urged his fellow members to speak out in the people's congresses not as individuals, but as representatives of their parties.[65] Leaders of the small parties also publicly expressed their impatience with the many promises they had received regarding the appointment of their members to high-level positions. Despite these assurances, only the Ministry of Supervision had a non-CCP vice minister.

The Democratic Elite's Response to Neo-Authoritarianism

The debate over "neo-authoritarianism" *(xin quanwei zhuyi)* was another impulse pushing Hu Yaobang's network toward more organized action. Neo-authoritarianism had been discussed periodically,[66] primarily in Shanghai and in Beijing at the Central Party School,[67] since the discourse on political reform in 1986. The resurgence of interest in political reform in late 1988–1989 provoked the supporters of neo-authoritarianism and the supporters of democratic reform into vigorous debates. Both sides saw democracy as essential for China's modernization, but while Hu's network and associates urged that democratic means be used to achieve democratic aims, the neo-authoritarians insisted that authoritarian means, especially the rule of a strong enlightened leader, were needed to overcome bureaucratic obstructions to economic reform and then to introduce democracy. The Hu network had looked first to Eastern Europe and subsequently to the West for inspiration; the neo-authoritarians, who were primarily younger scholars, were attracted to the four little dragons of East Asia—Taiwan, Singapore, South Korea, and Hong Kong—which, after a period of rapid economic development under authoritarian rule, were gradually moving in a democratic direction.

Both sides challenged orthodox Marxism-Leninism and sought to limit the power of the state in order to allow the development of a market economy. The neo-authoritarians believed that because the population was politically apathetic, to move directly from the old authoritarian or totalitarian path directly to democracy was impossible. First the state needed to move to a neo-authoritarian stage, in which a strong leader and the development of a market economy would produce a middle class. This class would then provide a social base for democracy. Through this sequential process these intellectuals sought to avoid the kind of chaos, *luan,* that China had experienced at the end of the Qing dynasty, when China's reformers attempted to move directly to democracy and instead provoked several decades of warlordism.

The democratic elite insisted that strong-man rule would lead only to more authoritarianism, as demonstrated by China's more recent history, and that a market economy would not necessarily lead to democracy. They maintained that neo-authoritarianism would become like the old authoritarianism unless societal pressure for political participation compelled China's leaders to move in a democratic direction. To members of Hu's network, economic growth and democratization were interdependent and interactive. They needed to be carried out simultaneously, not sequentially. They repeatedly predicted that if rising discontent and popular demands for change were not quickly addressed by political reforms within the system, then China's population would pursue these demands outside the system through demonstrations, strikes, and social turmoil—a warning that proved to be accurate only a few months later.

Debate on these views was conducted in late 1988 and early 1989 at various seminars, in the mainstream party newspapers, and in the semiofficial *World Economic Herald* and the nonofficial *Economic Weekly.* On both sides the participants ranged from the older generation of theorists to graduate students in the universities. The most articulate speakers for the neo-authoritarian view were Wu Jiaxiang, a Peking University graduate and a researcher in the General Office of the Central Committee, and members of the Institute for Economic Structural Reform. Both the institute and the General Office were under Zhao Ziyang's aegis. The neo-authoritarians' demands for a strong leader and market reforms bolstered Zhao's efforts to overcome the bureaucratic obstacles undermining his changes in the economic sector. In December 1988, Wu published *Deng Xiaoping: Theory and Practice,* in which he identified Deng's cat theory with neo-authoritarianism. In a series of articles in the *World Economic Herald* in early 1989, Wu responded to the criticisms of members of Hu Yaobang's network, which had been published in the same paper. Publication of opposing views in the same newspaper was unprecedented, and an indication of the emergence of a more pluralistic intellectual environment.

Wu Jiaxiang granted that a market did not automatically lead to the "spontaneous growth of a democratic political system," but he insisted that "without a relatively healthy market, it would be very difficult for a democratic political system to be generated."[68] He argued that to introduce democracy right away would entail making concessions to the electorate and various interest groups that would undermine the viability of the economic reforms. As a consequence, the political system would be mired in confusion and disruption from which it could not extricate itself. Another neo-authoritarian, Xiao Gongqin, from the history department of Shanghai Normal University, described the impact of the premature introduction of democracy in a society with a large uneducated population and a weak parliamentary system with a vivid agricultural analogy: "The condition for establishing a pluralistic democratic system is not ripe and establishing this system can be likened to pulling the shoots upward in order to help them grow."[69] An enlightened leader and intellectual elite were needed to guide the transition, which was described as a "visible hand" creating an "invisible hand."[70] Although this metaphor actually described the Confucian ideal, such an approach, it was claimed, had been used in the past in Western Europe and was being used at present in the four little dragons and in Latin America.

Several of the neo-authoritarians referred to the work of the American political scientist Samuel Huntington, whose book *Political Order in Changing Societies* had been translated into Chinese in 1987 in several different versions. Although these theorists cited Huntington's argument that an efficient government, capable of maintaining political order and stability, was necessary for modernization, they disregarded his concomitant emphasis on an impersonal government based on law, which did not accord with their stress on rule by a strong leader.[71] They also referred repeatedly to the successes of the four little dragons, but they ignored the fact that the four had begun to modernize with already semiprivatized economies and with markets that had not necessarily been created by a strong leader. In the case of Taiwan, the privatized economy had emerged despite the strong rule of Chiang Kai-shek.

Given China's Marxist ideology, Leninist party-state, and Stalinist model of development, the neo-authoritarians' stress on private ownership and nonideological approach could be considered relatively radical. But their emphasis on an enlightened leader appeared very conservative to the democratic elite. They believed the neo-authoritarians' plan to be merely another version of the political system that had existed in China since the early decades of the twentieth century. Their vehement opposition to neo-authoritarianism provoked them into a more forceful and direct articulation of their own views on democracy. By early 1989, moreover, they had lost faith not only in Deng Xiaoping, whose ability and willingness to carry out even administrative reforms they now doubted, but also in Zhao Ziyang, who they had hoped would assume Hu Yaobang's role in promoting political reform. They were especially dismayed by Zhao's

seeming support of neo-authoritarianism and his apparent winning of
Deng's support for it in March 1989. Deng supposedly believed that
neo-authoritarianism embodied his own political views. As the democratic elite became increasingly disenchanted with Zhao, Zhao became increasingly critical of their ideas. He feared that their strong
advocacy of political reforms would provoke the elders into opposing
all reforms, including the economic reforms to which he and his mentor Deng were so committed.

Consequently the tacit alliance that had emerged between Zhao and
the democratic elite after Hu Yaobang's purge fell apart in late 1988–
early 1989 as the democratic elite and younger theorist allies launched
a vigorous counterattack against the neo-authoritarians. They argued
that only democratic procedures and laws, not individual leaders, no
matter how enlightened, could establish authoritative rule and bring
stability. To introduce a market economy without changing the political structure, they believed, would lead not to democratization but,
rather, to increasing corruption as party bureaucrats used their control over resources for their own purposes. The younger theorist Rong
Jian, of People's University, argued that although neo-authoritarianism could lead to democracy in the four little dragons, in the
People's Republic, where economic life was still almost entirely controlled, a strong leader would only intensify the authoritarian nature
of the state and make movement toward democracy all the more difficult. Echoing members of the democratic elite, Rong warned that
China could no longer afford to postpone the introduction of democracy, both because of the current "worldwide tide of democracy"[72]
and, more important, because history had shown that "unless the
people's democratic demands can be met and realized through normal
means, they are bound to be vented through abnormal means, such as
demonstrations, protests, strikes, and even violent behavior." Rong
Jian even suggested that the degree to which the economy was freed
depended on the "degree to which political authoritarianism is itself
reformed and changed."[73] Here again was another warning of the consequences of not carrying out political reforms.

One area in which the democratic elite and the neo-authoritarians
agreed was on the need to join with other social groups in order to
produce any kind of fundamental change. Rong Jian, for example,
called for the development of the market and private property so as
to create the conditions for independence from political control and

to exert pressure upon the political leadership.[74] Similarly, the neo-authoritarian Xiao Gongqin observed that the market would not only help produce a middle class but would make possible an alliance of the middle class with the intellectuals, "including the stratum of the common citizens," which was necessary in order to prevent the "political corruption of the new authoritarianism, the degeneration of power and the retrogression of ideology."[75]

But despite these areas of agreement, Xu Liangying in particular was vociferous in denouncing neo-authoritarianism, which he called traditional despotism in a new guise, or the same rule by men rather than by law. His articles on the subject revealed the degree to which his views on democracy and those of his colleagues had changed since the Cultural Revolution. Xu admitted that it was only in the last ten years that he had read seriously on the subject of Western democracy. Before that he and his colleagues had not clearly understood the concept that the majority decides, but "the minority still receives the protection of the law and still enjoys all rights of citizens." Nor had they understood that to prevent the emergence of absolute power it was necessary that "the people's representatives [be] directly responsible to the voters" and that "restraints and balances [be] put on power." He characterized Hitler, Stalin, and Mao as unrestrained leaders who had "brought disasters . . . [to their countries] and even to all mankind." Prophetically, he called for depoliticization of the military, asserting that "interference by the armed forces in politics is strictly forbidden."[76] Wang Ruowang was also prophetic when in an interview with a Hong Kong journal he cited Khrushchev, a reference that could be considered an allusion to Gorbachev or even to Zhao Ziyang, as an example of an enlightened authoritarian leader who had not turned into a despot, but had been overthrown by the entrenched party bureaucracy because his reforms threatened their interests. Wang predicted that without a radical change in the political system, Deng's partial liberalization would also be undermined by entrenched interests.[77]

Although Yan Jiaqi had served as an advisor to Zhao Ziyang and had dedicated one of his books to him, he declared that the Cultural Revolution had proved that the search for the infallible man could lead only to disaster. On the contrary, as Yan had often explained, leaders were far from infallible: "Since man has all sorts of weaknesses and shortcomings, he must be subject to institutional restraints."[78] Without limited terms in office and predetermined procedures for correcting errors in a relatively timely way, China had been unable "to correct the mistakes of the Cultural Revolution until after Chairman Mao Zedong passed away."[79] Like Yan, Yu Haocheng observed that the debate on neo-authoritarianism was of "tremendous significance because it touches on the vital issue of whether we have learned the correct lesson from the calamity of the Cultural Revolution."[80]

Hu Jiwei emphasized that, like the neo-authoritarians, the advocates of democracy were not opposed to strong government. They too sought a strong government, but one that was democratic rather than autocratic. His view of democracy in early 1989 had become much more sophisticated than the one he had expressed earlier in the decade. He had moved through at least three stages: from talking about the need to listen to a variety of views, to seeking freedom of the press guaranteed by law and the establishment of a nonofficial press, to emphasizing the election of leaders according to democratic procedures. He acknowledged that "democratic elections may not necessarily choose leaders of the best quality, but they ensure that bad leaders will not be able to remain in power." Like Xu Liangying, he no longer defined democracy as solely majority rule, but recognized that the "minority of people who hold different opinions must also be respected and protected."[81] The transformation of Hu Jiwei's Marxist humanist vision into a belief in democratic institutions and the legal protection of minority views was typical of many members of Hu Yaobang's network. Although they were influenced by Western ideas, the evolution of their political beliefs was shaped principally by their Cultural Revolution experiences and their continuing persecution by the reformist Deng regime.

The "enfant terrible" of literary circles, the Beijing Normal University lecturer Liu Xiaobo, joined the democratic elite in the attack on neo-authoritarianism. Although Liu was very much an iconoclast and critical of members of the democratic elite for their desire to remain within the party establishment, his political ideas moved closer to theirs in early 1989, perhaps because the democratic elite was moving toward a more direct confrontation with the party leadership. The persistent belief in a virtuous leader rather than in a good system, Liu asserted, was a "most fatal weakness." To criticize corruption or even the officials engaged in corruption, he explained, "only conceals the corruption of the system itself." The "official profiteering" that had become so rampant had little to do, in his view, with the moral degeneration of party officials and their children; the corruption was due to the "absence of legal and institutional deterrence." He was especially critical of his fellow intellectuals who, he said, had always believed that the morality of the rulers rather than the political system was responsible for corruption and wrongdoing. He lamented that despite the lessons of the Cultural Revolution, which exposed the "utter ugliness" of the autocratic system, once again many intellectuals were "hoping for an enlightened ruler with absolute power to appear from within the despotic system to reshape the country." The intellectuals themselves, he charged, were to blame for their plight.[82]

The nonofficial journal *Economic Weekly* also became a prominent forum for the presentation of views for and against neo-authoritarianism. Wang Juntao, the deputy editor, leaned toward neo-authoritarianism and Chen Ziming, the publisher, toward democracy, and both views and others as well were presented in the weekly, exhibiting a pluralism similar to that in the *World Economic Herald*. One strong critique of neo-authoritarianism in the *Economic Weekly* denounced its ideas as "actually very old in China." Since the 1911 revolution, Yuan Shikai, Chiang Kai-shek, and Mao had espoused them.[83] Another critique, by Yan Jiaqi's wife Gao Gao, pointed out that although Mao was supposedly an "enlightened" leader, "the practice of enlightened rule can be such that it can be enlightened today and tomorrow, but on the day when power and interests are touched enlightenment will all but be squeezed out by autocracy." This happened, for example, when the "well-meaning criticisms" of the Hundred Flowers "were construed as malicious attacks on the party and socialism" and over half a million people were deprived of their rights in the anti-rightist campaign. This development "led not only to the 'Great Cultural Revolution,' but brought the nation to the brink of collapse."[84]

Other articles in the *Economic Weekly* attributed China's problems not to a weak political authority, but to a weak society. For nearly four decades the government had had too much power over the economy, the culture, and education, thereby reducing the people's authority. "The forces of people's participation in political affairs are very weak. Our country has conducted much political mobilization (from top-to-bottom movements) but what it lacks is political participation."[85] By the end of the decade, many members of the democratic elite had concluded that participation in political affairs was not just the prerogative of intellectuals but should be the prerogative of all classes. Such participation, moreover, as Fang Lizhi had stated earlier, was a right that was not conferred but must be won by the people.

The series of articles and debates on neo-authoritarianism culminated at a huge forum at People's University on April 3, 1989, lasting for over four hours. Organized by a student organization at the university, it was attended by 2,000 students, crammed into a classroom for only 800. In a highly charged confrontation, students cheered and jeered as each side spoke. On the democratic side were the younger theorists, such as Rong Jian and members of the Hu Yaobang network, and on the neo-authoritarian side were Wu Jiaxiang and researchers from the Central Committee General Office. The neo-authoritarians argued that with the introduction of democratic procedures, chaos would ensue; the democratic elite responded that only democracy, not autocracy, could ensure stability. Furthermore, said Wang Yizhou, the way to prepare the Chinese people for democracy was not through tutelage by a leader but through participation in democratic processes. Echoing Hu Jiwei, he asserted, "only by practicing democracy can it be mastered and applied."[86]

The forum proved to be the final debate between the two sides before the social discontent that both had been warning about erupted in Tiananmen Square just two weeks later. Despite their ideological differences, both sides were to participate in the events of Tiananmen, and both sides desired some of the same ends—a market economy, a strong middle class, ideological and interest pluralism, and genuine democracy. Though the debate between them was vociferous, they differed more from the elders than from each other. The neo-authoritarians were to participate in the Tiananmen protest in support of Zhao Ziyang; the democratic elite participated more in the hope of winning democratic rights. But in the June 4 crackdown and its aftermath, the elders made little distinction in their persecution of members on both sides of the debate.

Reaction to the Mao Craze

Another impetus to the democratic elite's more open confrontation with the Deng regime was an upsurge of interest in Mao and Mao's thought, evolving from the 1987 campaign against bourgeois liberalization. In addition to former Yan'an literary bureaucrats' efforts to resuscitate Mao's literary views, a series of reminiscences and lengthy sympathetic interviews with some of the radical ideologues of the original core group of the Cultural Revolution, such as Wang Li and Guan Feng, were published in 1988. A compassionate depiction of Mao in his last days, written by his nurse, and a long "neutral" description of Lin Biao by Lin Biao's secretary were also published at the end of 1988. In another attempt to prop up Mao's image, it became known that criticism of Stalin was no longer permitted. Wang Zhen demanded that Stalin's portrait not be removed from Tiananmen Square. Li Xiannian similarly complained that Mao's picture had not appeared on television as it usually did during the New Year's holidays.[87] Among the general population, increasing resentment against inflation and official corruption inspired nostalgia for the supposedly noninflationary, incorrupt Maoist era.

The reemergence of a neutral and even favorable view of Mao infuriated Yu Guangyuan. He condemned the publication of Maoist recollections of the Cultural Revolution without any rebuttals, while the history of the period by Yan Jiaqi and Gao Gao was suppressed; discussion of the Cultural Revolution, he said, should not be a "forbidden zone."[88] He proposed the establishment of a nongovernmental research institute to study and publish works on the Cultural Revolution. His proposal reveals that even the most loyal of government advisors was willing by early 1989 to contemplate action outside the official establishment and to acknowledge that a true picture of the Cultural Revolution could not be presented under official auspices.

An associate of the democratic elite, the poet and former rightist Shao Yanxiang, "welcomed" Wang Li's interview because he hoped that such an interview would reopen discussion on the Cultural Revolution and revive Ba Jin's proposal for a Cultural Revolution museum. Shao explained: "Only by increasing the degree of openness, making archives public, encouraging private research of history, and facing inevitable contention can we help clarify historical facts and expose the truth of history." This approach to history, especially the call for "private" research and the opening up of archives, clashed directly with the party's efforts to control historical research, especially on the Cultural Revolution. Shao, restating Yu Guangyuan's position, argued that if Wang Li could "clarify things" from his point of view, then the victims of the Cultural Revolution should also be able to clarify things from their point of view. Therefore he called for more study of the Cultural Revolution, so that "the occurrence of similar events can be minimized in the future even if it cannot be prevented." [89]

Even though there was still more criticism than praise of Mao and his statues were continuing to be demolished on university campuses, the renewed interest in him provoked members of the democratic elite and their younger associates to take countermeasures. The *Guangming Daily* investigative reporter Dai Qing, who, while supportive of the neo-authoritarian stance, on occasion joined the forums of the democratic elite, began investigating and writing about the victims of Mao's purges. Her first exposé concerned Mao's attack on the writer Wang Shiwei, who had been purged in 1942 at the very time that Mao had issued his Yan'an Talks and was killed five years later. Dai then wrote of Mao's attack on the former *Guangming Daily* editor Chu Anping, in the anti-rightist campaign. Liu Zaifu's journal *Literary Commentary* organized a discussion on Hu Feng, in which it detailed the negative consequences that had ensued for several generations of intellectuals from the persecution of Hu Feng and his disciples. The participants pointed out that Hu Feng was publicly vilified by former Yan'an bureaucrats, the very same officials now active in the effort to resuscitate Mao's thought. In the spirit of Ba Jin and Liu Zaifu, one participant exhorted his fellow intellectuals: "We need an interrogation of the soul." Other participants noted that in contrast to his accusers, Hu Feng had refused to persecute others, even those who had vilified him. In the summer of 1966, imprisoned under the harshest conditions and threatened with capital punishment, Hu refused to criticize Zhou Yang, who had led the campaign against him in 1955. [90] Several panelists urged the establishment of an "independent force of intellectuals outside the political system" to act as a check on dictatorial power as well as to express an independent view. [91] Such a recommendation was another indication that at least some intellectuals, especially among the democratic elite, were beginning to consider action outside the official establishment.

The New Enlightenment

In late 1988 the core group of Hu Yaobang's network attempted to establish its own nonofficial journal, *New Enlightenment* (Xin qimeng), organized by Wang Yuanhua, a scholar and former director of the Propaganda Department of the Shanghai Party Committee, the aesthetician Gao Ertai, and Wang Ruoshui. By registering the journal as a book series, published by an official publisher, the Hunan Educational Publishing House, the writers and editors involved were able to evade party censorship for a time. They published four issues until they were stopped just before the April–May 1989 demonstrations. Although to set up a journal outside official auspices was a nontraditional act, the founders' purpose, as stated in the first issue's postscript, written by its editor Wang Yuanhua, sounded very Confucian: "The life of theory lies in courage and sincerity which does not bow down to power and does not flatter."[92] Despite the radical changes in their views on political reform, the democratic elite still emulated, though not consciously, their literati predecessors in their concern for ideological issues and their emphasis on integrity. Although their rhetoric and concerns may have remained relatively traditional, by late 1988 they were beginning to act more like their East European counterparts in establishing media outlets and organizations outside the official sphere. Their actions had less to do with a conscious emulation of the East Europeans than with the increasing difficulty they were encountering in publishing their views in the party-controlled media.

The founders of the journal also organized a series of seminars without party authorization. The first was "Modernization and the New Enlightenment," held at Shanghai Normal University, attended by members of Hu Yaobang's network: Yu Haocheng, Li Honglin, Ge Yang, Ruan Ming, Zhang Xianyang, and Yu Guangyuan plus other associates such as Shao Yanxiang, Jin Guantao, and Pan Weiming, another former director of the Propaganda Department in Shanghai, who had been ousted in the anti–bourgeois liberalization campaign.

To mark *New Enlightenment*'s publication, its founders established the New Enlightenment salon on January 28, 1989, holding their meetings at the Universal Joy (Dule) Bookstore in Beijing. The salon was part of the democratic elite's move away from isolated protests toward more concerted efforts and more organized forms of political expression. In addition to those who had attended the earlier Shanghai meeting, other participants were Su Shaozhi, Wu Zuguang, Fang Lizhi, Wang Juntao, and the historian Bao Zunxin, who edited *Reading* (Dushu), an influential official journal on the social sciences, and who had also been involved in the "Toward the Future" series. Journals, seminars, and salons outside party control had been established in universities, institutes, and cities all over China since the mid-1980s. What made the New Enlightenment group so unusual was its membership—highly placed intellectuals involved in nonofficial activities.

Another new phenomenon of the late 1980s was the basement café of the Universal Joy Bookstore, where reformist intellectuals met. The bookstore had been opened in 1984 with private funds by a twenty-five-year-old woman, Yu Yansha. Early on, however, the store encountered official opposition. It was closed twice without notification in 1985, once for distributing the inaugural issue of a daring journal, *Youth Self-Study* (Qingnian zixue), published by the *China Youth News,* and again for distributing *Pioneer,* the magazine which had published Liu Binyan's "A Second Kind of Loyalty." Yu Yansha was also fined 15,000 yuan. She reopened the bookstore in 1986, during the intellectual relaxation. But after holding a reception to celebrate *New Enlightenment* and the establishment of the salon, the bookstore was again closed.[93]

Before *New Enlightenment* was shut down, however, it had made an impact. The first issue, published in October 1988, had a print run of 20,000 copies; the second issue, in December 1988, had a run of 10,000; the third issue, in February 1989, had a run of 10,000; and the fourth issue, in April 1989, printed 9,000 copies. The fourth issue was dedicated to the historian Li Shu, who had died in December 1988. The fifth issue, entitled "Reunderstanding Capitalism," and the sixth, "In Commemoration of the Seventieth Anniversary of May Fourth," were compiled and sent to the compositor but never published. The four published issues contained a total of nineteen essays, written mostly by the 1979 theory conference participants plus Liu Xiaobo and several younger colleagues, such as Jin Guantao and Bao Zunxin, and an older colleague, Li Rui, a former secretary of Mao, purged in 1959. Many of their articles asked why the May Fourth movement had failed to bring democracy and science to China. Some attributed this failure to the argument, put forth by the philosopher Li Zehou, that national survival had become more important than democracy and science. Others blamed the usual culprit, the traditional culture.[94] Wang Yuanhua blamed the "naiveté and theoretical immaturity of some Marxists at the time."[95] In addition they were said to be "greatly influenced by debased Soviet mechanistic theories of socialism" and "ultraleftist trends from Japan."[96] Thus leftism and the Soviet model were also held responsible for China's difficulty in developing democracy and science.

Many of the essays exhorted the intellectual community to become an independent force. Ruan Ming proclaimed: "The time has come for China's intellectuals to shed their long historical position of dependence and become their own masters."[97] Liu Xiaobo again chided his fellow intellectuals for groveling to and beseeching the authorities for their rights. Their pleas, he said, were "not an effort to win the freedom that one is entitled to, but rather . . . begging superiors for freedom." When Fang Lizhi had made a similar critique in 1986, his manner had been gentle and cajoling. Liu Xiaobo treated his fellow intellectuals with scorn. He mocked them for feeling no shame at their behavior and, in fact, feeling proud and shedding "copious tears of gratitude for this bestowal."[98] He urged them to abandon their suppliant attitude and to assert their independence from political authority.

Gao Ertai, who as a rightist had spent many years in labor reform camps, pointed out that just as some of the democratic ideas of Rousseau had led to the Terror of the French Revolution, so had some Marxist ideas, such as the dictatorship of the proletariat, led to Stalin's "large-scale bloody suppression."[99] Wang Ruoshui repeated his argument that such ideas and practices had generated alienation under socialism in China as well as in the Soviet Union. Li Honglin, as he had at the 1979 theory conference, continued to stress that the distortion of Marxism in practice had led to the loss of faith in Marxism. "The socialism that has been realized is not what the founders of Marxism envisioned and it has been left behind in the economic race with capitalism. This state of affairs causes a wavering of confidence in countries that have established a socialist system. In other places it has caused socialism to lose its appeal."[100]

The Three Petitions

At the Dule Bookstore celebration honoring *New Enlightenment,* Fang Lizhi had urged his fellow intellectuals to take more direct political action. He told them of a letter he had written to Deng Xiaoping on January 6, 1989, asking him to pardon Wei Jingsheng and other political prisoners in commemoration of the forthcoming anniversaries of the May Fourth movement, the French Revolution, and the

establishment of the People's Republic. Wei Jingsheng's case was particularly sensitive, because Deng had personally approved his sentencing. Nevertheless, Fang's example sparked the first organized political
efforts of the democratic elite, their associates, and like-minded intellectuals to confront the party publicly with alternative policies. In a
series of three petitions, they called for freedom of speech and a rule
of law as well as for the pardon of Wei Jingsheng. Although members
of Hu Yaobang's network did not initiate the petitions, their names
were on all three.

The first petition, sent to the Politburo and the National People's
Congress, was organized by a leader of the obscure poetry movement,
Bei Dao. Bei, a construction worker in the Cultural Revolution, had
participated in the April 5, 1976, protest and in the Democracy Wall
movement, during which he served as an editor of *Today* (Jin tian), a
journal of post-Mao literature. But after 1979 he had taken little part
in any political activity and had immersed himself in writing poetry,
becoming one of the few Chinese poets to gain a worldwide reputation. The impending tenth anniversary of Wei Jingsheng's imprisonment, however, had awakened in Bei Dao a sense of guilt for not having protested against the imprisonment of his fellow Democracy Wall
activist.[101] In January 1989, therefore, Bei organized a group of prominent literary intellectuals to petition for the release of Wei Jingsheng
and other political prisoners. The petition linked the demand for Wei's
release to the fortieth anniversary of the United Nations Declaration
on Human Rights, asserting that freeing Wei would be in keeping with
the spirit of the declaration.

Among the signers were Wei's colleagues from *Today,* former rightists who had actively called for democratic reform under Deng such
as the playwright Wu Zuguang and the poet Shao Yanxiang, and the
makers of "River Elegy" Su Xiaokang, Jin Guantao, and Wang Juntao
of SERI. Also included were members of the New Enlightenment
group, Wang Ruoshui, Su Shaozhi, and Bao Zunxin. Most surprising
were the signatures of several prominent writers who until then had
had little to do with politics, such as Bing Xin, a revered eighty-nine-
year-old writer; Xiao Qian, an essayist from the 1930s; several authors of wounded literature, such as the woman writer Zhang Jie;
and the literary critic Li Tuo. Other signers were philosophers and
historians who had concentrated primarily on philosophical issues,
such as Li Zehou, and scholars of premodern Chinese thought, such
as Pang Pu, Tang Yijie, and Zhang Dainian.

Even more challenging was the second petition, or open letter, of February 26, 1989, signed by forty-two intellectuals, mostly famous scientists. This document went even further in making a political statement. The signatories presented themselves as modern-day literati who had "inherited the tradition that 'every man has a share of responsibility for the life and death of the country' [and] cannot but worry about these problems." Although their language and style were traditional and some of their concerns, such as the corruption of the bureaucracy, sounded very Confucian, the four proposals they presented were nontraditional. The first called for political structural reform, by which they meant political democratization and rule of law. The second sought to guarantee the basic rights of citizens stipulated in the constitution, especially freedom of speech and freedom of the press, in the hope that "criticisms against leaders will not be repressed or retaliated against." The purpose of this proposal was to "prevent the historical tragedies, when people were punished for expressing views or publishing articles holding different political views, from happening again."[102] The third proposal concerned the release of political prisoners; "if people are no longer sentenced for ideological reasons, it will open a new political era for our country."[103] Fourth, the letter urged more funding for intellectuals' salaries and for research.

Xu Liangying initiated the second petition, which he drafted in the same period that his close friend Fang Lizhi was composing and sending his letter to Deng Xiaoping. Xu had been increasingly provoked by the prominence given to neo-authoritarian views. He emphasized, in an interview with a Hong Kong journal, that the only guarantee of stability and unity was not more political control, but democracy. Repression would backfire: "Using autocratic and coercive measures to suppress different views is bound to create chaos."[104] As unusual as the petition's proposals were the signatures on it. Included were the usual members of the democratic elite—Yu Haocheng, Zhang Xianyang, Li Honglin, Wu Zuguang, Shao Yanxiang, and Bao Zunxin— several of whom had also signed Bei Dao's petition. But the majority of the forty-two signers were natural scientists, some of them very well known, who hitherto had not spoken out politically.

The idea of circulating the petition among the scientific community began when one of Xu's old Zhejiang University classmates, Shi Yafeng, formerly a director of the Lanzhou Glaciology and Permafrost Institute, complained to Xu about the party's deterioration. They decided to get in touch with other Zhejiang University classmates and former underground comrades from the 1940s to see if they agreed with their proposals. Thirteen of the forty-two signers were their former classmates. Nine were committee members of the academic departments of the Academy of Sciences, among them Qin Linzhao, a well-known crystal physicist; Wang Ganchang, a nuclear and particle physicist who had contributed to China's development of the atomic and hydrogen bomb and had befriended Xu when he was labeled a rightist in 1957; Ye Duzheng, a former vice president of CAS and a famous meteorologist; and Hu Shihua, one of the founders of the system for China's computer software research. Half of those who signed were party members. Nine were NPC deputies and eight were CPPCC committee members. Xu had spent one to two hours talking with each person he contacted; only four or five refused to sign, not because they disagreed, but because they feared they might hurt their families. Xu's wife, Wang Laidi, a historian at the Modern History Institute of CASS who had incurred the wrath of Hu Qiaomu for her unorthodox interpretation of the May Fourth movement, also signed. After this second petition, Yuan Mu, spokesman for the State Council, insisted that only regular channels within the government be used to express views.

In mid-March a third petition appeared, this one signed by forty-three younger social scientists, humanists, and journalists. One of the initiators of this effort was the *Guangming Daily* journalist Dai Qing. This was not her first experience in organizing political action. Earlier that year, she and several journalist colleagues had published a book of interviews with experts opposing the Three Gorges project redirecting the Yangtze River. Aided by the *New Enlightenment* contributor Li Rui, who was also an engineer, the experts charged that Three Gorges, a huge engineering feat on the scale of Stalinist projects and supported by Soviet-educated officials, among them Premier Li Peng, would cause inestimable environmental and human damage. They urged that such an undertaking, affecting millions of lives, be debated publicly and not be decided by a few leaders behind closed doors. The book was another independent effort paid for by dozens of journalists and intellectuals, among them the philosopher Feng Youlan and Jin Guantao's controversial group, "Toward the Future." In the Soviet Union and Eastern Europe, the first organized challenges to the Leninist party-state had come from groups contesting environmental damage. Their environmental protests had gradually changed into organized political protest. The opposition to the Three Gorges project had the potential to be similarly transformed.

Co-initiator of the younger intellectuals' petition was the writer Su Wei, the director of the Institute of the Study of New Subjects of CASS. He contacted most of those who signed, including the political scientist Yan Jiaqi; another of the makers of "River Elegy," Yuan Zhiming; and editor of *Reading*, Wu Bin. In an interview at the time, Su Wei differentiated loyalty to one's country from loyalty to one's government in a manner reminiscent of Bai Hua. He explained that even though the opinion of the signers differed from that of the government, this did not mean they did not love their country.[105] He urged that the three petitions, with all their signatures, be published in the media; Xu Liangying had already sent his petition to the press. Although no newspaper or journal responded and the petitions were not published in the People's Republic, their existence nevertheless became public knowledge. Subsequently a group of students at Peking University established the Society of Contemporary Social Problems, with the undergraduate history student Wang Dan as its chairman. The organization hoped to study ways to promote democracy and to disseminate information on Wei Jingsheng, about whom the students had known little until the issuance of the three petitions.

These independently organized challenges to the party's policies by well-known, highly placed intellectuals infuriated not only the elders but also the reform officials. Zhao Ziyang and Hu Qili ordered the media not to publish the petitions or, for the next six months, any articles written by the signers. Furthermore, those signing the petitions were not to appear on television.[106] Official publications insisted that China had no political prisoners and reiterated the charge, first made in 1979, that Wei had leaked information to foreigners about China's imminent invasion of Vietnam. The official media blamed the petitions not on the famous intellectuals who had initiated and signed them but on a relatively unknown intellectual, Chen Jun. He had recently returned from the United States and supposedly had ties with the Alliance for Democracy in New York under the leadership of Hu Ping, the exiled philosopher who had won the 1980 elections to the local people's congress. The party charged that the Alliance was connected with Taiwan. It sought to show that the signers had been hoodwinked by this traitor, Chen, and had not necessarily agreed with the petitions to which they had affixed their names. Chen Jun had in fact helped Bei Dao gather signatures for the first petition, but he had not been its initiator.

Hu Qili visited a number of the signers to learn more about their motives. His attitude was polite and relatively tolerant toward those he questioned. A few wavered afterward, but despite the pressure the support for the petitions generally held. The signers were encouraged by their fellow intellectuals. The playwright Xia Yan, for example, phoned Bei Dao after the first petition appeared to express his support and his desire to sign. Shortly thereafter, top officials warned Xia against becoming involved in such activities.[107]

While the party media was fulminating against the "evil doings" of Chen Jun and a few others, the semiofficial and nonofficial press supported the petitioners' demands. An article in the *World Economic Herald* pointed out that since the end of the eighteenth century, Western countries had granted amnesty and special pardons to prisoners. It described this practice as "humane consideration" or "as a reward to a prisoner's heroic acts."[108] It noted that China's 1954 constitution included a provision for special pardons, though it had never been used. At the same time, some of the signers who had been asked to withdraw their names made a public statement to the effect that they had no intention of withdrawing. Subsequently they moved on to more organized political actions against party policies with which they disagreed.

The Democratic Salons

Students had also recently begun to organize their own independent activities, interrupted earlier by the crackdown on the 1986 demonstrations. On the afternoon of May 4, 1988, the Peking University alumnus Fang Lizhi arrived by bicycle with his wife Li Shuxian to celebrate the sixty-ninth anniversary of the May Fourth movement and the ninetieth anniversary of the university at a lawn seminar near the statue of Miguel Cervantes on the campus. About three hundred students and some alumni listened to Fang speak about science and democracy. This informal seminar had been arranged by a former physics graduate student of Li Shuxian, Liu Gang, who had also been involved in the 1986 student demonstrations.[109]

Earlier in the day Li Tieying, another Peking University graduate and a Czech-trained bureaucrat, Politburo member, and minister of the State Education Commission, had addressed 25,000 invited guests at the official celebration. He stressed the traditional virtues of discipline, honesty, and hard work. Fang's message at the informal seminar was in marked contrast to Li's.

Fang reiterated the argument for which Wei Jingsheng was still imprisoned: "China cannot have economic development without democracy!" He cautioned, however, that democracy must be developed gradually, so as not to cause disruption. Perhaps even more challenging to the elders was his comparison of East and West Germany, North and South Korea, and the People's Republic and Taiwan. Fang pointed out that in these divided countries, the socialist nations were the less successful.[110] His eloquence and humor electrified the crowd, and as he left he was mobbed by students seeking his autograph.[111] Whereas Fang was received with enthusiasm, Li Tieying was greeted with boos and catcalls when he tried to rationalize the government's inability to fulfill its repeated promises of more funds for education.

The demand for more funding for education, including intellectuals' salaries, was one of the issues that united the students and intellectuals in a common cause. The Peking University president Ding Shisun, at meetings of the NPC and the CPPCC, had repeatedly criticized the political leadership's neglect of education. He also criticized the leadership's belief that "ideological work" could prevent student protests.[112] Following Ding's criticisms, Peking University students had put up wallposters praising Ding and chastising Li Peng for his disregard of education. A few of the wallposters also criticized Zhao Ziyang for concentrating on economic reforms to the neglect of education, intellectual life, and human rights. Mocking Zhao's advice to intellectuals to supplement their meager salaries with second jobs, fifteen students marched to Tiananmen Square and offered to shine the shoes of the NPC deputies in order to earn extra income. Other university students, also protesting the treatment of education and intellectuals, staged a sit-in in front of the Great Hall of the People, where the NPC was meeting.[113] Informal student demonstrations in Tiananmen Square began again in the spring of 1988.

Although only five sessions of the lawn seminar at Peking University were held before they were stopped, shortly after the 1988 summer vacation they resumed as "democratic salons." Organized by the undergraduate history student Wang Dan and his friends, the salons convened on Wednesday afternoons and held fifteen sessions before the April 1989 demonstrations began. Because it was impossible to announce the seminars publicly, the number of participants varied from several dozen to as many as one hundred to two hundred. The democratic salons formed the first direct contacts between student activists and members of the democratic elite. Bao Zunxin, Wu Zuguang, Zhang Xiangyang, Xu Liangying, and other members of the elite were among the speakers. Ren Wanding, who had been the chief editor of *China's Human Rights* (Zhongguo renquan) during the Democracy Wall movement and had been imprisoned from 1979 to 1983, gave a seminar on the 1978–1979 movement.

The authorities, however, intervened on March 29, 1989, at the thirteenth gathering of the democratic salon. The meeting had been planned to mark the anniversary of Wei Jingsheng's arrest. Jiang Hong, a young professor in the Institute of International Relations of CASS, had been invited to be the principal speaker, but was ordered by the Beijing Party Committee, the Public Security Bureau, and the party committee at Peking University not to attend. Twenty plainclothes security guards monitored the gathering, took pictures, and taped the speeches. In response, an open letter signed by fifty-seven students was sent on April 3 to the university president and the university party committee, demanding the right to hold open seminars. It declared that the university should be a place where freedom of speech and academic freedom were fully implemented. At the next salon meeting on April 5, on the thirteenth anniversary of the April 5, 1976, protest, the organizers again defied the authorities by inviting Li Shuxian, who had more direct contact with the students, particularly through Wang Dan, than her husband Fang Lizhi. The participants discussed ways to promote political reform and made plans for their next meeting, which was to be held on the seventieth anniversary of May Fourth. In opposition to the party's emphasis on the patriotic legacy of May Fourth, they intended to focus on the movement's democratic features.[114] They also planned to invite Fang Lizhi, Su Shaozhi, Yan Jiaqi, and Wang Ruoshui to address them.

While the democratic salon at Peking University was perhaps the most famous, it was just one of a number of informal gatherings organized by independent student organizations under different guises on university campuses all over the country. Another relatively independent student organization at Peking University, for example, was the

Olympic Institute, established by science concentrators, among them Shen Tong. The group supposedly discussed scientific issues, but in reality debated political questions.[115] Another salon was the Tomorrow Association, organized by Li Lu at Nanjing University. These informal groups and their leaders were to become the key organizers of the spring 1989 student demonstrations in Beijing.

The students' desire for relatively independent political debates and organizations on their campuses was revealed in a survey taken by the Institute of Economic Structural Reform in the spring of 1989. Second only to student complaints about rising prices and official corruption were complaints about the lack of public forums where they could express their own concerns.[116] Reacting to these signs of discontent, the State Education Commission issued an internal document to the universities. In it the commission once again denounced Wei Jingsheng's "crimes" and Fang Lizhi's "reactionary speeches and acts," but, more significant, it instructed university officials to be on the lookout for possible student protests on the anniversaries of April 5 and May 4.[117] Thus the Deng regime anticipated some form of student protest in the spring of 1989. The leadership's fear of an impending social explosion was also reflected in its efforts to retighten controls over the meetings of the NPC and the CPPCC held that March.

The March 1989 Meetings of the NPC and CPPCC

At the Politburo meeting preceding the NPC, several elders expressed their growing concern over the activities of the democratic elite and potential student protests. Whereas earlier, most of the elders' criticisms of Zhao Ziyang had concerned his economic reforms, they now increasingly attacked him, as they had Hu Yaobang, for relaxing party controls over ideology and intellectuals. In particular, they were furious with him because he had given permission for Fang Lizhi to go abroad. Safely overseas, and able to speak more freely on many topics, Fang in 1988 had criticized officials and their children for having overseas bank accounts. Wang Zhen submitted a written statement to the meeting in which he called Fang a "counterrevolutionary" and urged his arrest. Although the Politburo did not act on Wang Zhen's proposal, Zhao, increasingly on the defensive, criticized those who had launched the petition drives for challenging the regime.[118] Zhao also went along with his fellow Politburo members in severely condemning the protests for independence and religious freedom that occurred in Tibet on the thirtieth anniversary of the Communist takeover there and in approving the imposition of martial law in Tibet in March. The use of martial law was justified by a member of the Ministry of Public Security, who explained that it was "an indispensable measure in modern state administration when it comes to dealing with foreign aggression, domestic riots, or serious natural calamities."[119] This same justification would be used just two months later for the imposition of martial law on China's own Chinese subjects in the Tiananmen demonstration. Yet with the exception of Wang Ruowang, who denounced the imposition of martial law in Lhasa, most of the democratic elite and the students were silent on Tibet.

Since the meetings of the National People's Congress had increasingly become forums where criticisms and new proposals circulating informally in official and intellectual circles were made public, party members attending the NPC were instructed to rebut immediately any remarks made there against party policies or socialism. Despite these instructions, however, some party delegates refused to comply. A nonparty standing committee member of the NPC, Huang Xunxing, for example, who had defected from Taiwan three years earlier, and two other delegates echoed the demands of the three petitions by proposing a review of the amnesty requests for prisoners.[120] At the meeting of the Beijing delegation, some even raised the issue of human rights, supposedly another "forbidden area." Nevertheless, the NPC delegates supported the government's imposition of martial law on the Tibetans, who were then regarded, even by the most reformist officials and intellectuals, as not protected by what were termed "universal human rights." At the other political extreme, NPC representatives of the "leftist" persuasion complained that the government had failed to promote "socialist spiritual civilization," especially among the youth, who they charged had been given inadequate attention.[121] They urged a return to the Yan'an values of patriotism, plain living, hard work, devotion to the motherland and the party, and a sense of duty. These values were to be reemphasized after the June 4 crackdown.

Despite their political disagreements, both the associates of the democratic elite and those of the elders attempted to use the 1989 NPC meeting to strengthen the congress as a check on executive power. Thirty Shanghai delegates, for example, submitted a letter in which they requested explanations for government errors in policy implementation.[122] A Liaoning delegate criticized the NPC Standing

Committee for the introduction of price reforms and the emphasis on the coastal economy before these issues were debated and adopted in the NPC. When a vote was taken on the proposal to grant legislative power to the people's congress in the special economic zone of Shenzhen so that it could formulate its own regulations, giving it greater authority than people's congresses elsewhere, more than 1,000 of the 2,688 members voted against it.[123] This was a much larger vote in opposition to a government request than ever before. Most of those voting against the proposal were from inland and northern provinces, who wanted to prevent even wider gaps between the special economic zones and the rest of the country. Still, though a sizable number of delegates may have been against certain economic reforms, this did not mean that they necessarily supported the efforts of the elders, led by Li Peng, to recentralize economic activities.

Several delegates suggested that the NPC select government leaders in a multicandidate election, a proposal that questioned the party leaders' authority to select themselves and their successors. Another extraordinary occurrence was the criticism by delegates of their chairman Wan Li for failing to carry out his constitutionally empowered authority to supervise the work of the State Council. Ironically, though Wan Li was a reformist official, unlike Peng Zhen, he was reluctant to challenge legislation submitted by his fellow reformer Zhao Ziyang, even if doing so would enhance the power of the NPC to check the executive branch. Wan Li acknowledged his ineffectiveness and then publicly criticized the detention by Customs of a petition, signed by 24,000 residents of Hong Kong, calling on the NPC to release Wei Jingsheng.[124]

Two significant pieces of legislation approved at the meeting had the potential to give ordinary citizens rights in fact as well as in theory. One was the "NPC Rules of Procedures," the first effort to codify congress procedures. This codification, begun in 1981, had been distributed to provincial people's congresses and government departments for discussion and had gone through ten drafts. The establishment of an agreed-upon set of procedures for dealing with political matters[125] had been a goal of the democratic elite since the early 1980s. The code specified procedures for conducting meetings and elections, making appointments, impeaching officials, and establishing investigative committees. Its implementation, however, would be stymied by the June 4 crackdown.

The other important legislation was the Administrative Litigation

Law, which codified the procedures to be used when ordinary citizens sued a party or a government official for infringement of rights. This law, in preparation for three years, was based on practices in foreign countries. Again it was the fruition of demands by the democratic elite and others that disputes between individuals and party cadres be dealt with in civil courts rather than in party offices. An NPC delegate who was also a private businessman explained that until then a private citizen who wanted to redress an injustice could only appeal to the very organization that had committed the injustice in the first place.[126] A handbook was to be published spelling out in simple language the legal procedures that ordinary people could use to sue officials.

The new law was also intended to protect the rights of lawyers who defended ordinary citizens against the party. The press was filled with reports of defendants' lawyers in such cases who had lost their rights and were even arrested for defending their clients. The passage of the Administrative Litigation Law was hailed in a *People's Daily* commentator article as overcoming the "erroneous idea of certain cadres who wrongly think that engaging in a lawsuit with common people is a matter beneath their dignity."[127] The *China Daily* praised the law as a "significant step towards the establishment of an independent judiciary system in a country where the will of [an] individual official often prevails over law." It acknowledged that many laws on paper were not implemented, but it urged: "We cannot let this happen [to the Administrative Litigation Law]."[128]

As if foreseeing the impending events, some delegates tried to draft a law safeguarding the rights of participants in demonstrations. Jiang Ping, a vice chairman of the NPC Law Committee and president of the University of Politics and Law in Beijing, prepared a motion for deliberation by the NPC Standing Committee that would amend China's criminal law to drop the charge of "counterrevolutionary" offense. He explained that because China was no longer in its revolutionary era, to call an offense counterrevolutionary was no longer appropriate. No action, however, was taken on his proposal.[129]

Perhaps the most direct challenge to the party at the NPC came from Hu Jiwei at a meeting of the two hundred Sichuan delegates, which Li Peng also attended. Hu used the occasion to criticize the State Council leadership, mainly Li Peng and his colleagues, for not paying attention to the need for political structural reform, and he warned of serious consequences if political reforms did not accompany economic reforms. Concerning the popular mood, he emphasized that freedom of the press provided people with a safe channel for venting their discontent. A free press, he asserted, was a "very good outlet for anger." Like his colleagues, he explained that if people did not dare to speak out, the situation could be explosive. He concluded: "Democratic authority is the best factor of stability, whereas autocratic authority is the most unstable factor."[130]

Despite Hu Jiwei's call at the NPC for freedom of the press, the *World Economic Herald* complained that it had been denied permission to cover the congress. Zhang Weiguo, head of its Beijing office and a major contact with the democratic elite, convened a forum to criticize the NPC delegates' lack of assertiveness in pushing for political democratization.[131] Yan Jiaqi complained that although voters could elect delegates to the district, township, and county congresses, they could not directly elect delegates to the NPC; almost all of those who participated were selected by the party leadership. The NPC was therefore accountable to the leadership, but not to the people. Once more, Yan criticized the party for acting as if it were still an underground organization involved in inner-party struggles and he exhorted party leaders to follow "constitutionally prescribed procedures."[132] Several NPC delegates, as well, called for direct election of deputies to the NPC as was done at lower levels and as was being done in the Council of People's Delegates in the Soviet Union.

Delegates to the CPPCC meeting used the occasion to criticize the increasing number of articles and reminiscences by Cultural Revolution activists. In addition, several of the literary and art members demanded specific legislation to protect the rights of writers and artists. In demands even more directly threatening to the elders, they also criticized the unjust treatment of Hu Yaobang and called for his return to political leadership.[133] A Beijing actress, Du Jingfang, asked: "What mistake did he make?" Wei Minglun, a director of the Sichuan Opera, called for the reinstatement of Liu Binyan's party membership. He pointed out that the corruption Liu had exposed over the past ten years had grown much worse.[134]

On March 26, soon after the two meetings, a forum of two hundred was convened in the Beijing Library to discuss ways to revise and implement the constitution. The meeting was organized by the Stone Group's think tank, headed by Cao Siyuan, in association with a number of semiofficial institutions, including the Research and Development Institute of the Capital (Shoudu) Iron and Steel Corporation, the *World Economic Herald,* the *New Observer,* and the editorial board of the "Democratic Studies" series. For several organizations to work together outside the party's authority to revise the constitution was an extraordinary step. The original 1954 constitution had been revised three times under the party's auspices, in 1966, 1975, and most recently in 1982. As with the previous revisions, the 1982 version had merely reflected the party's policies at that time.[135]

Since 1986 members of the democratic elite, particularly Yan Jiaqi, Yu Haocheng, and Cao Siyuan, as well as reform officials, newspaper editors, and other intellectuals had been calling for a constitution that defined the political system but omitted statements about current policies, priorities, and specific leaders. Yu Haocheng, in an article in the journal *Jurisprudence* (Faxue), denounced Mao's disregard of the constitution. "The solemn Constitution was reduced to a piece of scrap paper."[136] He also criticized the document because it included terms such as "party leadership" and "Marxism-Leninism," which he said did not belong in the constitution proper. In the 1982 constitution these phrases, along with the four cardinal principles, were moved to the preamble, where Yu declared they were not legally binding.[137] Cao Siyuan proposed removing not only the four cardinal principles but also Mao's name—as in "with Chairman Mao as the leader"—from the preamble, as well. Although Cao had studied with Su Shaozhi, Zhang Xianyang, and Yu Guangyuan, after graduation he worked for one of Zhao Ziyang's economic think tanks. By early 1989, however, he had moved well beyond Zhao's technocratic approach to reform. Among his goals were to restore the right to strike and to introduce a stipulation on the presumption of innocence before a court of law. Both Cao, in a series of articles in the *World Economic Herald,* and Yu Haocheng, in *Jurisprudence,* urged that the specific responsibilities and rights of citizens be spelled out in the constitution so that they could not be changed at will by political leaders.

The Death of Hu Yaobang

In the midst of these increasingly organized challenges to the party, Hu Yaobang was preparing to make a comeback. Described as despondent in the period after his purge, he had seldom participated in the meetings of the Politburo, of which he was still a member. Instead he had retreated to his home, where he practiced calligraphy and read ancient Chinese literature and Marxist texts. Yet he was not forgotten. Unlike what occurred under Mao, when a fallen official either became a nonperson or was treated as a villain, in the Deng era a purged victim, especially one purged from the heights of power, gained in stature. As Hu's image as a reformer and as a protector of intellectuals grew, the image of the elders, his former Long March companions, declined. Increasing public awareness of Hu's courage in rehabilitating and protecting controversial figures, his outspokenness in condemning the special privileges of party leaders, his reluctance to engage in political intrigue, his unmitigated criticism of the Cultural Revolution, his willingness to dispense with parts of the Marxist-Leninist canon, and his openness to new ideas, which had characterized his actions since his return to power after the Cultural Revolution, endeared him more and more to the urban populace. Whereas his former revolutionary colleagues constantly exhorted party officials to set a good example for others to follow, he was regarded as the only one who truly lived up to the party's ideals.

In late March Hu began to prepare a speech on the need to give greater support spiritually as well as financially to education and to intellectuals, which he planned to present at an enlarged Politburo meeting on April 8 convened to discuss education. He had done extensive research on the subject and had spoken with a number of intellectuals from his old networks. He told his old friend Li Rui that he regretted his inability to protect intellectuals from persecution in the past and that he was sorry for the denunciation of Liu Binyan in his 1987 self-criticism.[138] He incorporated some of his friends' suggestions into his speech. But at the Politburo meeting, he suddenly suffered a heart attack. He died a week later, on April 15, 1989.

The death of Hu Yaobang set off the social explosion that many of his followers and even his former revolutionary colleagues had been anticipating. The Tiananmen Square demonstration sparked by his death was unprecedented not only in bringing together students and intellectuals—both the democratic elite and the neo-authoritarians— but in linking them at times with workers, professionals, party members, and ordinary urban citizens. The participation of other social groups in political affairs, which the democratic elite had come to believe was necessary for the emergence of a democratic polity, was finally occurring.

11

The Democratic Elite and Tiananmen

The tacit compact between the democratic elite and the reform leadership made in the early days of the Deng Xiaoping regime was shattered beyond repair by the spring of 1989. The break was largely attributable to changes on the part of the democratic elite. Over the decade, most of them had moved from seeing themselves as the intermediaries between the people and leaders, responsible for upholding the ideology and reforming the regime from within, to calling for the establishment of democratic institutions through which the people themselves would assume some responsibility for political decision making by means of elections, legislatures, and a free press. The evolution of their views and their increasingly more independent and more organized stance derived not only from their exposure to Western ideas and institutions in the 1980s but, perhaps more important, from their own inability to carry out their responsibilities in the traditional literati manner because of the party's continuing repression. By the late 1980s many of them had concluded that political reform would not come from within the party without pressure from outside the party.

Even though the democratic elite had provided the intellectual underpinnings for student demonstrations during the 1980s, they themselves did not participate in any of them until the Tiananmen Square demonstration of spring 1989 and then not until mid-May, relatively late in the demonstration. The participation of the East European and Soviet intellectuals with students and workers in largely successful efforts to bring about changes in their societies had some influence on the actions of Chinese intellectuals. But their role in the 1989 demonstration was in no way comparable to that of their East European counterparts. The only ones who came close were Chen Ziming and Wang Juntao, who had established the independent think tank, SERI. Though they had participated in some of the seminars of the democratic elite, they represented a new kind of intellectual activist—as became clearer in the aftermath of Tiananmen.

China's intellectuals did not instigate the demonstrations; nor were they "black hands" manipulating the students behind the scenes, as the party was later to charge. Nevertheless their participation, though belated, revealed an acceptance of the fact that an enlightened intellectual elite was not sufficient to bring about a more modern and more humane society. Indeed, their experience in the Deng as well as in the Mao era had nearly demonstrated the opposite: that in China's decades-long effort to achieve this goal, its intellectuals had been ineffectual and at times even counterproductive.

Mourning Hu Yaobang

Hu Yaobang's death on April 15, 1989, evoked a genuine outpouring of grief from China's urban population, particularly its intellectuals and students, who had identified with Hu's efforts to redress the wrongs suffered by intellectuals and others during the Mao era. Like the students, the democratic elite and other intellectuals used the occasion of Hu's death to express dissatisfaction with the party's current policies and to press for political reform. Equally threatening to the elders was their call for a reappraisal of Hu's purge in January 1987, an implicit criticism of those who had dismissed him.

There was some similarity between the ceremonies surrounding Hu's death and those held for Zhou Enlai on April 5, 1976. On both occasions, young people used the opportunity to criticize the prevailing leadership and to call for change. In 1989 students at Peking University had been planning a pro-democracy demonstration to coincide with the seventieth anniversary of the May Fourth movement.[1] Hu's death pushed up their timetable. That the students organized themselves so quickly and effectively to mourn Hu's passing indicates that preparations had already been under way for some form of organized action. On April 15, the very day of Hu's death, a wreath-bearing ceremony in his honor took place at the university.

Just as some students used Hu's death for their own purposes, Zhao

Ziyang attempted to use it to retake the offensive in his power struggle with the elders and Li Peng, by regaining the support of the intellectuals and students he had lost in late 1988. During the preparations for the official funeral, to take place on April 22, another conflict arose between Zhao and the elders over whether or not Hu's name should be preceded by the words "great Marxist" in the eulogy and whether or not Hu's resignation should be reappraised. After soliciting views from others, Zhao decided to use the phrase, believing such a description might placate the students and intellectuals calling for Hu's reappraisal. Although Deng Xiaoping at first seemed to agree, some of the elders refused to accept the wording. By the evening before the funeral, therefore, when the fifth draft of Hu's eulogy was sent to Deng for approval, he deleted "great Marxist." Deng once again had given in to his elderly colleagues, but he was also influenced by reports from the Beijing Party Committee, particularly those of Mayor Chen Xitong and the party secretary Li Ximing, who depicted the students' ongoing ceremonies in honor of Hu as potentially disruptive.

Despite Deng's deletion, Zhao's eulogy for Hu Yaobang was a laudatory one. Zhao praised Hu for his respect for talented people, his appreciation of science and literature, and his leadership in the struggle against the "two whatevers" in the practice criterion discussion. He also lauded Hu for presiding over agricultural and urban reforms, opening up the coastal areas, and developing the commodity economy, policies that were more associated with Zhao than with Hu. Zhao concluded the eulogy by saying that Hu "loved the party and people deeply and the party and people deeply loved him." Implicit in Zhao's praise was criticism of the elders for having purged such an outstanding leader. The anger of Hu's family toward the elders for the way in which Hu had been treated was expressed in their invitations to the funeral, which included everyone except the elder Bo Yibo, who had led the denunciation of Hu at the enlarged Politburo meeting that had dismissed him. Bo attended the funeral anyway, but Hu's wife refused to shake hands with him.

Despite the Hu family's virtually open invitation to the funeral, it was announced that the public would be denied access to Tiananmen Square when the leadership, including the elders, entered the Great Hall of the People for the official funeral on April 22. Seventy thousand students plus 30,000 workers and others, however, occupied the square the night before the ceremony.[2] The students were far better organized than they had been in past demonstrations. They set out from the university area, the Haidian District, in northwest Beijing, the night before, sometimes marching and sometimes running, hand in hand. Directed by marshals, their regimented cordons stretched for miles through the city streets. In some places the residents lined up to cheer them on. Such spontaneous public support from ordinary citizens for a student demonstration was unheard of in the forty years of the People's Republic. The leaders of the march carried a huge portrait of Hu, depicted as a fighter for democracy and a friend of youth. When they marched into Tiananmen Square, Hu's portrait symbolically blocked out Mao's image hanging in front of the Gate of Heavenly Peace. The night in the square before the day of the official ceremony was spent in eulogizing Hu and debating political policies. Like their predecessors in the demonstration of April 5, 1976, the students repeatedly sang the "Internationale" and other revolutionary songs and recited poems they had learned in school.

At the unofficial mourning ceremony for Zhou Enlai, held thirteen years earlier, the demonstrators had demanded new leaders to replace the Gang of Four and had implicitly attacked Mao. In 1989 most of the students were asking for fundamental reform of the political system and a change in its values. Some of the participants wore headbands on which were written political slogans, such as "Long live democracy." Their definitions of democracy were often vague, and at times the student leaders acted autocratically toward both their fellow students and other social groups. Yet most of them defined democracy as a government which was responsible to the people and which guaranteed freedom of the press, a rule of law, the right to choose leaders directly, and human rights. Though a general definition, it contained some of the prerequisites for a democratic system. The words of their anthem, the "Internationale," were challenging to any regime. The second verse declared: "No one will give us deliverance; no god, no czar, no hero; We'll arrive at our freedom only by our hand."

As the official guests to the funeral entered the Great Hall around 9:00 A.M. on April 22, the demonstrators held up posters highlighting the constitution's promise of freedom of speech, assembly, and demonstration. Three students presented a petition to the leadership that, in addition to calling for freedom of press, asked for the establishment of nonofficial newspapers, a large increase in funds for education, improvement in the living conditions of intellectuals, a reassessment of the spiritual pollution and the anti–bourgeois liberalization campaigns, a reversal of verdicts on those wrongfully accused, and a fair account of their demonstration in the media. Although the demands were radical even in the context of the Deng regime, the way in which they were presented was very traditional. Three student leaders knelt on the stairs to the hall for almost forty minutes with the petition held over their heads, just as supplicants at court had once waited for the dynastic ruler to accept their appeal. Whereas at times in the past Confucian officials might have accepted such a petition, no party leader came forward now. The dignitaries appeared to be uncertain how to handle the demonstration; their indecision further intensified the emotional pitch of the demonstrators.

Some members of the democratic elite participated in the unofficial ceremony for Hu Yaobang. About twenty editors and reporters from the *Science and Technology Daily,* among them the deputy editor Sun Changjiang, a participant in the theory conference, were present. The editors of the *New Observer* sent a wreath in the name of their journal, and a wreath from the editors of the *World Economic Herald* referred to Hu as a "great Marxist," in defiance of the elders' rejection of such a description. In addition, the democratic elite held their own memorial service for Hu a few days earlier, on April 19. Their commemoration, in the form of a seminar, was convened by the Beijing office of the *Herald,* headed by Zhang Weiguo, and the *New Observer,* whose editor, Ge Yang, presided. These two journals had been major forums for Hu's intellectual network over the decade. The seminar was held in the conference room of the Ministry of Culture, of which Wang Meng, a Hu Yaobang appointee, remained the minister. It was attended by about forty-five members of Hu's network and others, who presented a view of Hu in direct opposition to that of the party.

Many of those who came—Hu Jiwei, Yu Guangyuan, Qin Chuan, Wu Mingyu, Sun Changjiang, Su Shaozhi, Feng Lanrui, Tong Dalin, Zhang Xianyang, Li Honglin, and Yan Jiaqi—had participated in the 1979 theory conference. Yu Haocheng, on the very day of the seminar, had been summoned to the Public Security Bureau to be interrogated about articles of his published in Hong Kong journals. Others had been associated with Hu's intellectual network over the decade, such as Xu Liangying, former propaganda director Zhu Houze, and Li Rui, whom Hu had rehabilitated after almost twenty years of labor reform and imprisonment, and Pan Weiming, the purged propaganda chief in Shanghai. Dai Qing from the *Guangming Daily* and Chen Ziming, publisher of *Economic Weekly* as well as the head of SERI, also participated.

Recalling their contacts with Hu over the past decade, members of his network made the reappraisal of him that the party had refused to undertake. Yan Jiaqi compared the party's unjust treatment of Hu to the Gang of Four's unjust treatment of Zhou Enlai.[3] Others praised Hu's integrity and openness, implying that these qualities were thoroughly absent in his Long March colleagues. Feng Lanrui depicted Hu as unusual among the leadership in that he had admitted and corrected his mistakes and responded readily to others' ideas.[4] Zhu Houze noted Hu's openness and appreciation of people with talent. Zhang Xianyang described Hu's manner as humane and democratic. He recounted Hu's efforts in the 1957 anti-rightist campaign to reduce its scale and to protect its victims.[5] Ge Yang hailed Hu for reversing the verdicts against thousands of victims of the party's purges. She herself, sent away for labor reform in the 1957 anti-rightist campaign, had also been one of his rehabilitees. She noted that when Hu had been purged in January 1987, she again was put on the party's black list, on the day of her seventieth birthday. Only Hu's protection, she implied, had allowed her and her colleagues to function as freely as they had. Dai Qing, despite her neo-authoritarian stance, had increasingly participated in the activities of the Hu network. She observed that her study of party history had shown that the party had treated unjustly not only intellectuals such as Wang Shiwei and Chu Anping but also most of its party secretaries, from Chen Duxiu to Qu Qiubai to Hu Yaobang. She asked whether there might be something inherently wrong with a political system that was responsible for such injustices, expressing some of the same doubts about it that the democratic elite had expressed over the past ten years.[6]

The *World Economic Herald* Controversy

The *World Economic Herald*'s decision to publish the proceedings of the seminar in honor of Hu Yaobang sparked a controversy that impelled other members of the democratic elite and their colleagues to join the student demonstration. That its editor, Qin Benli, wanted to publish the accolades to Hu is not surprising, given the close association of his newspaper with Hu's intellectual network as well as with Zhao Ziyang's think tanks. Just before Hu's death, Qin had published controversial articles stressing the need for pressure from below in order to influence the leadership at the top. One of these, written by Wen Yuankai with two others, pointed out that the economic reforms had brought about a "more extensive social transformation from below to above." But, the writers complained, "the old political structure is still obstructing and restraining social development." They therefore called for political reforms—a government based on separation of powers, enhancement of the National People's Congress, an independent judiciary, freedom of the press, and acknowledgment of different political views and political factions—to break down the obstructions. They also called for the elimination of the "abominable practices" of resolving political differences by means of political movements and dictatorial mandates and demanded the abolition of the personal files and residence registration by which the party enforced its controls. Finally, the authors took the unusual step of urging their fellow intellectuals to "work together with the workers, the peasants, and the people at all strata . . ."[7]

Qin's instructions to Zhang Weiguo were to devote as many pages of the *Herald* as needed to the speeches made at the seminar reappraising Hu. Qin also decided to publish the issue a day earlier than normal, so that it would appear on the day of Hu's official memorial service. The Shanghai Propaganda Department learned of his plan, and ordered Qin to show them the final proofs for the issue; upon seeing them, the department recommended that several hundred characters be deleted. When Qin refused, Jiang Zemin, then the mayor of Shanghai, criticized Qin for ignoring party discipline. Qin finally agreed to some deletions, but before his orders were received, 160,000 copies of the issue had already been printed in its original form and sent to Beijing.[8] The Shanghai Party Committee suspended Qin as editor on April 26 and sent in a task force to rectify the paper. Despite these actions, when the next issue, number 440, appeared, instead of bearing the wording approved by the task force, "In Commemoration of May Fourth," in the top right corner of the front page, it bore the more defiant inscription: "We Need an Environment Where We Can Speak Freely."[9]

On May 1, Qin convened the editorial board at his home to compose a protest statement. Several hundred copies of the completed

statement were issued on May 2. His associates phoned foreign corre-
spondents to ask for their support. Even though Jiang Zemin had
hinted that Qin might be reinstated if he made a self-criticism, Qin
refused. Zhang Weiguo also refused, saying that the party had no jurisdiction over the paper because it was run without state money.[10]
He noted that there were at least forty-seven similar newspapers
jointly run by their members rather than by the party or government,
and all should control their own activities.[11] The next issue, number
441, scheduled to appear on May 8, was held up by the Shanghai
Party Committee because the front page had a denunciation of Qin's
firing and a statement by the China World Economic Association, the
Herald's sponsor, that only it, and not the Shanghai Party Committee,
had the power to dismiss Qin and change the staff. Issue number 441
was finally published on May 11, without the criticism of Qin's firing,
but with articles equally bold in protesting the party's interference in
the *Herald*'s affairs. Although the staff prepared the May 15 issue,
number 441 proved to be the *Herald*'s last before it was shut down.[12]

The staff then broke new ground in bringing a civil suit against
Jiang Zemin, for "harming the reputation of the *World Economic
Herald*." Two civil litigation experts from People's University volunteered their services, and the Civil Law Department at the University
of Politics and Law volunteered to help file the writ. This was the first
time that a Chinese newspaper had sued a party leader, and indicates
that the Administrative Litigation Law, just passed in March, may
have had some influence. The suit encouraged other journalists and
intellectuals to bring charges against party units they believed had infringed on their rights.

At the same time, a wave of outside support was building for Qin
and his paper that ultimately was to enlarge the Beijing demonstration
beyond a student movement. Dai Qing encouraged Qin to continue
his struggle with the Shanghai party authorities and contacted *China
Youth,* the *Guangming Daily,* and Chen Ziming of the *Economic
Weekly* to support him. Several hundred journalists from the party's
national papers, including the *People's Daily, Workers Daily, Farmers
Daily,* and the Women's Federation paper, sent a petition to the Shanghai Party Committee protesting Qin's treatment.[13] The *Asia-Pacific
Economic Forum,* the weekly connected with the CASS of Guangzhou, held a press conference in Beijing to voice public support for
the *Herald.* Yan Jiaqi and Xu Liangying drafted an "open letter" to

the Shanghai Party Committee entitled "Defend Freedom of the Press," signed by fifty intellectuals, among them Su Shaozhi, Yu Haocheng, Zhang Xianyang, Bao Zunxin, and Su Xiaokang. Many had written for the *Herald*. Their letter stated that the party's action was contrary to Article 35 of the constitution which guaranteed the freedom of the press.

The *Herald*'s experience provoked journalists for the first time in the People's Republic to organize themselves for concerted political action. Journalists were the first professional group to join the student demonstration with their own demands. On May 4 about five hundred journalists took to the streets with banners calling for support for the *World Economic Herald* and freedom of the press. On May 9, a petition was delivered to the Chinese Journalists Association, signed by more than a thousand journalists, asking for a "dialogue on press reform." Since the mid-1980s they had tried in vain to get a law protecting the press by working within the system; now they would seek the same goal through public protest.

The Role of the Media

In addition to the *Herald,* a few other newspapers played a crucial role in helping to expand the social base of the spring 1989 demonstration. One of these was the *Science and Technology Daily*. Its chief editor, Lin Zixin, an old revolutionary journalist, and its deputy editor, Sun Changjiang, published the first factual accounts of the demonstration, with a large photo of students paying their respects to Hu Yaobang. Copies were quickly posted on the walls of Peking University, drawing huge crowds. Lin had allowed the first reports about the demonstration because his newspaper had been overlooked when other senior editors were called to a meeting with Hu Qili at which he ordered them not to report on the demonstration. On the same day that Hu Qili met with the editors, *Science and Technology Daily* ran its first story. It continued to report on the demonstration even after its editors became aware of Hu Qili's order.[14]

When the *Science and Technology Daily*'s editors and journalists returned to their offices after Hu Yaobang's funeral on April 22, they were determined to report on the students' unofficial ceremony as well as on the official ceremony. The younger journalists, in particular, were so committed to giving the unofficial ceremony full coverage that at a meeting lasting well into the early morning of April 23, they persuaded a majority of the staff to threaten to resign if that could not be done. At the urging of Sun Changjiang, Lin finally agreed. On April 24, an article entitled "Under Wind and Rain, Sing a Song to Say Goodbye to You" reported on the 100,000 participants at the unofficial funeral and told of their demands for a quicker pace for democratization. The issue also carried five photos of the unofficial ceremony and other stories on it as well. The other official media, by contrast, reported only on the official funeral. The unofficial ceremony was not mentioned.

When the authorities attempted to stop the distribution of this issue through the mail, the *Science and Technology Daily* staff personally carried stacks of the paper to post offices around Beijing. Seth Faison, then a reporter at the *South China Morning Post,* observed that "the *Science and Technology Daily's* coverage, like a tiny leak in the dike of official control, led to further journalistic risk-taking, which eventually turned into a flood of reports on the peaceful protest movement."[15] On April 27, Ge Yang's *New Observer* presented an objective account of the student demonstration. One by one, newspapers such as *Workers Daily, Farmers Daily,* and *Beijing Youth News* began to report more objectively on the demonstration, though none of them gave as comprehensive an account as the *Science and Technology Daily* continued to provide. On May 6, in a move to bolster his political position, Zhao Ziyang told Hu Qili and others that there was "no big risk to open up a bit by reporting the demonstrations and increase the openness of news."[16] With this loosening of control, other newspapers gave fuller accounts of the demonstration as well. This was not the first time since the demonstration began that Zhao had taken a position at odds with his mentor Deng and the elders. When Zhao had returned from a visit to North Korea at the end of April, he had criticized the Shanghai Party Committee's handling of the *Herald* affair.[17]

Zhao's encouragement of fuller media coverage of the demonstration, especially in the *People's Daily,* the party's premier mouthpiece, gave the public the impression that the demonstration had received the party's imprimatur.[18] Supposing the risk to have lessened, over a million of Beijing's inhabitants were emboldened to join in. The journalistic profession's show of solidarity with the student protesters, moreover, seemingly without punishment, further encouraged other professional groups, bureaucrats, academics, workers, and ordinary citizens to participate. The media's relatively objective coverage was instrumental in transforming the demonstration from a student effort into an urban protest, extending beyond Beijing to virtually all of China's major cities.

The other event that was to expand the demonstration beyond the student community, but for opposite reasons, was the *People's Daily's* April 26 editorial, based on a speech that Deng had made a day earlier. His speech relied on information filtered to him through Li Peng from Mayor Chen Xitong and Beijing party secretary Li Ximing. The editorial itself was originally written by the Beijing propaganda director, Xu Weicheng, and then with instructions from Deng was revised by a committee under Hu Qili. It characterized the demonstration as a premeditated conspiracy to bring about political disorder and blamed an "extremely small number of people with ulterior purposes," whose goal was "to sow dissension among the people, plunge the whole country into chaos and sabotage the political situation of stability and unity."[19] This charge against the students provoked sizable segments of other urban classes to join the demonstration.

The editorial also expressed the elders' alarm, as revealed in Deng's speech the day before, that the demonstration might turn into another Cultural Revolution. Deng warned that the disturbance must not be allowed to spread to secondary schools or to society at large. He also feared that the demonstration might be a forerunner of the political ferment then occurring in Eastern Europe. Of China's demonstrators, he said: "Those people . . . have been influenced by the liberalized elements in Yugoslavia, Poland, Hungary and the Soviet Union . . . Their motive is to overthrow the leadership of the Communist Party and to forfeit the future of the country and the nation."[20] While the events in Eastern Europe had helped to inspire China's demonstrators, they frightened China's elders.

As his fellow elders had urged in earlier demonstrations, Deng threatened to dispatch troops to put down the protest. Nevertheless, in late April the leadership still hesitated to use force, not because of its tolerance of what was happening, but because of disagreement between the elders and Zhao Ziyang on how to respond to the demonstration. The elders advocated forceful repression, but Zhao advocated a more moderate response to the demonstrators' demands, which initially Deng allowed him to attempt. The leadership also hesitated to use force because of upcoming events involving the outside world, particularly the meeting of the Asian Development Bank scheduled for early May, to be attended by Taiwan's finance minister, Shirley Guo, the first official from Taiwan to participate in an official meeting in Beijing, and the official visit of Mikhail Gorbachev planned for May 15–18, the first trip to China by a Soviet general secretary since the Sino-Soviet break in 1960. Both of these meetings would bring the international media to China.

Although dissatisfaction was widespread in urban areas, it is unlikely that other groups would have joined the students' demonstration unless they had sensed the hesitation of the top leadership to react. In addition, people had learned from previous campaigns in the Deng era that there were fewer personal costs for expressing grievances and demands than there had been in the Mao era. This seemingly lessened threat of retribution and lessened sense of fear fueled a massive protest of ordinary urban residents, turning the demonstration into the largest and longest in the history of the People's Republic.

The Private Sector

An important group of demonstrators came from the burgeoning private sector, spawned by Deng's economic reforms. These participants were protesting not only inflation and corruption but also the leadership's unwillingness to define property and legal rights. The members of this group ranged from the Flying Tigers motorcycle brigade, which sped through Beijing delivering messages among the various groups, to the street vendors, who provided students with free food and clothing. Another source of support came from the Shekou special economic zone, which donated more than HK$210,000.[21] In the mid-1980s, Shekou citizens of cadre rank and above had begun electing their top officials directly. This record of political reform, which accompanied Shekou's economic reforms, may explain its willingness to make contributions. The All-China Federation of Trade Unions was another source of funding for the demonstration. Zhu Houze, secretary of the federation, had continued to participate in the forums of the democratic elite after he had taken his new job. He was one of the few reform officials to become directly involved in the demonstration. On May 19, just a day before the imposition of martial law, his federation donated 100,000 yuan to the demonstrators. The demonstration also received financial support from overseas Chinese, especially in Hong Kong, and from Chinese students studying abroad.

Wan Runnan, the head of the Stone Group, was the largest financial contributor, donating about 200,000 yuan.[22] He also provided an advanced communications network of photocopiers, computers, fax machines, cellular phones, public address systems, and printing equipment. More significant, he and other Stone employees—including the head of Stone's think tank, Cao Siyuan, and Zhou Duo, a sociologist and former student of Yu Guangyuan and Su Shaozhi—actively participated in the Tiananmen demonstration. Through Cao, Zhou, and his in-laws Feng Lanrui and Li Chang, Wan had contact with the democratic elite. He was a prime example of a member of the Red Guard generation who had successfully made the transition from revolutionary to entrepreneur. He had been born in 1946 in Jiangsu and graduated from Qinghua University in 1970. After participating in the Cultural Revolution, he worked as a software engineer in the Computer Research Institute of CAS. He also studied computer science in the United States and Japan. In 1984 Wan left his institute and with six other scientists established Stone, which is the English transliteration of *sitong,* meaning "moving in four directions." With a loan of 20,000 yuan, about $5,440, from Evergreen Township, Wan and the others set up shop in half of a vegetable store in Haidian District on Zhongguancun Street, China's Silicon Valley. They developed a printer that was compatible with the IBM-PC and sold its new technology to Mitsui. Its prized product was a Chinese-English electronic typewriter, which it had both designed and developed. Stone became one of few Chinese corporations to export its technology to advanced countries.

In contrast with China's state industries, the Stone corporate culture and spirit respected the individual and encouraged the full use of its employees' skills. Its brochure emphasizes: "Our personnel are placed where their talents can be put to maximum use." Many of Stone's employees literally bought their way out of their previous work units with payments of several thousand dollars because, as they explained, Stone gave them an opportunity to put their ideas into practice.[23] Of the programmers working at Stone's Beijing plant in 1988, a noticeable proportion were women. Although Stone gave most of its employees only one-year contracts, offered no housing, and provided fewer benefits than state firms, its salaries were higher

and the company contributed 20 percent of its profits toward bo-
nuses.

By the time of the 1989 demonstration, Stone employed about 900
people and had 27 subsidiaries and offices in Japan, the United States,
and Europe. The company accounted for 80 percent of China's production of word processors and had 600 stores, 40 wholesale centers,
and 100 maintenance shops. Although part of its success can be attributed to its technological and entrepreneurial skills, part of it was
also due to the preferential treatment it received from reform officials,
especially Zhao Ziyang, who protected Stone against charges of steal-
ing ideas brought against it by former colleagues in CAS. The establishment of a new experimental zone in Beijing in which firms involved in foreign trade received a three-year tax exemption and
another three-year tax reduction also proved very helpful to Stone.

Whereas in the Cultural Revolution Wan had rebelled against the
party in the name of Mao's utopia, in the Deng period he challenged
the party in the name of democracy. Like the other entrepreneurial
participants, he too wanted property and legal rights, but he believed
that economic reforms could only be secured if they were accompanied by political reforms. His participation in the demonstration may
have been primarily to support Zhao Ziyang against the elders, but it
was also, he explained later, because entrepreneurs felt very insecure.
Even when they made "a lot of money," they were eager for political
reform that would ensure stability, which he believed would be provided by a democratic system.[24] These views had underlain his establishment of the Stone think tank, which had lobbied not only for a
bankruptcy law but also for making the constitution a more democratic document. Wan also believed that the formation of a strong
middle class was needed to provide a social base for the development
of democracy.[25] Until the 1989 demonstration, China's private sector
was generally thought to be only interested in making money. But the
participation of important entrepreneurs in the movement revealed
that some of China's new business class also wanted political change
and had the financial and personnel resources to support it.

The Role of Workers and Others

Another new element in the 1989 demonstrations was the participation of workers. Although there had been workers among the Democracy Wall activists, most of them probably would have been intellectu-

als or officials had they not been deprived of an education by the Cultural Revolution. As in 1986, the 1989 student demonstrators initially sought to prevent workers from participating, both for strategic reasons and for reasons of status. The students were aware of the elders' fear of a Solidarity-like movement in China, revealed as recently as Deng's April 25 speech, in which Deng tried to assure his colleagues that because China did not have to worry about the church and the workers, they need not fear a Solidarity in China. He explained that they only had to contend with students. But by mid-May, despite his assurance, workers and other urban groups had literally pushed themselves into the demonstration.[26]

The Beijing Workers Autonomous Federation, reaching 20,000 members, was established during the demonstration, with its headquarters located at the far northwest corner of Tiananmen Square. The group was headed by Han Dongfang, a twenty-seven-year-old railway worker who had a high school education. Apart from a small, short-lived workers' group set up in Taiyuan, Shanxi, which had carried out a strike in the winter of 1980, Han's federation was the first independent labor organization in the People's Republic. After word of the 1989 demonstrations spread, autonomous workers' federations were quickly organized in other major cities that May. Because of Li Peng's imposition of tight controls over the money supply in late 1988 and early 1989 and the subsequent closing of a number of private and collective enterprises, many members of the autonomous workers' federations were unemployed workers or small shopkeepers from rural as well as urban areas.

On May 31, three workers who had been members of a preparatory committee to establish the Beijing Workers Autonomous Federation were arrested. Even though their headquarters was far away from the student headquarters, which was close to the Monument of the People's Heroes at the center of Tiananmen Square, the incident became known. About 2,000 students gathered at Beijing Normal University and joined with others to march to the Public Security Bureau to demand and win the workers' release. The alliance between intellectuals—even if so far primarily students—and workers that the elders had feared appeared to be forming.

As the demonstration continued, its participants came to include almost all segments of the urban population in Beijing and in China's other major cities. The content of the protests was extremely diverse.

The workers, entrepreneurs, and ordinary citizens were more concerned with economic issues; students and intellectuals, with political issues. One protest expressed by virtually all the participants was the outcry against corruption, directed especially at party officials and their children who had used the economic reforms to serve their own interests. The same outcry had also been heard in the 1985 demonstration against Japanese goods and militarism, and in the 1986 demonstration for democratization. Another important issue for all groups was the country's accelerating inflation. Such concerns revealed the general desire of urban residents to gain more control over their lives. As the democratic elite had warned prior to the demonstration, the party's unwillingness to establish institutionalized channels through which the population could express its views and be responded to had forced it to go outside the political system in order to be heard. The urban residents as well as the students turned to demonstrations, sit-ins, parades, and chants to express what they were unable to express within the Leninist political structure.[27]

The Role of the Democratic Elite

Although members of Hu Yaobang's network had observed and been somewhat influenced by the demands of the Democracy Wall activists and several had openly supported the activists, few had joined that movement or any other demonstration during the Deng era. In general, members of the democratic elite had feared that demonstrations would provoke a backlash from the elders and undermine Deng's reforms. By 1989, however, they no longer believed that Deng would carry out the political reforms they now felt were necessary to sustain the economic reforms and to make possible a more humane, modern society. For the first time, therefore, some of them joined the student and urban protests, though their role was peripheral. They were able to influence their fellow intellectuals during the demonstration, and their ideas may have influenced some of the student leaders beforehand, but they were unable to influence the course of the 1989 demonstration itself.

Direct contacts between students and the democratic elite had been minimal before the demonstration and did not become much closer once it began. Although the party later charged that Fang Lizhi and his wife Li Shuxian had manipulated Wang Dan, the student co-leader with Wu'er Kaixi, Fang and Li publicly kept their distance from the demonstration precisely to prevent such an accusation. When members of the democratic elite joined the demonstration in mid-May, moreover, it was relatively late, at a time when even the original student leaders had lost control of the movement. The major contribution of the democratic elite proved to be issuing and signing petitions in support of the demonstrators and at times participating in protest marches. In this the most active participants were Yan Jiaqi, Yu Haocheng, Li Honglin, Xu Liangying, Su Shaozhi, Liu Zaifu, and those associated with them, such as Bao Zunxin, Dai Qing, Wen Yuankai, Su Xiaokang, and other creators of "River Elegy."

The petitions that they issued and signed, though worded simplistically, expressed many of the ideas about which they had been writing. A petition on the eve of May 4, for example, declared that the students' demands for democracy, reform, and opposition to autocracy and corruption were a continuation of the May Fourth spirit, and that the students' peaceful demonstration was a right protected by China's constitution. In response to the elders' arguments that China was not ready for democracy, the petition asserted: "We cannot accept the absurd views that democracy must be delayed because the quality of the Chinese nation is too low. Facts have proved that it is precisely those officials, who are afraid of democracy, who lack the quality of democracy." It continued by reiterating the view, so often expressed by Yu Haocheng, that democracy, freedom, human rights, and rule of law "are the precious fruit of human civilization, and are prerequisites for building socialism. We oppose the act of refusing to accept them under the pretext of 'Chinese national conditions.'" The petition concluded with the demand that reform of the political structure begin immediately by holding free elections for the people's congresses at all levels.[28]

On May 16, when rumors of an imminent crackdown were widespread, members of the democratic elite plus famous literary figures such as Ba Jin and Ai Qing and over a thousand other intellectuals issued an open statement in which they urged party leaders not to use "high-handed policy and force" against the students.[29] They advised the regime to learn from the negative consequences of past repressions, from the attack on Hu Feng in 1955 to the dismissal of Qin Benli in 1989. They argued that stability could best be achieved by democratic means, rather than by using force, and insisted that the demonstration was not directed against the party and socialism but was a result of China's movement toward democracy. The next day a group of only eleven intellectuals, led by Yan Jiaqi and Bao Zunxin, issued a more radical statement, reflecting perhaps the increasing radicalism of the students' demands as well as their increasing fear of a crackdown, in which they called for the "stepping down" of Deng Xiaoping and Li Peng. Although the Qing dynasty had been overthrown for over seventy-six years, they charged that there was still a "titleless emperor" on the throne, "an old, muddleheaded dictator." [30]

The majority of researchers at CASS became involved in the demonstration in one way or another. Some signed petitions in support of students, others marched to the square. Among them were hitherto apolitical intellectuals, such as the philosopher Li Zehou, the historian Liu Danian, and the writer Qian Zhongshu. At one point even Hu Qiaomu's old friend Hu Sheng, the president of CASS, signed a "Letter of Appeal" of noted Beijing intellectuals that urged the government to hold a dialogue with the students and to refrain from violent measures. Other signatories were leaders of the small parties—Fei Xiaotong, Zhou Gucheng, Lei Jieqiong, and Qian Weichang.

The issuance and signing of petitions to the leadership was very much in the literati tradition, but intellectuals' participation in demonstrations with other classes had not been common either in the dynastic period or in the People's Republic. Beginning in mid-May, writers, professors, artists, scientists, and members of the democratic elite marched alongside students, workers, entrepreneurs, and ordinary citizens. On May 17, Yan Jiaqi, Yu Haocheng, Su Shaozhi, and Bao Zunxin demonstrated in Tiananmen Square in support of the students. During the students' hunger strike from May 13 to 19, famous intellectuals such as Bing Xin and Ai Qing and writers who had been criticized during the Deng period such as the poet Ye Wenfu went to the square to express their support. There Ye also announced his withdrawal from the party, to the applause of all those who heard him. On May 20, the day that martial law was officially implemented, the playwright Wang Peigong, the author of "Us," announced his withdrawal from the party as well, in a letter to the Work Committee of the Ministry of Culture. He explained that for twenty years he had been an obedient party member, but the party leaders' actions since April had fully exposed their "stupidity." They "ignore the cry of the masses . . . even going to the length of openly resorting to armed forces with the people taken as the enemy."[31] In the Soviet Union by the spring of 1989 a public announcement of withdrawal from the party was greeted as an everyday occurrence, but in China for a party member to withdraw, let alone make a public announcement, was rare. The leadership treated it as a traitorous act. Only party leaders could dismiss members from the party; one could not resign of one's own accord. On the day that Wang Peigong resigned from his party unit in the army, eighteen young writers in the army from Shandong also withdrew.[32]

At the end of April, under Wang Dan and Wu'er Kaixi's leadership, students had established the first autonomous student union, and other autonomous unions followed their lead. Ninety prominent intellectuals established the Beijing Intellectuals Autonomous Federation on May 23, with members of the democratic elite, including Yan Jiaqi, Bao Zunxin, Yu Haocheng, Li Honglin, Su Shaozhi, Liu Zaifu, and Su Xiaokang, forming its core leadership. Like the students' autonomous union, they demanded that the party recognize their independent status.

Zhao Ziyang's Think Tanks

Another highly placed group of intellectuals participating in the demonstration were from Zhao Ziyang's think tanks. They joined the movement more to bolster Zhao's position in his power struggle and to continue the economic reforms than to fight for democratization. Those most actively involved came from the Research Center for the Reform of the Political Structure, led by Zhao's secretary Bao Tong; the Institute for Economic Structural Reform, headed by Chen Yizi; the Rural Development Research Institute, led by Du Runsheng; the China International Trade and Investment Corporation (CITIC); the Beijing Young Economists Association; the Institute of Economics at CASS; plus the proponents of neo-authoritarianism in the Policy Research Office of the Central Committee.

Throughout the past decade the democratic elite and Zhao Ziyang's think tanks had reinforced each other in pushing for economic reforms. They often participated in the same seminars, and there was also some overlap in personnel. Bao Tong had been at the theory conference and Yan Jiaqi had for a time been a member of Bao Tong's group drafting the political reform program that Zhao presented at the Thirteenth Party Congress. Bao Tong had had Zhao intervene to protect Yan when he was attacked in the 1987 anti–bourgeois liberalization campaign. When Hu Yaobang was purged in January 1987, Zhao assumed political patronage for the democratic elite, even though their political views differed from his.

The democratic elite's emphasis on political reform and Zhao's think tanks' emphasis on economic reform kept the two groups from uniting to pursue their goals together before the 1989 demonstration. Still, Bao Tong and his associates were not wholly disinterested in political reform. Bao Tong, in an article in *Seek Truth from Facts* in March of 1989 had repeated Deng's argument of August 18, 1980, that systems were more fundamental than leaders in determining the viability of a political structure.[33] The inaugural issue of the journal *Reform of the Political Structure,* a mouthpiece of Bao Tong's political reform group, which appeared in early 1989, contained an article by its chief editor Du Guang, a former rightist, entitled "Rendering the Party Multidimensional." It described the reform of political structures under way in Eastern Europe and the Soviet Union, particularly the formation of new political entities of workers and intellectuals. Arguing that the Soviet bloc was catching up with China's reforms, Du pressed China to compete by introducing a multiparty system. He also urged eliminating party cells from government and industrial units, a change that had been called for in the Thirteenth Party Congress report, but not implemented effectively. Another article in the inaugural issue, written by a military officer in the Jilin District, favored ending political departments and political commissars in the army in order to emphasize professionalism. Bao Tong, however, banned the distribution of this issue at the last minute, though a few hundred copies had already been circulated.[34]

Just before the demonstration began, some members of Zhao's think tanks participated in a seminar entitled "Theory and Practice of the Ten Years of Reform," held on April 2 in Beijing. The participants called for political reforms to accompany economic reforms, but like Zhao at the Thirteenth Party Congress, they interpreted political reform to mean providing access to different expert opinions and placing some constraints on political power. Their intent was primarily to counter the power of Li Peng and the elders rather than to implement a separation of powers or freedom of the press.

Although Zhao's encouragement of objective press coverage of the demonstration also had more to do with his internal struggles than with a genuine desire for democracy, his conduct during the demonstration and afterward revealed that he was more open to the students' demands than were Deng and his elder colleagues. Zhao's more conciliatory response to pressure from below was evident not only in his positive evaluation of Hu Yaobang in his funeral eulogy but also in speeches he gave in early May after his return from North Korea. On May 3, in a speech for the seventieth anniversary of May Fourth, Li Peng had directed Zhao to add the slogan "oppose bourgeois liberalization," but Zhao refused to include it. More significant, his speech the following day before the Asian Development Bank, drafted by Bao Tong, defiantly called the student demonstration "patriotic," just as the students themselves were calling it, and urged that China's problems be resolved through democratic and legal means. His emphasis was in marked contrast to Deng's threat of violence in his April 25 speech and to the depiction of the demonstration as a conspiracy in the *People's Daily* April 26 editorial. Zhao delivered his speech without arranging for the usual vetting by Deng and the Politburo, thereby infuriating not only the elders but also his mentor Deng. The elders consequently declared, as the Maoists had during the Cultural Revolution, that the party was speaking with "two voices."

In his May 16 talk with Gorbachev, Zhao revealed that a 1987 Central Committee decision had given Deng the authority to make all crucial decisions. In giving the Soviet leader this information, Zhao shifted the responsibility for the handling of the student movement onto Deng, and in doing so he lost Deng's support in his power struggle with the elders. At an enlarged meeting of the Politburo on May 19, when it was decided to use military force against the demonstrators, Zhao Ziyang objected. He then resigned as general secretary.

Members of Zhao's think tanks leaked news of what was happening behind closed doors to the demonstration's leaders in an effort to defuse the demonstration and perhaps to save the economic reforms as well as Zhao. From May 13, when the hunger strike began and Gorbachev's arrival was imminent, Yan Mingfu and several other reform officials tirelessly sought to gain the help of the student leaders, the democratic elite, and especially Wang Juntao to try to persuade the demonstrators to leave the square. By this time, however, it was already too late. The leaders, Wang Dan and Wu'er Kaixi, might have been persuaded to leave. But the hunger strike had brought more and more people, many from outside Beijing, into the square, and the demonstration, expanding to over a million people, was out of the control of its initial leaders and advisors.[35]

During the demonstration there was more tacit agreement between Zhao's think tanks and the democratic elite than there had been earlier. Both groups agreed on the need to open a dialogue between the party leaders and the demonstrators, and both groups wanted the demonstrators to leave the square in order to prevent bloodshed and a rollback of the economic reforms. Although the members of the democratic elite were disillusioned with Zhao, they preferred to keep him and his associates in power than find them replaced by the elders and the military. Nevertheless these two groups, because of their divergent goals, did not unite in a concerted effort to guide the demonstrators in constructive negotiations with the political leadership. Even if they had been able to join in such an undertaking, whether they would have had enough authority with the demonstrators or with the elders to achieve the beginnings of political dialogue is questionable.

There was, however, one organized effort during the demonstration in which the two groups together tried to use constitutional procedures to stop the impending military crackdown. Hu Jiwei and Cao Siyuan led an attempt to convene an emergency session of the standing committee of the NPC to review Li Peng's announcement on May 19 of the imposition of martial law. Cao had informed Hu Jiwei as a member of the NPC's Standing Committee about the articles in the constitution—Article 29, which stipulated that martial law could only be imposed when the state faced a foreign invasion or serious armed riot; Article 61, which called for the convening of the NPC at any time the standing committee deemed necessary; and Article 57, which stipulated that the NPC was the highest organ of state power with the right to remove the premier—that would warrant calling an emergency session. Hu then entrusted Cao and his Stone think tank with the task of collecting the necessary signatures from other standing committee members. Hu sought to resolve China's current crises "through legal procedures."[36]

Hu Jiwei's leadership of such an effort was consistent with his views in the late 1980s. In a May article in the *World Economic Herald*, just before it was suspended, he pointed out that with a forum for arguing things out and a chance for appeal, "tragedies that should not have taken place are prevented."[37] Within three days, May 21–24, forty-six members of the standing committee signed or gave their approval over the phone. Their number exceeded the one-third of standing committee members needed to call an emergency meeting.[38] Among those giving approval, in addition to Hu himself, were Zhou Gucheng, Qin Chuan, Li Yining, the economist Dong Fureng, Liu Danian, Ma Hong, and Wang Meng. With the signatures of the standing committee in hand, Hu wrote on May 24 to the deputy head of the NPC Standing Committee, Peng Chong, asking him to convene a meeting immediately. Peng Chong responded, however, that the standing committee could not be convened without permission of the Politburo, an open acknowledgment of the party's control over the NPC. Cao also sent an announcement of the proposal for a NPC emergency meeting to the Beijing media, but only the *Wenhui News* in Hong Kong published it.

Members of Zhao's think tanks also joined in the call for an emergency meeting of the NPC Standing Committee, in the belief that it would help Zhao in his political struggle. On May 21, even before Hu Jiwei formally requested a meeting of the NPC Standing Committee, Zhao had cabled its chairman, Wan Li, to return home from a visit to the United States and Canada ahead of schedule. Wan Li's reformist image and praise of the student movement while abroad had raised hopes that he might be able to resolve the crisis peacefully. But just as Wan Li was about to return he received another cable, this time from Li Peng and the Politburo Standing Committee, urging him to continue his visit. Wan Li returned, but was waylaid by Jiang Zemin in Shanghai. On May 27 Wan publicly announced his support for the imposition of martial law.

Although virtually from the beginning of the Deng era the democratic elite had tried to make the NPC the country's supreme authority, their efforts had had little success. Hu Jiwei's attempt had been the best organized, but Deng and the elders continued their unconstitutional practices of overriding or ignoring NPC demands with which they disagreed. Thus the brief united front of the democratic elite and Zhao's think tanks to use constitutional means against unconstitutional acts was of no avail against the party elders, who were supported by the military.

On June 3–4, 1989, consequently, the military advanced on Tiananmen Square, smashing through roadblocks put up by the demonstrators and Beijing citizens and shooting randomly at those in their path. It is estimated that they killed over a thousand people on the way to the square.[39] There, the military's first target appeared to be the headquarters of the Beijing Workers Autonomous Federation. Worker demonstrators were killed or jailed indiscriminately. The remaining four hundred or so students, however, through an arrangement worked out between the military and four prominent intellectuals still in the square—Zhou Duo of Stone; Liu Xiaobo, the literary critic; Gao Xin, a journalist from Beijing Normal University; and Hou Dejian, a pop singer from Taiwan—were allowed to evacuate peacefully.

The Ineffectiveness of the Democratic Elite

Neither the democratic elite nor the student leaders knew how to bring about concrete results from the great popular enthusiasm and dramatic symbolism of the demonstration. Some of them engaged in quixotic actions, such as the open letter of Yan Jiaqi, Bao Zunxin, and a few others asking Li Peng to resign: "If a head of the government, who has been discarded by the people, refuses to resign of his own accord, people can dismiss him through the stipulations contained in the Constitution." They argued that since "no armed riot" had occurred, the imposition of martial law "violate[d] the Constitution."[40] Their failure to organize a movement to bring pressure on the leadership was primarily due to their lack of experience in working with other social groups, even with the students, whose goals were closer to theirs than any of the other groups. Although the writings of certain members of the democratic elite were well known to some of the student leaders and they might have had more credibility with the students than did members of Zhao's think tanks, they could only offer advice. They did not have the necessary contacts or organizational skills to make their advice a reality. Beginning in mid-May, they counseled the students to discontinue the hunger strike, leave the square, return to their campuses, and carry out efforts there to establish their own student organizations and newspapers. Again some of the student leaders, such as Wang Dan and Wu'er Kaixi, agreed. But others, along with the rank and file, did not. To them such advice amounted to capitulation.

Although the democratic elite's efforts may have been inadequate, the students also intentionally avoided cooperating with them and with other intellectuals, for strategic reasons. They knew from Deng's April 25 speech that an alliance with the intellectuals and/or with the workers would antagonize the elders more than a demonstration made up purely of students. In addition, as the elders and Li Peng rejected their demands, the students became increasingly radicalized and idealistic. Beginning with the hunger strike, they saw themselves more and more in the tradition of their literati and May Fourth predecessors, willing to risk death for their cause. Their slogans in mid-May calling for Deng and Li Peng to "step down," though echoed by Yan Jiaqi and Bao Zunxin, further widened the gap between them and most of the other democratic elite. The students were also influenced by Western rock music and by a desire for individual and sexual liberation like that of their Western and overseas Chinese counterparts, which the democratic elite had trouble understanding. Both the students and the democratic elite wanted a more democratic polity, but neither group knew how to shift from demonstration and rhetoric to organization and negotiation to achieve its goals.

Even if a closer alliance had been established between the democratic elite and the students, however, it still might have been impossible to achieve the more limited goals of founding relatively independent student organizations and student newspapers. The elders, who ultimately won the power struggle, regarded even these moderate demands as an infringement and a threat to their authority. To give in on such matters, they feared, would lead to the unraveling of the whole system of control upon which they based their leadership. Moreover, by mid-May the demonstration had assumed a dynamic of its own that no single individual or group could control or mobilize for its own goals. Most important, neither the student leaders, the democratic elite, nor the entrepreneurial participants were numerous enough, strong enough, or experienced enough to establish an alternative political organization or party. Despite all the changes that had occurred in a decade of economic reform, in 1989 China had no organizations comparable to the Solidarity movement in Poland or the Charter 77 in Czechoslovakia. Nor did China have a tradition of civil society, as Czechoslovakia and Hungary did, to sustain such a movement.

The weakness of the organizations of the students and the democratic elite and their lack of connections with other social groups, particularly the working class, weakened their ability to mobilize popular pressure for specific purposes. Their weakness was in large part due to the repressive nature of the regime, but it also stemmed from their own earlier choice not to contemplate, let alone establish, any alternative political group outside the party until the late 1980s. Finally, no matter how concrete their proposals, how closely they worked with other groups, or how well organized they might have been, it is unlikely that they could have achieved even their moderate demands as long as the elders and especially Deng were able to mobilize the military might of the state against them.

The Return of the Elders and Their Spokesmen

The elders saw the establishment in mid-May of autonomous federations of students, workers, intellectuals, and ordinary citizens not as new institutions but as replicas of the Red Guard organizations that had so brutally attacked them in the Cultural Revolution. Their fear that the demonstration might spark a repetition of those terrible years was evident in Deng Xiaoping's April 25 speech and in Chen Yun's note to Deng in early May, advising that unless strong action were taken to suppress the student movement, it would "only grow bigger, and if workers join in, the consequences will be unimaginable."[41]

The elders—Chen Yun, Yang Shangkun, Bo Yibo, Peng Zhen, Li Xiannian, Wang Zhen, Deng Xiaoping, and at times Deng Yingchao, Zhou Enlai's wife—reacted as they had in the past when they believed themselves threatened. As they had during the 1986 student demonstrations when they purged Hu Yaobang, they cast aside regular party procedures, took ad hoc action, and refused to negotiate. Although there were subtle differences among them, their overall approach was summarized in Chen Yun's speech on Beijing television on May 26, in which he declared: "We the veteran comrades must step forward boldly . . . We must never make concessions."[42] That Deng Xiaoping and the elders resorted to the military to put down the demonstration and resolve their inner-party struggle was consistent with their past actions. Not only had they used force to gain power initially, but as recently as December 1986, Yang Shangkun and Wang Zhen had threatened to use military force unless Hu Yaobang suppressed the student demonstrators. Deng Xiaoping had expressed admiration for President Jaruzelski's forceful suppression of the Solidarity movement in Poland in 1981. Military troops had been used in March 1989 to quell nationalist and religious demonstrations in Tibet. When faced with widespread demonstrations that they regarded as a repudiation of Marxism-Leninism, the party, socialism, and themselves and when confronted by a disobedient general secretary, the self-appointed guardians of the Leninist party-state fought back by the military means they had invariably used in the past.

Deng Xiaoping's feeling of desperation during the demonstration was revealed by his decision to turn for help to the very elders who had opposed some of his reforms. His alliance with them against the demonstrators returned the elders to the center of power after the June 4 crackdown and led to the revival of the Leninist controls that Hu and Zhao had gradually loosened. Deng and his elderly colleagues recommended their usual bromide for any disruption—ideological education. This kind of indoctrination had nothing in common with the education in modern science and technology that Deng had been pushing since 1974. Rather, as Deng explained in a speech to army units on June 9, "What I mainly mean by education here is ideological and political education, and not merely education in school."[43] This speech plus Deng's selected works, along with the selected works of Chen Yun and Peng Zhen, issued after June 4, became the focus of study for the whole population in a reversion to forced ideological remolding and political study sessions of the Mao era. Deng blamed the 1989 demonstration not only on Hu Yaobang's and Zhao Ziyang's tolerance of bourgeois liberalization but also on the influence of events in Eastern Europe and the Soviet Union, where the leaders had not repressed Western ideas, thereby causing "turmoil" in their societies. The elders' old friend, the Romanian dictator Nicolae Ceausescu, was one of the few world leaders to congratulate China's leadership on the June 4 crackdown. But when he met his end in December after his army turned against him, the People's Liberation Army, including senior officers, also became a major focus of the remolding.

Accordingly, the elders' specialists in indoctrination, particularly Deng Liqun, Hu Qiaomu, and Wang Renzhi, director of the Propaganda Department, also regained center stage. They were joined by their old associates, the literary watchdogs from Yan'an. At the same time that they worked at reindoctrinating students, intellectuals, the military, and the urban population, they also sought retribution against those who had pushed them aside. The desire for revenge was palpable even in Hu Qiaomu's July 1 speech at the celebration of the sixty-ninth anniversary of the party's founding. Hu complained that under Hu Yaobang and Zhao Ziyang, he had been deprived of his right to speak by those who regarded themselves as "advocates of freedom and democracy."[44] Although he called for freedom of speech in criticizing the "corrupt" ways of the party, he made clear that there would be no freedom of speech for those who had prevented him from speaking earlier.

The elders' spokesmen, who after June virtually took over the party's national media, were assisted by several former Cultural Revolution activists who had once been their persecutors. Xu Weicheng, who had been a member of a Gang of Four writing group, was elevated from directing propaganda in Beijing to be a deputy director of the Propaganda Department for the country as a whole. Some younger theorists, such as He Xin, aged forty, who before the demonstration had expressed some reformist views, afterward attacked their former colleagues with a vengeance.[45] For them, the switch in policy was an opportunity for upward mobility. The philosopher Xing Bensi similarly criticized his colleagues. Xing was promoted from his post as the director of the Institute of Philosophy at CASS to the position of vice president at the Central Party School, and He Xin became affiliated with CASS. They are examples of intellectuals who bend with every shift in the political wind. But they were the exceptions in 1989, and they were shunned by their fellows. Unlike during the Mao period, the majority of intellectuals neither joined the ranks of the elders' spokesmen nor betrayed their colleagues with criticisms and accusations.

Deng Liqun eclipsed Hu Qiaomu as the major spokesman for the elders in the aftermath of June 4. Languishing in the Central Advisory Commission since the Thirteenth Party Congress, he suddenly became active in all areas of ideology and the media. In addition to people who had worked for the Gang of Four and others active in the campaigns of the Deng era, he gathered around him a coterie of those who had written essays during the Soviet-Chinese ideological disputes before the Cultural Revolution. They revived the ideological methods of the Mao period.

The Ideological Crackdown

Ideological indoctrination, which had been erratic and at times had virtually stopped during the decade of reform, became mandatory and intensive after June 4 for everyone from the party hierarchy, including the army, all the way down to the kindergartens. Party groups that had been eliminated in some government offices, organizations, and enterprises under Zhao Ziyang were reintroduced in order to carry out renewed indoctrination as well as other party functions. The purpose of these efforts was to prevent the "democratic socialism" emerging in Eastern Europe and the "bourgeois liberalism" of the West from taking root in China.

A major theme of the indoctrination was to reidentify patriotism with loyalty to the party, as had been done in the campaign against Bai Hua in 1981. The efforts of Bai Hua and others to define patriotism as identification with one's country rather than with the party-state had been reflected in a banner held high in the 1989 demonstration: "We love our country but we hate our government." A commentator article in the *Guangming Daily* after June 4, however, countered that patriotism was "closely linked to and inseparable from ardent love for the CPC and the socialist system." [46] The former mayor of Tianjin, Li Ruihuan, expressed the party's view at a national symposium: because "the party is the most prominent representative of the people's interests, . . . the party's ears, eyes, and mouth are naturally the people's ears, eyes and mouth." [47] Li had been known as a reformer, but he became a new member of the Standing Committee of the Politburo after June 4, taking Hu Qili's place in charge of propaganda.

The elders' definition of patriotism after June 4 also included respect for China's traditional culture. They themselves had no great reverence for traditional culture; they knew little about it and in their revolutionary days and during the Maoist era they had totally rejected it. But their praise of traditional culture was now used to condemn the openness of the democratic elite, including the "River Elegy" group and the philosopher Li Zehou who had given moral support to the demonstrators. The elders charged them with regarding everything associated with Chinese culture as bad and everything associated with foreign culture as good. At the same time, by praising the authoritarian aspects of Confucian culture—discipline, obedience, and collectivism—the elders used tradition to tighten controls. Western democratic systems, whether of the American, British or Japanese variety, were deemed incompatible with Chinese culture.

The elders again asserted that democracy was beyond the understanding of the Chinese people. An *Economic Daily* article stressed:

"China should also take into account . . . its people's limited capacity to withstand political and psychological strains."[48] The patronizing, patriarchal view drew as much on the elitist nature of the Leninist state as on that of the traditional state. An *Outlook* article further explained: "When many people are still preoccupied by the daily toil for basic survival, it is impossible to expect from them a high degree of democratic participation." Because of their low education level, "if a so-called democracy is forcibly implemented, interference from various factors will give rise to individualism, factionalism and anarchy, and lead to de-facto nondemocracy and even chaos." The population, moreover, lacked "democratic practice, experience and habit," a failing the party blamed not on themselves but on the people.[49]

The elders specifically sought to counter the argument of the democratic elite as well as that of the neo-authoritarians that an emerging middle class could become the social base for a democratic system. One of the elders' spokesmen pointed out that China still did not have a genuine middle class. A study by the former director of the Institute of Sociology at CASS, He Jianzhang, was cited as proof. It indicated that 70 percent of the owners of private businesses were based in rural areas and had originally been farmers or cadres of the former people's communes. In the urban areas about half were jobless youth, about a quarter had worked for public organizations, and another quarter were retired or dismissed employees or housewives.[50] The study concluded that owners of private businesses therefore could not be considered members of a middle class. The implication was that there had been little change in the class structure, and certainly none of the kind that gave rise to the bourgeoisie in Western democracies.

Accompanying the repudiation of the democratic elite and Western political culture was the revival of Mao's thought that had already begun in the fall of 1988. Mao's *Selected Works* reappeared on bookshelves alongside the selected works of the elders. Accordingly, the Maoist stress on class struggle and people's dictatorship was reemphasized in the media and in new organizations and journals, such as *Current Tide* (Dangdai sichao) and *Pursuit of Truth* (Zhenli de zhuiqiu), which suddenly came on the scene to articulate the views of the elders and their spokesmen.

Mao's view that literature must be subordinated to politics was also stressed, as it had been in the campaign against bourgeois liberalization. His Yan'an Talks once again became dogma, and writers were urged to become closer to the masses and more cognizant of their social responsibilities. The subjective spirit and literary innovations advocated by Liu Zaifu and Wang Meng were denounced. *Seek Truth from Facts* accused Liu Zaifu of wanting to create a language revolution in which "the autocratic style of 'speaking like a mouthpiece'" was transformed into the "'independent' style of 'speaking for oneself.'"[51] Wang Meng was specifically castigated for writing about loneliness, confusion, absurdity, and illusions, all deemed corrosive to the people's spirit.

The Targets of the June 4 Crackdown

After the military crackdown, troops were stationed at Beijing's eight major universities, CASS, and the national media, important centers of support for the student demonstrators. Those who headed the universities from which many of the demonstrators had come, such as the president of Peking University, the prominent mathematician Ding Shisun, and the president of the University of Politics and Law, Jiang Ping, a former rightist who had defended the students during the demonstration, were removed from their posts along with scores of younger professors. Most of the members of those institutions, from the presidents to the janitors, were forced to write detailed statements about their activities during the demonstration. A large number of students and professors lied about their own activities and those of their friends, a clear indication of the decreasing fear and alienation that Wang Ruoshui had observed years earlier. The sense of alienation had only intensified after the crackdown. A survey taken after June 4 by the CPPCC revealed that only 20 percent of Peking University students agreed with the leadership ideologically. Some 40 percent said that they disagreed, and the remaining 40 percent simply chose to remain silent.[52]

At CASS, where it was estimated that two thousand of its members had participated in the demonstration or had signed petitions supporting it, disciplinary measures were taken against 120 academics; the punishments ranged from imprisonment to dismissal to warnings. The CASS president, Hu Sheng, who had tacitly approved of the participation of his members and had even tried to protect some of them, was spared punishment because of his venerable party background and his close association with Hu Qiaomu, but real power at CASS was passed to new officials appointed after the crackdown.

Virtually all the major media, including the more orthodox *Liberation Army Daily* and the *Beijing Daily,* were purged and filled with Yan'an ideologues and their associates or members of the army's General Political Department, directed by Yang Shangkun's younger half-brother Yang Baibing. Even in Guangzhou, where relatively few demonstrations had occurred, special work teams were sent to the major newspapers. The editor-in-chief of the *Guangzhou Daily* was replaced, and its subsidiary, the *Guangzhou Youth News,* was closed down altogether. Party work groups were sent in to rectify the *Guangming Daily, China Youth, Workers Daily,* the Ministry of Culture, the All-China Federation of Trade Unions, the Youth League, the Women's Federation, and the central radio, film, and television studios.

At the *People's Daily,* the director and the editor-in-chief, Qian Liren and Tan Wenrui, were replaced by Gao Di, a vice president of the Central Party School, and Shao Huaze, from the army's General Political Department. Almost all the members of the editorial board of the *People's Daily* were purged, and many were replaced by staff from the *Liberation Army Daily,* provincial newspapers, and Deng Liqun's followers. The party's premier mouthpiece thus came under the elders' control. Yang Baibing, who after the crackdown became secretary general of the Military Affairs Commission, extended his authority beyond the army, not only into the media but, through the launching of another nationwide "Learn from Lei Feng" campaign, into schools, factories, farms, and intellectual circles. The elders and their spokesmen knew only how to reimpose the bankrupt symbols of the Mao era.

Sun Changjiang was removed as deputy editor of *Science and Technology Daily.* The *New Observer, World Economic Herald,* and *Economic Weekly* were suspended. Some of their editors and journalists escaped abroad. Ge Yang, who had been abroad for a conference during the demonstration, remained in exile in the United States. Others went into hiding or were arrested. Zhang Weiguo, the head of the Beijing office of the *Herald,* spent twenty months in jail. When he was released in early 1991, he continued to demand freedom of speech. Without a job and under constant surveillance, he was threatened with another arrest for talking with foreign journalists and for refusing to hand over a manuscript he was writing on the founder of the *Herald,* Qin Benli, who had died on April 15, 1991. Eventually, because of his continuing defiance of the authorities, Zhang was rearrested for a brief time in August 1991. In 1993, he was allowed to go to the United States.

Four categories of intellectuals were singled out for attack—Hu Yaobang's intellectual network, Zhao Ziyang's advisors and members of his think tanks, advocates of neo-authoritarianism, and controversial writers. A few, such as Su Shaozhi, Liu Zaifu, Yan Jiaqi and his wife Gao Gao, and most of the makers of "River Elegy," were able to escape abroad. Li Honglin, Yu Haocheng, and Cao Siyuan were imprisoned for almost a year. Others in Hu Yaobang's network such as Yu Guangyuan, Zhang Xianyang, Wu Mingyu, and Tong Dalin were eased out of their positions and spent most of their time at home. Hu Jiwei was harshly condemned for his efforts to convene the NPC Standing Committee and was removed from his positions in the congress.

The works of Fang Lizhi, Li Shuxian, Liu Binyan, Bao Zunxin, Su Xiaokang, Bei Dao, Liu Zaifu, Wang Juntao, Chen Ziming, and others were banned. Works about Hu Yaobang and Zhao Ziyang were also forbidden. In addition, publishing houses were rectified, and township and private bookstores threatened with closure. It was reported that thousands of books were burned in Xi'an, Shanxi, reminiscent of the first Qin emperor's burning of the books in the same area. Hu Yaobang's network was finally silenced, though not totally repressed.

Zhao Ziyang's think tanks, such as the Rural Development Research Institute, the CITIC International Research Center, and the Beijing Young Economists Association, were purged, and some of their members arrested. The Institute of Economic Structural Reform was similarly purged, but several of its leaders, among them Chen Yizi, were able to escape abroad. Bao Tong, Zhao Ziyang's political secretary, was arrested shortly after the imposition of martial law, and his institute for the reform of the political structure was purged and dismantled. He was finally brought to trial in July 1992, and sentenced to nine years in prison, reduced to seven because of the time he had already served, supposedly for leaking state secrets. He was actually a scapegoat for Zhao Ziyang, who was too closely associated with Deng Xiaoping to be tried. Although Zhao refused to make a self-criticism, he was allowed a relatively relaxed form of house arrest. Yan Mingfu and Hu Qili temporarily lost their official positions; they were reappointed to much less influential positions in June 1991.

Wang Meng, who unlike the other cabinet ministers did not pay his respects to the martial law troops, resigned as minister of culture in August 1989; he was replaced by the Yan'an literary bureaucrat He Jingzhi as acting minister of culture and head of its party group.

Members of the democratic elite and the student leaders were tried in early 1991. Bao Zunxin was sentenced to five years, but was released in 1993 because of ill health. The student leader Wang Dan was sentenced to six years, but was also released in 1993; his co-leader was able to flee abroad. The major proponent of neo-authoritarianism, Wu Jiaxiang, was arrested; he was finally tried and released in August 1992. Dai Qing was jailed for almost a year. The eight small parties returned to their former compliant stance. Their efforts to introduce a truly multiparty system ceased. At the time of the imposition of martial law, Peng Zhen invited the chairmen of the eight small parties to a dinner, at which he sought their backing for the imposition of martial law and the dismissal of Zhao Ziyang. Although most of them tried to assume a neutral position, none expressed any resistance to the crackdown publicly.

Writers, particularly the authors of wounded literature and the editors of literary journals, as in the Mao years, were treated more severely than those in other creative or academic fields. Although Wang Ruowang had done no more in the spring of 1989 than lead a march, along with Bai Hua, of writers and journalists in Shanghai calling for freedom of expression, he was arrested. The arrest was his third for political dissent, once by the Guomindang and twice by the Communist Party. He was imprisoned in the same cell in which he had been locked up twenty years earlier during the Cultural Revolution. When he was released over a year later, his health had become impaired. He still had to report to the Public Security Bureau each week, and in May 1991 he and his wife were taken in for interrogation for forty-eight hours on suspicion of being supporters of an underground human rights journal. He was allowed to go abroad in 1992. Liu Binyan was still in the United States at the time of the crackdown and Liu Zaifu was able to flee abroad, but all their books were banned from sale and from libraries. Liu Xinwu, who had led a procession of the entire staff of *People's Literature* in the demonstration, was replaced and censured for his story "The Schoolmaster," the first story to criticize the Cultural Revolution. His post at *People's Literature* was taken over by the old Yan'an writer Liu Baiyu. The editors of the *Literary*

Gazette were purged and their posts also filled with followers of the Yan'an literary bureaucracy.

ACFLAC and the Writers Association were purged of their top leaders and reorganized. Lin Mohan was made the head of the federation. With Hu dead, Zhao out of power, and the elders resurrected, these old "new" literary officials could renew their crusade against nonconformist writers begun back in Yan'an. Those who had tormented Wang Shiwei in Yan'an, Hu Feng and his followers in 1955, the rightists in 1957, and literary figures throughout the Mao era once more assumed positions of authority from which they could pursue unorthodox writers and retaliate against those who had eclipsed them during the reform era. The persecutors from Yan'an—Liu Baiyu, Lin Mohan, Chen Yong, and their associates—were again in charge of investigating writers and drawing up lists for criticism.

The crackdown was also used to renew attacks against literary figures persecuted off and on during the Deng era. The poet Ye Wenfu, criticized in 1981 for his poem "General, You Cannot Do This," was briefly arrested in July 1989 for dedicating a poem to the demonstrators as well as for his public resignation from the party. The playwright Wang Peigong of "Us," who had also publicly resigned from the party, was arrested for a brief time as well. Even Ai Qing, one of the few survivors of the 1942 Yan'an rectification, was once more on a blacklist for having engaged in bourgeois liberalization and having comforted fasting students from his wheelchair. The older writers Xia Yan and Zhang Guangnian, who had expressed regret for their harassment of writers in the Maoist period, found themselves under attack in the crackdown aftermath.

The political philosopher Li Zehou, who had merely signed a few petitions and comforted students on the hunger strike, was subjected to intense criticism in the media, primarily because of his belief that China had something to learn from the Western essence *(ti)*. His ideas had great appeal to China's educated youth, which may explain why the party singled him out for public attack. Fang Lizhi and Li Shuxian sought refuge in the American embassy in Beijing for a year, before the Chinese government allowed them and their two sons to leave the country. Fang's former colleague from Keda, Wen Yuankai, who had tried repeatedly to persuade the students to leave the square, lost his job and was unable to have even his scientific papers published.

Although the student and intellectual leaders were interrogated, subjected to arrest, deprived of their jobs, and put under surveillance, they were not executed as were scores of workers who had participated in the demonstration. Nor were they ostracized and sent away for labor reform, as they had been in the Mao era. Most of those killed in the June 4 crackdown were workers or bystanders. The four intellectuals who arranged for the students who remained in the square to leave peacefully were subsequently imprisoned. Three of them were released within the year. Hou Dejian was returned to Taiwan, from which he had defected in 1981. Gao Xin was able to go to the United States. Zhou Duo tried to open up a private business venture, but the regime, fearing that he would use the proceeds for political purposes, forced him out of business and denied him a job. He too eventually went to the United States. Liu Xiaobo was imprisoned for almost two years. When he was released in February 1991, he was placed under surveillance. He too was denied a job until he went abroad in 1992 on a fellowship.

Yet despite the milder treatment of students and intellectuals in comparison with the Mao period, China's democratic elite felt weighed down by an oppression comparable to that of earlier years. Even when some of them were able to speak out again on economic matters, after Deng Xiaoping's trip to Guangzhou and Shenzhen in early 1992 to whip up support for continuing economic reforms, they spoke primarily about the need to move to the market in accordance with Deng's policy. Xu Liangying, Yu Haocheng, and Hu Jiwei continued to demand political reforms, but they were the exceptions. The more organized, independent political stance that the democratic elite had been moving toward in late 1988 and early 1989 appeared to have been successfully thwarted by the elders. With a large portion of the democratic elite abroad or removed from positions of influence at home, their decade-long effort to revise the ideology and change the political structure seemed to have come to an end.

12

A New Kind of
Intellectual Activist

If the June 4 crackdown revealed how little China's political system and leadership had changed over the decade, the demonstration itself revealed how much Chinese society had changed in the same period. Deng Xiaoping did not seem to understand that the economic reforms and the opening to the outside world he had encouraged would inevitably give rise to an increasingly independent, pluralist society that the party could not fully control. The 1989 demonstration was unprecedented in the history of the People's Republic not only because of its multiclass nature but because of the role played by a new genre of intellectual. At the same time that the democratic elite was moving toward a more organized political identity, certain members of the Red Guard generation were already much further along in assuming such a stance. Although they were acquainted with some members of the democratic elite and were also intellectuals, their different experiences in the Cultural Revolution and in the Deng era had led them to a more independent, activist political role. They more closely resembled the intellectuals who played a leading role in overthrowing the Communist systems in the Soviet Union and Eastern Europe.

Wang Juntao and Chen Ziming of the *Economic Weekly* and SERI exemplify this new intellectual. Their approach involved a fundamental transformation of the traditional relationship between intellectuals and the state. The democratic elite had used ideological revision, political discourse, and high-level contacts to press for change, much in the tradition of their literati ancestors. Only in the late 1980s did they begin to organize themselves to achieve specific political aims. Wang, Chen, and their associates, by contrast, from the Cultural Revolution on, pursued political goals through organizational activities. Whereas the democratic elite had sought to bring about political change from the top down, Wang and Chen worked from the bottom up. Though they too tended to see politics as the preserve of the intellectuals, they demanded a voice in government for those outside the establishment, for ordinary citizens who wished to participate in decisions that affected their lives. But Wang and Chen also differed from most of their former Red Guard colleagues in that they took part in establishment as well as nonestablishment activities.

Their nonestablishment stance was not necessarily the one they would have chosen for themselves; it was forced upon them by the times in which they grew up.[1] Chen, born in 1950, and Wang, born in 1958, were children of the elite. Chen Ziming came from an intellectual family of many generations; Wang Juntao was the son of a dean of an army defense college. But both participated in the Cultural Revolution, and both were imprisoned for their actions. Chen was imprisoned for the first time in 1975, though he was a Red Guard, for having criticized the Gang of Four in a letter to a friend. Just before he was to be transferred to labor reform, however, he passed through Beijing and joined the April 5, 1976, demonstration in Tiananmen Square, where he quickly assumed a leadership role. When the demonstrators were stopped by the militia, Chen seized a loudspeaker to urge the militia to take the side of the people rather than of the party.[2] He was then pushed forward by the crowd to represent them in negotiations with the authorities for the release of protestors who had been arrested.[3] Because Chen did not give his name and no one knew who he was, he became known as "crew-cut shorty," owing to his prison haircut and small stature. Wang Juntao was also prominent in the April 5 demonstration. He led his high school class into the square and recited a poem that he had written for the occasion. Because of his leading role, Wang too was sent away for labor reform.

Both men were released shortly after Mao's death in September 1976, and they subsequently participated in the Democracy Wall movement in 1978–79. With friends, they published one of the most influential journals of that movement, *Beijing Spring* (Beijing zhichun). Their political views were relatively moderate. They sought to bolster the reform leaders against the remaining Maoists. After Deng consolidated his power in early 1979 and no longer needed their grass-roots support, however, he suppressed the movement and their journal. Subsequently they resumed their studies, Chen studying chemistry at the Chemical Engineering College and then doing graduate work at the Biophysics Institute of CAS, and Wang studying physics at Peking University. Both were members of the Youth League. Wang became an alternate member of its Central Committee, already on his way to a powerful political position. He had been among the small number of Democracy Wall activists whom Hu Yaobang had invited to his home during the movement in an effort to try to convince them to cease their activities.

Both Chen and Wang could have easily become part of the party establishment, but they chose instead to run as nonofficial candidates in the 1980 elections for the local people's congresses. In his November 3, 1980, campaign speech, Wang declared that even if he were not elected, the goal of political democratization was one that he would fight for all his life.[4] Chen had made a similar commitment in a 1979 article in *Beijing Spring,* in which he declared that he was "determined to offer his entire life to the people's cause."[5] Although some elements of their election campaigns appeared similar to those in the West— the use of campaign staffs, policy platforms, brochures, speechmaking, and debates—these were techniques they had learned as Red Guards.

Despite having graduated from prestigious institutions in scientific fields, Chen and Wang, because of their unorthodox political records, were unable to find positions appropriate to their skills. Wang quit his job as a low-level nuclear technician in 1983, resigned from the Youth League in 1984, and began wandering the country. He went to Wuhan, where he tried without much success to convince the dean of Central China Normal College to establish a school there to train cadres in democratic practices. At the same time, Chen and several former colleagues from *Beijing Spring* did research on China's traditional and Western civil service systems, in the hope of establishing a civil service in the People's Republic. In 1985 Chen and his wife Wang Zhihong set up two private correspondence schools that taught business skills to administrators. With lucrative returns from the schools, they, again with their former *Beijing Spring* colleagues, founded a variety of politically oriented enterprises.[6]

In fall 1986, Chen established the Social and Economic Research Institute (SERI), the first social science think tank in Beijing not under government auspices. SERI was much more than an unofficial version of CASS and Zhao Ziyang's think tanks; it was an expression of Chen's and Wang's belief that intellectuals should be independent of the government. Officials and intellectuals might have common goals, as Chen saw it, but they should "contend but not clash and cooperate but remain independent of each other."[7] Though independent, SERI still had to have an official registration in order to operate. Using the traditional method of family connections, Chen was able to register SERI with the Beijing city government.[8] He and his colleagues also established a publishing company that translated Western books on economics, society, psychology, and politics and brought out original works by pioneering Chinese political thinkers. They produced several dozen avant-garde book series, as other groups of intellectuals around the country were also doing.[9] In March 1988 they established China's first independent public opinion polling center—Opinion Research Center of China (ORCC)—which adopted the most advanced techniques, taught to its employees by three returned students trained in survey research at the University of Michigan. ORCC's polls revealed the emergence of a pluralistic society in China. One of its surveys, of NPC delegates in April 1980, to which 1,100 of the 3,000 delegates responded, was so highly regarded that it was reported on in the major party newspapers, including the *People's Daily.* The purpose of all of Chen's enterprises was to explore ways to make China's political system more democratic.

When Wang Juntao returned to Beijing in 1986 he joined his old friend's projects, and in 1988 he became an associate editor of the *Economic Weekly,* which Chen had bought from the United Association of Economists. The journal came with the official registration they needed in order to operate. He Jiadong, a former rightist, became its publisher. He had earlier been deposed as deputy director of the official Workers Publishing House for having published Liu Binyan's "A Second Kind of Loyalty." In a short time Wang, Chen, and He had made the *Economic Weekly,* a rather academic journal, into one of the most outspoken and lively political forums in China, on the order of the *World Economic Herald.* Wang also wrote a weekly column for the journal. By the late 1980s, like their counterparts in Eastern Europe and the Soviet Union, Chen and Wang had built a network of independent organizations. Other relatively independent research centers and independent newspapers and journals were established all over China by the late 1980s as well, but Chen and Wang's enterprises were perhaps the largest and the most influential. Together these organizations contained the seeds for the development of a civil society.

SERI, located in the university area of Haidian, was staffed with many of Chen and Wang's former Red Guard associates from the early days of the April 5 protest, the Democracy Wall movement, and especially from *Beijing Spring*. Chen had used the occasion of Wang Juntao's marriage in December 1986 to Hou Xiaotian, a graduate of the Beijing College of Economics, to persuade his old allies who attended the wedding to join him. Among them were Min Qi and Li Yimin, who also had been imprisoned in 1976 and had been members of the editorial board of *Beijing Spring*. Min Qi conducted the first nationwide public opinion survey, released in 1987.[10] It revealed that ordinary Chinese knew little about specific political institutions, but knew quite a bit about their political leaders. Moreover, they believed that they had the right to criticize the abuses of party leaders. Although the sample was skewed toward the urban and the educated, it showed an urban population restive over failed promises of reform and feeling a general discontent.

SERI drew on the services of several dozen full-time paid researchers, many of whom, like Wang and Chen, had served prison terms and could not be employed by official institutes. In addition, SERI employed hundreds of professors, graduate students, and prominent academics who at the same time also worked in official institutes and wrote for official publications. By the late 1980s, the activities of Wang and Chen attracted highly placed reform intellectuals and reform-minded officials associated with Hu Yaobang and Zhao Ziyang, most of whom had kept their distance from them when they were Democracy Wall activists. In late 1988 not only were the members of the democratic elite becoming more independent and more politically organized, but nonofficial institutes like SERI had achieved a degree of respectability. Li Honglin and Bao Zunxin, for example, asked Chen to fund a journal they wished to start. Members of the democratic elite and reform officials attended seminars held at SERI; members of SERI attended the democratic elite's seminars, as well. Moreover, both groups invited members of the newly emerging urban and rural entrepreneurial class to their seminars. Wang and Chen were able to extend their influence, therefore, inside and outside the intellectual and official establishment. Despite the financial success of their enterprises, they continued to lead frugal lives, paying themselves the standard Chinese workers' salary and pouring their profits back into their research projects, seminars, and publishing ventures.[11]

Wang and Chen did not always agree politically. Toward the end of the 1980s, Wang advocated a more gradual approach, believing that the success of China's reforms required that reform leaders such as Zhao Ziyang have sufficient power to carry out economic and political changes. He appeared to be moving in a neo-authoritarian direction. Chen shared this view to some extent, but feared that an enlightened leader with too much power could easily turn into an unenlightened despot. Chen published an article in the *Economic Weekly* underlining the "shortcomings" in the neo-authoritarian view. He noted that China had had strong political leaders—Yuan Shikai, Chiang Kai-shek, and Mao—"but there never appeared a stable social order. There were frequent civil wars before 1949 and numerous movements after it." He called the desire for a strong leader an "infatuation with idealized political models." What China needed was "the art of politics to balance and compromise, not a stubborn adherence to ideologies and models."[12] Their journal attempted to embody this view. In addition to articles advocating democracy or neo-authoritarianism, it published a wide spectrum of political opinions. The April 9, 1989, issue stated that a climate of tolerance should be maintained even for those views one found intolerable,[13] another rare perspective in the People's Republic.

Because SERI and many younger intellectuals in the nearby universities were in frequent contact, it is not surprising that Wang, Chen, and several other members of the institute played an important role in the 1989 Tiananmen Square demonstration. One of their liaisons with the students was Chen Xiaoping, a deputy chairman of the Department of Constitutional Law at the University of Politics and Law. As a third-year law student during the 1985 student demonstration, Chen Xiaoping had put up a wallposter reading: "China's constitution guarantees freedom of expression and assembly. Yet they tear down posters and arrest peaceful demonstrators. China should either follow its own laws or face up to its actual policies honestly, and delete these bogus rights from the constitution."[14]

Another liaison was Liu Gang, a physics graduate student at Peking University. As an undergraduate he had attended Keda in Anhui, where he met Fang Lizhi; he later did graduate work with Fang's wife Li Shuxian at Peking University. Liu participated in the 1986 student demonstrations and helped organize the campaign in which Li Shuxian was elected to the local people's congress in the Haidian District in 1987. He became associated with SERI in 1988 and helped initiate the lawn, later democratic, salon, at Peking University in May of that year. Subsequently he helped organize similar salons at other area universities, including Qinghua, People's University, and the University of Politics and Law. The leaders of these salons became the core group that led the early phase of the 1989 demonstration. Both Liu Gang and Chen Xiaoping also helped organize the student funeral procession following Hu Yaobang's death. Whereas the democratic elite and other intellectuals did not become directly involved with the demonstration until the hunger strike in mid-May, some members of SERI became involved at the beginning and held daily meetings with the student leaders. Liu Gang also helped organize the first of the autonomous organizations, the Beijing Students Autonomous Federation, established in late April, and Chen Xiaoping helped organize the Beijing Citizens Autonomous Federation, established in mid-May.

When the demonstration began, Wang Juntao was out of town. He and Chen Ziming early on had decided to support it, but they too did not become directly involved until the hunger strike. They hesitated at first because, like Fang Lizhi, they feared that their participation might provoke the party into charging that the demonstration was a "conspiracy." Yet by mid-May and especially after the imposition of martial law, Wang and Chen literally lived in the square and were in daily contact with the protest leaders. Their direct access to the students contrasted with the marginal role played by most intellectuals, including the democratic elite, who supported the student demonstrators with petitions and perhaps by participating in the marches, but were not in direct contact with the students during the demonstration. The *Economic Weekly* reported accurately on the protests and continued to conduct public opinion surveys. These surveys, particularly those from May 13 through May 20, revealed the support of Beijing's citizens for the demonstration and their disillusionment with the way the government was handling it.

The personal involvement of Wang and Chen with the demonstrators came about in large part because of the efforts of Zhao Ziyang's ally Yan Mingfu, the director of the United Front Work Department. Yan contacted Wang and Chen as well as other intellectuals known to be influential with students in order to get their help in persuading the students to stop their hunger strike and evacuate the square before Gorbachev's arrival on May 15. In a three-hour meeting with Yan on May 13, Wang sought to negotiate an agreement whereby the students would evacuate the square and return to their universities in return for the party's allowing some independence to student organizations and newspapers and for the party's repudiation of the April 26 editorial.[15] Through such a compromise Wang hoped to bolster Zhao's position and to prevent both the elders' return to power and any use of the military.

Despite the independent stance of Wang and Chen, underlying their relatively moderate counsel was their belief, like that of the democratic elite, that reform could still be achieved within the existing political system. Equally important, they had concluded that student demonstrations in and of themselves could be more destructive than constructive. For this reason, among others, Wang Juntao had not participated in the 1986 student demonstrations, even though he had returned to Beijing by that time. Past experience had convinced him that without a realistic, specific program such demonstrations could have counterproductive results, including the purge of enlightened leaders, as happened in 1987 with Hu Yaobang. Chen similarly decided that emotional large-scale protests could "bring results extremely inimical to stability."[16] Both men also knew that the kind of democracy that the students were calling for was not possible right away. They therefore sought to use the 1989 demonstration to achieve small, realizable political changes, as they had done with their nonofficial enterprises, and then gradually increase the pressure for political reforms. They urged the student leaders to accept more limited goals rather than seeking the immediate achievement of a democratic polity or the overthrow of the leadership.

The student leaders Wang Dan and Wu'er Kaixi initially accepted the moderate counsel of Wang and Chen, whose advice was in the same spirit as that they were receiving from members of the democratic elite and Zhao Ziyang's think tanks. Wang Juntao patiently and persistently tried to persuade Chai Ling, the leader of the hunger strike, to discontinue the strike. But by the time she finally called it off, the number of demonstrators had expanded into the millions in Beijing, and the movement had spread to other major cities in China. Controlling its momentum had already become impossible—for Wang Dan and Wu'er Kaixi or for anyone else. Moreover, Yan Mingfu had been unable to get the party leadership's acquiescence to even the seemingly moderate demands for more independent student organizations and newspapers, let alone the repudiation of the April 26 editorial. To the leadership, particularly the elders, to give in on these demands would have meant a loosening of Leninist controls and an acknowledgment that they had erred. Such concessions would have further undermined their authority. Without a willingness to compromise on both sides and with a movement that had taken on a dynamic of its own, the demonstrators and elders were on a collision course that culminated in the imposition of martial law on May 20 and the military crackdown on June 4. No one, not even savvy political organizers with the access and influence of Wang and Chen, could have controlled the forces already set in motion by mid-May.

The Role of Wang and Chen after Martial Law

Although the names of Wang and Chen were not on the "most wanted list" issued after the crackdown, they were pursued and finally captured in October 1989. At the first major trial of the leaders of the 1989 demonstration held in February–March 1991, they were charged with "masterminding" the demonstration and encouraging "counterrevolutionary activity." They were each sentenced to thirteen years in prison, the longest sentences among the major defendants. Wang and Chen had indeed been active in the later stages of the demonstration, but there was little evidence that they had "masterminded" the demonstration. Nor was credible evidence presented of "counterrevolutionary" activity. Their writings during the demonstration were as moderate in tone as their advice to the students to withdraw from the square. Wang Juntao on May 7 had expressed the hope that the demonstration could be resolved by peaceful, positive means. His tone was temperate: "All sectors of society must learn tolerance and restraint of one's sentiments, must resort to reason and not to violence."[17] In contrast to the relatively radical nature of the political views he had voiced in the 1980 political campaign, Wang counseled the demonstrators to take a flexible, moderate stance toward the leadership. His approach was more temperate than that of some members of the democratic elite. He did not sign Yan Jiaqi's and Bao Zunxin's petition calling for Deng Xiaoping and Li Peng to step down.

The commentary articles in the *Economic Weekly* reinforced this moderate approach. A commentary of May 21, 1989, blamed the existing political system, evolved from the guerrilla movement with its hierarchical structure, unified ideology, control of all areas of life, and repeated political campaigns, for the social disturbances and political instability with which the regime was now confronted. But instead of calling for its overthrow, the article spoke of making the existing system "flexible, self-adjustable, and able to integrate all kinds of interests . . . [in order] to attain political stability."[18] The commentary did, however, point out that the nation could not be equated with the party or its leaders. In the current crisis, it endorsed the efforts of Hu Jiwei and Cao Siyuan to convene the NPC immediately. Settling the conflict by constitutional means would allow the demonstration to "move democracy from the streets into the hall of the People's Congress."[19]

On June 4, the day of the crackdown, the *Economic Weekly* pleaded that "differences within the leading group" be settled "according to procedures and within the scope prescribed by the Party Constitution." It urged that two or more different opinions be allowed to coexist: "The key to guaranteeing social stability lies in maintaining a basic balance of the interests of various social strata." These interests are not maintained by use of military force and threats, which "are for dealing with enemies and are usually ineffective." Once again, the *Economic Weekly* asserted: "Major state affairs cannot be settled on the streets and can only be settled by depending on democracy and law. A government and a ruling party can achieve long-term order and stability of the country only if they are skillful at resolving contradictions instead of intensifying them."[20] The goal was to end the demonstration through negotiation and compromise to prevent a military showdown.

Although Wang and Chen urged compromising with the existing political system in the short run, in the long run they still sought a democratic polity. At a symposium held at SERI in early April, shortly before the demonstration, Wang Juntao observed that the changes going on in the socialist world had shown that socialism was inferior and, therefore, that China was "'at a time of making a choice of new civilizations.' The old pattern, which has been proven to be outdated, does not work."[21] In a series of articles that he wrote for the *Economic Weekly* around this time he expressed the fear, as had members of the democratic elite just before the demonstration, that China's worsening economic situation would "turn into social and political problems," whose outcome, he warned, would depend on whether China would "be able to establish new political conditions capable of dispelling the dangers of the situation." He noted: "What primarily has allowed countries to successfully weather some critical times has been the fact that some representatives of the people's will [have] . . . used their power in a salient way . . . [to] convey independently and wisely the fundamental interests of the people."[22] This was the course that he and his associates had pursued since the Democracy Wall days.

Yet despite their moderate counsel, these two men represented a much greater danger to the elders and their supporters than did the students, the democratic elite, or even the labor leaders. It was above all the actions of Chen and Wang, rather than their ideas, that the elders found most threatening. At a symposium on April 23, planned before the demonstration, Chen had urged intellectuals "to move forward from a political consciousness" to become an organized group in order to achieve tangible results.[23] Wang and Chen tried to build such an organization during the demonstration and especially after the imposition of martial law. They attempted to link various autonomous groups into a unified political alliance that could negotiate with the party. Their goal was to transform the demonstration in the streets into an organized political movement that could achieve concrete political results.

Most of the intellectuals and students kept their distance from the workers during the demonstration. But perhaps because of their experience with all classes of people in the Cultural Revolution, Wang, Chen, and their allies were in direct contact with some workers. Most of the small number of intellectuals advising the Beijing Workers Autonomous Federation and the official All-China Federation of Trade Unions had been somehow associated with Wang and Chen in the past. Liu Jiamin, another former Red Guard who had also been imprisoned during the Cultural Revolution and had written for *Beijing Spring* during the Democracy Wall movement, was a professor at the Chinese Workers Movement Institute, a training college for cadres of the federation. He had long been an advocate of trade union autonomy. Another ally, Li Jinjin, a lecturer in law at Peking University, became a legal advisor to the Beijing Workers Autonomous Federation. Liu and Li, along with Wang, Chen and other associates, actively defended the workers who, unlike the students and intellectuals, were imprisoned without trials while the demonstration was still under way. When the Beijing Workers Autonomous Federation, led by Han Dongfang, pressed for the release of three workers by the Public Security Bureau, Li Jinjin and others helped in the effort. Wang and Chen then sought to coordinate the activities of the Beijing Workers Autonomous Federation with the other autonomous groups of intellectuals, students, and ordinary citizens in Beijing.

On May 19, Wang, Chen, Liu Gang, Chen Xiaoping, Zhou Duo, and other colleagues wrote "A Letter to the People," in which they warned of the impending imposition of martial law and urged the various autonomous groups to join together and begin strikes of all kinds across the country.[24] On May 22, Wang and Chen gathered the leaders of the autonomous organizations together at the Monument of the People's Heroes to announce the establishment of an alliance of their groups that included the Beijing Workers Autonomous Federation. On May 23 they held a meeting with the heads of the autonomous organizations at the Marxist-Leninist Institute of CASS, at which they founded the Joint Liaison Group of All Circles in the Capital to Protect the Constitution in an effort to form a united front to stop the entrance of troops into the square. They helped in building barricades and roadblocks as well as urging Beijing citizens to use personal persuasion with the soldiers to block the military's approach. The Joint Liaison Group published a news sheet, News Flash (Xinwen kuaifeng), and held meetings every morning at CASS to discuss strategy with the autonomous organization leaders.

Breaking more new ground, Wang and Chen were also in contact with Zhu Houze, secretary of the official All-China Federation of Trade Unions, to gain his cooperation in staging a nationwide strike in another attempt to prevent the use of the military.[25] At the last moment Zhu withdrew his support for the strike. The potential consequences of such an action, perhaps more than any other development of the 1989 demonstration, must have acutely frightened the elders, who since the early 1980s had been obsessed with the specter of an alliance between intellectuals and workers on the order of Poland's Solidarity movement. As Deng's April 25 speech indicated, the elders believed that they could handle a purely intellectual or student movement, but they very much feared an intellectual-worker alliance. The contacts of Wang and Chen with workers' unions, official as well as unofficial, came closest to making the elders' fears a reality. That the workers' tent headquarters in the square was one of the first targets of the army forces on June 4 and that scores of workers were either summarily executed or imprisoned without trial and received longer sentences than the student and intellectual participants was not only a manifestation of the elders' contempt for ordinary workers but also evidence of their real fear of losing power. If workers could organize and work for their own rights, then they would have no need of a Communist Party to represent them.

By the end of May, realizing the futile nature of their resistance, Wang helped the leaders of the demonstration flee Beijing. At the same time he and others tried to persuade the remaining demonstrators to evacuate the square. They had little influence, however, over the newly arriving students from the provinces, who planned to remain until the June 20 meeting of the National People's Congress. Initially Wang and Chen did not want to flee or go into hiding. They had refused several invitations to go abroad in the past in the belief that they could be effective politically only if they remained in China. On June 6, nevertheless, they fled the capital. Several of their associates—Liu Gang, Chen Xiaoping, Min Qi, Li Jinjin, and leaders of the Beijing Autonomous Workers Federation—were soon arrested. Wang and Chen themselves, betrayed by one of their former colleagues, were captured in south China in October. To elude the authorities even for four months was surprising, given that they had been under surveillance by the Public Security Bureau through most of the Deng period. Their success in avoiding capture for a time indicated that they were helped by a broad network of allies or ordinary citizens who had lost their belief in the party.

Wang and Chen may have had greater and more direct influence with the student demonstrators than any other intellectual or adult group, but neither they nor anyone else instigated or manipulated the demonstration as the authorities charged. The demonstration began spontaneously and had its own dynamic that no group or individual could control. The efforts of Wang and Chen to build a civil society before the demonstration and, during the demonstration, to organize a political alliance of students with other social groups, including workers, however, may explain why they received the most severe sentences of the intellectual Tiananmen participants.

Although the elders considered such acts "counterrevolutionary activity," Wang and Chen had not called for the overthrow of the leadership or the party. On the contrary, they had tried to work out a peaceful solution that would be acceptable to both sides. Though some intellectuals sympathetic to the students felt that Wang and Chen had used the demonstration and the student demonstrators to achieve their own political goals, Zhou Duo, one of the four intellectuals who had negotiated the peaceful withdrawal from the square on June 4, and who had been at Wang's side during the critical mid-May negotiations with Yan Mingfu and the student leaders, described Wang and Chen as "mediators" who "never advocated the overthrow of the government." Zhou called Wang an "outstanding man in terms of wisdom, personality and experience . . . Very few people are close to perfect but Wang Juntao is close . . . [He] is very even-tempered and not easily excitable. He likes to argue but never gets angry. Many people cursed the Government and party during that time but even after the massacre, Juntao never cursed the party."[26] For the elders and their associates, however, the attempts of Wang and Chen to bring together diverse social groups and establish an alternative political organization could only be viewed as treasonous.

The Trials

In February 1991 Wang and Chen were each sentenced to thirteen years in prison. Liu Gang, who was ranked third on the list of the twenty-one "most wanted" students, was sentenced to six years, and other associates received from three to five years. That Wang and Chen received the stiffest sentences can also be viewed as the elders' retribution for their actions ever since the Democracy Wall movement.

At their trials Wang and Chen acted as defiantly as they had throughout their lives. Although they knew the consequences of refusing to confess, they categorically denied the charges against them. Wang not only defended his own actions but also defended the demonstrators. He did not always agree with them, he said, but he upheld their basic right as citizens of the People's Republic to voice their legitimate opposition to their leaders. He explained in a letter to his lawyers: "The dead are unable to defend themselves. Many of them intended to fight for China and her people, for truth and justice. I decided to take my chances to defend some of their points, even if I did not agree with all of them at the time." He also urged that the "legitimate rights of citizens . . . be protected." He continued: "I got angry when the public prosecutor accused me of being counterrevolutionary by opposing leaders. A defense should not be limited to saying 'I do not oppose leaders,' but should allow for the legitimate right to oppose leaders." His goal, he declared, had not been to overthrow the leaders. He expressed admiration for most of them: "I respect our elder generation very much—it is ironic that today I face a sentencing from them ... What I want to safeguard are principles and conscience."[27] Chen presented a vigorous defense as well and refused to show repentance for his actions. At one point his argument became so impassioned that the judge called for an adjournment.[28]

No matter how moving or persuasive the prisoners' arguments, their sentences, as was the usual practice in political cases, had already been determined by the authorities. When Wang's wife, Hou Xiaotian, rushed to the dock to embrace her husband before he was taken away, she was punched by the police several times and her brother, who tried to protect her, was also pushed away.[29] She herself was detained for five months after June 4 merely for being Wang's wife and while in detention became ill from having to sleep on a cement floor. When she was released, she was denied housing and medical treatment. She was also repeatedly threatened with another arrest for daring to speak with foreign journalists about her husband.

After their sentencing, both Wang and Chen appealed their cases, but the lawyers who had so vigorously defended them at their trials were put under great pressure not to handle the appeals. Chen's lawyers were effectively disbarred by the Ministry of Justice, which confiscated their licenses.[30] In his appeal, prepared by his wife, Wang explained that he had been reluctant to play an active role in the 1989 demonstration because of the failure of previous student movements. But ultimately he had decided to participate, in the hope that he could "provide the movement with solid ideas and factual input instead of empty slogans."[31] His efforts to help the students achieve concrete results in 1989 had proved no more successful than the previous demonstrations in which he and Chen participated.

In prison, Wang and Chen acted as they had since the Cultural Revolution—defiant in asserting their rights and those of their fellow citizens. Wang contracted hepatitis B and Chen suffered from other ailments, for which they were both refused adequate medical treatment. Both men then carried out hunger strikes until their prison conditions and medical treatment improved. Hou Xiaotian worked to draw world attention to the plight of Wang, Chen, and other political prisoners, who she said were living in circumstances that would reduce them to "idiots and mad men."[32] After an outcry from foreign governments and international human rights groups, the prison conditions of Wang and Chen began to improve slightly in 1992, but Hou Xiaotian reported that Wang continued to be critically ill with hepatitis.

Their associate Liu Gang also acted defiantly. He spoke for an hour in his own defense at his trial, stating that what he had been forced to admit under prison interrogation, where he was threatened with death and torture, was invalid. When Liu had been placed with other prisoners before his trial, he had organized his fellow inmates to carry out passive resistance by singing the "Internationale" and other songs of protest. They even commemorated the first anniversary of the June 4 crackdown by going on a hunger strike. As a result, Liu Gang was put in solitary confinement. For several days his arms were lashed behind him, and for two months he was shackled with leg irons. He was sent to a prison camp in the Northeast where he was subjected to life-threatening punishment. By contrast, their colleague Chen Xiaoping made a self-criticism and was released in February 1991. Nevertheless, he lost his job, his right to live in Beijing, and his party membership and was forced to return to his hometown in rural Hunan.

Nearly all of Wang's and Chen's colleagues from their *Beijing Spring* days refused to comply with the authorities' efforts to force them to confess or to betray their colleagues. Some members of SERI escaped abroad, others were imprisoned, and still others were reduced to doing menial work. SERI was closed down, and all of its papers, equipment, and files confiscated. Han Dongfang was imprisoned without a trial, but he was handed over to his family on April 28, 1991, because he was desperately ill with tuberculosis. He was allowed to travel to the United States in 1992 for medical treatment.

Ren Wanding, the human rights activist of the Democracy Wall movement, was sentenced to seven years in prison. Like Wang and Chen, he too had urged students and workers to unite, but his stiff sentence had more to do with his past actions than his participation in the 1989 demonstration. Ren had been released from prison in 1983, but had only started to speak out again in 1988, on the tenth anniversary of the Democracy Wall movement. He published an op-ed piece in the *New York Times* on December 26, 1988, and sent a letter to the U.N. Commission on Human Rights in which he urged the international community to make its investments in China conditional on the amelioration of China's human rights abuses and the improvement of prison conditions for political prisoners. His public appeal for help from abroad in dealing with repression in China had infuriated the elders in 1979 and did so again in late 1988.

Yet of all those brought to trial, Wang Juntao and Chen Ziming were regarded as the most dangerous. Their activist political life outside the party's control and their organizational skills in linking social groups, generations, and reformers inside the political system with democratic activists outside the political system represented something new in China—an effort to establish an organized alternative to the party. Even if some of their views in the late 1980s tended toward neo-authoritarianism, their ability to construct an independent network of activities—a think tank, a publishing company, a journal, and a polling agency—was as significant for the process of democratization as the democratic elite's efforts in the party media to inform the public about democratic ideas and the need for political reform. The democratic elite worked through words and only belatedly through organized action; Wang and Chen expressed through their actions, even during the Cultural Revolution, a desire to live as free citizens in an unfree society.

The seeds of a civil society that Wang and Chen and others of their Red Guard generation tried to plant may eventually flower. They nurtured their seeds with methods different from those of the democratic elite; their efforts may one day prove even more conducive to bringing spring to China.

A Change in the Role of the Democratic Elite

China's 1989 demonstration inspired subsequent demonstrations in Eastern Europe and the Soviet Union in which intellectuals played a significant role in ushering in the new polities of the post-Communist era. Their seeming success provoked members of China's democratic elite to ask why they had been so ineffectual in their efforts to reform China's Leninist party-state. A partial explanation was that the Leninist party-state had been imposed on Eastern Europe by the Soviet Union and had never been as powerful or as deeply rooted as the party-state that came to power internally in China as well as in the

Soviet Union. Another explanation was that because Eastern Europe and Russia had a religious background similar to that of the West and had several more centuries of contact with the West, they had much more in common with the West than did China. Yet members of the democratic elite pointed out that their ethnic and Confucian brethren in Taiwan were developing opposition parties, an outspoken press, and an assertive legislature, disproving the view of both the elders and others that Western institutions were inappropriate for a nation with Chinese traditions and culture.

Another explanation was that in comparison with the Soviet party-state, which had been in the process of change since the thaw of the mid-1950s, culminating with the Gorbachev era, China's party-state was much stronger and more repressive, making it much less susceptible to change. Moreover, members of China's democratic elite differed from their East European and Russian counterparts in important ways. As descendants of the Chinese literati as well as former Marxist-Leninists, they tended to see democracy as the preserve of the elite and the educated. By 1989 they were willing to join with the students and even with the "money-grubbing" entrepreneurs whom they had once disdained in a common political effort, but few of them gave much attention to the workers, let alone the peasants, as participants in their efforts to build democracy in China.

Even though the party had brutally persecuted the democratic elite, their families, and their colleagues for over two decades, most of them were despondent at the thought of being expelled from the party and were overjoyed to be asked to reregister. They believed that they could only function effectively within the political and intellectual establishment. The decision of East European and Soviet intellectuals such as the Czech playwright Vaclav Havel, the Polish philosopher Adam Michnik, and the Soviet physicist Andrei Sakharov to opt out of the party establishment voluntarily and join the opposition to work for political change, was utterly alien to them. The intellectuals of the Cultural Revolution generation, represented by Wang Juntao and Chen Ziming, came closest to asserting their independence by opting out of the Youth League, trying to establish connections with workers and other groups, and setting up a nonofficial intellectual base. Yet they too worked with the establishment in order to maintain their independence. And they too believed that only intellectuals could bring democracy to China. Although some members of the democratic elite, such as Liu Binyan and Su Shaozhi, publicly acknowledged their own shortcomings after the 1989 crackdown, Liu Xiaobo's critique of the elite for seeking to remain in the party establishment, no matter how badly it treated them, was accurate.

Though not well versed in or in sympathy with traditional culture, the democratic elite during the Deng decade of reform nevertheless embodied the Confucian ideal of intellectuals who felt a responsibility, even at the risk of their own careers, to make their society more humane by trying to persuade their leaders to be less abusive. By the late 1980s, however, owing to their disillusionment with continuing repression at home and an awareness of the democratizing tide sweeping the outside world, some members of the elite gradually began to change their view of their role in relation to the government. As they shifted their emphasis from revising ideology to establishing institutions and laws to curb the abuse of political power and, by the end of the decade, to joining in concerted efforts with others to bring this about, they also inexorably undermined their own role in the political establishment.

One extreme expression of the change came from the Stone executive Wan Runnan, former chairman of the Federation for a Democratic China, to which many of the exiled democratic elite belong. Wan urged its members to remain independent and not accept amnesty from the party. Since the party, he declared, "will not voluntarily give up its one-party dictatorship, it will have to be forced into doing so by an opposition party that operates democratically." Therefore the federation "must organize a political force. Without organization, it would be impossible for us to change China's political structure." [33] Only an organized alternative party, and not social explosions or demonstrations, he maintained, could express and achieve the demands of China's urban population.

This view may be held by only a small number of the democratic elite. Most of those still in China and not under arrest or on probation were reregistered as party members in 1991. Even some exiles hoped to be reregistered as party members. Despite the terrible abuses they and their families had endured from the party for decades, they still wanted to be part of the ruling elite. The traditional concept of loyalty to the government and its leaders remained deeply embedded in China's political culture, even among those individuals and groups who had disagreed most vigorously with the government's policies.

Yet these same intellectuals, so pleased to be reregistered in the party, still had a changed conception of their role. Early in the post-Mao era, some had made distinctions between the party, the state, the nation, and the people. By the late 1980s, members of the democratic elite also questioned their role as the intermediaries between the government and the people, and in spring 1989 some of them had moved completely over to the side of the people. Through their words, they expressed themselves in opposition to the party-state. They even began to form and participate in alternative organizations. In the context of China's history, if this line of thinking and action continues and spreads, a radical, even revolutionary, change in the intellectuals' view of their relationship with the state could result.

Their continuing persecution in the Deng era, albeit milder than in the Mao era, made members of the democratic elite unwilling to rely any longer on the tolerance of political authorities, the assumption of a benign government, or a democratic style of leadership. Time after time they had seen tolerance turn to animosity when they displeased a political leader or when leaders with a democratic style, such as Hu Yaobang and Zhao Ziyang, were purged or defeated in a power struggle. Even the channels opened between themselves and the political leadership at the beginning of the decade were closed down when the leaders did not want to hear what they had to say.

Members of the democratic elite consequently no longer assumed that the party-state was dedicated to the public good or that enlightened leaders would produce enlightened policies. They no longer expected the party-state to discipline or restrain itself of its own accord, and they no longer believed that the traditional methods of ideological remonstrance or moral persuasion could check the abuse of political power. Moreover, informal procedures and good connections with some leaders did not protect them from retaliation by other leaders. They gradually moved toward the view that only institutional and legal checks on the power of the state and a broader base of support from below could protect them as individuals and protect society as a whole.

Most important, this view had gained adherents outside the intellectual community, as was demonstrated by the support of China's urban population for the demonstrations in the spring of 1989. Their support may have been motivated more by economic than by political concerns, but like the students and intellectuals, they too desired more control over their lives. In addition, fundamental forces at work in China in the 1980s—growing professionalism, rising educational levels in the urban sector, the decentralization of political as well as economic power, and continuing opening to the outside world—had the potential to lead the urban community toward a similar change in vision.

As long as the elders and their successors seek economic, scientific, and technological modernization, they must rely on professionals, intellectuals, and skilled workers, thereby making it impossible to eliminate altogether the forces pushing for political change. Although the June 4 crackdown showed that this process is not a consistent or inevitable one, if China's modern history, including the Mao era, is any guide, a period of retrenchment and reaction is sooner or later followed by one of reform and liberalization, in which calls for political reform as well as for economic reform resume, as happened in early 1992. But unless reform means more than merely a period of intellectual relaxation and intellectual debate as in the past, it will be succeeded by yet another period of repression.

The experience of the democratic elite indicates that no matter how energetic, brave, or talented its members may be, or whether they are in or outside the establishment, they will have little chance to express themselves or to influence policy making unless the political system itself is changed. And if and when that should happen, they will no longer be an elite class, endowed by tradition with the responsibility to rule; they will be one of a number of different groups participating in the political process. Their words and actions may help to create a polity in which they lose their preeminent status, but one in which they may finally have a real and sustained voice. Such a polity would need to allow for the development of a pluralistic society, with limits on political power, in which the government is held accountable by means of competitive elections, laws, a legislature, and a relatively free press. These are the institutions that the democratic elite called for under Deng Xiaoping for almost ten years and that Wang Juntao and Chen Ziming tried to generate in beginning to build a civil society.

Such institutions are not completely unknown in China. The late Qing and Republican eras saw the beginnings of a civil society, but their roots were very fragile. The historians William Rowe and Mary Rankin and the political scientist David Strand have shown[34] that autonomous organizations existed but were relatively weak and unable to provide a foundation for a civil society and pluralistic politics. With the imposition in 1949 of the Communist Party as the only functioning political organization, these other organizations, already enfeebled by the Guomindang, the Japanese, and the civil war, were easily crushed. In 1989, even if the demonstration had toppled the leadership, there was no viable alternative to the party that could have taken its place. Neither the eight small parties nor any members of the democratic elite were ready to assume leadership. In the Soviet Union, at the time of the August 1991 coup attempt when Gorbachev was put under house arrest, there were a number of legitimately elected leaders, particularly Boris Yeltsin, who had been elected president of the Russian Republic by an overwhelming majority, and various independent political groups already active in the Supreme Soviet that could take charge. Perhaps the closest equivalent to a political organization outside party control in the People's Republic were the new nonofficial groups that Chen, Wang, and others had established since the mid-1980s and the alliance of autonomous social federations that Wang and Chen had brought together briefly during the 1989 demonstration. But these groupings were just beginnings and were very fragile. Moreover, they had no solid social base.

Thus the democratic elite, the Wang-Chen group, and the 1989 demonstrations shook up the system and increased popular awareness of political issues, but they were unable to lead to any fundamental change in China's Leninist party-state like that which occurred soon thereafter in Eastern Europe and the Soviet Union. The East European demonstrations were successful at least in part because the East Europeans had some form of organized alternative leadership outside the control of the party-state. Whether it was Charter 77, which became the Civic Forum in Czechoslovakia, the Solidarity movement in Poland or the Democratic Russia party, these groups and their leaders were able to replace the Communist Party in their countries; in China, neither the democratic elite nor even the democratic activists were able to establish strong socially based organized alternatives to the Communist Party leadership.

Nevertheless the decade of reform under Deng not only marked the beginning of a change in the intellectuals' view of their relationship with the state; it also marked a period in which certain sectors of the population gained some experience with competitive elections, secret ballots on the local level, a strengthening of the NPC, limited terms of office for some officials, open political debate, periodic assertions of autonomy by the eight small parties, and the beginnings of a semi-independent press and autonomous organizations. The underpinnings for these changes remain. Even though the party continues to control the military and most jobs, housing, medical treatment, and education, the seeds for these changes have been sown. The ground may be frozen most of the time, but when the political winters periodically turn into spring, some of the seeds produce democratic shoots. That their growth has been stunted has more to do with the internal dynamics of the power struggle in the top leadership and the repressive Leninist political system than with their inability to grow in China.

Despite chilling blasts, the roots grow a little stronger each time the blast subsides. When China's shoots finally flower, they may not look the same as those in the West or those in Japan; their colors and configurations may be quite different. The Deng decade has demonstrated, however, that China's soil can nourish democratic seedlings. It has also demonstrated that continued growth and potential flowering depend not only on the political climate, China's openness, and the development of the nonstate economic sector but also on the persistence of China's democratic elite, nonofficial activists, and their successors. As many have pointed out, it took democratic institutions three or more centuries to be established in the West. After almost a century of effort, the roots of China's democracy are still fragile, the atmosphere still uncertain, and portions of the soil still unfertile. But by the end of the Deng decade, having been nurtured by the democratic elite and the nonofficial activists and by the economic reforms, the roots had become stronger and the shoots a bit taller. Others will continue the cultivation, perhaps using different methods, so that the seeds the democratic elite and others have sown over the Deng decade of reform may someday truly flower.

Notes

Index

Notes

Abbreviations

FBIS   Foreign Broadcast Information Service (until April 1, 1981, entitled *Daily Report: People's Republic of China;* from April 1, 1981, *Daily Report: China*)

JPRS   Joint Publications Research Service
  –C   JPRS Report: China
  –PSMA   JPRS China Report: Political, Sociological and Military Affairs
  –RF   JPRS China Report: Red Flag
  –TPRC   JPRS Translations on the People's Republic of China

1. The Democratic Elite

1. See Arif Dirlik, "Chinese Historians and the Marxist Concept of Capitalism: A Critical Examination," *Modern China* (January 1982), 105–132.
2. Wm. Theodore de Bary, *The Liberal Tradition in China* (Hong Kong: Chinese University Press, 1983).
3. Rudolf Wagner of Heidelberg University has suggested the term "murmurings."
4. Benjamin Schwartz, *China's Cultural Values* (Tempe: Center for Asian Studies, Arizona State University, 1985).
5. Tang Tsou, *The Cultural Revolution and Post-Mao Reforms* (Chicago: University of Chicago Press, 1986), pp. 3–66.
6. See Andrew Nathan, *Chinese Democracy* (New York: Knopf, 1985), for an analysis of the historical roots of democracy in China.
7. De Bary, *The Liberal Tradition in China,* p. 84.

8. Vera Schwarcz, *The Chinese Enlightenment* (Berkeley: University of California Press, 1986).

9. See Ding Xueliang, "Political Appeals and Social Consequences," Ph D. dissertation, Department of Sociology, Harvard University, 1992.

10. Ba Jin, *Random Thoughts,* trans. Geremie Barmé (Hong Kong: Joint Publications, 1984), p. 96.

11. Ibid.

12. Deng Xiaoping, "On the Reform of the System of Party and State Leadership," August 18, 1980, in *Selected Works of Deng Xiaoping (1975–1982)* (Beijing: Foreign Languages Press, 1984), pp. 302–325.

13. Schwartz, *China's Cultural Values,* pp. 1–23.

14. Gail W. Lapidus, "State and Society: Toward the Emergence of Civil Society in the Soviet Union," in *Politics, Society, and Nationality inside Gorbachev's Russia,* ed. Seweryn Bialer (Boulder: Westview Press, 1989).

2. Hu Yaobang's Intellectual Network

1. Yang Zhongmei, *Hu Yaobang: A Chinese Biography,* ed. Timothy Cheek (Armonk, N.Y.: M. E. Sharpe, 1988), chap. 13. Much of the background on Hu comes from this source.

2. Liu Binyan, with Ruan Ming and Xu Gang, *"Tell the World"* (New York: Pantheon, 1989), p. 74.

3. Author's conversation with Liu Binyan in 1988.

4. Ding Panshi, "He Had Deep Love for His Comrades—Comrade Yaobang as I Understand Him," *Zhongguo qingnian bao,* May 25, 1989, p. 2, JPRS–C, no. 89071, July 7, 1989, p. 7.

5. Author's conversation with Liu Binyan in 1988.

6. Author's conversation with informant.

7. Talk by Liu Binyan, December 13, 1988, Yenching Auditorium, Harvard University.

8. "Refuting Yao Wenyuan's Theory of Substitution," *Renmin ribao,* March 15, 1977, FBIS, March 17, 1977, p. E7.

9. Deng Xiaoping, "Speech at the Opening Ceremony of the National Conference on Science," March 18, 1978, in *Selected Works of Deng Xiaoping (1975–1982)* (Beijing: Foreign Languages Press, 1984), pp. 101–116.

10. The complete process is described in a New China News Agency release, November 15, 1978, FBIS, November 22, 1978, pp. E22–23.

11. "It Is Absolutely Impermissible to Attack Scientific and Technical Personnel," *Guangming ribao,* October 10, 1978, p. 1, FBIS, October 20, 1978, p. E20.

12. "Crippling Talent Is a Crime against the Revolution," *Renmin ribao*, October 10, 1978, p. 3, FBIS, October 18, 1978, p. E27.

13. "Science and Democracy," *Renmin ribao*, May 4, 1978, p. 2, FBIS, May 17, 1978, p. E17. Special commentator article originally published in *Theoretical Trends*.

14. "It Is Imperative to Make Research in Social Sciences Prosper as Never Before," *Renmin ribao*, March 11, 1978, p. 3, FBIS, March 23, 1978, p. E7.

15. "Criticize the Cultural Despotism of the 'Gang of Four' and Actively Promote 'A Hundred Schools of Thought Contend,'" *Zhexue yanjiu*, no. 4 (1978), 9–12, JPRS–TPRC, no. 72735, January 31, 1979, p. 11.

16. Ibid., p. 12.

17. Ibid., pp. 13–14.

18. Zhou Yang, "The Development Plan for Philosophy and Social Sciences and the Policy of Letting 100 Flowers Bloom and 100 Schools of Thought Contend," *Zhexue yanjiu*, October 25, 1978, pp. 2–11, JPRS–TPRC, no. 72912, March 2, 1979, p. 100.

19. For further discussion of literature in the post-Mao era, see, among others, works by Leo Ou-fan Lee, Perry Link, and Michael Duke.

20. Wang Min, interview with New China News Agency, April 7, 1978, FBIS, April 10, 1978, p. E16.

21. Su Ching and Wang Chia-fu, "A Civil Code Must Be Drafted," *Renmin ribao*, November 24, 1978, p. 3, FBIS, December 5, 1978, p. E6.

22. New China News Agency, November 27, 1978, FBIS, November 29, 1978, p. E13.

23. Beijing Domestic Service, November 30, 1978, FBIS, December 1, 1978, p. E8.

24. "Promote Democracy and Realize the Four Modernizations," *Renmin ribao*, January 3, 1979, FBIS, January 4, 1979, p. E3.

25. Ibid., p. E5.

26. For an analysis of this topic, see Michael Schoenhals, "The 1978 Truth Criterion Controversy," *China Quarterly*, no. 126 (June 1991), 243–268.

27. *Renmin ribao*, February 7, 1977, p. 1.

28. Quoted in Schoenhals, "The 1978 Truth Criterion Controversy," p. 251, regarding Deng Xiaoping's meeting with Deng Liqun and others.

29. Deng Xiaoping, "Persist in the Party's Line and Improve Working Methods," February 29, 1980, speech, *Hebei ribao*, July 3, 1983, pp. 1, 3, FBIS, July 15, 1983, p. K10.

30. See Schoenhals's translation of a transcript of Wu Lengxi's phone call to Hu Jiwei in "The 1978 Truth Criterion Controversy," p. 261.

31. Sun Changjiang, "From the Criterion of Practice to the Criterion of Productive Forces," *Renmin ribao*, May 9, 1988, p. 5, FBIS, May 18, 1988, p. 27.

32. Dan Chen, "On Ba Jin and Random Thoughts," *Shehui kexue*, March 15, 1990, pp. 67–80.

33. Lin Chun and Li Yin-ho, "It Is Necessary to Bring Democracy into Full Play and Consolidate the Legal System," *Zhongguo qingnian*, no. 3 (1978), reprinted in *Renmin ribao*, November 13, 1978, FBIS, November 15, 1978, p. E2.

34. Ibid., p. E3.

35. Ibid., p. E9.

36. Ibid., p. E10.

37. Ibid., p. E2.

38. On the Democracy Wall activists, see Roger Garside, *Coming Alive* (New York: McGraw-Hill, 1981); Andrew Nathan, *Chinese Democracy* (New York: Knopf, 1985); and James Seymour, *The Fifth Modernization* (Stanfordville, N.Y.: Human Rights Publishing Group, 1980). This section concentrates on a comparison of the Democracy Wall activists with the democratic elite.

39. See George Black and Robin Munro, *Black Hands of Beijing* (New York: John Wiley and Sons, 1993), for biographies of Wang Juntao and Chen Ziming.

40. Jin Sheng, "Human Rights, Equality and Democracy—Commenting on the Contents of 'Move on the Fifth Modernization,'" *Tansuo*, January 29, 1979, pp. 4–7, JPRS–TPRC, no. 73787, June 29, 1979, p. 33.

41. Ibid., p. 36.

42. Jin Sheng, "Human Rights, Equality and Democracy," part 3, *Tansuo*, March 11, 1979, pp. 1–4, JPRS–TPRC, no. 73421, May 10, 1979, p. 32.

43. Mu Yi, "Don't We Chinese People Have Our Own Thought?" *Tansuo*, January 29, 1979, pp. 8–16, JPRS–TPRC, no. 73787, June 29, 1979, pp. 40–41.

44. Ibid., p. 44.

45. Ibid., p. 45.

46. "Do We Want Democracy or New Dictatorship?" *Tansuo* (special ed.), March 25, 1979, pp. 1–4, JPRS–TPRC, no. 73421, May 10, 1979, p. 29.

47. Ibid., pp. 29–30.

48. Deng Xiaoping, "Emancipate the Mind, Seek Truth from Facts and Unite as One in Looking to the Future," in *Selected Works of Deng Xiaoping (1975–1982)*, pp. 157–158.

49. Ding Xueliang, "Political Appeals and Social Consequences," Ph.D.

dissertation, Department of Sociology, Harvard University, 1992, p. 171.

50. This method is inadequate, because it provides only a general account of what was discussed at the theory conference. Nevertheless, much of the information on the procedures and content of the conference has been provided to me by Ruan Ming and Su Shaozhi, both of whom were participants and who have verified other accounts.

51. Zhang Xianyang and Wang Guixiu, "On the Nature of the Line of Lin Biao and the 'Gang of Four,'" *Renmin ribao*, February 28, 1979, FBIS, March 1, 1979, p. E7. In my article "Hu Yaobang's Intellectual Network and the Theory Conference of 1979," *China Quarterly*, no. 126 (June 1991), I incorrectly identified Wang Guixiu as Zhang's wife.

52. Wang Ruoshui, "An Important Lesson of the 'Cultural Revolution' Is That We Must Oppose the Personality Cult," *Jing bao* (March 1989), 66–69, JPRS–C, no. 89078, July 27, 1989, p. 4.

53. Ibid., p. 7.

54. Li Honglin, *Lilun fengyun* (Theoretical storms) (Beijing: Sanlian chubanshe, 1985), pp. 284–285. This is a collection of Li's articles written in the late 1970s and early 1980s.

55. Guo Luoji, "Let There Be a Full Emancipation of the Mind," *Renmin ribao*, January 23, 1978, p. 3, FBIS, February 3, 1978, pp. E14–15.

56. Guo Luoji, "Political Questions Can Be Discussed," *Renmin ribao*, November 14, 1979, p. 3, FBIS, November 19, 1979, p. L11.

57. Ibid., p. L12.

58. Ibid., p. L13.

59. Ding Xueliang, "Political Appeals and Social Consequences."

60. Su Shaozhi's speech, "On the Stages of Social Development after the Proletariat Has Seized Power," with a few revisions, was published in *Jingji yanjiu* (May 1979).

61. Liu Mingming, "Ultra-left Thinking Remains Barrier to Reform," *Jing bao* (October 1987), 42–46, JPRS–C, no. 87060, December 11, 1987, p. 13.

62. A copy of this speech was given to me by participant Ruan Ming.

63. Deng Xiaoping, "Uphold the Four Cardinal Principles," in *Selected Works of Deng Xiaoping (1975–1982)*, p. 181.

64. Ibid., p. 178.

65. Ibid., p. 183.

66. Ibid., p. 184.

67. Ibid., p. 180.

68. *Xuanchuan dongtai xuanbian, 1979* (Selections from Propaganda trends, 1979) (Beijing: Zhongguo shehui kexue chubanshe, 1981), p. 14.

69. Ibid., p. 15.
70. Ibid., p. 16.
71. Li Honglin, *Lilun fengyun,* p. 172.
72. Ibid., p. 183.
73. Ibid., pp. 183–184.
74. Ibid., p. 184.
75. Li Shu, "Thirty Years of Research in Social Sciences in China," *Lishi yanjiu,* November 15, 1979, pp. 3–10, JPRS–PSMA, no. 75064, February 5, 1980, p. 35.
76. Ibid., p. 36.
77. Ibid., p. 37.
78. Ibid., p. 36.
79. "The Political Science and Sociology Group of the Beijing Area Academic Symposium" *Guangming ribao,* October 24, 1979, pp. 1–3, FBIS, October 29, 1979, p. L7.
80. Ibid., p. L8.
81. Liang Fen, "Take a Correct Approach toward the Question of So-Called Human Rights," *Gongren ribao,* August 11, 1979, p. 3, FBIS, August 24, 1979, pp. L1–2.
82. Ibid., p. L1.
83. Ibid., p. L3.
84. Ibid.
85. "Strengthen the Legal System, Develop Democracy, Accelerate the Four Modernizations," *Renmin ribao,* July 5, 1979, FBIS, July 10, 1979, p. L6.
86. Ibid.

3. Political Openness, Literary Repression

1. Ruan Ming's copy of Deng Xiaoping's unpublished speeches, pp. 242–244. Li Weihan had married Deng's second wife.
2. Ibid.
3. Ruan Ming's copy of Hu Yaobang's unpublished speeches, pp. 248–254.
4. Ibid.
5. Ibid.
6. Deng Xiaoping, *Selected Works of Deng Xiaoping (1975–1982)* (Beijing: Foreign Languages Press, 1984), p. 303.
7. Ibid., p. 310.
8. Ibid., p. 311.
9. Ibid., p. 312.
10. Ibid., p. 315.

11. Ibid., p. 316.

12. Ibid., pp. 319, 323.

13. Ibid., p. 324.

14. Liao Gailong, "The '1980 Reform' Program of China," *Qishi niandai* (March 1981), FBIS, March 16, 1981, p. U12.

15. Ibid, p. U9.

16. Ibid.

17. Ibid., p. U11.

18. Feng Shen, "On Democratization," *Sixiang jiefang,* January 5, 1980, pp. 16–19, JPRS–PSMA, no. 75962, June 30, 1980, p. 64.

19. Ibid., p. 66.

20. Ibid., p. 67.

21. Shao Yanxiang, "One Should Never Look Forward to a 'Good Emperor,'" *Beijing wanbao,* August 7, 1980, p. 3, JPRS–PSMA, no. 76883, November 25, 1980, p. 38.

22. Ibid., p. 39.

23. Liao Mosha, "It is Good to Talk about the Emperor," *Beijing wanbao,* August 23, 1980, p. 3, JPRS–PSMA, no. 76883, November 25, 1980, p. 43.

24. *Dangfeng wenti* (The problem of party style) (Beijing: Zhongyang dangxiao chubanshe, 1981), p. 88, cited in Stuart Schram, "'Chinese Socialism': The Deng Experiment and the Future of Marxism-Leninism," paper presented at the International Conference on a Decade of Reform under Deng Xiaoping, Brown University, November 1987, p. 16.

25. Lu Zhichao, "Democracy Is Both a Means and an End," *Zhexue yanjiu,* December 25, 1980, pp. 6–12, JPRS–PSMA, no. 77613, March 18, 1981, p. 24.

26. Ibid., p. 29.

27. Ibid., p. 30.

28. Ibid.

29. Ibid., p. 31.

30. Interview in *Jing bao,* September 10, 1989, pp. 56–59, JPRS–PSMA, no. 89112, November 22, 1989, p. 58.

31. Yu Haocheng, "Achieving Freedom of the Press Is an Important Problem," *Dushu,* 1 (1981), 26–29, JPRS–PSMA, no. 77495, March 3, 1981, p. 20.

32. Ibid., p. 21.

33. Ibid., p. 22.

34. *Beijing ribao,* January 23, 1981, FBIS, January 26, 1981, p. L28.

35. Yu Xianyu, "The Legalization of Democracy and the Democratization of the Law," *Wenhui bao,* January 16, 1981, p. 3, JPRS–PSMA, no. 77968, April 30, 1981, p. 12.

36. Ibid., pp. 12–13.
37. Ibid., p. 13.
38. Ibid., p. 14.
39. Chen Chao, "Yi ben jieshao qimeng sixiangjia fan fengjian de jikan" (A collection introducing enlightened thinkers opposing feudalism), *Renmin ribao,* October 30, 1980, p. 5. The collection was edited by the Graduate Research Department of the History of Western Philosophy of CASS.
40. Guo Luoji, "Commenting on the Crisis of Faith," *Wenhui bao,* January 18, 1980, p. 3, JPRS–PSMA, no. 75320, March 17, 1980, p. 23.
41. Ibid., p. 24.
42. Ibid., p. 28.
43. Wang Ruoshui, "Marxism and Emancipation of the Mind," *Renmin ribao,* August 1, 1980, p. 5, JPRS–PSMA, no. 76474, September 23, 1980, pp. 28–30.
44. Ru Xin, "Does Humanism Mean Revisionism?—A Further Understanding of Humanism," *Renmin ribao,* August 15, 1980, p. 5, FBIS, August 21, 1980, pp. L11–12.
45. Wang Ruoshui, "On Estrangement," *Journalist Front,* no. 8 (1980), translated in *Selected Works on Studies of Marxism,* no. 12 (May 1981), edited by the Institute of Marxism-Leninism-Mao Zedong Thought of CASS.
46. Ruan Ming, "Ren de yihua dao ren de jiefang" (From man's alienation to man's liberation), originally in *Xin shiqi* (The new period), no. 1 (1981); reprinted in *Xinhua wenzhai,* no. 4 (1981), 17–20.
47. Wang Ruoshui, "On Estrangement," pp. 5–6.
48. Ibid., p. 6.
49. Ibid., p. 8.
50. Ibid., p. 10.
51. Ibid., p. 12.
52. Ibid., p. 16.
53. Yan Beiming, "A Discussion of Confucian Humanitarianism," *Wenhui bao,* August 3, 1981, p. 3, JPRS–PSMA, no. 79073, September 25, 1981, p. 42.
54. Author's conversation with Bai Hua, who worked with Wang Juntao in the late 1980s as a pollster.
55. Hu Ping, Wang Juntao et al., eds., *Kaituo—Beida xueyun wenxian* (Exploration—Peking University student movement materials) (Hong Kong: Tianyuan shuwu, 1990), p. 80.
56. Ibid., p. 84.
57. Ibid., p. 86.

58. Ibid., p. 87.

59. Ibid., p. 84.

60. Ibid., p. 109.

61. Although the Central Committee had ordered the official media not to publish the writings of the candidates not endorsed by the party, this article was reprinted in *Qingnian wengao* (*Youth*'s draft articles), published internally at CASS. Reprinted in *SPEAHRhead,* no. 12/13 (Northern Winter/Spring 1982), 38.

62. Ibid., p. 39.

63. "Opinions from the People's Deputies," *Beijing Review,* October 6, 1980, p. 27.

64. *Ming bao,* May 4, 1981, FBIS, May 4, 1981, p. W7.

65. Ibid., p. W8.

66. *Ming bao,* May 5, 1981, FBIS, May 6, 1981, p. W1.

67. Ibid.

68. Ibid., p. W2.

69. "Make an Effort to Depict the Heroic Deeds in Socialist Modernization," *Renmin ribao,* January 20, 1981, FBIS, February 9, 1981, p. L15.

70. Jia Chunfeng and Teng Wensheng, "On Strengthening Stability and Unity," *Guangming ribao,* February 16, 1981, FBIS, March 5, 1981, p. L19.

71. Perry Link, ed., *Stubborn Weeds* (Bloomington: Indiana University Press, 1983), p. 248.

72. Hu Yaobang, "Speech at Playwriting Forum (12 and 13 February 1980)," *Hongqi,* October 16, 1981, pp. 7–25, JPRS–RF, no. 79712, December 22, 1981, p. 26.

73. Ibid., p. 27.

74. *Guangjiao jing* (Wide angle) (May 1980), 31.

75. Feng Mu, "The Question of Innovations in Literature," *Renmin ribao,* February 11, 1981, p. 5, JPRS–PSMA, no. 77797, April 9, 1981, p. 50.

76. Ibid., p. 53.

77. Ibid., p. 51.

78. Feng Mu, "Random Chat on the Creation of New Poems," *Guangming ribao,* April 21, 1981, p. 4, JPRS–PSMA, no. 78576, July 22, 1981, p. 60.

79. Ibid., p. 63.

80. Ding Zhenhai, "The Question of 'For Whom' Is Still a Fundamental Question," *Hongqi,* May 16, 1981, pp. 13–17, FBIS, June 26, 1981, p. K19.

81. Ibid., p. K20.

82. Xia Yulong and Liu Ji, "It Is Also Necessary to Eliminate Erroneous 'Leftist' Influence on the Science and Technology Front," *Jiefang ribao,* June 2, 1981, p. 4, FBIS, June 11, 1981, p. K8.

83. Translated in Howard Goldblatt, ed., *Chinese Literature for the 1980s* (Armonk, N.Y.: M. E. Sharpe, 1982), p. 107.

84. Liu Binyan, *People or Monsters,* ed. Perry Link (Bloomington: Indiana University Press, 1983), p. 26.

85. Ibid., p. 43.

86. Liu Shaotang, "A Few Points I Feel Are Worthy of Attention in Literary and Artistic Works at Present," *Beijing wenyi* (April 1980), JPRS–PSMA, no. 76736, October 31, 1980, p. 88.

87. Ibid., p. 89.

88. *Wenyi bao* (October 1980), 24.

4. The Campaign against Bai Hua and Other Writers

1. The background information on Bai Hua is based on Richard Kraus, "The Political Authority of a Writer," in *China's Establishment Intellectuals,* ed. Carol Lee Hamrin and Timothy Cheek (Armonk, N.Y.: M. E. Sharpe, 1986), pp. 185–211.

2. Author's conversation with Bai Hua, summer 1986.

3. Ibid.

4. Bai Hua and Peng Ning, "Kulian" (Unrequited love), *Shiyue,* no. 3 (October 1979).

5. Translated in Michael Duke, *Blooming and Contending* (Bloomington: Indiana University Press, 1985), pp. 136–137.

6. Ibid., p. 144.

7. Author's conversation with Bai Hua, summer 1986.

8. Benjamin Schwartz, *China's Cultural Values* (Tempe: Center for Asian Studies, Arizona State University, 1985).

9. Bai Hua, "No Literature without a Breakthrough," *Renmin ribao,* Nov. 13, 1979, p. 3, JPRS–PSMA, no. 74748, Dec. 11, 1979, p. 101.

10. Ibid., pp. 98, 101.

11. Howard Goldblatt, ed., *Chinese Literature for the 1980s* (Armonk, N.Y.: M. E. Sharpe, 1982), p. 67.

12. Deng Xiaoping, "Opposing Wrong Ideological Tendencies," in *Selected Works of Deng Xiaoping (1975–1982)* (Beijing: Foreign Languages Press, 1984), p. 359.

13. Ibid., p. 356.

14. Zhang Changhuan, "The Issues and Lessons of 'Bitter Love,'" *Jiefang-jun bao,* May 15, 1981, p. 3, FBIS, May 29, 1981, p. K6.

15. Ibid., p. K8.

16. Author's conversation with Bai Hua, summer 1986.
17. Zhongguo Xinwenshe, May 25, 1981, JPRS–PSMA, no. 78286, June 12, 1981, p. 40.
18. *Zhengming*, August 1, 1981, p. 16, JPRS–PSMA, no. 79035, September 22, 1981, p. 93.
19. Ibid., p. 94.
20. Gu Yan, "Develop Healthy Literary and Art Criticism," *Renmin ribao*, June 8, 1981, p. 4, FBIS, June 10, 1981, p. K6.
21. *Wenyi bao*, May 22, 1981.
22. *Dagong bao* (Hong Kong), August 4, 1981, p. 2, FBIS, August 11, 1981, p. W5.
23. *Zhengming*, July 1, 1981, JPRS-PSMA, no. 78847, August 27, 1981, p. 67.
24. Deng Xiaoping, "Concerning Problems on the Ideological Front," in *Selected Works of Deng Xiaoping (1975–1982)*, p. 369.
25. Ibid., p. 370.
26. Ibid., p. 369.
27. Deng Xiaoping, "Suggestions on the Drafting of the 'Resolution on Certain Questions in the History of Our Party,'" *Hongqi*, July 1, 1983, pp. 2–15, JPRS–RF, no. 84307, September 13, 1983, p. 7.
28. Ibid., p. 10.
29. Ibid., p. 15.
30. Zheng Yong, "We Must Make Criticism and Self-Criticism," *Guangming ribao*, August 9, 1981, p. 3, FBIS, August 20, 1981, p. K6.
31. Ibid.
32. Commentary, "China Needs to Strengthen Literary and Art Criticism," Zhongguo Xinwenshe, August 26, 1981, FBIS, August 28, 1981, p. K6.
33. *Zhongguo qingnian bao*, September 1, 1981, p. 4, FBIS, September 17, 1981, p. K3.
34. Ibid., p. K5.
35. Hu Qiaomu, "Some Problems on the Present Ideological Front," *Hongqi*, December 1, 1981, pp. 2–22, FBIS, December 15, 1981, p. K19.
36. Ibid., p. K20.
37. "On the Erroneous Tendency of 'Unrequited Love,'" *Renmin ribao*, October 7, 1981, FBIS, October 14, 1981, p. K4.
38. Ibid.
39. Ibid., p. K6.
40. Chen Bo, "Films Should Contribute toward Developing a Socialist Spiritual Civilization," *Hongqi*, October 1, 1981, pp. 29–33, FBIS, October 28, 1981, p. K8.
41. Bai Hua, "Letter on 'Unrequited Love,'" *Renmin ribao*, December 24, 1981, p. 4, FBIS, December 29, 1981, p. K3.
42. Ibid.

43. Ibid., p. K4.
44. Ibid.
45. Ibid., p. K2.
46. *Liaoning ribao,* August 17, 1981, FBIS, August 26, 1981, p. K18.
47. Sun Changjiang, "The Attitude of Marxists toward Historical Experience," *Renmin ribao,* September 11, 1981, p. 5, FBIS, September 30, 1981, p. K22.
48. Sun Changjiang, *Zhenli de qiusuo* (Quest for truth) (Shanghai: Shanghai renmin chubanshe, 1989), p. 3.
49. Hu Qiaomu, "Some Problems on the Present Ideological Front," p. K6.
50. Ibid., p. K20.
51. Ibid., p. K21.
52. Ibid., p. K23.
53. Ibid., p. K29.
54. Author's conversation with Bai Hua, summer 1986.
55. Chen Bo, "Films Should Contribute toward Developing a Socialist Spiritual Civilization," p. K8.
56. This letter was obtained by the Taiwan *Zhongyang ribao,* November 20, 1981, p. 3, FBIS, November 30, 1981, p. V1.
57. Ibid., p. V2.
58. Ibid., p. V3.
59. Jin Xi and Yong Ren, "China's Theoreticians Step Up Study of Mao Zedong's Philosophical Thought," *Beijing ribao,* December 26, 1981, p. 1, FBIS, January 8, 1982, p. K5.
60. Hu Yaobang, "Speech at the Mass Meeting to Honor the Centenary of Lu Xun's Birth," *Hongqi,* October 1, 1981, pp. 2–6, JPRS–RF, no. 79619, December 9, 1981, p. 5.
61. Xinhua, December 29, 1981, FBIS, December 30, 1981, p. K10.
62. Zhongguo Xinwenshe, March 26, 1982, JPRS–PSMA, no. 80866, May 20, 1982, p. 113.
63. Ibid., p. 114.
64. Zhu Jian, "A Visit to Bai Hua in the Spring Rain," Zhongguo Xinwenshe, April 23, 1982, FBIS, April 26, 1982, p. K13.
65. *Zhengming,* no. 5 (1982), 33–34, JPRS–PSMA, no. 81484, August 9, 1982, p. 31.
66. Hu Qiaomu, "On Bourgeois Liberalization and Other Issues," *Hongqi,* no. 8 (1982), JPRS–RF, no. 81062, June 16, 1982, pp. 18–19.
67. Sun Jingxuan, "Dangerous Tendency and Profound Lesson," *Wenyi bao,* November 22, 1981, pp. 34–38, FBIS, January 26, 1982, p. K10.
68. Ibid., p. K11.
69. Ibid., p. K13.
70. Ibid., pp. K13–14.

71. Deng Xiaoping, "Concerning Problems on the Ideological Front," in *Selected Works of Deng Xiaoping (1975–1982)*, p. 367.

72. *Zhengming*, February 1, 1982, pp. 20–24, JPRS–PSMA, no. 80510, April 7, 1982, p. 63.

73. *Zhengming*, January 1, 1982, pp. 30–32, JPRS–PSMA, no. 80257, March 8, 1982, p. 72.

74. Translated in Helen F. Siu and Zelda Stern, eds., *Mao's Harvest* (New York: Oxford University Press, 1983), p. 161.

75. *Zhengming*, February 1, 1982, JPRS–PSMA, no. 80510, April 7, 1982, p. 67.

76. *Zhengming*, March 1985, pp. 34–38, JPRS–PSMA, no. 85054, June 5, 1985, p. 103.

77. For background on Wang Ruowang, see Kyna Rubin, "Keeper of the Flame: Wang Ruowang as a Moral Critic of the State," in *China's Intellectuals and the State*, ed. Merle Goldman with Timothy Cheek and Carol Lee Hamrin (Cambridge: Council on East Asian Studies, Harvard University, 1987), pp. 233–250.

78. Wang Ruowang, "A Gust of Cold Wind in the Spring," *Guangming ribao*, July 20, 1979, p. 4, FBIS, August 14, 1979, pp. L16–21.

79. Wang Ruowang, "On 'Governing by Doing Nothing' in Literature and Art," *Hongqi*, September 2, 1979, pp. 46–52, JPRS–RF, no. 74503, November 1, 1979, p. 85.

80. Ibid., p. 86.

81. Originally published in *Shouhuo*, no. 1 (1980); reprinted in *Dong xiang*, May 16, 1981, pp. 18–20, JPRS–PSMA, no. 78450, July 6, 1981, p. 40.

82. *Zhengming*, no. 5 (1982), JPRS–PSMA, no. 81560, August 17, 1982, pp. 97–98.

83. *Shidai de baogao*, December 25, 1981, pp. 46–51, JPRS–PSMA, no. 81068, June 16, 1982, p. 59.

84. De Min, "A Good Momentum," *Renmin ribao*, August 21, 1982, p. 1, FBIS, August 25, 1982, p. K4.

85. Zhao Yiya, "Communist Ideology Is the Core of Socialist Civilization," *Jiefangjun bao*, September 27, 1982, p. 1, FBIS, September 29, 1982, p. K4.

86. Ibid., p. K6.

87. *Jiefangjun bao*, September 27, 1982, FBIS, October 4, 1982, p. K2.

88. Ibid., p. K6.

89. Ibid., p. K8.

90. Commentator, "A Scientific Understanding and Handling of Questions Concerning Class Struggle," *Jiefangjun ribao*, October 8, 1982, FBIS, October 12, 1982, p. K6.

91. *Ming bao,* October 22, 1982, p. 5, FBIS, October 22, 1982, p. W3.
92. "A Different Opinion on 'the 16 Years' Proposition—Summaries of Statements Made at Forum Convened by This Journal's Editorial Department," *Anhui wenxue,* no. 2 (June 1982), 71–76, 79, JPRS–PSMA, no. 82070, October 25, 1982, p. 76.
93. Yu Dong, "A Noteworthy Question of Principle," *Wenyi bao,* April 7 1982, pp. 50–51, JPRS–PSMA, no. 82070, October 25, 1982, p. 69.
94. "The Key to the Present Implementation of the Policy toward Intellectuals," *Renmin ribao,* October 21, 1982, p. 1, FBIS, October 22, 1982, pp. K7–8.
95. Yu Yizu, "Preliminary Evaluation on an Article in *Wenyi bao,*" *Shidai de baogao* (August 1982), 43–51, JPRS–PSMA, no. 82556, December 29, 1982, p. 64.
96. Editorial Department, "Self-Criticism for Publishing an Article with Grave Mistakes," *Jiefang ribao,* November 16, 1982, p. 1, FBIS, November 22, 1982, p. K4.
97. "Put Right the Various Types of Anti-Intellectual Prejudice," *Jiefangjun bao,* January 8, 1983, FBIS, January 10, 1983, p. W5.

5. The Revival and Suppression of Political Discourse

1. "Hu Yaobang's Report to the 12th Party Congress," Xinhua, September 7, 1982, FBIS, September 8, 1982, p. K12.
2. Ibid., p. K15.
3. Xu Bing, "Building a High Level of Socialist Democracy Is Important Guarantee for Developing a Socialist Spiritual and Material Civilization," Beijing Radio, October 3, 1982, FBIS, October 6, 1982, p. K10.
4. Zhang Youyu, "Build a High Level of Socialist Democracy," *Renmin ribao,* September 14, 1982, p. 5, FBIS, September 24, 1982, p. K7.
5. Ibid., p. K8.
6. Yu Haocheng, "The New Constitution Has Developed Socialist Democracy," *Renmin ribao,* December 20, 1982, p. 5, FBIS, December 28, 1982, p. K15.
7. Li Honglin, "The Authority of Democracy," *Renmin ribao,* March 1, 1982, p. 5, FBIS, March 12, 1982, p. K16.
8. Ibid., p. K17.
9. *Beijing ribao,* May 31, 1982, p. 3.
10. Zhou Yang, "Carry Forward the Spirit of the 12th CPC National Congress," *Renmin ribao,* January 5, 1983, FBIS, January 12, 1983, p. K22.
11. Xinhua, January 7, 1983, FBIS, January 14, 1983, p. K17.

12. Zhao Xun, "Some Ideas Concerning Reform of the China Federation of Literature and Art Circles," *Guangming ribao*, February 19, 1983, FBIS, March 3, 1983, p. K7.

13. Hong Tianguo, "Pay Attention to Developing the Role of Intellectuals in Building the Four Modernizations," *Renmin ribao*, January 20, 1983, p. 4, JPRS–PSMA, no. 83026, March 8, 1983, pp. 32–33.

14. Lu Jiaxi, "Strive to Create a New Situation in the Field of Science," *Renmin ribao*, September 23, 1982, p. 3, FBIS, September 30, 1982, p. K7.

15. Zhang Guangnian, "The Glorious Duty of Literary and Art Circles," *Renmin ribao*, September 29, 1982, p. 5, FBIS, October 1, 1982, p. K12.

16. Qiang Xiaochu, "Maintaining Political Unity with the Central Committee Is the Guarantee for Creating a New Situation," *Renmin ribao*, October 20, 1982, p. 2, FBIS, October 22, 1982, p. K12.

17. This article was called to my attention by David Kelly, the foremost Western interpreter of Wang Ruoshui's thought and the development of Marxist humanism in China. *Wenhui bao*, January 17, 1983, p. 3, JPRS–PSMA, no. 82880, February 16, 1983, pp. 45, 55–56.

18. Su Shaozhi, "Develop Marxism under Contemporary Conditions," *Selected Studies on Marxism*, no. 2 (1983), 23.

19. Ibid., p. 32.

20. Hu Yaobang, speech of March 13, 1983, Xinhua, March 13, 1983, *Summary of World Broadcasts*, March 13, 1983, p. BII/3.

21. Ibid., p. BII/4.

22. Ibid.

23. Ibid., p. BII/6.

24. Ibid., pp. BII/6–7.

25. Zhou Yang, "Examination of Several Theoretical Questions about Marxism," *Renmin ribao*, March 16, 1983, pp. 4–5, JPRS–PSMA, no. 83267, April 15, 1983, p. 58.

26. Ibid., p. 60.

27. Ibid., p. 62.

28. Information on the response to Zhou Yang's speech comes from Wang Ruoshui and Su Shaozhi, who were in the audience.

29. Author's conversation with Wang Ruoshui, summer 1986.

30. Ru Xin, "New Tasks Faced by Marxist Philosophy," *Renmin ribao*, July 20, 1983, p. 5.

31. Su Shaozhi, "Shekeyuan Ma-Lie Suo" (The Marxist-Leninist Institute of CASS), manuscript, p. 5.

32. Deng Xiaoping, *Fundamental Issues in Present-Day China* (Beijing: Foreign Languages Press, 1987), p. 30.

33. Ibid., pp. 30–31.
34. Ibid., p. 32.
35. Ibid., p. 33.
36. Ibid., p. 35.
37. "It Is Imperative to Eliminate Spiritual Pollution in Building Civility in Villages and Towns," *Renmin ribao*, November 8, 1983, pp. 1–2, FBIS, November 14, 1983, p. K6.
38. "Leading Cadres Must Take the Lead in Resisting Spiritual Pollution," *Jingji ribao*, October 28, 1983, p. 1, JPRS–PSMA, no. 84831, November 28, 1983, p. 82.
39. Jin Ping, "Eliminate Spiritual Pollution, Make Economic Science Flourish," *Guangming ribao*, November 20, 1983, p. 3, FBIS, December 8, 1983, p. K9.
40. Liu Guoguang, "Eliminating Spiritual Pollution in the Field of Economics," *Jingji ribao*, November 8, 1983, p. 3, FBIS, November 17, 1983, p. K7.
41. Lin Mohan, "On Humanism and Other Issues," *Guangming ribao*, December 25, 1983, pp. 1, 3, JPRS–PSMA, no. 84019, March 5, 1984, p. 29.
42. Xue Zhongxin, "Questions and Answers on 'Alienation' and Humanism," *Banyue tan*, November 25, 1983, pp. 26–28, JPRS–PSMA, no. 84023, March 28, 1984, p. 34.
43. *Zhengming*, February 1, 1984, pp. 6–11, FBIS, February 7, 1984, p. W6.
44. Xinhua, November 17, 1983, FBIS, November 18, 1983, p. K9.
45. "Problems in Economic Reforms Cannot Be Regarded as Spiritual Pollution," *Gongren ribao*, December 12, 1983, p. 1, FBIS, December 21, 1983, p. K1.
46. "The Most Important Political Guarantees," *Renmin ribao*, November 4, 1983, p. 1, FBIS, November 9, 1983, p. K5.
47. "Build Spiritual Civilization, Oppose Spiritual Pollution," *Renmin ribao*, November 16, 1983, FBIS, November 17, 1983, p. K4.
48. Xinhua, November 28, 1983, FBIS, December 2, 1983, p. K1.
49. Xinhua, December 23, 1983, FBIS, December 29, 1983, p. K14.
50. Lin Mohan, "Eliminating Spiritual Pollution and Boosting Socialist Literature and Art," *Hongqi*, December 26, 1983, pp. 33–35, FBIS, January 18, 1984, p. K1.
51. Liu Baiyu, "Eliminate Spiritual Pollution, Promote the Prosperity of Literature and Art Creation," *Hongqi*, January 1, 1984, pp. 23–25, FBIS, January 31, 1984, p. K1.
52. "Importance of Eliminating Spiritual Pollution on the Theoretical Front," November 24 forum, *Renmin ribao*, December 1, 1983, p. 5.
53. Author's conversation with Wang Ruoshui, April 1989.

54. Stuart Schram has analyzed this speech, as well as the spiritual pollution campaign, in depth in his *Ideology and Policy in China since the Third Plenum, 1978–1984* (London: Contemporary China Institute, School of Oriental and African Studies, 1984).

55. Wang Ruoshui, "My Views on Humanism," *Jing bao,* June 10, 1984, pp. 24–32, FBIS, August 10, 1984, p. W15–16.

56. Ibid., p. W17.

57. Wang Ruoshui, "The Pain of Wisdom," reprinted in *Jing bao* (May 1985), 25–27, JPRS–PSMA, no. 85083, August 16, 1985, p. 148.

58. *Zhengming,* January 1, 1984, pp. 9–12, FBIS, January 26, 1984, p. W4.

59. Xinhua, November 5, 1983, FBIS, November 7, 1983, p. K18.

60. Ibid., p. K19.

61. "Eliminating Spiritual Pollution Is Also a Kind of Emancipation of the Mind," *Renmin ribao,* November 12, 1983, p. 1, FBIS, November 14, 1983, p. K4.

62. Jin Ping, "Eliminate Spiritual Pollution, Make Economic Science Flourish," FBIS, p. K9.

63. See Xing Bensi, "The Alienation Issue and Spiritual Pollution," *Renmin ribao,* November 5, 1983, p. 5, FBIS, November 7, 1983, p. K9.

64. Wang Meng, "Be an Ordinary Soldier in the Ranks of the Party," *Hongqi,* November 16, 1983, pp. 17–19, FBIS, December 12, 1983, p. K17.

65. Zhang Zhixiu and Lin Yantian, "Correctly Conduct Criticism and Self-Criticism, Conscientiously Solve the Contradictions within the Party," *Hongqi,* November 1, 1983, pp. 2–6, FBIS, December 2, 1983, p. K8.

66. Xinhua, November 9, 1983, FBIS, November 14, 1983, p. K11.

6. Radical Revisions of Ideology and Political Procedures

1. See Hong Yung Lee, *From Revolutionary Cadres to Party Technocrats in Socialist China* (Berkeley: University of California Press, 1991).

2. Xinhua, November 19, 1984, FBIS, November 21, 1984, p. K7.

3. "Cultivate Revolutionary Guts, Temper the Ability to Make Decisions—To Intellectuals Newly Elected to Leading Posts," *Guangming ribao,* September 3, 1984, p. 1, FBIS, September 19, 1984, pp. K11–12.

4. Su Shaozhi and Ding Xueliang, "Marx's Predictions on the Era of Information," *Renmin ribao,* August 24, 1984, p. 5, FBIS, September 14, 1984, p. K12.

5. Ibid., p. K14.

6. Ibid., p. K17.

7. "Carry Out in a Deep Going Way Education in Thoroughly Negating the 'Cultural Revolution,'" *Hongqi,* July 16, 1984, pp. 14–15, JPRS–RF, no. 84017, September 19, 1984, p. 23.

8. "Eliminate 'Leftist' Pernicious Influence and Correct Weakness and Laxity," *Renmin ribao,* April 1, 1984, p. 1, FBIS, April 2, 1984, p. K1.

9. *Zhengming,* July 1984, pp. 56–58, JPRS–PSMA, no. 84061, September 11, 1984, p. 115.

10. Li Honglin, "Socialism and Opening to the Outside World," *Renmin ribao,* October 15, 1984, p. 5, FBIS, October 17, 1984, p. K9.

11. Lu Binyan, "Certain Questions Concerning the Relationship between Party Policies and State Laws," *Faxue Jikan* (July 1984), 3–7, JPRS–PSMA, no. 84068, October 15, 1984, pp. 32–33.

12. Ibid., p. 35.

13. Ibid., p. 36.

14. Ibid., p. 37.

15. "Bold Attempt at Reforming the Cadre System," *Renmin ribao,* November 13, 1984, p. 1, FBIS, November 14, 1984, p. K10.

16. Su Shaozhi, "Shekeyuan Ma-Lie Suo," manuscript, p. 6.

17. "Theory and Practice," *Renmin ribao,* December 7, 1984, p. 1, FBIS, December 7, 1984, p. K1.

18. "More on Theory and Practice," *Renmin ribao,* December 21, 1984, p. 1, FBIS, December 21, 1984, p. K2.

19. *Zhengming,* March 1, 1985, pp. 6–10, JPRS–PSMA, no. 85044, May 15, 1985, pp. 100–102.

20. Ibid., p. 102.

21. Yuan Ying, "Eliminate the Pernicious 'Leftist' Influence, Promote the Prosperity of Literary Creation," *Renmin ribao,* December 10, 1984, p. 7, FBIS, December 14, 1984, p. K3.

22. Ibid., p. K2.

23. Ibid., p. K3.

24. Hu Qili, speech given at the Fourth Congress of the Chinese Writers Association, Xinhua, December 29, 1984, FBIS, December 31, 1984, p. K5.

25. Zhang Guangnian, speech, ibid., p. K8.

26. Wang Meng, "The Golden Age of Socialist Literature Has Come," *Renmin ribao,* January 6, 1985, p. 3, FBIS, January 14, 1985, p. K17.

27. *Zhengming,* March 1985, pp. 11–12, JPRS–PSMA, no. 85054, June 5, 1985, p. 97.

28. Ibid., p. 98.

29. Ke Ling, "Concentrate Efforts on Rooting Out Stubborn 'Leftist' Disease," *Renmin ribao,* December 31, 1984, p. 7, FBIS, January 9, 1985, p. K9.

30. Author's conversation with Liu Binyan, summer 1986.

31. *Zhengming,* February 1, 1985, pp. 6–10, FBIS, February 7, 1985, pp. W1–8.

32. Ding Ximan, "Only by Enhancing Morale Can There Be Great Prosperity," *Wenyi bao,* no. 11, November 7, 1984, pp. 5–6, FBIS, December 27, 1984, p. K23.

33. Bai Hua, "March Rapidly Forward," *Renmin ribao,* December 31, 1984, p. 7, FBIS, January 4, 1985, p. K4.

34. *Zhengming,* July 1985, pp. 44–45, JPRS–PSMA, no. 85101, September 27, 1985, p. 108.

35. Ibid., pp. 108–109.

36. Ibid., p. 110.

37. Author's conversation with Liu Binyan, summer 1986.

38. Liu Nan, "A Prelude to the Reform of China's Literary Circles," Zhongguo Xinwenshe, January 7, 1985, FBIS, January 10, 1985, p. K12.

39. Xinhua, January 9, 1985, FBIS, January 10, 1985, p. K11.

40. Liao Mosha, "Keep an Eye on the 'Leftist Specter,'" *Liaowang,* February 4, 1985, p. 41, JPRS–PSMA, no. 85063, June 25, 1985, p. 34.

41. Deng Youmei, "We Have Arrived at the Best Time for Literature and Art Creation," *Renmin ribao,* February 4, 1985, p. 7, FBIS, February 12, 1985, p. K7.

42. Chen Dengke, "The Spring Breeze Caresses Our Faces, Enthusiasm Is Running High," *Renmin ribao,* February 4, 1985, p. 7, FBIS, February 8, 1985, p. K15.

43. Ibid., p. K16.

44. Liu Binyan, "Freedom of Creation," *Jing bao* (February 1985), 6–8, JPRS–PSMA, no. 85090, September 11, 1985, p. 126.

45. *Xinwen jizhe,* no. 1, 1985; reprinted in *Zhengming,* June 1, 1985, FBIS, June 6, 1985, p. W6.

46. *Kaituo* (Pioneer), no. 1 (March 1985).

47. For a biography of Ni Yuxian, see Anne F. Thurston, *A Chinese Odyssey* (New York: Charles Scribner's Sons, 1991).

48. "A Second Kind of Loyalty," *Zhongguo baokan,* February 13, 1985, p. 4, JPRS–PSMA, no. 86004, January 15, 1986, p. 36.

49. Liu Xiaobo's critique of Liu Binyan appeared in Hong Kong journals. See Geremie Barmé and Linda Jaivin, eds., *New Ghosts, Old Dreams: Chinese Rebel Voices* (New York: Times Books, 1992), p. 177.

50. Hu Yaobang, "On the Party's Journalism Work," *Renmin ribao,* April 14, 1985, pp. 1, 2, 3, FBIS, April 15, 1985, p. K8.

51. Ibid.

52. Twenty percent was actually more than was currently used.

53. Hu Yaobang, "On the Party's Journalism Work," FBIS, p. K9.

54. Ibid., p. K3.

55. Ibid., p. K12.

56. Su Shaozhi, "Shekeyuan Ma-Lie Suo," manuscript, p. 6.

57. Xinhua, March 10, 1985, FBIS, March 12, 1985, p. K1.
58. Xinhua, April 18, 1985, FBIS, April 19, 1985, p. K23.
59. Hu Yaobang, "On Some Questions Concerning Current Literature and Art Work," *Zhengming,* October 1, 1985, pp. 62–66, FBIS, October 4, 1985, p. W1.
60. Author's conversation with Su Shaozhi.
61. Hu Qiaomu, "Carry Forward Patriotism," *Zhongguo qingnian bao,* July 3, 1985, pp. 1, 2, FBIS, July 15, 1985, p. K9.
62. Xinhua, June 29, 1985, FBIS, July 1, 1985, p. K3.
63. Xinhua, June 30, 1985, FBIS, July 2, 1985, p. K6.
64. Liu Binyan, "Our Changing Atmosphere," *China Reconstructs* (May 1985), 35.
65. Liu Binyan's self-evaluation was published in *Neibu cailiao* (Internal materials), September 3, 1985, translated in *Chinese Law and Government,* 21, no. 2 (Summer 1988), 23.
66. Ibid., p. 27.
67. Ibid., p. 29.
68. Ibid., p. 31.
69. Lu Keng, interview with Hu Yaobang on May 10, 1985, *Baixing,* June 1, 1985, pp. 3–16, translated in *An Interview with Hu Yaobang* (New York: Sino Daily Express, 1985), p. 41.
70. Ibid., p. 43.
71. Ibid., p. 46.
72. Hu Jiwei, "Study Journalism in the Period of Socialist Construction," *Renmin ribao* (overseas ed.), August 4, 1985, p. 2, FBIS, August 7, 1985, p. K17.
73. Ibid., p. K14.
74. Ibid., p. K16.
75. *Zhengming,* June 1, 1986, pp. 6–10, FBIS, June 12, 1986, p. W9.
76. Xinhua, May 30, 1985, FBIS, June 3, 1985, p. K3.
77. *Qunyan,* November 7, 1985.
78. *Baixing,* October 16, 1985, pp. 3–5, JPRS–PSMA, no. 86004, January 15, 1986, p. 50.
79. Zhang Xianliang, *Half of Man Is Woman,* trans. Martha Avery (New York: Viking, 1988).
80. *Dagong bao,* April 3–9, 1986, p. 7, FBIS, April 3, 1986, p. W6.
81. Zhang Xinxin, "My Views on the Depiction of Sexual Psychology in 'The Other Half of Man Is Woman,'" *Wenyi bao,* December 28, 1985, p. 2, JPRS–PSMA, no. 86057, July 7, 1986, p. 79.
82. Ibid.
83. Wang Ruoshui, "On 'Revolutionary Humanism,'" *Gongren ribao,* June 21, 1985, FBIS, June 24, 1985, p. K2.

84. Zhang Xianyang and Wang Guixiu, "Master Marxist Theory in Light of New Realities," *Renmin ribao,* November 1, 1985, p. 5, FBIS, November 8, 1985, pp. K10–11.

85. Xinhua, March 19, 1985, FBIS, March 20, 1985, p. K4.

86. Sun Ziyu, "Science's Prosperity and Academic Freedom," *Hongqi,* May 1, 1985, pp. 33–35, JPRS–RF, no. 85014, July 11, 1985, p. 59.

87. An article originally in *Wenhui bao,* excerpts in "Free Exchange of Thought Leads to Academic Progress," *China Daily,* February 12, 1985, p. 4.

88. Ma Ding, "Ten Major Changes in China's Study of Economics," *Gongren ribao,* November 2, 1985, FBIS, May 22, 1986, pp. K3–6.

89. Ibid., p. K8.

90. Deng Weizhi, "Caution Is Required in Criticizing Theoretical Liberalism," *Wenhui bao,* April 2, 1986, p. 3, JPRS–PSMA, no. 86057, July 7, 1986, p. 73.

91. Yu Guangyuan, "Marxism and the Socialist Construction," *Wenhui bao,* April 2, 1986, p. 3, JPRS–PSMA, no. 86057, July 7, 1986, p. 24.

92. Ma Ding, "Ten Major Changes in China's Study of Economics," *Shijie jingji daobao,* April 7, 1986, pp. 12–13.

93. *Zhengming,* June 1, 1986, pp. 6–10, FBIS, June 12, 1986, p. W9.

94. Xu Jingchun, "Leaders Should Rise Up to Protect the Initiative and Enthusiasm of Explorers," *Shijie jingji daobao,* May 12, 1986, p. 6, FBIS, May 21, 1986, p. K1.

7. Beyond the Limits of Discourse

1. Chen Haodi, "Create an Atmosphere of Democracy, Harmony, and Trust," *Liaowang* (overseas ed.), June 2, 1986, pp. 4–6, FBIS, June 4, 1986, p. K5.

2. Ibid., p. K6.

3. "Steadily Carry Out Policies, Solve Problems on the Basis of Seeking Truth from Facts," *Liaowang* (overseas ed.), August 4, 1986, pp. 7, 8, FBIS, August 13, 1986, p. K10.

4. *Beijing Review,* June 30, 1986, p. 6.

5. Mi Bohua, "Free Airing of Views and Social Progress," *Guangming ribao,* July 13, 1986, p. 1, FBIS, July 24, 1986, p. K9.

6. "The Legal System Is an Important Matter Which Has a Bearing on the Overall Situation," *Liaowang* (overseas ed.), July 21, 1986, pp. 9–11, FBIS, August 13, 1986, p. K15.

7. Author's conversation with Wu Guoguang, a former writer of commentator articles for the *People's Daily.*

8. "The Chinese Leadership Stratum Attaches Major Importance to Mak-

ing a Democratic and Scientific Process out of Policy-Making," *Liao-wang* (overseas ed.), August 11, 1986, pp. 6–7, FBIS, August 20, 1986, p. K10.

9. Ibid., p. K11.
10. Liu Chiang, "Wan Li Meets Liu Binyan," *Jing bao,* September 10, 1986, pp. 26–28, FBIS, September 19, 1986, p. K2.
11. Ibid. Liu Binyan has confirmed the accuracy of this account.
12. Su Shuangbi, "Several Questions Concerning the Promoting of the 'Contention of a Hundred Schools of Thought,'" *Guangming ribao,* April 30, 1986, p. 3, FBIS, May 19, 1986; p. K8.
13. Yu Haocheng, "The Double Hundred Policy and Its Guarantee by the Legal System," *Renmin ribao,* May 30, 1986, p. 5, FBIS, June 2, 1986, p. K11.
14. Sun Jiazheng, "Relaxation, Tolerance, and Something Else," *Xinhua ribao,* June 23, 1986, p. 1, FBIS, July 8, 1986, p. K11.
15. Ibid., p. K12.
16. Du Feijin, "Talking about the 'Double Hundred' Policy and Its Guarantee by the Legal System," *Renmin ribao* (overseas ed.), June 15, 1986, p. 2, FBIS, June 25, 1986, p. K17.
17. Leng Dong, "How Can the Party's Voice Be Relaxed and Harmonious," *Zhengming,* September 1986, pp. 36–37, JPRS–PSMA, no. 86086, December 18, 1986, p. 28.
18. Xiang Pu, "Media Reform Stirs Lively Public Debate," *China Daily,* September 29, 1986, p. 4.
19. Sun Xupei, "Socialist Press Law Is a Law for the Protection of Freedom of the Press," *Wenhui bao,* August 30, 1986, p. 2, FBIS, September 12, 1986, p. K3.
20. Ibid.
21. Jiang Zaizhe, "Deng Xiaoping Enriches and Advances the Thought on Leadership System," *Mao Zedong sixiang yanjiu* (Chengdu), no. 4 (1986), 29–32, JPRS–PSMA, no. 87011, March 13, 1987, p. 21.
22. "Beijing Journal Discusses Reform of the Political Structure, Pointing Out That Its Essence Is Democratization," *Dagong bao* (Hong Kong), August 7, 1986, p. 3, FBIS, August 13, 1986, p. W5.
23. Yan Jiaqi, speech delivered at the Fairbank Center, Harvard University, fall 1987.
24. A number of Yan Jiaqi's articles are translated in David Bachman and Dali L. Yang, ed. and trans., *Yan Jiaqi and China's Struggle for Democracy* (Armonk, N.Y.: M. E. Sharpe, 1991).
25. Yan Jiaqi, "Reflections on the Goodness or Evil of Human Nature," *Xin guancha,* no. 17, September 10, 1986, pp. 15–16, JPRS–PSMA, no. 86081, November 6, 1986, p. 62.

26. Ibid., p. 63.

27. Yan Jiaqi, "Significance of a Fully Opened Cultural Domain to China's Modernization," *Nanfang ribao*, September 14, 1986, p. 1, 2, JPRS–PSMA, no. 86085, December 12, 1986, p. 18.

28. Ibid., p. 21.

29. Ibid.

30. Ch'iu Ch'iu-liang, "Yan Jiaqi Discusses Political Structure and Political Reform," *Jiushi niandai* (The nineties) (December 1986), 40–47, JPRS–PSMA, no. 87020, April 8, 1987, p. 42.

31. Ibid., p. 39.

32. Gu Wen, "Beginning the Talk with the 'Rubber Stamp,'" *Gongren ribao*, September 27, 1986, p. 3, FBIS, October 17, 1986, p. K4.

33. Yu Haocheng, "The Double Hundred Policy and Its Guarantee by the Legal System," *Renmin ribao*, May 30, 1986, p. 5, FBIS, June 2, 1986, p. K10.

34. Yu Haocheng's 1986 interview with *Jing bao*, "Questioning the 'Third Echelon,'" reprinted in *China Spring Digest* (November–December 1987), 64.

35. Ibid., p. 66.

36. Yu Haocheng, "On Tolerance," *Wenhui bao*, May 25, 1986, p. 2, JPRS–PSMA, no. 86065, August 27, 1986, p. 26.

37. Ibid., p. 27.

38. Fang Bin, "Wang Ruoshui Case Not Yet Settled," *Jing bao*, no. 9, September 10, 1986, pp. 39–41, FBIS, September 24, 1986, p. K4.

39. Li Honglin, "Modernization and Democracy," *Shijie jingji daobao*, June 2, 1986, pp. 12–13, FBIS, July 29, 1986, p. K27.

40. See Chapter 10.

41. Wang Ruoshui, "The Double Hundred Policy and Civil Rights," *Huasheng* (Voice of China), August 8, 1986, reprinted in *Zhengming*, September 1, 1986, *Summary of World Broadcasts*, September 10, 1986, FE8360, pp. BII/8–9.

42. Su Shaozhi, "Reform of the Political System and Opposition to the Influence of Feudalism," *Renmin ribao*, August 15, 1986, p. 5, FBIS, August 21, 1986, p. K7.

43. Kung Shuangyin, "Director of the Research Institute of Marxism-Leninism-Mao Zedong Thought under the Academy of Social Sciences of China on Political Reform," *Dagong bao* (Hong Kong), September 17, 1986, p. 2, FBIS, September 29, 1986, p. K16.

44. Su Shaozhi, "My Humble Opinions on Reforming the Political System," *Dushu*, September 10, 1986, pp. 3–9.

45. Yang Baikui, "Some Questions on China's Political Structural Reform," *Guangzhou yanjiu*, no. 2 (1987), 30–33, FBIS, May 11, 1987, p. K9.

46. Xinhua, July 11, 1986, FBIS, July 14, 1986, p. K10. James Seymour discusses their activities in his *China's Satellite Parties* (Armonk, N.Y.: M. E. Sharpe, 1987).

47. Xu Hong, "Power Should Be Placed under the Supervision of the People," Zhongguo Xinwenshe, July 30, 1986, FBIS, July 31, 1986, p. K2.

48. Information on this forum and on Zhu Houze's speech was provided by the political scientist Feng Shengbao, who attended the forum.

49. Deng Weizhi, "On the Issue of Diversification in the Development of Marxism," *Shehui kexue,* June 15, 1985, pp. 2–5, JPRS–PSMA, no. 86083, November 26, 1986, p. 43.

50. Deng Weizhi, "Enhance Liberal Atmosphere," *Jiefang ribao,* May 21, 1986, p. 4, JPRS–PSMA, no. 86065, August 27, 1986, pp. 37–39.

51. Cheng Danghong, "Huan Xiang Calls Attention to the Great Harm of Overestimating the Maturity of the Socialist System," *Shijie jingji daobao,* September 29, 1986, p. 1, FBIS, October 14, 1986, p. K2.

52. "Zhu Houze Discusses Theoretical Problems," *Wenzhai bao,* June 29, 1986, p. 6, FBIS, July 14, 1986, p. K23.

53. Hu Sheng, "Several Questions Concerning the Strengthening of the Study of Social Science," *Hongqi,* no. 9, May 1, 1986, pp. 3–11, FBIS, May 28, 1986, p. K19.

54. "'Cultural Revolution Has Lessons for All,'" *China Daily,* August 29, 1986, p. 4, FBIS, August 29, 1986, pp. K4–5.

55. Liu Zaifu, "Breaking Through and Deepening Literature in the New Period," *Renmin ribao,* September 8, 1986, p. 6, FBIS, September 18, 1986, p. K16.

56. Ibid., p. K20.

57. Wang Yongzhi and Xia Chunping, "Relaxation and Harmony Signify National Progress," Zhongguo Xinwenshe, July 17, 1986, FBIS, July 21, 1986, pp. K13–14.

58. Wang Meng, "It Is an Admonition and a Spiritual Asset," *Renmin ribao,* October 13, 1986, p. 7, FBIS, October 17, 1986, p. K1.

59. Wang Ruoshui, "The Double Hundred Policy and Civil Rights," *Huasheng,* August 8, 1986, p. 12, reprinted in *Zhengming,* September 1, 1986, *Summary of World Broadcasts,* September 10, 1986, FE8360, p. BII/12.

60. Wang Jiren, "Literature Is Not Merely Repentance," *Renmin ribao,* September 22, 1986, p. 7, FBIS, October 1, 1986, p. K8.

61. Li Honglin, "Modernization and Democracy," *Shijie jingji daobao,* June 2, 1986, pp. 12–13, FBIS, July 29, 1986, p. K28.

62. Yin Jindi, "An Interview with Chen Yong," *Liaowang* (overseas ed.), October 13, 1986, pp. 34–35, FBIS, October 17, 1986, p. K2.

63. Wu Jianguo, "'Reflections' on the Question of Freedom," *Hongqi,* Sep-

tember 1, 1986, pp. 32–38, JPRS–RF, no. 86020, October 15, 1986, p. 54.

64. Ibid., p. 58.

65. Ibid., p. 59.

66. *Zhengming,* December 1, 1986, pp. 9–12, FBIS, December 12, 1986, p. K12.

67. Wang Zhen, "Study, Uphold, and Development Marxism," *Lilun yuekan,* no. 10, October 25, 1986, pp. 1–2, FBIS, November 14, 1986, p. K14.

68. *Zhengming,* December 1, 1986, pp. 9–12, FBIS, December 12, 1986, p. K12.

69. Author's conversations with Ruan Ming, Liu Binyan, and Wang Ruoshui.

70. "Building Spiritual Civilization," *Liaowang,* September 15, 1986, p. 4, FBIS, September 29, 1986, p. K15.

71. "We Must Be Clear about Priorities in Political Structural Reform," *Jingji ribao,* September 24, 1986, p. 1, FBIS, October 3, 1986, p. K7.

72. *Zhengming,* September 1, 1986, pp. 6–10, JPRS–PSMA, no. 86079, October 17, 1986, p. 43.

73. Ruan Ming, *Deng Xiaoping diguo* (The empire of Deng Xiaoping) (Taiwan: Shibao chuban, 1992), p. 184.

74. Deng Xiaoping, "Remarks at the 6th Plenary Session of the Party's 12th Central Committee" (September 28, 1986), *Beijing Review,* no. 26, June 29, 1987, p. 14.

75. *Wenhui bao,* March 21, 1987, p. 1, FBIS, March 23, 1987, p. K13.

76. Author's conversation with Ruan Ming.

77. *Newsweek,* October 6, 1986.

78. Yu Guangyuan, "Marxism and the Building of the Spiritual Civilization," *Renmin ribao,* October 18, 1986, p. 5, FBIS, October 30, 1986, p. K11.

79. "More Discussion, Less Criticism," *Renmin ribao,* October 28, 1986, p. 1, FBIS, October 30, 1986, p. K16.

80. Ibid., p. K17.

81. *Zhengming,* December 1, 1986, pp. 9–12, FBIS, December 12, 1986, p. K14.

82. Li Legang, "Only by Promoting Political Democracy Is It Possible to Open Up the Road to Modernization," *Shijie jingji daobao,* November 3, 1986, p. 1, 13, JPRS–PSMA, no. 87009, February 23, 1987, p. 36.

83. Hu Sha, "Several Questions Regarding the Correct Appraisal and Treatment of Western Culture," *Guangming ribao,* November 22, 1986, pp. 1, 4, FBIS, December 11, 1986, p. K17.

84. Zhou Xiuqiang, "Approach Correctly the Civilization Created during

Bourgeois Rule," *Renmin ribao,* December 15, 1986, p. 5, FBIS, December 18, 1986, p. K15.

85. Yu Guangyuan, "Actually Build Up Spiritual Civilization in Regard to Opening Up to the Outside World," *Liaowang* (overseas ed.), October 8, 1986, p. 10, FBIS, October 9, 1986, p. K9.

86. Min Qi, "On the Function, Form, and Structure of Democracy," *Zhong-guo qingnian bao,* December 2, 1986, p. 4, FBIS, December 19, 1986, p. K11.

87. Ibid., p. K12.

88. Jiang Yaochun, "A Dialogue with Liu Binyan," *Minzhu yu fazhi,* September 20, 1986, pp. 12–13, JPRS–PSMA, no. 87002, January 14, 1987, p. 73.

89. Author's conversation with Wang Ruowang, summer 1986.

90. Information on Fang Lizhi's career comes from *Ziran bianzhengfa tongxun* (Journal of the dialectics of nature), November 6, 1986; Orville Schell, *Discos and Democracy* (New York: Pantheon Books, 1988); Fang Lizhi, *Bringing Down the Great Wall* (New York: Knopf, 1991); and discussion with James Williams, Fang's principal translator.

91. Orville Schell, "China's Andrei Sakharov," *Atlantic,* May 1988, p. 36.

92. Author's conversation with Fang Lizhi.

93. Fang Lizhi, speech delivered at Tongji University, November 18, 1986, in "Between Party and Principle: The Exit and Voice of Fang Lizhi, Liu Binyan, and Wang Ruowang," *Chinese Law and Government,* ed. James Tong, 21, no. 2 (Summer 1988), 88–89.

94. Ibid., p. 92.

95. Transcript reprinted in the *Washington Post,* January 18, 1987, p. C4.

96. *Ziran bianzhengfa tongxun,* November 4, 1986.

97. Xu Liangying, "Essay on the Role of Science and Democracy in Society," in Xu Liangying and Fan Dainian, *Science and Socialist Construction in China* (Armonk, N.Y.: M. E. Sharpe, 1982), p. 219.

98. Ibid., p. 218.

99. Ibid., p. 219.

100. Xinhua, December 3, 1986, FBIS, December 23, 1986, p. K19.

101. *Der Spiegel,* January 12, 1987, pp. 100–102, FBIS, January 21, 1987, p. K13.

102. *Agence France Presse,* January 6, 1987, FBIS, January 6, 1987, p. K2.

103. *New York Times,* January 11, 1987, p. E2.

104. Benedict Stavis, *China's Political Reforms* (New York: Praeger, 1988), p. 95. Also a useful analysis of the political discussion in Shanghai.

105. Ibid., p. 98.

106. *Washington Post,* January 11, 1987, p. A28.

8. The Campaign against Bourgeois Liberalization

1. *Beijing Review,* June 29, 1987, p. 15.
2. Deng Xiaoping, *Fundamental Issues in Present-Day China* (Beijing: Foreign Languages Press, 1987), p. 162.
3. Ibid., p. 164.
4. Zhongguo Xinwenshe, January 1, 1987, FBIS, January 2, 1987, p. K2.
5. Ibid., p. K3.
6. Ruan Ming, *Deng Xiaoping diguo* (The empire of Deng Xiaoping) (Taiwan: Shibao chuban, 1992), p. 189.
7. *Beijing Review,* June 29, 1987, p. 15.
8. Ibid., p. 16.
9. Ibid.
10. Ibid.
11. There were rumors that Yang Shangkun had threatened to send in troops against the demonstrators.
12. "Put Lofty Ideals into Practice in the Course of Wholeheartedly Serving the People," *Jiefangjun bao,* March 5, 1987, p. 1, FBIS, March 18, 1987, p. K22.
13. Ruan Ming, *Deng Xiaoping diguo,* pp. 200–203.
14. Author's conversation with Liu Binyan in 1988.
15. *Guangjiao jing* (Hong Kong), Feb. 16, 1987, pp. 6–9, FBIS, Feb. 20, 1987, p. K8.
16. *Zhengming,* May 1, 1987, pp. 10–11, FBIS, April 30, 1987, p. K1.
17. Lu Keng, *An Interview with Hu Yaobang* (New York: Sino Daily Express, 1985), p. 33.
18. *Zhengming,* May 1, 1987, pp. 10–11, FBIS, April 30, 1987, p. K1.
19. *Jiushi niandai,* June 1, 1987, pp. 30–32, FBIS, June 9, 1987, p. K9.
20. "Take a Clear-cut Stand in Opposing Bourgeois Liberalization," *Hongqi,* February 1, 1987, FBIS, February 19, 1987, p. K7.
21. Xinhua, January 27, 1987, FBIS, January 29, 1987, p. K11.
22. "Defend the Current Good Situation," *Zhongguo qingnian bao,* December 23, 1986, FBIS, December 24, 1986, p. K2.
23. "It Is Necessary to Proceed from Reality in Building Socialist Democracy," *Zhongguo qingnian bao,* December 25, 1986, FBIS, December 29, 1986, p. K8.
24. Li Jinkun and Cao Xiurong, "Several Experiences Concerning Marxist Education among University Students," *Hongqi,* February 1, 1987, pp. 17–22, FBIS, February 26, 1987, p. K15.
25. Ibid., p. K16.
26. "Questions and Answers on Opposing Bourgeois Liberalization," *Banyue tan,* February 25, 1987, pp. 6–9, FBIS, March 13, 1987, p. K12.

27. Li Zhun and Ding Zhenhai, "Uphold and Develop the Marxist Theory of Literature and Art through New Practice," *Hongqi*, January 16, 1987, pp. 17–23, JPRS–PSMA, no. 87021, April 19, 1987, p. 34.

28. Zhao Fusan, "Some Thoughts on Certain Aspects of Modern Western Culture," part 1, *Renmin ribao*, March 23, 1987, p. 5, FBIS, April 8, 1987, p. K32.

29. Ibid., part 2, *Renmin ribao*, March 24, 1987, p. 5, FBIS, April 15, 1987, p. K24.

30. Li Zhun, "The 'Modern Sense of Loneliness' and Socialist Literature and Art," *Guangming ribao*, June 30, 1987, p. 3, JPRS–C, no. 87038, August 25, 1987, p. 23.

31. Aang Kejia, "National Pride, Worshipping and Fawning on Things Foreign," *Guangming ribao*, February 21, 1987, p. 1, FBIS, March 4, 1987, p. K4.

32. Hou Mingan, "Roundup on Theoretical Discussion Meeting on Adhering to the Four Cardinal Principles and Opposing Bourgeois Liberalization," *Guangming ribao*, May 11, 1987, p. 3, FBIS, May 27, 1987, p. K4.

33. Gao Guang, "The Two-Party System Does Not Tally with China's National Conditions," *Guangming ribao*, May 28, 1987, p. 3, FBIS, June 12, 1987, pp. K8–9.

34. "Socialist China Cannot Advocate the Separation of the Legislative, Executive, and Judicial Powers," *Guangming ribao*, April 12, 1987, p. 3, FBIS, May 8, 1987, p. K11.

35. See Tony Saich, "The Chinese Communist Party at the Thirteenth Party Congress: Policies and Prospects for Reform," *Issues and Studies*, 25, no. 1 (January 1989), 11–40.

36. Talk with Chinese Journalists Association, September 3, 1986, in Fang Lizhi, *Bringing Down the Great Wall* (New York: Knopf, 1991), pp. 126–127.

37. Xinhua, February 25, 1987, FBIS, February 27, 1987, p. K12.

38. "Uphold the Four Cardinal Principles, Firmly Enforce Party Discipline," *Renmin ribao* (overseas ed.), January 25, 1987, p. 1, FBIS, January 27, 1987, p. K12.

39. *Wenhui bao*, April 7, 1987, p. 2, FBIS, April 8, 1987, p. K12.

40. "Take Practical Measures to Strike at Illegal Publication Activities," *Guangming ribao*, July 13, 1987, p. 1, FBIS, July 27, 1987, p. K13.

41. Xue Muqiao, "Continue to Push Forward the Science of Marxism," *Renmin ribao*, March 20, 1987, p. 5, FBIS, April 9, 1987, p. K34.

42. Hu Peizhao, "Adopt a Correct Attitude toward Western Economics," *Guangming ribao*, March 7, 1987, p. 3, FBIS, March 24, 1987, p. K27.

43. Yao Zengyin, "We Must Correctly Deal with Western Economics," *Qunyan,* January 7, 1987, pp. 16–18, FBIS, March 4, 1987, p. K39.

44. Xinhua, March 15, 1987, FBIS, March 16, 1987, p. K3.

45. Xinhua, March 14, 1987, FBIS, March 16, 1987, p. K9.

46. Author's conversation with Feng Shengbao, who was on one of the sub-committees of Zhao's political reform group.

47. "Speeches from Zhuozhou Conference, 1987," *Wenyi lilun yu piping,* January 24, 1990, pp. 60–68, JPRS–C, no. 90029, April 20, 1990, p. 34.

48. Yi Ren, "The Ins and Outs of the Zhuozhou Conference," *Wenyi lilun yu piping,* January 24, 1990, reprinted in *Renmin ribao,* February 14, 1990, p. 3, JPRS–C, no. 90029, April 20, 1990, p. 3.

49. Wu Guoguang and Charles Burton, manuscript, November 5, 1990, p. 6.

50. Zhao Ziyang, speech at meeting of Propaganda, Theoretical, Press, and Party School Cadres, May 13, 1987, Xinhua, July 8, 1987, FBIS, July 10, 1987, p. K3.

51. Ibid., pp. K5–6.

52. Ibid.

53. Ibid., p. K7.

54. Ruan Ming, *Deng Xiaoping diguo,* p. 210.

55. Liu Mingming, "Ultra-left Thinking Remains Barrier to Reform," *Jing bao* (October 1987), 42–46, JPRS–C, no. 87060, December 11, 1987, p. 14.

56. Ruan Ming, *Deng Xiaoping diguo,* p. 210.

57. *Zhengming,* September 1, 1987, pp. 12–14, FBIS, September 8, 1987, p. 22. The attacks on Yu Guangyuan are discussed by Su Shaozhi in his manuscript "Shekeyuan Ma-Lie Suo," p. 26.

58. *Huaqiao ribao* (China daily news), September 8, 1987. Wu Zuguang's letter was written on August 10, 1987, and was originally published in *Jing bao* (September 1987).

59. See the work by Stanley Rosen, ed., "Youth Socialization and Political Recruitment in Post-Mao China," *Chinese Law and Government,* 20, no. 2 (Summer 1987).

60. *Beijing Review,* August 31, 1987, p. 6.

61. The drafting process is described in Xinhua, November 3, 1987, FBIS, November 9, 1987, p. 24.

62. Wu Guoguang, "The Issues of Participation in the Political Reform: Pressures and Limitations," in *China: The Crisis of 1989,* vol. 2, ed. Roger V. Desforges (Buffalo: Council on International Studies and Programs, State University of New York, 1990), pp. 241–242.

63. Author's conversation with Feng Shengbao.

64. *Beijing Review,* November 9–15, 1987, p. xvii.
65. Ibid., pp. xix–xx.
66. Ibid., p. xx.
67. Ibid.
68. Ibid., p. xxi.
69. Ibid., p. xxii.
70. Stuart Schram, "China after the 13th Congress," *China Quarterly,* no. 114 (June 1988), 184.

9. The Return of the Democratic Elite

1. *South China Morning Post* and *Hong Kong Standard,* September 3, 1988, p. 7, FBIS, September 8, 1988, pp. 26–27.
2. Agence France Press, June 16, 1988, FBIS, June 17, 1988, pp. 25–26.
3. Wu Guoguang and Gao Shan, "Promote the Institutionalization of Socialist Democratic Politics in Our Country," *Hongqi,* November 4, 1987, pp. 43–48, FBIS, December 16, 1987, p. 14.
4. Ibid., p. 17.
5. Ibid., p. 18.
6. Yan Jiaqi, "'Separation of Party and Government Work' in China as Viewed from a Comparative Angle," *Wenhui bao,* March 23, 1988, p. 3, FBIS, April 14, 1988, p. 45.
7. Liu Juishao, "Yan Jiaqi Refuses to Serve Another Term," *Wenhui bao,* April 29, 1988, p. 7, FBIS, April 29, 1988, p. 13.
8. Yan Jiaqi, "From 'Non-procedural Politics' to 'Procedural Politics,'" *Shehui kexue,* August 15, 1988, pp. 3–7, JPRS–C, no. 88075, November 23, 1988, p. 38.
9. Ibid., p. 41.
10. Yan Jiaqi, "China Is No Longer a Dragon," *Renmin ribao,* May 23, 1988, p. 5, FBIS, June 8, 1988, p. 30.
11. Ibid., p. 31.
12. Ibid., p. 32.
13. *South China Morning Post,* June 20, 1988, p. 9, FBIS, June 20, 1988, p. 42.
14. Yuan Zhiming, "Random Talk on Power Worship," *Guangming ribao,* May 22, 1988, p. 3, FBIS, June 16, 1988, p. 25.
15. Xinhua, November 17, 1988, FBIS, November 22, 1988, p. 30.
16. Xinhua, April 1, 1988, FBIS, April 1, 1988, p. 35.
17. "Give Play to the Supervisory Role of the Media," *Renmin ribao,* May 22, 1988, p. 1, FBIS, May 26, 1988, p. 25.
18. Beijing Domestic Service, September 19, 1988, FBIS, September 23, 1988, p. 32.

19. Gan Xifen, "Many Voices, One Direction," *Shijie jingji daobao,* March 28, 1988, p. 15.

20. Peng Jianfen, "Press Reform Vital to Democratic Construction," *Shijie jingji daobao,* April 4, 1988, p. 15.

21. Yin Jindi, "For the Sake of the Flowering of Literature and Art," *Liaowang* (overseas ed.), April 10, 1989, pp. 3–5, FBIS, April 20, 1989, pp. 35–36.

22. Yang Lianghua and Qi Xin, "Minister of Culture Wang Meng Forecasts Cultural, Art Work in 1988," *Renmin ribao,* January 1, 1988, p. 2, FBIS, January 21, 1988, p. 14.

23. Huang Zhaocun, "Take Advantage of Guangdong's Strong Points in Reform and Opening Up—A Talk with Wang Meng Yesterday," *Yangcheng wanbao,* February 7, 1988, p. 1, FBIS, February 22, 1988, p. 13.

24. "Gain Fresh Understanding of Culture and Art Production under the Conditions of a Commodity Economy," *Guangming ribao,* February 29, 1988, p. 11, FBIS, March 16, 1988, p. 23.

25. Xinhua, November 17, 1987, FBIS, November 17, 1987, p. 28.

26. Yu Guangyuan, "The System of Socialist Commodity Economy Is the Foundation and Center of the New Economic System," *Jingji yanjiu,* no. 1, January 20, 1988, pp. 3–8, FBIS, March 8, 1988, pp. 36–37.

27. Su Shaozhi and Wang Yizhou, "Policy Making Must Be Open," *China Daily,* January 20, 1988, p. 4, FBIS, January 21, 1988, p. 9.

28. Yi Li, "'Retrogression' or 'Progress'?" *Liaowang* (overseas ed.), November 30, 1987, p. 1, FBIS, December 17, 1987, p. 15.

29. Zhongguo Xinwenshe, March 3, 1988, FBIS, March 9, 1988, p. 24.

30. Ibid., p. 25.

31. Xinhua, January 25, 1988, FBIS, January 26, 1988, p. 7.

32. "Emancipate the Mind," *Guangming ribao,* May 11, 1988, p. 1, FBIS, May 24, 1988, p. 21.

33. Hong Zhaolong, "Studying the Scientific Attitude of Marx and Engels toward the 'Manifesto,'" *Guangming ribao,* February 29, 1988, p. 3, FBIS, March 9, 1988, p. 19.

34. Ren Xinwen, "Roundup on Viewpoints Put Forward at Symposium on Restudying Capitalism," *Guangming ribao,* June 20, 1988, p. 3, FBIS, July 6, 1988, p. 44.

35. "Reunderstanding Capitalism and Socialism," *Liaowang* (overseas ed.), July 18, 1988, pp. 3–5, FBIS, July 25, 1988, p. 30.

36. Zhang Weiguo, "The Fruit of Science and Technology Grows on the Trees of Commodity Economy," *Shijie jingji daobao,* August 8, 1988, p. 2, FBIS, August 16, 1988, p. 34.

37. "The Idea and Slogan of Using Science to Save the Nation Should Be Reevaluated," *Renmin ribao* (overseas ed.), December 6, 1987, p. 2, FBIS, December 8, 1987, p. 17.

38. Zhang Weiguo, "Li Honglin on Reunderstanding Socialism," *Shijie jingji daobao,* April 11, 1988, p. 7, FBIS, April 28, 1988, p. 20.

39. Yu Wujin, "Several Paradoxes in Contemporary Chinese Culture," *Renmin ribao,* August 22, 1988, p. 5, FBIS, August 26, 1988, pp. 22–23.

40. Yang Yu, "Freedom and Zero Gravity," *Renmin ribao,* April 26, 1988, p. 5, FBIS, May 5, 1988, p. 26.

41. Su Dongbin, "China Is Heading toward 'New Socialism,'" *Guangming ribao,* March 27, 1989, p. 3, FBIS, April 11, 1989, p. 22.

42. Zhang Shuyi, "Statism—The Root Cause of All Defects of the Old System," *Shijie jingji daobao,* August 15, 1988, p. 15, FBIS, September 1, 1988, pp. 21–22.

43. Zhang Shuyi, "Democracy's Form of Realization Should Be Stressed," *Shijie jingji daobao,* April 25, 1988.

44. Gong Xiangrui, "The Key to Political Reforms Lies in the Introduction of Democratic Politics," *Shijie jingji daobao,* April 18, 1988, FBIS, May 11, 1988, pp. 21–22.

45. Cao Siyuan, "Thought on the Reform of the NPC System," *Shijie jingji daobao,* November 7, 1988, p. 13, FBIS, November 23, 1988, p. 23.

46. Ibid., pp. 24–25.

47. *Shijie jingji daobao,* October 31, 1988, p. 1, JPRS–C, no. 88079, December 14, 1988, p. 65.

48. Wang Ruoshui, "The Cult of the Individual and Intellectual Alienation," *Jing bao* (April 1988), 24–27, and (May 1988), 40–44; translated by David Kelly in ms., p. 2.

49. Ibid., p. 17.

50. Ibid., p. 18.

51. Chen Jinluo and She Dehu, "Social Groups Are an Important Force for Building Socialist Democratic Politics," *Renmin ribao,* April 29, 1988, p. 5, FBIS, May 12, 1988, p. 28.

52. Li Anshan, "Some Opinions on the Political Reform in China," *Xin guancha,* September 10, 1988, pp. 14–15, JPRS–C, no. 88078, December 8, 1988, p. 2.

53. Rong Jian, "Decline of Chinese Intellectuals Analyzed," *Lilun xinxi bao,* August 15, 1988, p. 3, JPRS–C, no. 88075, November 23, 1988, p. 6.

54. Su Shaozhi, "Some Problems of the Political Reform in China," *China Information,* 3, no. 2 (Autumn 1988), 36.

55. Su Shaozhi and Wang Yizhou, "Two Historic Tasks of Reform," *Renmin ribao,* March 5, 1988, p. 5, FBIS, March 9, 1988, p. 23.

56. This Guangdong provincial congress was described in *Dagong bao,* February 4–10, 1988, p. 2, FBIS, February 5, 1988, pp. 12–13.

57. Zhongguo Xinwenshe, October 28, 1988, FBIS, October 31, 1988, p. 31.

58. Peng Qiyan and Han Jiyou, "A Vice Governor Elected on the Direct Recommendation of the Delegates—An Interview with Liu Yuan," *Gongren ribao*, February 1, 1988, p. 2, FBIS, February 24, 1988, p. 24.
59. Li Li, "Multicandidate Election in Provinces," *Beijing Review*, 31, no. 37, September 12–18, 1988, p. 4.
60. Yan Xiaoming, "'We Know Why We Cast This Vote': An Eyewitness Report on the Election in Dingxiang County, Shanxi," *Renmin ribao*, November 27, 1987, p. 1, FBIS, December 8, 1987, pp. 15–16.
61. "Start with Developing Democracy at the Grass-Roots Level," *Renmin ribao*, November 27, 1987, p. 1, FBIS, December 8, 1987, pp. 15–16.
62. "Work Report of the Standing Committee of the NPC," *Renmin ribao*, April 19, 1988, pp. 2, 3, FBIS, April 27, 1988, p. 15.
63. Yu Zhongmin, "Political Democracy and Citizens' Right to Criticize," *Renmin ribao* (overseas ed.), April 21, 1988, p. 2, FBIS, April 25, 1988, p. 21.
64. Wang Houde, "Increase Transparency and Enhance the Degree of Opening Up," *Renmin ribao*, January 2, 1988, p. 5, FBIS, January 6, 1988, p. 11.
65. Xinhua, April 1, 1988, FBIS, April 1, 1988, p. 11.
66. Yau Shing-mu, "Voting for President, Vice Chairmen," *Hong Kong Standard*, April 9, 1988, pp. 1, 6, FBIS, April 12, 1988, p. 27.
67. Ibid., p. 26.
68. "Sense of Democracy of Chinese People's Deputies Is Still Insufficient According to a Sample Survey," Zhongguo Tongxunshe, June 27, 1988, FBIS, June 28, 1988, p. 20.
69. Zhang Xiaogang, "NPC Deputies Surveyed on Opinions," *China Daily*, July 9, 1988, p. 4, FBIS, July 11, 1988, p. 43.
70. "Unity Journal Discusses Political Reform," *China Daily*, February 29, 1988, p. 4, FBIS, February 29, 1988, p. 27.
71. Zhongguo Tongxunshe, April 1, 1988, FBIS, April 4, 1988, p. 47.
72. Xinhua, March 30, 1988, FBIS, April 1, 1988, p. 31.
73. Lin Caifen, "Wu Zuguang Sharply Criticizes CPC," *Ming bao*, April 11, 1988, p. 5, JPRS–C, no. 88026, May 31, 1988, p. 25.

10. The Beginning of Organized Opposition

1. Zhang Yide, "The *Guangming ribao* Editorial Department Holds a Forum Commemorating the Tenth Anniversary of the Discussion on Truth Criterion," *Guangming ribao*, May 7, 1988, p. 1, FBIS, May 17, 1988, p. 22.
2. Yu Guangyuan, "Commemorating the Tenth Anniversary of the Discussion on the Question Regarding the Criterion of Truth," *Renmin ribao*, May 6, 1988, p. 5, FBIS, May 12, 1988, p. 24.

3. Yang Xiguang, "There Is No End to Emancipation of the Mind," *Guangming ribao,* May 7, 1988, p. 2, FBIS, May 17, 1988, p. 24.
4. Ibid., p. 25.
5. Tao Kai, "Verify Truth by Experience and Gain Fresh Knowledge with Experience," *Guangming ribao,* May 5, 1988, p. 2, FBIS, May 17, 1988, p. 25.
6. "Emancipation of the Mind and Criterion of Practice," *Hongqi,* May 1, 1988, pp. 2–7, FBIS, May 26, 1988, p. 19.
7. "The Inside Story and New Interpretation of the Discussion on the Criterion of Truth on the Mainland," *Liaowang* (overseas ed.), May 16, 1988, pp. 3–5, FBIS, May 18, 1988, p. 19.
8. "He Shang" (River elegy) is described in detail by Frederic Wakeman in "All the Rage in China," *New York Review of Books,* March 2, 1989.
9. On the "cultural fever" discussion, see Leo Ou-fan Lee, "The Crisis of Culture," in *China Briefing 1990,* ed. Anthony J. Kane (Boulder: Westview Press, 1990), pp. 83–106.
10. *Ningxia ribao,* September 28, 1988, p. 1, FBIS, December 12, 1988, p. 25.
11. *Jing bao,* December 10, 1988, pp. 14–17, FBIS, December 16, 1988, p. 24.
12. *Boston Globe,* October 9, 1988, p. 15.
13. Li Chengdao, "Thoughts on Reading 'River Elegy,'" *Renmin ribao,* November 4, 1988, p. 3, FBIS, November 9, 1988, p. 44.
14. "Chinese Thinkers' Research Center of Nanjing University Holds Forum on 'River Elegy,'" *Guangming ribao,* November 20, 1988, p. 3, FBIS, December 14, 1988, p. 19.
15. Zhou Rong, "Behind the Scenes of the Chinese Literature and Art Congress," *Guangjiao jing,* November 16, 1988, pp. 6–9, FBIS, November 25, 1988, p. 26.
16. *Wenhui bao,* November 1, 1988, p. 1, FBIS, November 1, 1988, p. 21.
17. *Zhengming,* December 1, 1988, pp. 13–14, FBIS, December 6, 1988, p. 25.
18. Zhejiang Provincial Service, October 22, 1988, FBIS, October 31, 1988, p. 35.
19. Xia Yan, "Enhance Vigor, Promote Literature and Art," *Renmin ribao,* November 15, 1988, p. 5, FBIS, November 16, 1988, p. 25.
20. *Jing bao,* December 10, 1988, pp. 14–17, FBIS, December 16, 1988, p. 25.
21. "Forge Ahead in Unity to Promote the Flowering of Literature and Art," *Guangming ribao,* November 8, 1988, p. 1, FBIS, November 22, 1988, p. 24.
22. Author's conversation with Su Shaozhi.

23. "On Freedom to Discuss Theoretical Problems," Su Shaozhi's speech at the Theoretical Discussion Meeting marking the tenth anniversary of the Third Plenum of the Eleventh Central Committee, p. 1. Quotations are from the full text of the original speech, given to the author by Su Shaozhi.

24. Ibid., p. 3.

25. Ibid., pp. 3–4.

26. Ibid., p. 5.

27. Ibid.

28. Ibid., p. 6.

29. Ibid., p. 7.

30. Ibid., p. 9.

31. Ibid., p. 10.

32. *Jiushi niandai,* March 1, 1989, pp. 53–55, FBIS, March 2, 1989, p. 16.

33. Yu Guangyuan, Hu Qili et al., eds., *Mengxing de shike* (The Moment of awakening) (Beijing: Zhongwai wenhua chuban gongsi, April 1989).

34. Ibid., p. 1.

35. Ibid., pp. 105–143.

36. Ibid., pp. 246–278.

37. "Conversation with Wen Yuankai," in *Yan Jiaqi and China's Struggle for Democracy,* ed. and trans. David Bachman and Dali L. Yang (Armonk, N.Y.: M. E. Sharpe, 1991), p. 131.

38. Ibid., p. 134.

39. Ibid., p. 129.

40. Yu Haocheng, "Protection of Human Rights Is a Just Cause in the Advance of Mankind," *Shijie zhishi,* December 1, 1988, pp. 2–5, JPRS–C, no. 89018, March 1, 1989, p. 1.

41. Ibid., p. 2.

42. Ibid.

43. Ibid., p. 4.

44. Cao Siyuan, "The Safe Way to Political Structural Reform," *Shijie jingji daobao,* November 21, 1988, p. 11, FBIS, December 8, 1988, p. 34.

45. Ibid.

46. Ibid., p. 35.

47. Li Anshan, "Some Opinions on the Political Reform in China," *Xin guancha,* September 10, 1988, pp. 14–15, JPRS–C, no. 88078, December 8, 1988, p. 1.

48. Du Gui, "The Press Represents Different Social Interests," *Shijie jingji daobao,* March 28, 1988, p. 15.

49. Ibid.

50. *Jing bao,* January 10, 1989, pp. 28–32, FBIS, January 27, 1989, p. 22.

51. Zhang Kewen, "Poll Reveals NPC Deputies' Views on Press Law,"

China Daily, December 30, 1988, p. 4, FBIS, December 30, 1988, p. 24.

52. Wang Furu, "A Journalist Should Take the Overall Situation into Consideration," *Zhongguo jizhe,* November 15, 1988, p. 1, FBIS, December 29, 1988, p. 33.
53. Hu Jiwei and Chang Dalin, "Exploring China's Theories on Democracy," *Renmin ribao,* December 30, 1988, p. 5, FBIS, January 6, 1989, p. 28.
54. Ibid., p. 27.
55. Zhang Binfu, "The Degree of Democracy and the Criterion for Measuring It," *Guangming ribao,* October 24, 1988, p. 3, FBIS, November 25, 1988, p. 33.
56. Zheng Yefu, "Democracy Poorly Understood in China Even by Intellectuals," *Lilun xinxi,* July 18, 1988, p. 2.
57. Fang Lizhi, *Bringing Down the Great Wall* (New York: Knopf, 1991), pp. 255–256.
58. Zhang Weiguo, "Whither the State Ownership System?" *Shijie jingji daobao,* April 3, 1989, p. 10, FBIS, April 25, 1989, pp. 48–49.
59. Zhang Xianyang, "Marxism: Reflection and Transcendence," *Wenhui bao,* January 25, 1989, p. 2, FBIS, January 30, 1989, p. 37.
60. Ibid., p. 38.
61. *Zhengming,* March 1, 1989, pp. 57–59, JPRS–C, no. 89048, May 18, 1989, p. 2.
62. *South China Morning Post,* December 1, 1988, p. 13, FBIS, December 1, 1988, p. 16.
63. *Hong Kong Standard,* December 9, 1988, p. 6, FBIS, December 9, 1988, pp. 23–24.
64. *South China Morning Post,* January 30, 1989, p. 8, FBIS, January 30, 1989, p. 27.
65. Chang Hong, "Nonparty Members Urged to Consolidate Views," *China Daily,* January 4, 1989, p. 1, FBIS, January 5, 1989, p. 37.
66. For background and detailed discussion of neo-authoritarianism, see Stanley Rosen and Gary Zou, eds., "The Chinese Debate on the New Authoritarianism," *Chinese Sociology and Anthropology* (Winter 1990–91, Spring 1991, and Summer 1991); see also the unpublished manuscript by Michael Sullivan at the University of Wisconsin–Madison.
67. Mark P. Petracca and Meng Xiong, "The Concept of China's Neo-Authoritarianism," *Asian Survey* (November 1990), 1099.
68. Rosen and Zou, "The Chinese Debate on the New Authoritarianism" (Winter 1990–91), 38.
69. Xiao Gongqin, "Checks and Balances by Authority: The Only Way to

Success in China's Reform," *Shijie jingji daobao,* March 13, 1989, p. 11, FBIS, March 24, 1989, p. 43.

70. Liu Jun, "A Brief Introduction to the Debate on 'Neo-Authoritarianism,'" *Guangming ribao,* March 17, 1989, p. 3, FBIS, April 6, 1989, p. 31.

71. See Pei Minxin's interview with Samuel Huntington in *Shijie jingji daobao,* March 27, 1989.

72. Rosen and Zou, "The Chinese Debate on the New Authoritarianism" (Winter 1990–91), 59.

73. Ibid., p. 60.

74. Ibid., p. 65.

75. Ibid., pp. 74–75.

76. Xu Liangying, "Antidemocracy Countercurrent in China," *Jiushi niandai,* May 1, 1989, pp. 71–73, JPRS–C, no. 89070, July 6, 1989, p. 36.

77. Interview with *Jiushi niandai,* December 1, 1988, pp. 65–75, JPRS–C, no. 89033, April 12, 1989, p. 4.

78. Yan Jiaqi, "Democracy the Only Road to Prosperity for China," part 2, *Xinhua wenzhai* (February 1989), 134–137, JPRS–C, no. 89088, August 21, 1989, p. 8.

79. Ibid., p. 9.

80. Yu Haocheng, "The Rule of Law Must Replace the Rule of Man," *Faxue,* March 10, 1989, pp. 2–5, JPRS–C, no. 89078, July 27, 1989, p. 59.

81. Hu Jiwei, "Establish Democratic Authority," *Jingjixue zhoubao,* March 5, 1989, p. 5, FBIS, March 17, 1989, p. 16.

82. Liu Xiaobo, "Part II: Contemporary Chinese Intellectuals and Politics," *Zhengming,* April 1989, pp. 78–81, JPRS–C, no. 89088, August 21, 1989, pp. 10–11.

83. Qin Xiaoying, "Jumping Out of the Vicious Cycle of History," *Jingjixue daobao,* March 12, 1989, p. 5, FBIS, March 28, 1989, p. 45.

84. Gao Gao, "Improve the Social Control System Taking the Rule of Law as the Main Body," *Jingjixue zhoubao,* March 12, 1989, p. 5, FBIS, March 28, 1989, pp. 31–32.

85. Li Wei, "'New Authority' Going Astray," *Jingjixue zhoubao,* March 26, 1989, p. 7, FBIS, April 7, 1989, p. 16.

86. *Dagong bao,* April 18, 1989, p. 2, FBIS, April 19, 1989, p. 28.

87. *Zhengming,* April 1, 1989, pp. 12–13, FBIS, April 4, 1989, p. 54.

88. Zhang Weiguo, "Yu Guangyuan on Scientific Nature," *Shijie jingji daobao,* March 27, 1989, p. 2, FBIS, April 12, 1989, p. 25.

89. Shao Yanxiang, "I Am Glad to Read 'An Interview with Ill Wang Li,'" *Xin guancha,* February 10, 1989, pp. 15–16, JPRS–C, no. 89020, March 8, 1989, pp. 5–6.

90. Wan Quanzhou, "Self-Reflection by Mainland Intellectuals," *Zhengming,* March 1989, pp. 66–67, JPRS–C, no. 89065, June 26, 1989, p. 71.
91. Ibid., p. 72.
92. *Xin qimeng,* no. 1 (October 1988), 92.
93. See *Zhengming,* April 1989, pp. 14–15, JPRS–C, no. 89070, July 6, 1989, pp. 7–9.
94. *Xin qimeng,* no. 4 (April 1989), 9–10.
95. *Xin qimeng,* no. 1 (October 1988), 11.
96. Ibid., pp. 12–13.
97. Ibid., p. 61.
98. Ibid., p. 76.
99. *Xin qimeng,* no. 4 (April 1989), 75.
100. *Xin qimeng,* no. 2 (December 1988), 42.
101. Author's conversation with Bei Dao in April 1989.
102. Michel Oksenberg, Lawrence Sullivan, and Marc Lambert, eds., *Beijing Spring, 1989* (Armonk, N.Y.: M. E. Sharpe, 1990), p. 170.
103. Ibid., p. 171.
104. *Jiushi niandai,* April 1989, pp. 21–23, JPRS–C, no. 89080, July 31, 1989, p. 2.
105. *Baixing,* April 1, 1989, pp. 5–6, FBIS, April 11, 1989, p. 18.
106. *Zhengming,* April 1, 1989, pp. 9–10, FBIS, April 5, 1989, p. 32.
107. *Jiushi niandai,* April 1, 1989, pp. 48–50, FBIS, April 7, 1989, p. 20.
108. Li Shuguang and Qu Xinjiu, "Reprieve: Historical Origin, Theoretical Development, and Its Reality," *Shijie jingji daobao,* March 27, 1989, p. 16, FBIS, April 10, 1989, p. 25.
109. Interview with Li Shuxian, October 1992, by Mark Griffith, in Griffith, "The Student Movement before Tiananmen," unpublished paper.
110. Liang Shuohua, "Interview with Fang Lizhi on 1 June 1988 in Beijing," *Mingbao yuekan* (July 1988), 15–24, JPRS–C, no. 88061, October 3, 1988, p. 2.
111. Described in *Dagong bao,* May 5, 1988, p. 2, FBIS, May 5, 1988, p. 20.
112. *South China Morning Post,* April 8, 1988, p. 1, FBIS, April 8, 1988, p. 40.
113. *Hong Kong Standard,* April 11, 1988, p. 5, FBIS, April 12, 1988, p. 46.
114. *Baixing,* May 16, 1989, pp. 13–15, JPRS–C, no. 89090, August 25, 1989, p. 53.
115. See Shen Tong, with Marianne Yen, *Almost a Revolution* (Boston: Houghton Mifflin Co., 1990).
116. *Baixing,* May 16, 1989, pp. 12–14, JPRS–C, no. 89090, August 25, 1989, p. 51.

117. *Zhengming,* April 1, 1989, pp. 9–10, FBIS, April 5, 1989, p. 33.

118. Ibid., p. 32.

119. Hao Chiyong, "Martial Law—An Indispensable Emergency Measure in Modern State Administration," *Renmin gongan bao* (People's security paper), March 24, 1989, p. 3, FBIS, April 3, 1989, p. 38.

120. *South China Morning Post,* March 25, 1989, p. 8, FBIS, March 27, 1989, p. 26.

121. Xinhua, March 29, 1989, FBIS, March 31, 1989, p. 28.

122. Xinhua, March 30, 1989, FBIS, March 31, 1989, p. 20.

123. *Hong Kong Standard,* April 6, 1989, p. 5, FBIS, April 6, 1989, p. 26.

124. Ibid.

125. Zhongguo Xinwenshe, March 29, 1989, FBIS, April 4, 1989, p. 42.

126. Xinhua, March 30, 1989, FBIS, April 4, 1989, p. 21.

127. "An Important Step in Building Democratic Politics," *Renmin ribao,* April 10, 1989, p. 1, FBIS, April 11, 1989, p. 15.

128. Wang Gangyi, "New Law Will Give People More Rights," *China Daily,* April 13, 1989, p. 4, FBIS, April 13, 1989, pp. 18–19.

129. *South China Morning Post,* March 31, 1989, p. 10, FBIS, March 31, 1989, p. 25.

130. Zhongguo Xinwenshe, March 27, 1989, FBIS, March 27, 1989, p. 48.

131. Dai Weicheng, "NPC Deputies Less Than Assertive in Pushing for Political Democratization," *Shijie jingji daobao,* March 27, 1989, p. 2, JPRS–C, no. 89078, July 27, 1989, p. 1.

132. Zhang Weiguo, "Yan Jiaqi Calls for the Replacement of Revolutionary Politics by Democratic Politics," *Shijie jingji daobao,* April 3, 1989, p. 11, JPRS–C, no. 89078, July 27, 1989, p. 3.

133. *Ming bao,* March 28, 1989, p. 8, FBIS, March 28, 1989, p. 23.

134. Ibid., p. 24.

135. See Andrew Nathan, *Chinese Democracy* (New York: Knopf, 1985), for a discussion of China's constitutions and the historical roots of China's democratic movements.

136. Yu Haocheng, "The Rule of Law Must Replace the Rule of Man," *Faxue,* March 10, 1989, pp. 2–5, JPRS–C, no. 89078, July 27, 1989, p. 59.

137. Ibid., p. 61.

138. Author's conversation with Li Rui in 1993.

11. The Democratic Elite and Tiananmen

1. See Shen Tong, with Marianne Yen, *Almost a Revolution* (Boston: Houghton Mifflin Co., 1990).

2. *New York Times,* April 23, 1989, p. A1.

3. Kate Wright, "The Political Fortunes of Shanghai's 'World Economic

Herald,'" *Australian Journal of Chinese Affairs,* no. 23 (January 1990), 124.

4. *Baixing,* May 1, 1989, pp. 3–6, FBIS, May 3, 1989, p. 40.
5. Ibid., p. 41.
6. Kuang Yan, "Dai Qing, the Rebellion 'Reporter,'" *Guangming ribao,* September 13, 1989, pp. 1–2, FBIS, September 25, 1989, p. 35.
7. Wen Yuankai et al., "Preliminary Notions about China's Reforms in the Next Decade," *Shijie jingji daobao,* April 10, 1989, p. 10, FBIS, May 2, 1989, pp. 32–34.
8. "The Truth about the Case of *Shijie Jingji Daobao,*" Xinhua, August 18, 1989, FBIS, August 21, 1989, p. 23.
9. Ibid., p. 24.
10. *Ming bao,* May 7, 1989, p. 2, FBIS, May 8, 1989, pp. 29–30.
11. Ibid., p. 30.
12. Author's conversation with Zhu Xingqing, former deputy editor-in-chief of *Shijie jingji daobao,* in 1993.
13. Kuang Yan, "Dai Qing, the Rebellion 'Reporter,'" FBIS, p. 36.
14. Seth Faison, "The Changing Role of the Chinese Media," in *The Chinese People's Movement,* ed. Tony Saich (Armonk, N.Y.: M. E. Sharpe, 1990), p. 148.
15. Ibid., pp. 146–147.
16. Chen Xitong, "Report on Checking the Turmoil and Quelling the Counterrevolutionary Rebellion," June 30, 1989, Xinhua, July 6, 1989, FBIS, July 6, 1989, p. 28.
17. *Ming bao,* May 14, 1989, p. 8, FBIS, May 15, 1989, p. 51.
18. See Andrew G. Walder, "The Political Sociology of the Beijing Upheaval of 1989," *Problems of Communism* (September–October 1989), 38–39.
19. "It Is Necessary to Take a Clear-Cut Stand against Disturbances," *Renmin ribao,* April 26, 1989, FBIS, April 25, 1989, pp. 23–24.
20. Michel Oksenberg, Lawrence Sullivan, and Marc Lambert, eds., *Beijing Spring, 1989* (Armonk, N.Y.: M. E. Sharpe, 1990), p. 204.
21. *South China Morning Post,* September 15, 1989, p. 1, FBIS, September 15, 1989, p. 9.
22. "Wan Runnan—'Entrepreneur' Bent On Subverting the Government," *Beijing Review,* June 18–24, 1990, p. 24.
23. Author's interviews at Stone in Beijing, summer 1988. For more information on Wan Runnan, see Dorothy Solinger, "Urban Entrepreneurs and the State," in *State and Society in China,* ed. Arthur Rosenbaum (Boulder: Westview Press, 1992).
24. Interview with Wan Runnan in *China Forum,* February 1992, p. 2.
25. Wan Runnan, "Creating the Environment—Creating a Momentum—Returning to China," *Jiushi niandai* (February 1990), 32–33, JPRS–C, no. 90026, April 9, 1990, p. 6.

26. A few students made contact with workers earlier. See Shen Tong, *Almost a Revolution.*

27. See Jeff Wasserstrom and Joseph Esherick, "Acting Out Democracy," *Journal of Asian Studies,* 49, no. 4 (November 1990), 835–865.

28. *Ming bao,* May 3, 1989, p. 8, FBIS, May 3, 1989, p. 30.

29. Zhongguo Xinwenshe, May 19, 1989, FBIS, May 19, 1989, p. 36.

30. *Ming bao,* May 18, 1989, p. 8, FBIS, May 18, 1989, p. 47.

31. *Ming bao,* May 31, 1989, p. 9, FBIS, May 31, 1989, p. 66.

32. *Zhengming,* June 1, 1989, pp. 10–12, FBIS, May 31, 1989, p. 71.

33. Xinhua, March 14, 1989, FBIS, March 15, 1989, p. 38.

34. *South China Morning Post,* March 16, 1989, p. 10, FBIS, March 16, 1989, pp. 27–28.

35. Author's conversation with Zhou Duo, one of the participants in the discussions with Yan Mingfu, April 1992 in Beijing.

36. Xinhua, July 5, 1989, FBIS, July 6, 1989, p. 45.

37. Hu Jiwei, "There Will Be No Genuine Stability without Press Freedom," *Shijie jingji daobao,* May 8, 1989, p. 3, FBIS, June 1, 1989, p. 42.

38. *Wenhui bao,* May 31, 1989, p. 2, FBIS, May 31, 1989, p. 38.

39. The Chinese Red Cross issued a civilian death count of 2,600 immediately after the crackdown. The *New York Times,* June 6, 1989, reported a minimum of several hundred killed. The total number, which may never be known, may be 1,500 or more.

40. Yan Jiaqi and Bao Zunxin, "Solve the Current Problems in China along the Track of Democracy and Legal System," *Ming bao,* May 26, 1989, p. 2, FBIS, May 26, 1989, p. 11.

41. *South China Morning Post,* May 4, 1989, pp. 1, 13, FBIS, May 4, 1989, p. 29.

42. Beijing Television Service, May 26, 1989, FBIS, May 26, 1989, p. 15.

43. "Our Most Serious Error and Lesson," *Jingji ribao,* June 21, 1989, p. 1, FBIS, June 30, 1989, p. 28.

44. Speech on July 1, 1989. See *Jiushi niandai* (August 1990), 72, JPRS-C, no. 90082, November 6, 1990, p. 5.

45. See Geremie Barmé and Linda Jaivin, eds., *New Ghosts, Old Dreams: Chinese Rebel Voices* (New York: Times Books, 1992), pp. 260–264, 408–410.

46. "Step Up Education on Patriotism," *Guangming ribao,* June 21, 1989, p. 1, FBIS, June 30, 1989, p. 27.

47. Xinhua, November 25, 1989, FBIS, November 27, 1989, p. 19.

48. Zheng Wen, "China Can Never Copy Wholesale the Western Democratic System," *Jingji ribao,* July 18, 1989, p. 3, FBIS, August 1, 1989, p. 24.

49. Wang Guofa, "Democracy Should Not Go beyond Social Develop-

ment," *Liaowang,* August 7, 1989, p. 17, FBIS, August 21, 1989, pp. 32–33.

50. Xinhua, January 26, 1990, FBIS, January 31, 1990, p. 19.
51. Dong Xuewen, "On the Essence of Liu Zaifu's Theory of 'Literary Subjectivity,'" *Qiushi,* January 1, 1991, JPRS–C, no. 91012, March 5, 1991, p. 14.
52. *Ming bao,* December 26, 1989, p. 2, FBIS, December 26, 1989, p. 12.

12. A New Kind of Intellectual Activist

1. The source for much of the background information on Wang Juntao and Chen Ziming is "Rough Justice in Beijing," *News from Asia Watch,* January 17, 1991, based on interviews Robin Munro and others conducted with associates of Wang and Chen who escaped to Hong Kong after the crackdown. See George Black and Robin Munro, *Black Hands of Beijing* (New York: John Wiley and Sons, 1993), for full biographies.
2. Chen Ziming, "Recollections of the 5 April Movement," *Beijing zhichun,* January 9, 1979, pp. 25–30, JPRS–TPRC, no. 73728, June 20, 1979, p. 29.
3. "China: Defense Statement of Chen Ziming," *News from Asia Watch,* June 10, 1992, p. 3.
4. Hu Ping, Wang Juntao et al., eds., *Kaituo—Beida xueyun wenxian* (Exploration—Peking University student movement materials) (Hong Kong: Tianyuan shuwu, 1990), p. 81.
5. Chen Ziming, "Recollections of the 5 April Movement," JPRS–TPRC, p. 27.
6. The *Wall Street Journal,* February 13, 1991, p. 20, reported that Chen Ziming and Wang Zhihong had an enrollment of 250,000 correspondence students, whose tuition brought in more than two million dollars.
7. "China: Defense Statement of Chen Ziming," p. 7.
8. Ding Xueliang, "Political Appeals and Social Consequences," Ph.D. dissertation, Department of Sociology, Harvard University, 1992.
9. Ibid.
10. Andrew Nathan, testimony to the Commission on Broadcasting to the PRC, June 4, 1992, pp. 1–2; Min Qi, *Zhongguo zhengzhi wenhua* (Chinese political culture) (Kunming: Yunnan renmin chubanshe, 1989).
11. *Wall Street Journal,* February 13, 1991, p. 20.
12. Chen Ziming, "Shortcomings in the Structure of the Neo-Authoritarian Theory," *Jingjixue zhoubao,* April 30, 1989, p. 7, FBIS, May 18, 1989, p. 85.
13. Tu Wentao, "Tolerance and Democracy," *Jingjixue zhoubao,* April 9, 1989, p. 5, JPRS–C, no. 89099, September 27, 1989, p. 22.

14. *Amnesty International Bulletin,* December 1990, p. 13.
15. Author's conversation with Zhou Dou, April 1992. Zhou put Yan Mingfu in contact with Wang Juntao.
16. "China: Defense Statement of Chen Ziming," p. 12.
17. This quotation was cited by Wang Juntao's wife, Hou Xiaotian, in conversation with the author, April 1992.
18. "Written on the Fifth Day after the University Students' Hunger Strike Started," *Jingjixue zhoubao,* May 21, 1989, p. 1, FBIS, June 6, 1989, p. 52.
19. Hou Xiaotian, "Return My Husband—A Cry for Justice for Wang Juntao," *Jiushi niandai* (December 1990), 31–33, JPRS–C, no. 91001, January 8, 1991, p. 9.
20. Chen Fei, "China: Calm Is Needed," *Jingjixue zhoubao,* June 4, 1989, p. 1, FBIS, June 16, 1989, p. 17.
21. "Court Verdict by Beijing Municipal Intermediate Court on Wang Juntao," *Jing bao,* March 10, 1991, pp. 60–61, FBIS, March 13, 1991, p. 13.
22. Quoted by Hou Xiaotian in "Return My Husband," JPRS–C, p. 8.
23. "Guilt by Association: Chinese Trials," *News from Asia Watch,* July 25, 1991, p. 5.
24. *Jing bao,* March 10, 1991, pp. 60–61, FBIS, March 13, 1991, p. 14.
25. Author's conversation with Bai Hua, a pollster at SERI who was with Wang Juntao in the square, in 1992.
26. *South China Morning Post,* June 10, 1991, p. 17, FBIS, June 10, 1991, p. 22.
27. The letter was published in the *South China Morning Post,* March 2, 1991. "The Case of Wang Juntao," *News from Asia Watch,* March 11, 1991, pp. 18–19.
28. *Jing bao,* March 10, 1991, pp. 28–31, FBIS, March 11, 1991, pp. 27–28.
29. *Hong Kong Standard,* February 14, 1991, p. 1, FBIS February 14, 1991, p. 12.
30. "Guilt by Association," p. 2.
31. "On the Prosecution of Wang Juntao: An Appeal from Hou Xiaotian, His Wife," *Human Rights Tribune,* 2, no. 2 (April 1991), 17.
32. *Hong Kong Standard,* May 30, 1991, FBIS, May 30, 1991, p. 17.
33. Interview with Wan Runnan in *China Forum* (February 1992), 2.
34. William T. Rowe, "The Public Sphere in Modern China," *Modern China,* 16, no. 3 (July 1990), 309–329; David Strand, *Rickshaw Beijing* (Berkeley: University of California Press, 1989); Mary Rankin, "The Origin of a Chinese Public Sphere," paper presented at the Fairbank Center for East Asian Research, Harvard University, 1991.

Index

ACFLAC. *See* All-China Federation of Literary and Art Circles

Administrative Litigation Law, 298, 309

Agriculture, 41; decollectivization of, 17, 28, 62, 169; family responsibility system in, 117–118, 121, 123, 166, 169, 199; metaphors from, 1. *See also* Peasants

Ai Qing, 84, 106, 216, 318, 319, 336

Alienation *(yihua),* 3, 11, 74, 75–77, 115, 131, 332; debate on, 116–121, 122, 124, 126, 127, 128, 130, 264, 287; ideological, 75, 119; political, 76, 119

All-China Federation of Journalists, 215, 217

All-China Federation of Literary and Art Circles (ACFLAC), 87, 93, 115, 119, 139, 141, 147, 165; Fifth Congress of, 152, 260–262, 263, 264; and June 4 crackdown, 336

All-China Federation of Trade Unions, 172, 233, 251, 252, 261, 313, 333, 348, 349

Anhui Literature (Anhui wenxue), 107, 110, 111

Anti–bourgeois liberalization campaign, 18, 20, 204–237, 238, 239, 243, 260, 261, 263, 265, 283, 285, 306, 321, 331

Anti-rightist campaign, 3, 17, 37, 137, 206, 235, 258; fear of another, 199, 224; and intellectuals, 23, 101, 140, 159, 284; opposition to, 26; victims of, 6, 12, 15, 21, 28, 60, 85, 86, 87, 103, 198, 216, 281, 307; writing about, 32, 34, 51, 81

Anti–spiritual pollution campaign, 121, 122–223, 124–132, 151, 210, 216, 260, 306; and elders, 18, 20; opposition to, 209, 231, 261, 263; restraints on, 124–127, 208; targets of, 143, 145, 178; and writers, 137–138, 139, 141, 143, 159, 164, 168, 178, 193

April Forum (Siwu luntan), 46

Asian Development Bank, 313, 322

Asian Pacific Economic Times, 270

Authoritarianism, 4, 5, 14, 123, 275, 278, 330

Ba Jin, 15, 141, 143, 193, 250, 284; and 1989 demonstrations, 318; *The Family,* 12; and obedience to Mao, 75, 90; proposal for Cultural Revolution museum, 129, 221, 283; *Random Thoughts,* 39, 102, 183, 184

Bai Hua, 2, 112, 113, 115, 116, 117, 119, 152; campaign against, 88–103, 105, 106, 107, 108, 126, 129, 132, 139, 143, 153, 209, 330; "Clouds of Yunnan," 103; and 1989 demonstrations, 335; and patriotism, 90, 95, 98, 118, 291, 330; self-criticism of, 98–99, 102, 103, 105, 130; "The Story of King Goujian," 130; "Tonight the Starlight Glitters," 89; "Unrequited Love" (Kulian), 89–95, 96, 97, 99, 100, 101, 102, 103, 144, 247, 259; and Writers Association, 142–145, 226

Bao Tong, 49–50, 189, 219, 224, 226, 227, 228, 232, 240, 320–321; and 1989